1996
Year A

D1515259

AN ALMANAC OF PARISH LITURGY

SOURCEBOOK

FOR SUNDAYS AND SEASONS

Lawrence E. Mick

Mark Francis, CSV
Jerry Galipeau
J-Glenn Murray, SJ

LITURGY TRAINING PUBLICATIONS

ACKNOWLEDGMENTS

Texts of original opening prayers for Mass based on the scripture readings of the day, copyright ©1983, 1986, 1987, 1988, 1990, 1991, 1992, 1994 International Commission on English in the Liturgy, Inc. (ICEL). All rights reserved.

Texts taken from the Italian sacramentary, *Messale Romano,* copyright © 1983, Libreria Editrice Vaticana, are translated by Peter Scagnelli.

Inserts for the eucharistic prayers from the French *Textes propres pour la prière eucharistique,* copyright © 1978, A.E.L.F., Paris are translated by James A. Wilde.

Sourcebook for Sundays and Seasons, 1996, copyright © 1995, Archdiocese of Chicago: Liturgy Training Publications, 1800 North Hermitage Avenue, Chicago IL 60622-1101; 1-800-933-1800, FAX 1-800-933-7094. All rights reserved.

Printed in the Unites States of America

ISBN 1-56854-066-3

The Gospel of Matthew, the predominant gospel read on the Sundays of Year A, was written about AD 85–90 for a Christian community, probably in present-day Syria. Although the gospel bears the name of the apostle Matthew, who was a Jewish tax-collector, the writer was probably an early Christian teacher and church leader who may have based his work on a collection of Jesus' sayings compiled by the apostle. Because the Gospel of Matthew begins with Jesus' human genealogy, the evangelist often is represented by a winged human figure.

CONTENTS

RESOURCES

Developing a Liturgical Tradition

The Hispanic Mística

African American Spirituals

ADVENT

CHRISTMAS

WINTER ORDINARY TIME

Foreword

WELCOME to *Sourcebook for Sundays and Seasons, 1996!* The book you are holding may not feel very heavy, but years of experience, study, cogitation, argument and instinct, seasoned with affection and delight, are packed into these pages. If you are new to *Sourcebook,* you are about to discover a treasure chest of information, instructions, ideas and good common sense. If you are one of *Sourcebook*'s longtime friends, thank you for your confidence in us.

■ WHAT'S NEW? Jerry Galipeau has added to the musical suggestions and selections in this year's book. A native of Boston, Jerry has served in parishes in Florida and Illinois; he currently is director of music and liturgy at St. Marcelline's parish in Schaumburg, Illinois. He is a team member for institutes of the North American Forum on the Catechumenate, on whose board of directors he also serves.

This year *Sourcebook* presents some of the wisdom and viewpoints of African American and Hispanic Catholics regarding the celebration of the church's liturgy. J-Glenn Murray, a Jesuit priest and liturgist, shares the African American focus through the lens of the spirituals. Mark Francis, a Viatorian priest and professor of liturgy, in consultation with José Castillo, the coordinator of Hispanic programs for Chicago's Office for Divine Worship, offers insights into the Hispanic worldview.

■ WHAT'S THE SAME? Lawrence E. Mick remains as principal author and compiler. In addition, he has written one of the introductory articles for this year's book, offering an excellent primer on how to establish a parish liturgical tradition. Larry is a priest of the archdiocese of Cincinnati and has served as a pastor, campus minister, retreat-house staff member and resource person in the area of liturgy. Larry also travels the country offering workshops for priests and liturgy planners. You may know his series on liturgy in *Today's Parish* magazine or his writing in the *Faith Alive!* series from Catholic News Service, published in many diocesan newspapers. Larry has published several titles with The Liturgical Press: *To Live as We Worship* (1984), *Understanding the Sacraments Today* (1987; also published in leaflet form), *Penance: The Once and Future Sacrament* (1987) and *RCIA: Renewing the Church as an Initiating Assembly* (1989).

The general intercessions are selected from those composed, adapted or assembled by Timothy Fitzgerald over the last several years. Tim is a priest of the diocese of Des Moines and is associate director for education at the Center for Pastoral Liturgy at the University of Notre Dame. Tim is a frequent author for LTP; his works include *Confirmation: A Parish Celebration* and *Infant Baptism: A Parish Celebration.*

And again, Rita Corbin's artwork graces the cover and inside of this year's book. Rita has been working in religious and liturgical art for many years. You may be most familiar with her work from *The Catholic Worker.*

Because *Sourcebook for Sundays and Seasons* evolves much as an almanac does, the work of many previous authors and compilers remains a part of this book. The hands of G. Thomas Ryan, Peter Scagnelli, Peter Mazar, Mary Beth Kunde-Anderson, David Anderson, Barry Moorehead, Neil Kraft and Anthony DiCello all may still be detected herein. *Sourcebook* is richer for their contributions, and so, we hope, is your parish's liturgical life.

■ WHO BRINGS IT ALL TOGETHER? Many people work hard and long to transfer this book from a stack of papers (a big stack!) and a couple of floppy disks into the book you are now reading. Copy editing throughout production was provided by Deborah Bogaert. David Philippart, editor of *Liturgy 90* and *Environment & Art Letter,* reviewed the manuscript and offered his insights.

LTP's graphics department takes all these words and makes them into a thing of beauty. Jane Kremsreiter, a former staff member, designed the 1991 book. Mary Bowers made some modifications to the original design and Ana Aguilar-Islas designed the cover. Judith Sweetwood did the layout for this year's book, and Mark Hollopeter did the typesetting.

Work on the 1997 book has already begun, but we are interested in hearing your comments and suggestions at any time.

Victoria M. Tufano
Editor

Welcome!

WELCOME to the year of our Lord 1996, another round of days given to us to serve the Lord and celebrate God's merciful love. That love is most fully celebrated during the great Triduum, culminating in the Easter Vigil. This year the Easter Vigil will be celebrated during the night of April 6. As the *Exsultet* proclaims, "This is the night"—the night when the people of Israel are freed from slavery, the night when the pillar of fire destroys the darkness of sin, the night when Christians everywhere are restored to grace, the night when Jesus Christ breaks the chains of death. Just as the death and resurrection of Christ is the axis on which the history of the world turns, this is the night on which the rest of the year turns, the night that gives meaning to all the other nights and days. This is the center point of our liturgical year. Based on this date, Ash Wednesday will begin the Paschal cycle on February 21 this year, and Pentecost Sunday will bring it to a conclusion on May 26.

This year marks the twenty-fifth anniversary of the introduction of the revised *Rite of Confirmation*. The confusion over the proper understanding and appropriate age for celebrating this sacrament continues around the country and shows little hope of resolution in the near future. Perhaps this sacrament will only find its true place as parishes gain more experience with the *Rite of Christian Initiation of Adults* and the celebration of the unified rites of initiation at the Easter Vigil.

In this edition of the *Sourcebook,* we have chosen to focus on a broader issue of liturgical renewal, namely, the development of a local liturgical tradition. Those who use *Sourcebook* are the prime agents in the shaping of such a tradition in parish worship. We hope that our discussion of this process will stimulate local conversations and planning that will lead to solid decisions as parishes continue on the road of renewal.

■ THE LITURGICAL YEAR: The liturgical calendar is a framework within which we, as Christians, seek to celebrate and experience anew the central mysteries of our redemption. Each member of the church appropriates those mysteries in varying degrees, but the liturgical year enables us to celebrate these realities communally and thus to grow together as the Body of Christ. The calendar's schedule of special days and seasons nudges us to continue to enter more deeply into the faith that we celebrate as each day of the year passes by.

Besides the worship services that mark each feast and season, the liturgical year should provide the framework for both parish activities and family observances. The synoptic gospel used in a given year's cycle (Matthew in 1996) might be the basis of adult education programs. The emphasis on death and the End Time during November might suggest a workshop on funerals or other issues of death and dying during that month. Viewing Lent as a time of parish "retreat" might prompt evenings of recollection for various parish committees and ministries during the Forty Days, while understanding Easter as an extended celebration might suggest parish parties and picnics during the Fifty Days. A deepening awareness of the unique character of each of the liturgical seasons and the various feasts and saints' days can help Christians create a healthy balance between work and festivity, penance and rejoicing in the course of the year.

■ SUNDAYS: Sunday is the primordial Christian feast day. It is our constant celebration of the paschal mystery, the central reality of our lives. This mystery is celebrated more richly at the Easter Vigil, of course, so Sunday is often called a little Easter. It might be more accurate to call Easter the great Sunday, since Sunday is the more ancient feast.

The observance of the Sunday is the foundation of the liturgical year, and nothing must be allowed to destroy or impair this regular pattern of worship. The liturgical reforms mandated by the Second Vatican Council strongly promoted this precedence of Sunday. The sanctoral feasts that can eclipse Sunday were trimmed, and numerous reminders have been issued about keeping the Sunday central in parish life and worship. (See page *x* for other notes on Sunday precedence and rest.)

■ SEASONS: Lent begins two weeks earlier than in 1995, giving us just a bit more than six weeks of Ordinary Time between the Christmas cycle and the Paschal cycle. The fluctuation of the date of Easter, which comes on the Sunday after the full moon that comes on or after the spring equinox, reminds us of the ancient links between our calendar and the lunar calendar.

Earlier in the liturgical year, planners, preachers and decorators will be challenged again, as Christmas and New Year's Day both fall on Monday. That means that Advent will be as short as it ever can be, with the fourth week being only one day, Christmas Eve. Planners should begin even earlier than usual to prepare Advent and Christmas so that these back-to-back feasts will be celebrated well. Because New Year's Day is a Monday, it will not be a day of obligation this year; but it is still a day many find important for prayer and worship, so it should be planned well.

■ YEAR A: Especially in Ordinary Time, Matthew will be our principal guide. Matthew's gospel is arranged over 38 Sundays this year. We draw from the gospel of John for one Sunday in Ordinary Time, three in Lent, all the Sundays of Easter except the Third Sunday (which uses Luke's Emmaus story), Trinity Sunday and the Feast of the Body and Blood of the Lord. Homilists and those who prepare the liturgy would do well to spend some time early in 1996 looking at their favorite commentaries on Matthew and John.

■ YEAR II: This is Year II in the weekday lectionary, a year when we hear many selections from the books of Samuel and Kings and from the prophets. From the Christian testament, we read from 1 Corinthians, Galatians, Ephesians, Philippians, 2 Thessalonians, 2 Timothy, James, 2 Peter and the three letters of John. During the final weeks of the year, we will listen to the book of Revelation.

Each week should be previewed:

> The continuous reading during the week is sometimes interrupted by the occurrence of a feast or particular celebration. In this case the priest, taking into consideration the entire week's plan of readings, is allowed either to combine omitted parts with other readings or to give preference to certain readings. (*General Instruction of the Roman Missal,* #319; see also the introduction to the lectionary—#82 in the 1981 edition.)

This *Sourcebook* includes notes at the beginning of weeks that are so affected.

■ FEASTS "LOST" AND "FOUND": Every year, certain feasts are "lost" because of the precedence of Sunday, the Triduum and the days immediately surrounding it. This year only two feasts

give way: The Nativity of the Blessed Virgin Mary and the feast of the Archangels, both in September. Eleven obligatory and twenty optional memorials are omitted this year. This leaves about 150 possible observances from the proper of saints in liturgical year 1996 (and some of those days commemorate two or even three saints). Many days on the universal Roman calendar are listed as optional memorials. Each parish should review these days and decide which will be observed this year. To these universal and national feasts, those who prepare the liturgy also should add the parish's own local festivals and any ember days (page *xvi*).

■ OTHER CHARACTERISTICS OF 1996:

- Thanksgiving Day this year falls after the feast of Christ the King, in contrast to last year. This will provide a challenge for planners, since Thanksgiving weekend will also be the beginning of Advent. Thanksgiving's place between Christ the King and the First Sunday of Advent suggests linking the celebration of the harvest with the harvest of God's people at the End Time, for which we long during Advent.

- Several other weekends this year will need special attention, too. Immaculate Conception falls on a Friday, resulting in a Friday–Saturday celebration just before the usual Saturday–Sunday Masses. Christmas is on a Monday, and so is the Solemnity of Mary, the Mother of God. The latter feast will not be a holy day of obligation but should be celebrated well. Near the end of the year, All Saints and All Souls fall on Friday and Saturday, creating a very full schedule of Masses that weekend. Good celebration of these significant days, especially when there is no obligation to attend, requires good catechesis as well as careful planning so that the feasts are true celebrations for those who come.

- This year is a presidential election year in the United States, which will surely get increasing attention as the year passes. While planners and preachers should never allow the liturgy to become a platform for particular candidates at any level, parishioners should be encouraged to vote responsibly and to pray for the election of candidates who will truly serve God and the people. Appropriate petitions in the general intercessions should model the proper approach to such prayer and such decisions.

Sourcebook in 1996

THIS year, *Sourcebook* has four new contributing authors. Jerry Galipeau has updated the music notes. He is director of music and liturgy at St. Marcelline parish in Schaumburg, Illinois, and is a member of the board of the North American Forum on the Catechumenate. J-Glenn Murray, SJ, offers a variety of insights from the African American worship experience. Fr. Murray is a teacher of liturgy and homiletics at Saint Mary's Seminary and a staff member of the Office for Pastoral Liturgy for the Diocese of Cleveland. Mark Francis, CSV, offers insights from the Hispanic tradition in consultation with José Castillo. Fr. Francis is a member of the faculty at Catholic Theological Union in Chicago, and Mr. Castillo is on the staff of the Office for Divine Worship for the Archdiocese of Chicago.

As always, this almanac is a combination of the new and the old. You will find much here that is familiar, with insights and suggestions from past writers and contributors. There are several features worth noting:

- Besides the comments on saints' days when appropriate, this *Sourcebook* offers comments on the readings of the day. It is hoped that these brief suggestions will be helpful both to daily presiders (priest, deacon or lay) and to teachers and others who plan daily liturgies. They are not meant to be exhaustive or restrictive; there are many possible insights to be gleaned from any set of readings. But these comments are provided as a starting point for those who find them useful.

- There are many suggestions this year for linking church and home. These are mostly found in sections titled "Taking It Home," though some are also found in the calendar sections. One of the most important goals of the liturgical renewal is to reconnect our worship with our daily lives. A major step in that direction is taken when individuals and families link their prayer and home activities to the community's worship. We would be happy to hear from users of *Sourcebook* about ways they have found to link worship and home life; good ideas deserve to be shared.

- There are various suggestions in this *Sourcebook* drawn from different ethnic communities. The new sections by our contributing authors expand this material this year. We hope to continue adding to these ideas, for we believe that there is much in the African American, Hispanic and other ethnic traditions that could be of use to the broader Catholic community. Again, we welcome input from readers who have suggestions to share.

Using this Sourcebook

THIS publication is not intended to substitute for the official liturgical books or for pastoral good sense. It stands as a companion to the official books, bringing together guidelines and resources from a number of separate sources. Its goal is simply to help a parish implement the official rites in a pastorally sensitive and liturgically sound fashion.

With this *Sourcebook,* the official liturgical books, the diocesan calendar and other sources in hand, the pastoral leadership of each parish should determine the parish calendar early in the new liturgical year and distribute it to all. This can help every parish group begin shaping their plans around the liturgical year. It might also encourage a sense of anticipation among parishioners as we approach the Triduum, the parish's patronal feast and other significant days.

■ COVER PAGES: Each season's cover page is designed for photocopying; it might be used for the parish bulletin or for participation booklets. The artistic images are meant to suggest themes of the season, inviting us into the rich images that mark our liturgical year.

■ INTRODUCTION TO EACH SEASON: These pages attempt to provide an overall view of the season and a sense of the images and themes that shape each season. Suggestions are also given for ways to prepare the parish community for the season's celebrations and for ways to help worshipers carry the spirit of the liturgy to their homes and daily lives.

■ CALENDAR: A day-by-day calendar appears immediately after each seasonal overview, guiding planners and preachers in the task of celebrating the season on each day within it. These suggestions presume that one has read the seasonal introductions first. The texts, music and ritual order should have a certain consistency throughout the season.

■ LITURGICAL TEXTS: Sample prayer texts follow each seasonal calendar. The intercessions (models, not prescriptions) were composed by Timothy Fitzgerald or selected by him from one of these sources: *Intercessions for the Christian People,* by Gail Ramshaw (Collegeville: Pueblo Books/The Liturgical Press, 1988), *The Book of Common Prayer,* the Divine Liturgy of St. John Chrysostom, the Divine Liturgy of St. James of Jerusalem and the Liturgy of St. Basil the Great, the Eucharistic Prayer for Masses of Reconciliation I, *Veritas Book of Blessing Prayers* (Dublin: Veritas Publications, 1989), Eucharistic Prayers III and IV, *The Promise of His Glory: For the Season All Saints to Candlemas* (Collegeville: The Liturgical Press, 1991) and Matthew, chapter 5.

The prayers for each Sunday are from the International Committee on English in the Liturgy (hereafter referred to as ICEL). Inserts for the eucharistic prayers were translated from the French by James A. Wilde. The texts for the lighting of the Advent wreath at Mass were composed by Larry Mick, and the other texts provided are translated or composed by Peter Scagnelli. The texts which take hold in your local community can help to define the given season year after year.

■ ART: The images gracing these pages (which may be photocopied for local, non-commercial use) are once again the work of Rita Corbin, whose images have appeared for years in *The Catholic Worker* and in other publications. Rita's work grows out of her own appreciation for the traditions and feasts of the church and her own living out of the Christian message in solidarity with the poor.

Scheduling

SUNDAYS: An ongoing obstacle to good celebration in many parishes is the scheduling of more Masses than the parish really needs. This puts a constant strain on parish resources, both human and financial, often leading to celebrations that are poorly prepared and weakly celebrated. These schedules often came about when "convenience" was the primary criterion for how many Masses were offered. As we have begun to appreciate more fully the role of the assembly in worship and the value of common worship in forming and sustaining the community's identity, many have begun to question the need for so many Masses every Sunday. Half-empty church buildings with people scattered around the space detracts from the assembly's identity and makes its essential role in worship more difficult.

Though some parishes have a real need for several Masses, many do not need the number currently scheduled. Parish leaders should take a good look at the size of the weekend worshiping community and then schedule only as many Masses as are really needed to accommodate the usual numbers in the space available. The basic ideal is a single Sunday Mass at which the whole assembly gathers. Even if work schedules might demand some other option most weeks, there is great value to periodic festivals at which only one Mass is celebrated, so that the whole parish can form one assembly and experience concretely their unity in Christ. This is required normally during the Triduum but may also be appropriate for other occasions.

This must be handled with a great deal of sensitivity, for it places the need for the community to gather as one at a higher level than the convenience of every individual member. Karl Rahner wrote:

> If, as J. A. Jungmann always insisted, the Sunday celebration is to be seen in the first place as a responsibility of the parish as such and not, properly speaking, the individual's wholly personal responsibility . . . we might perhaps arrange a splendid and beautiful common celebration only in the evening of Sunday or even on Saturday. We could then say that any particular individual (a bus conductor, for instance, who has to work at this time) has no need at all to attend Mass on that Sunday, since this is not primarily his own private and personal religious obligation, but, if he has any obligation at all, it is as a member of this parish, which can in fact choose to have a joint celebration and at a time which, from the nature of the case, cannot be convenient to every individual. ("The Sunday Precept in an Industrial Society," *Theological Investigations XIX* [New York: Crossroad, 1983], p. 158)

■ SEASONS FOR THE WHOLE CHURCH: After more than thirty years of efforts at liturgical renewal, there is still much to be done in most parishes to make the whole liturgical year a vital reality for the entire assembly. Parish staff and other parish leaders must share a common conviction of the importance of fully observing the feasts and seasons of the year. This will be communicated to parishioners gradually over time, as the dynamics and rhythm of the liturgical year affect all areas of parish life.

The degree of awareness of the liturgical year will be manifested in practical decisions about scheduling. The Triduum will be central to the parish's calendar, the days at the end of Lent and in the Easter octave will be free of business-as-usual, the great feasts will become the traditional days for parish socials, and liturgies such as Evening Prayer will be seen as the preferred format for regular prayer before parish meetings (for example, Evening Prayer may be held at 7:00 each night before meetings begin at 7:30).

■ THE EASTER TRIDUUM: The schedule of these holy days is described beginning on page 123. These central holy days of the year should be fully observed by every member of the assembly. It is an anomaly of our tradition that these days are not listed as holy days of obligation, even though they are the holiest days of the year. Perhaps that is because our ancestors considered these days so central that putting an obligation on them seemed superfluous. In any case, the result is that we are challenged to develop an awareness of the centrality of these days that will draw the assembly instinctively to gather for these central celebrations.

Observance of the paschal fast on Friday and Saturday will help prepare the community for the initiation sacraments at the Easter Vigil. The entire Easter Vigil is to take place at night. Other opportunities for common prayer beyond the main liturgies of these days should be available, and suggestions and materials should be provided for domestic prayer as well.

■ CHRISTMAS: This feast does draw the assembly almost instinctively; few Catholics celebrate Christmas because it is a day of obligation. The schedule of Masses should be determined by the anticipated numbers of participants; no more Masses than necessary should be scheduled, and every one of them should be a full and rich celebration. Then the other hours of the festival are to be kept sacred by all through the liturgy of the hours, domestic prayer and social gatherings. Christians need to relearn how to make Advent different from Christmas and how to keep Christmas throughout the season until Ordinary Time begins again.

Developing a Parish Liturgical Tradition

IT has been more than three decades since we began the reform of the liturgy mandated by the Second Vatican Council. The task was, in many respects, unprecedented. This is not to say that the church has never undergone liturgical reform before—there have been numerous periods of reform in our history, some minor and some major. But this reform is unique in at least three aspects.

First of all, it came after a period of about four hundred years of relatively unchanging liturgy. There were many small changes made over the course of those centuries, but the overall impression was of a liturgy that was fixed and immutable. This made the experience of liturgical reform traumatic for many.

The second difference in this reform is that it seeks to reverse the pattern of increasing uniformity in the Roman Rite that developed through several centuries and reached its height following the Council of Trent. The liturgical renewal envisions a liturgy more closely tied to the local culture and life of the people, which means much more variety than the pre–Vatican II Roman Rite allowed.

The third difference is the scope of the reform. It involves not just the Mass but every sacrament and ritual in the church's repertoire. And all of this has been undertaken in a relatively short period of time, aided by modern means of communication, in contrast to previous reforms, which often spread gradually from one area to another.

RITUAL AND CHANGE

All of this has been upsetting to many Catholics, resulting in resistance to change and the alienation of some members of the assembly. But some disorientation and unease is inevitable in liturgical renewal. Liturgy is ritual, which by definition is traditional, patterned behavior; much of the power of ritual comes from a sense that it transcends the moment, having roots in the history of the people. Thus creating new ritual is almost a contradiction. Rituals need to be old rather than new, traditional rather than innovative. And such rituals define the community's very identity: These people are those who do thus and so. Changing ritual patterns, therefore, inevitably disrupts the assembly's prayer life and its communal identity. It should be no surprise that many find the renewal difficult and painful.

Yet renewal is needed, so we have had to face the challenge of changing ritual patterns and even creating "new" rituals (almost all of which are ancient, actually, but were new to us). The goal is to establish firm patterns of prayer and worship that can become "traditional" for us again. This is not a quick process, and we have a long way to go in this liturgical renewal.

■ THE PROCESS OF RENEWAL: The first step in our renewal was the creation of new ritual books. In the years since Vatican II, we have seen a prodigious output of revised orders of worship, including the sacramentary and lectionary for Mass, all the other sacraments, the *Rite of Christian Initiation of Adults,* the *Liturgy of the Hours,* the *Book of Blessings* and many others. These books are based on the riches of our liturgical past but attempt to meet the needs of the contemporary church. Producing and translating them required the long-term efforts of many scholars from all over the world.

Once the books were received, the second stage was the implementation of the changes they required. This process is really still going on, even though we now have had many of the books for a quarter-century. Most parishes would make significant improvements in their worship if they just implemented fully the visions contained in the ritual books now in hand. The introductions to these books often present a strong and clear vision for understanding and celebrating the renewed rites.

The third stage of the renewal is for the new patterns of prayer and worship to become the living possession of the communities that use them. This involves a combination of several factors: There must be local adaptation of the rituals to reflect the culture and daily lives of the worshipers; there must be a long enough time using the new rituals for them to begin to feel traditional; and there must be a balance between ongoing change and relative stability that will enable the worshipers to relax with the rituals and be able to pray through them without having to worry about what comes next and what their response should be. Ritual patterns work best for prayer when they become largely unconscious, that is, when the worshipers can perform the ritual without focusing on the ritual itself. Then they are able to focus on encountering the Lord through the ritual.

■ FADS AND GIMMICKS: While there are many conscientious parish leaders who have worked hard and with great sensitivity to foster true liturgical renewal on the local level, it must also be admitted that some worship leaders have resorted to fads and gimmicks in their attempts to make worship "relevant." Such mistakes were inevitable, given the general lack of liturgical education before Vatican II. The task of reform was necessarily entrusted to many who had little or no training to prepare them for such a vast undertaking.

The use of gimmicks has been, all in all, rather limited in light of the scope of the reform. Much criticism has been leveled by some against the whole process of reform, and they make great outcry over isolated examples of abuses. The actual practice in most parishes, however, bears little resemblance to the extremes they attack.

What has been more common is a sense among liturgy planners that variety and innovation are the keys to lively liturgy, that to keep the worship experience fresh and exciting, ritual elements and texts must be continually varied. While there is certainly a need for some variety, as indicated by the changeable elements of the ritual (e.g., readings and prayers) and the variety of options within many rites (e.g., the penitential rite), too much variety and a sense of constant change is debilitating to the assembly's ability to enter into the ritual and engage in true prayer. Even when the changes are valid and needed, if they are introduced too rapidly and without adequate explanation, they may seem like fads or gimmicks to many.

■ A SOLID LITURGICAL TRADITION: What is needed is a solid local liturgical tradition that is based on the reformed ritual books, is carefully adapted to the local situation and embraces a balance of consistency and variability that truly enables the worshiping assembly to enter into the prayer of the church.

Such a tradition must develop organically. It cannot be imposed all at once, nor can it develop erratically, with changes introduced capriciously. Ritual patterns develop much as plants grow; a healthy plant needs firm roots and time to grow gradually. Changes in ritual patterns must be deliberate improvements, not just variety for the sake of change. And they must come gradually enough for people to assimilate the changes without too much consternation.

DEVELOPING A PARISH TRADITION

Developing such a tradition in a parish is a long-term process. It requires a steady commitment by the parish staff and worship committee, with a shared vision of the goals to be sought.

■ BEGIN WITH EVALUATION: The first step in the process should be a thorough evaluation of the worship life of the parish. Before goals can be set and strategies can be devised, it is important to determine what is solid in the parish's worship and what needs improvement. There are various ways to approach such an evaluation. Perhaps the most effective is to ask a team of experts from outside the parish to come observe the parish's worship over several weeks. Then they can give objective feedback that is not distorted by personal relationships and feelings about individuals who lead the worship. Some diocesan worship offices provide such a service. If that is not available in your diocese, check with area colleges and/or other parishes that have good worship to see if a team can be assembled for this task. Parishes should be willing to pay a reasonable stipend for such work, of course.

If an outside team is not used, another approach is to talk with a number of randomly selected parishioners to hear their experiences of worship in the parish. The main limitation of this approach is the lack of education and formation in liturgy among many parishioners, which can result in feedback that has little to do with good liturgy. Nevertheless, knowing what the assembly thinks and feels about the parish's worship is always valuable.

An essential part of the evaluation process is to read or reread the basic texts that ought to be shaping our worship since Vatican II. These provide the norms against which we can measure our current practice. The following list includes the major works that should be studied carefully (the first eight are included in LTP's *The Liturgy Documents,* third edition):

General Instruction of the Roman Missal
Introduction to the Lectionary
General Norms for the Liturgical Year and the Calendar
Directory for Masses with Children
Environment and Art in Catholic Worship
Music in Catholic Worship
Liturgical Music Today
Fulfilled in Your Hearing
Introductions to each sacrament, including *Rite of Christian Initiation of Adults*
Circular Letter concerning the Preparation and Celebration of the Easter Feasts
Introduction to the *Book of Blessings*

At the end of the evaluation, a list should be created that indicates what is solid in each ritual and in each season of the year. For each area, parish leaders should then set both long- and short-term goals in light of the norms expressed in the ritual books. These should be crafted so that changes can be introduced gradually and deliberately, moving the parish toward the long-term goals.

SOME EXAMPLES OF THE PROCESS

I offer here several examples of how a parish might go about developing a solid local liturgical tradition. It would take a full volume to treat every area that a parish team should examine and address, but the following examples should make the approach clear.

■ THE RESPONSORIAL PSALM: Ideally, the assigned psalm would be sung at every Mass. Reciting the psalm has all the appeal of reciting "The Star-spangled Banner." The psalm is meant to be a musical element between two readings, not another text to be read. If the parish is currently reciting the psalm, there are several steps that might move the assembly gradually toward the ideal.

The first step might be to begin singing the psalm in full one Sunday a month. This would allow time for musicians and cantors to practice and would only require the assembly to learn one short refrain each month. An alternative would be to begin singing just the refrain each week, with the verses being read above soft instrumental music, especially if the parish does not yet have trained cantors.

The second step would be to sing the psalm in full each week but to use the common seasonal psalms. This means that the musicians, cantors and assembly would only need to learn new music once every few weeks. The common psalms (found in the lectionary at #175) may not match the readings every week, but they do embrace the spirit of the liturgical season.

The third step might be to begin learning one new psalm each month while continuing to use the common psalms for the other Sundays. Over a period of two years, the assembly would learn two dozen psalms in addition to several common psalms.

The fourth step would be to sing the assigned psalm each week. If the parish has already learned two or three dozen psalms, this will not mean learning a new psalm each week. And by this point, the parish will have gotten used to picking up a sung refrain without too much effort.

Obviously, this process will take several years from beginning to end. Attempting to achieve the ideal too quickly will lead to resistance from the assembly and frustration on the part of the leaders. What is required is a firm and steady plan of progress that gradually enables the assembly to grow into its proper role in the singing of the responsorial psalm.

■ COMMUNION UNDER BOTH SPECIES: The goal that is evident in the official books as well as in the long tradition of the church is to offer communion under the species of both bread and wine at every Mass. If your parish is not currently offering communion from the cup at all, several steps will again be necessary.

The first step might be to recruit and train new eucharistic ministers. This will be necessary in order to have sufficient ministers to offer the cup regularly without over-scheduling the current ministers.

The second step is a sensitive and thorough catechesis of the assembly on the reasons for receiving communion under both species. Such catechesis should be multi-form, including bulletin inserts, homilies and presentations in catechetical classes and adult education programs. To devote the homily to this topic assumes that the readings lend themselves to such a focus, but there are numerous Sundays throughout the year when that would be possible. It is recommended that such homilies be given more than once, because people come to understand and accept such changes at different rates. It may be valuable to speak about the meaning of sharing both bread and cup several times a year over several years until the assembly fully assimilates the practice.

The third step might be to offer the cup at all Masses one weekend a month. This beginning gives the ministers time to work out refinements in procedures and movements so that the communion rite is celebrated prayerfully. It also gives the assembly time to get used to the practice gradually. This step will require only a few new ministers, so time will be available to continue recruiting and training more. It is much better to begin this way rather than offering the cup every week but only at one Mass; with that approach most of the parish will not become accustomed to the practice.

The fourth step would be to increase the distribution of both species to twice a month or every other week at all the Masses. The next step, offering both species at all Sunday Masses, could be taken as soon as enough ministers are recruited and trained. The final step would be to extend the use of the cup to all the parish Masses, not only those on Sundays.

■ HOLY THURSDAY: Nowhere is a solid liturgical tradition more important than during the Triduum. These central days of the liturgical year involve many rituals used only once a year. If the assembly is to enter into them deeply, they must be traditional in the best sense. For this example, we will focus only on Holy Thursday. Rather than outlining specific steps, I will suggest here a number of issues that should be addressed, perhaps over several years.

The first issue is the very character of the celebration on Holy Thursday. Is it clearly the entrance into the Triduum? Or has it been viewed primarily as a celebration of the institution of the eucharist and/or the ministerial priesthood? What music would help express its character as the first moment of the Three Days? Does the homily make it clear that this celebration is an integral part of the Triduum? Is catechesis offered to the assembly in the weeks before the Triduum to help them understand it and enter into it more deeply?

The unique ritual for this liturgy is the washing of feet. How well is this carried out? Who is included and why? If the parish has been washing hands instead of feet, how can it move back to the proper ritual? Can it be done in a way that involves more than a few representatives of the assembly?

Do you receive the holy oils at the beginning of the Mass? Is this ritual carried out with beauty and dignity? Does it help focus the celebration as part of the Three Days?

Is the best bread and wine used on this night? Can bread be baked by members of the assembly for this celebration?

How is the procession at the end of Mass carried out? What should be our traditional song and tune for this procession? Is the eucharist taken to a chapel of reservation outside the church, as the ritual books require? If not, can we find a space to use for this purpose? Are decorations in the chapel modest and appropriate for the Triduum? Is adoration well attended? What kind of parish prayer is offered during it?

How is the church stripped? Can it be more thorough, so that the space is truly bare for Good Friday?

■ EASTER SEASON: One of the main challenges of the Easter season is learning how to celebrate well for the whole Fifty Days. Various steps can be taken to help the assembly grow into this season, beginning by making it clear throughout the season that it is still Easter.

A key area is music. Are Easter hymns part of every Mass? Is the Gloria sung throughout the season? Is there an Easter alleluia used throughout? Should we sing the double alleluia at the dismissal throughout the season?

The decorations for the season also set the tone. Do the Easter flowers last throughout the Fifty Days? What types of flowers could be used that will last? Can the budget be adjusted to allow replacing flowers as the season progresses, even if this means having fewer flowers at the beginning? What other elements of the decor, such as banners, drapery and vestments, say "Easter" clearly?

Mass planning during Easter should keep Easter themes and images dominant. Do Mother's day, the month of May, First Communion or Confirmation override Easter? How can we integrate them into the season?

Preaching is crucial for helping the assembly sustain the spirit of Easter. Do the homilies preached every Sunday provide mystagogy for the neophytes and for the whole assembly? Do the homilies speak of Easter and what it means to live resurrected life?

Various rituals can also help to unify the season. Is the sprinkling rite used at all the Sunday Masses? Should the assembly stand through the eucharistic prayer during Easter, in imitation of the early Christians, who did not kneel during Easter? Are baptisms celebrated at Mass, reminding us that Easter is the prime season for initiation?

LOCAL FEASTS

Beyond the universal feasts that make up the liturgical calendar, it is important for a parish to develop local celebrations for days that have particular significance to the local community. Two of these are the anniversary of the dedication of the parish church building and the celebration of the feast of the parish patron saint.

If these days are not currently celebrated by the whole parish, a gradually increasing focus on these days will be needed to lead people to an awareness of their importance and to develop a parish tradition of rich celebration.

The first step might be simply to announce each of these days several weeks before the date and offer an evening eucharist or sung evensong if the date falls on a workday. This will signal the parish leadership's view that all parishioners are encouraged to take part.

Good planning of the celebrations themselves is also crucial, so that those who do come will be likely to gather again next year. Here again, though, things could develop gradually. Simply having musical accompaniment for the feast might be an improvement over previous years. In subsequent years, all the parish musicians might be invited to collaborate, and a special parish song might be chosen or even commissioned.

Beyond the liturgical celebrations, these days might well be the best days for parish picnics, dances or dinners, so that these feasts become prime community-building days for the parish. Over time, then, the local feasts of the parish can become major events to which all look forward each year.

A LONG-TERM EFFORT

These few examples may already have the parish worship committee ready to resign! The task is a large one, and it is easy to feel overwhelmed, but there is no short-cut to developing a solid local liturgical tradition. Long-term commitment is essential.

In carrying on the process of renewal, consistency is important. Changes should be deliberate and focused toward the long-range goals. This does not mean that we will never reverse ourselves. Some adjustments will be needed as we continue to learn and recognize that some steps we have taken were missteps. But these should be the exception, and the assembly should not feel that it is at the mercy of the changing whims of parish leaders.

If new staff members are interviewed (pastor, musician, liturgist), they should be asked if they accept the long-range goals that have been embraced by the parish leadership. One of the most devastating experiences for an assembly is to have a change of leadership and find that all the goals have changed.

Liturgical renewal does not mean just using new rites. Those rites must become part of a living tradition in the parish. Renewal means bringing new life to the parish's worship pattern. A consistent pattern, based on a solid understanding of rites, is the only thing that will do.

Latino Seasonal Traditions: The Hispanic Mística and the Liturgy

NEARING the end of the second millennium, the church has become more conscious of the way culture has influenced liturgy throughout Christian history. In previous ages, many of our ancestors in faith took for granted that all our inherited forms of prayer were divinely ordained (the same was also true, of course, of economic and political structures as well). Our worship changed so slowly that the majority of Catholics never realized that many of the liturgical practices they thought were universal were really quite particular and very much influenced by local traditions, languages and symbols. Even after the Council of Trent, when rigid liturgical uniformity was highlighted as a supreme value, the Roman Rite was experienced in different ways due to its cultural context. The Mass in Italy, Ireland and Austria might have been identical according to the liturgical books, but the arrangement and appointments of the worship space (its art and environment), the music used at the celebration and the folk customs associated with particular feasts before and after the celebration in church all made the universal rite particular and meaningful to a given people.

During the latter part of the nineteenth and the beginning of the twentieth century, national parishes were established in the United States to celebrate the faith in ways familiar to the many immigrant groups pouring into the country from Southern and Eastern Europe and to preserve their cultural identity in an environment that pressured all groups to assimilate. Even though the Mass always was celebrated in Latin, pastoral effectiveness demanded that preaching and other ministry be done in the language of the people, using their symbols, celebrating their saints. In short, even for the "unchanging" Tridentine liturgy to have been effective, it had to celebrate the mystery of Christ using the cultural forms of the people at worship.

Today the Catholic church in the United States is experiencing a similar pastoral/liturgical challenge brought on by another wave of immigration. In addition to the growing number of Asians (Vietnamese, Koreans, Laotians, Filipinos) and a new sensitivity to African American cultural differences, the Hispanic presence is being felt more and more in parishes around the country. Unlike some cultures only recently evangelized or others that are not traditionally Catholic, the various Hispanic groups that are coming to this country already possess what can be called a "Catholic culture." It would be a mistake, though, to think that all Hispanic groups are the same (even the term *Hispanic* is not universally accepted as a collective name; some prefer to be called *Latino*). However, peoples as diverse as Mexicans, Cubans and Bolivians not only share a common language, they also have a common *mística*. The term *mística* is used here to describe the Hispanic world view that is conditioned by centuries of contact with the gospel. The Hispanic *mística* is the way Latinos conceive of their place in the world and of their relationship to God and to other human beings. The term also refers to a spirituality that comes from deeply held values such as the dignity of the individual, the centrality of the family and the importance given to feeling and sentiment in living an authentically Christian life.

Mark R. Francis, CSV, with José Castillo

It must also be acknowledged that the *mística* is a product of the clash of three cultural worlds: the European, Native American and African. Through the *mestizaje* (mixing) of the Iberian conquerors with the native peoples of America and the slaves from Africa, a new *raza* was born: a people that incorporates aspects of all three cultures. This *mestizaje* is especially evident in the Hispanic approach to liturgy and prayer and influences the way Latinos interpret the traditional Catholic liturgical year.

The lens through which many Hispanics interpret their Catholic faith is popular religion. Rituals and beliefs handed down in the home and expressive of the *mística* form a large part of popular religion and serve to give a more human face to the more formal catechism of the official church. Popular religious practice can be as simple as a mother or father blessing their children before they run out the door to play. It can also take the form of the home altar, or *altarcito*, which highlights the sacredness of the home and is usually tended by the mother of the family.

Popular religious practices tend to be dramatic and emotional. Some of them, such the Nativity and Easter plays, find their origins in the first catechetical efforts of the Franciscan, Dominican and Augustinian missionaries to teach the faith by means of drama. Attending to the people's own religious customs—some of which differ from group to group—is an important aspect of ministry with Hispanics and is crucial for clues on how to inculturate the liturgy.

The purpose of the sections of this year's *Sourcebook* titled "The Hispanic *Mística* and the Liturgy" is to note how a particular part of the liturgical year is celebrated by some Hispanic groups. These descriptions are not meant to exhaust the richness of the Hispanic traditions represented by the various peoples who are now part of the Catholic church in the United States. Rather, the brief reflections on the Hispanic customs of a given season are written for the pastoral minister who may not be familiar with some of these traditions but who wants to be sensitive to their appropriate incorporation in the worship life of the parish.

Finally, these reflections are not limited to the liturgy, strictly speaking, but are addressed to the wide range of customs that contextualize the various celebrations of the liturgical year. It has been said that successful Hispanic religious celebrations are a holistic experience; they appeal to all the senses and cannot be limited to what is done in church. This is summed up by the expression of the three M's: *Misa, Musa, Mesa—Mass,* or liturgical celebration; *muse,* meaning some form of artistic expression such as dance, poetry reading and music; and *table,* the special food that is associated with a given celebration. This holistic approach to liturgy is something that many of us who belong to mainstream U.S. culture have undervalued. In welcoming and encouraging the Hispanic *mística* in parish celebrations, especially in multicultural settings, we will all be enriched.

FOR FURTHER READING

This annotated list of works is chosen to offer a range of resources for those working as liturgical ministers in Hispanic parishes.

Virgilio Elizondo, *Christianity and Culture.* San Antonio: Mexican American Cultural Center (MACC), 1975.
A classic reference work on the interrelationships of culture and faith with specific reference to the Hispanic (Mexican) community.

Rosa María Icaza, "Prayer, Worship and Liturgy in a U.S. Hispanic Key," in Alan Figueroa Deck (ed.) *Frontiers of Hispanic Theology in the United States.* Maryknoll: Orbis, 1992, pp. 134–54.
With a concern to link liturgy with the evangelization of culture, the author presents some of the basic characteristics of the *mística* and how they are expressed liturgically and in popular religion.

Mexican American Cultural Center, *Faith Expressions of Hispanics in the Southwest,* Revised Edition. San Antonio: MACC, 1990.
This handy booklet describes many traditional Hispanic customs common to the American Southwest, many of which are also common among Hispanics in other parts of the country.

Arturo Pérez, *Popular Catholicism: a Hispanic Perspective.* Collegeville: The Liturgical Press, 1988.
The best short work available on Hispanic liturgy in the United States, it describes well how the *mística* expresses itself in worship.

Spirituals: A Source of Protest and Praise

IN the liturgical document *Plenty Good Room,* African American spirituality is identified as contemplative, holistic, joyful, communitarian and emotive. Another adjective could be added: musical. As James Cone has written:

> In Africa and America, black music was not an artistic creation for its own sake; it was directly related to daily life, work, and play. Song was an expression of the community's view of the world and its existence in it. Through music, Africans recorded their history, initiated the young into adulthood, and expressed their religious beliefs. (The Spirituals and the Blues: An Interpretation [Seabury, 1972])

In short, music was and is intrinsic to our African American spirituality. Jon Michael Spencer recalls the power of this elemental characteristic in his book *Protest and Praise: Sacred Music of Black Religion* (Fortress, 1990). He reminds us that at the height of our enslavement, we protested our captivity and sang of freedom not only in that great by and by, but here and now. In those heady days of the abolitionist movement, we sang the hymnody from such great liturgical books as Edwin F. Hatfield's *Freedom's Lyre.* While others at the turn of the century were celebrating a new century, we were concerned about ushering in the kingdom. We sang the great hymns of Henry Sloane Coffin, Ambrose White Vernon, Mabel Mussey and Mornay Williams. During the Civil Rights Movement, we sat at counters, we marched in the streets, we boycotted, and we continued to sing. We dug deep into our past and brought forth those songs of protest that had galvanized our forebears in days gone by. Even when not on bended knee in

church, we sang. We sang the blues and were moved from lament to praise.

This praise continues to this day. For it, too, has long been a part of our heritage. Though our praising drums were taken away from us, we shouted and clapped and moaned and stomped in rhythm. Underlying all this activity was praise. We hear it today in the heavenly anthems of the Primal Pentecostals, in the testimony of the Holiness churches, and in the powerful singing of the Gospel in gospel. In addition, through our long history our preachers have sung their sermons and so stirred our souls that we were able not only to survive but thrive (Spencer, *Protest and Praise*). Singing is, indeed, in our sanctified soul.

Of particular interest in our singing is the place of spirituals. W.E.B. DuBois in his *Souls of Black Folk* (Literary Classics of the United States, 1986) called them "the singular spiritual heritage of the nation and the greatest gift of the Negro people." Malcolm X wrote in his *Autobiography* (Grove, 1965),

> The white man has taught us to shout and sing and pray until we *die,* to wait until *death,* for some dreamy heaven-in-the-hereafter, when we're *dead,* while this white man has his milk and honey in the streets paved with golden dollars right here on *this* earth!

Recent research such as that of Cheryl Kirk-Duggan (*A Troubling in My Soul,* ed. Emilie Townes [Orbis, 1993]) gives a fuller picture, however. It is clear that in the spirituals

> The singers talked "face to face" with Old Testament heroes and heroines, and their New Testament cosuffering Jesus. Slaves appropriated basic theological ideas

J-Glenn Murray, SJ

to express their religious cosmology and passion for freedom. The spiritual's core message focused on the protest hermeneutic of survival and hope.

Spirituals have been, in fact, a constant source and resource for understanding who we African Americans are before God and one another. They have been a source of hope and survival for us black Catholics as well. Now is the time for them to be a resource for the whole church. Pope John Paul II challenged us to do this when he spoke to African American Catholics assembled in New Orleans in October of 1987:

> Your black cultural heritage enriches the church and makes her witness of universality more complete. In a real way the church needs you just as you need the church, for you are part of the church and the church is part of you.

What the black religious experience brings to the table, then, is a notion of protest against injustice of any kind and praise of a God who in Jesus Christ is:

> King of Kings, and Lord of Lords,
> Jesus Christ, the first and the last,
> No man works like him!

It is for these reasons that we suggest a renewal in singing these songs of "protest and praise" throughout the liturgical year, at home in family gatherings and at liturgy, especially during the preliminary gathering.

The document *In Spirit and Truth,* a reflection by the U.S. Bishops' Committee on the Liturgy regarding the celebration of the eucharist in African American parishes, mentions the idea of a preliminary gathering. The drafters of this text envision this period as a time of building up the community. It is a time wherein those gathered might indeed come to some sense of their being in the unique presence of God. It is a time of witness and praise. It may be a time of welcome. Given the times in which we live— a time of lamentable proportions and near nihilism, as Cornel West suggests (*Race Matters* [Beacon, 1993])—it might do us well to recapture the genius of our ancestors and sing in protest.

The spirituals recognized a world in which there was pain and suffering. They were aware of a world in which people were longing for a land flowing with milk and honey. The spirituals were songs of protest, survival and hope against the injustice in which our progenitors were mired. Our own time is not much different. Today, we live in an age of violence and destruction. We long for safe shelter and shade. Would it not be important for us to denounce this evil, to establish through song a world view in Christ in whom there is no east or west, but one great family bound by love?

Bibliography

RITUAL BOOKS

I. The Roman Missal has been published in several parts, mostly to distinguish the various ministries. These volumes form the core of any parish's liturgical library:

A. *Sacramentary:* 1985 (The Liturgical Press, Catholic Book Publishing Company).

Complementary volumes:

The Book of the Chair (various publishers) contains the portions of the sacramentary used at the presider's chair on Sundays.

Collection of Masses of the Blessed Virgin Mary (Catholic Book Publishing Company)

Sacramentary Supplement (Catholic Book Publishing Company) is a collection of the propers for saints who have been added to the calendar since the sacramentary was published.

Forthcoming publication:

As *Sourcebook* went to press, the bishops of the United States were still working toward approving a revision of the sacramentary. After the bishops approve, their approval must be confirmed by Rome. After that, a date for publication will be determined.

B. *Lectionary for Mass:* The 1970 edition is still in use (various publishers, some with individual volumes for each year of Sundays).

Complementary volumes:

The *Lectionary for Masses with Children* provides readings for Sundays, feasts and weekdays in the Contemporary English Version. Various publishers have produced editions of this lectionary.

A new lectionary was published in Latin in 1981; its introduction is published in English (USCC, also in the LTP collection, *The Liturgy Documents*).

The Book of Gospels: The gospels from the lectionary have been published separately (Catholic Book Publishing Company).

The *Simple Gradual* was published in English in 1968, and its collection of psalms has made its way into many available hymnals.

Forthcoming publication:

A revised lectionary for the United States.

C. *Roman Calendar:* When the current (1969) calendar was implemented in the dioceses of the United States, several dates proper to this country were added. That list continues to grow. The calendar and the "General Norms for the Liturgical Year and the Calendar" are reprinted at the front of the sacramentary.

Complementary volumes:

Liturgy Documentary Series, #6: Norms Governing Liturgical Calendars (USCC, 1984). The "General Norms" and the calendar are accompanied by the commentary released by the Vatican in the early 1970s and updated to 1984, by the principles for particular calendars, and by clarifications issued by the Vatican.

Roman Calendar: Text and Commentary (USCC, 1976) has much of the same, but in an earlier version. It is one of the few places in English to find the Litany of the Saints.

Dioceses are mandated to issue annual calendars, with local feasts and norms. Many publishers issue annual calendars and ordos, some with regional editions.

II. *The Liturgy of the Hours:* 1975 (4 vols., Catholic Book Publishing Company; 2 vols., Daughters of Saint Paul). A treasure for all Catholics.

Complementary volumes:

Christian Prayer is a one-volume excerpt from the full collection. (Catholic Book Publishing Company)

Shorter Christian Prayer (Catholic Book Publishing Company) is a simplified, pocket-size edition to help introduce the assembly to this form of liturgical prayer.

A *Supplement* with new memorials to be observed in the United States was published by Catholic Book Publishing Company in 1987.

III. *The Roman Ritual,* published in one volume before Vatican II, has since been published in several volumes, one for each sacrament or rite. The increased number of options and adaptations made this necessary. Every parish, every presider and every planning group needs a full set of the current editions at hand (with the possible exception of the *Rite of Religious Profession*).

A. *Rite of Christian Initiation of Adults:* 1988 (LTP, The Liturgical Press, USCC, Catholic Book Publishing Company). This includes the rite for the Reception of Baptized Christians, formerly published in a separate booklet.

B. *Rite of Baptism for Children:* 1970 (The Liturgical Press, Catholic Book Publishing Company). The Canadian bishops published a handsome edition of this book with separate rites "within Mass" and "outside Mass." Copyright restrictions prohibit bulk sales in the United States, but individual copies can be obtained from the Canadian Catholic Conference.

C. *Rite of Marriage:* 1970 (The Liturgical Press, Ave Maria Press, Catholic Book Publishing Company). The Canadian edition (Canadian Catholic Conference) includes suggested texts for the rite of reception at the entrance and other texts which make it the best volume currently available.

> Forthcoming publication:
>
> The Vatican issued a new edition in 1990. ICEL and the U.S. bishops' conference are working on the U.S. adaptation. Presumably, this will be the next section of the ritual to be published.

D. *Order of Christian Funerals:* 1989 (LTP, The Liturgical Press, Catholic Book Publishing Company). The Canadian edition (Canadian Conference of Catholic Bishops, 1990) includes a fine re-ordering of the "Vigil and related rites and prayers," placing them in chronological order. It also contains important appendices: prayers for the end of the day, after vigil and visitation; norms for cremation and ritual directives for a funeral liturgy in the presence of the ashes (Canada received an indult to make this possible).

E. *Rite of Penance:* 1975 (The Liturgical Press, Pueblo Publishing Company, Catholic Book Publishing Company).

F. *Pastoral Care of the Sick: Rites of Anointing and Viaticum:* 1983 (LTP [Spanish and English], The Liturgical Press, Catholic Book Publishing).

G. *Holy Communion and Worship of the Eucharist Outside Mass:* 1976 (Catholic Book Publishing Company).

H. *Rite of Religious Profession:* 1988 (LTP).

I. *Book of Blessings:* 1989 (The Liturgical Press, Catholic Book Publishing Company). This book contains numerous blessings and prayers, including several rites once published separately: the orders for crowning an image of the Blessed Virgin Mary, for the commissioning of extraordinary ministers of the eucharist, and for the installation of a pastor.

> Complementary volumes:
>
> *Catholic Household Blessings and Prayers:* 1988 (USCC). This is the first attempt by the U.S. bishops since *A Manual of Prayers,* issued by the Baltimore Council of 1888, to provide a standard prayer book for the whole country.
>
> *Shorter Book of Blessings:* 1990 (Catholic Book Publishing Company). An abridged form of the *Book of Blessings,* it contains most of the blessings that take place outside of Mass.

IV. The *Roman Pontifical* includes those rites normally celebrated by a bishop. The *Blessing of Oil and Consecration of Chrism* has been included in the sacramentary. The rites for confirmation and for a church dedication, at least, should be in every liturgical library:

A. *Roman Pontifical,* Part I: 1978 (ICEL). Contains the now outdated rites of initiation, confirmation, the institution of readers and acolytes, the various ordination rites, and several blessings of persons (blessing of an abbot/abbess and consecration to a life of virginity).

> Complementary volumes:
>
> *Confirmation:* 1973 (USCC). Excerpted from the fuller pontifical.
>
> Forthcoming revision:
>
> Revised ordination rites were published in Latin in 1990 and currently are being translated.

B. *Dedication of a Church and an Altar:* 1989 (USCC). An important resource for parishes undergoing renovation or construction; useful for parishes preparing for each year's anniversary.

V. Other official books:

The *Ceremonial of Bishops:* 1989 (The Liturgical Press). While not a liturgical book of texts, it is an official compilation of rubrics and of emendations made since the various ritual books were published. The notes are useful for charting celebrations for every parish.

LITURGICAL DOCUMENTS

The Code of Canon Law (Canon Law Society of America, 1983) contains a significant amount of legislation pertaining to the celebration of the liturgy.

Documents on the Liturgy, 1963–1979: Conciliar, Papal and Curial Texts (Collegeville: The Liturgical Press, 1982). A fine translation and compilation of everything official. The massive index makes this a gold mine of information.

The Liturgy Documents: A Parish Resource, third edition, (LTP, 1991). The most recent translations of Roman liturgical documents are included along with documents of the Bishops' Committee on the Liturgy.

HISTORY AND CELEBRATION OF THE LITURGICAL YEAR

Adam, Adolf, *The Liturgical Year: Its History and Its Meaning After the Reform of the Liturgy* (Collegeville MN: Pueblo/The Liturgical Press, 1981). One of the best studies available.

Alexander, J. Neil, *Time and Community* (Washington DC: The Pastoral Press, 1990). Serious essays on such topics as the lenten lectionary in the fourth century and the origins of candlemas.

Baldovin, John, *Worship: City, Church and Renewal* (Washington: The Pastoral Press, 1991). See chapters on feasting the saints and on a calendar for a just community—all founded on careful scholarship of our ancient Christian heritage.

Bishops' Committee on the Liturgy Secretariat, National Conference of Catholic Bishops, *God's*

Mercy Endures Forever: Guidelines on the Presentation of Jews and Judaism in Catholic Preaching (USCC, 1988). Includes specific notes on the various liturgical seasons.

_____ , *Holy Days in the United States: History, Theology, Celebration* (USCC, 1984). With additional notes on the days in the American proper calendar as of 1984.

_____ , *Study Text 9: The Liturgical Year: Celebrating the Mystery of Christ and His Saints* (USCC, 1984).

Carroll, Thomas, and Halton, Thomas, *Liturgical Practice in the Fathers* (Collegeville MN: Glazier/The Liturgical Press, 1988). Carefully chosen quotations and commentary on the various seasons and feasts as they developed in the first centuries.

Congregation for Divine Worship. "Circular Letter Concerning the Preparation and Celebration of the Easter Feasts," (Washington DC: USCC). Issued by the Vatican in 1988, it is an excellent compendium of liturgical principles applicable in these weeks.

Huck, Gabe. *The Three Days: Parish Prayer in the Paschal Triduum* (LTP, revised edition, 1992).

Hynes, Mary Ellen. *Companion to the Calendar* (Chicago: Liturgy Training Publications, 1993). A daily and seasonal guide to the saints and mysteries that make up the calendar of Christians, with additional notes on the calendars of Jews and Muslims and the national days of the United States and Canada. For homes, schools, and parishes.

Irwin, Kevin. A trilogy of exhaustive guides to every day, to every liturgical text in the seasons (Collegeville: Pueblo/The Liturgical Press):
   Advent & Christmas: A Guide to the Eucharist and Hours, 1986.
   Lent: A Guide to the Eucharist and Hours, 1985.
   Easter: A Guide to the Eucharist and Hours, 1991.

Jackson, Pamela, *Journeybread for the Shadowlands* (Collegeville: The Liturgical Press, 1993). An unusual and useful set of reflections on the readings for the various rites of the RCIA throughout the year.

Martimort, A. G., et al., *The Church at Prayer* vol. 4, The Liturgy and Time (Collegeville MN: The Liturgical Press, 1986). See especially the essays by Pierre Jounel on Sunday and the year.

Metford, J. C. J., *The Christian Year* (New York: Crossroad, 1991). A masterful summary, with many nuggets of fascinating detail, organized season by season.

Nelson, Gertrud Mueller, *To Dance With God: Family Ritual and Community Celebration* (Mahwah, NJ: Paulist, 1986). A helpful collection of essays on celebration and suggestions for family rituals for each season.

Nocent, Adrian, *The Liturgical Year,* 4 vols. (Collegeville MN: The Liturgical Press, 1977). Excellent commentaries on the liturgical seasons and scriptures.

Parsch, Pius, *The Church's Year of Grace,* 5 vols. (circulating in various editions, most notably: Collegeville: The Liturgical Press, 1957). While commenting on the old calendar, this work still offers enormous assistance to readers, especially when looking for guidance to the previous generations' approach to the seasons and saints.

Pawlikowski, John T., and Wilde, James A., *When Catholics Speak about Jews* (LTP, 1987). Notes for homilists, catechists and intercession writers—arranged by the liturgical year.

Power, David, ed., *The Times of Celebration,* Concilium, #142 (New York: Seabury Press, 1981). Groundbreaking essays on time, seasons, Sundays and local calendars.

The Saint Andrew Bible Missal (Brooklyn: William J. Hirten Co., 1982). Contains insightful introductions to the liturgical seasons and to the readings, as well as attention to Christian initiation.

Schmemann, Alexander. *Great Lent: Journey to Pascha.* (Crestwood NY: St. Vladimir's Seminary Press, 1974). A classic, with universally applicable meditations on fasting, discipline, celebration and Lent as pilgrimage.

Sourcebooks from LTP (Texts of all kinds from over the centuries to enliven the various days and the season's overall development.):

An Advent Sourcebook, O'Gorman, Thomas, ed., 1988.
A Christmas Sourcebook, Simcoe, Mary Ann, ed., 1984.
A Lent Sourcebook: The Forty Days, Baker, J. Robert, Evelyn Kaehler and Peter Mazar, eds., 1991 (2 vols.).
A Triduum Sourcebook, Huck, Gabe, and Mary Ann Simcoe, eds., 1983.
An Easter Sourcebook: The Fifty Days, Huck, Gabe, Gail Ramshaw and Gordon Lathrop, eds., 1988.
A Sourcebook about Christian Death, Sloyan, Virginia, ed., 1990. For November or for the period of mourning after death.
A Baptism Sourcebook, Baker, J. Robert, Larry J. Nyberg and Victoria M. Tufano, eds. 1993.
A Liturgy Sourcebook, Huck, Gabe, ed., 1994
A Marriage Sourcebook, Baker, J. Robert, Kevin Charles Gibley, Joni Reiff Gibley, eds. 1994

Stevenson, Kenneth. *Jerusalem Revisited: The Liturgical Meaning of Holy Week* (Washington DC: The Pastoral Press, 1988).

Talley, Thomas J., *The Origins of the Liturgical Year* (Collegeville MN: Pueblo/The Liturgical Press, 1986).

Thurston, Herbert, and Attwater, Donald, *Butler's Lives of the Saints,* 4 vols. (Westminster MD: Christian Classics, 1981). The most complete publication on the saints in English. While the changes in the Roman Calendar have shifted several observances, this is invaluable for researching additions to the litany of the saints and for discovering the dates of saints not in the current Roman Calendar.

Walsh, Michael, *Butler's Lives of the Saints: Concise Edition* (New York: Harper Collins, 1991). This has about one-seventh of the material found in the full edition, but all recent canonizations and calendar shifts are listed in the complete index of saints.

Weiser, Francis X., *Handbook of Christian Feasts and Customs* (various editions, including: New York: Paulist Press, 1963). Contains abridged materials from his earlier volumes: *The Christmas Book, The Easter Book,* and *The Holyday Book.* All are invaluable for their references to once-popular traditions.

MUSIC RESOURCES

I. Hymnals

Cantate Domino (New York: Oxford University Press, 1980). The European ecumenical hymnal (the first edition was produced in the 1920s). An invaluable resource.

Catholic Book of Worship III (Ottawa: Canadian Conference of Catholic Bishops, and Toronto: Gordon V. Thompson, Limited, 1980). The Canadian national Catholic hymnal.

The Catholic Liturgy Book (Baltimore: Helicon Press, Inc., 1975). A fine, early attempt at a service book, well edited.

The Collegeville Hymnal (Collegeville: The Liturgical Press, 1990). Contains new seasonal psalm settings and contributions by many Benedictine authors and composers.

Flor y Canto (Portland: Oregon Catholic Press, 1990). Compiles music from the liturgical traditions of the European, Caribbean and American Spanish-speaking cultures.

Gather, Second Edition (Chicago: GIA Publications, Inc., 1994). The "contemporary" companion to Worship.

Gather Comprehensive (Chicago: GIA Publications, Inc., 1994). Combines the contents of *Gather, Second Edition* with 250 "traditional" selections.

The Hymnal 1982 (New York: The Church Pension Fund, 1985). The Episcopalian hymnal. There's more chant in this volume than in any Catholic hymnal.

Hymnal for Catholic Students (Chicago: GIA Publications, Inc., and LTP, 1988). A basic book for grade-school students in parochial schools and religious education programs. Children can learn this repertoire and then carry it with them throughout their lives. The *Leaders' Manual* of this book is fundamental reading for anyone interested in public worship.

Hymnal for the Hours (Chicago: GIA Publications, Inc., 1989). A gold mine of hymnody.

ICEL Resource Collection (Chicago: GIA Publications, Inc., 1981). Hymns in the public domain and settings of service music for the rites by contemporary composers.

Lead Me, Guide Me, A Hymnal for African American Parishes (Chicago: GIA Publications, Inc., 1987).

Songs of Zion (Nashville: Abingdon, 1982) Music from the black gospel and spiritual traditions.

Lutheran Book of Worship (Minneapolis: Augsburg Publishing House, 1978).

Peoples Mass Book (Schiller Park IL: World Library Publications, Inc., 1984). A basic collection with lots of Lucien Deiss.

Worship, Third Edition (Chicago: GIA Publications, Inc., 1986). Well-rounded American Catholic service book and hymnal.

II. Musical Resources for Liturgy of the Hours

The publications listed here provide full settings for the liturgy of the hours. Titles listed in the "hymnals" section may also offer orders of service, prayer texts, and musical settings of invitatories, office hymns, psalms, intercessions and canticles.

Christian Prayer, organ accompaniment. Various composers (Washington DC: ICEL, 1978).

Holden Evening Prayer. Marty Haugen (Chicago: GIA Publications, Inc., 1990).

Hymnal for the Hours (Chicago: GIA Publications, Inc., 1989).

Light and Peace (Morning Praise and Evensong). David Haas (Chicago: GIA Publications, Inc., 1986).

Nightsong: Music for Evening Prayer. Howard Hughes, SM (Schiller Park IL: World Library Publications, 1989).

O Joyful Light. Michael Joncas (Phoenix: North American Liturgy Resources, 1985).

Praise God in Song: Ecumenical Daily Prayer. Compiled and edited by John Allyn Melloh, SM, and William G. Storey with original music by David Clark Isele, Howard Hughes, SM, and Michael Joncas (Chicago: GIA, 1979).

Praise God in Song: Ecumenical Night Prayer. Compiled and edited by John Allyn Melloh, SM, and William G. Storey with original music by David Clark Isele, Howard Hughes, SM, and Michael Joncas (Chicago: GIA, 1982).

Worship, Third Edition, Liturgy of the Hours Leaders' Edition (Chicago: GIA, 1989).

III. Psalm Resources

These collections of responsorial psalmody are available as individual publications. Many contain reprintable refrains.

The Gelineau Gradual. Responsorial psalms for the lectionary for Mass for the Sundays and principal feasts of the liturgical year. (Chicago: GIA Publications, Inc., 1977).

The Gelineau Gradual, Volume II. Responsorial Psalms from the lectionary for Mass for the rites of the church. (Chicago: GIA Publications, Inc., 1979).

The Grail Gelineau Psalter. 150 Psalms and 18 Canticles (Chicago: GIA Publications, Inc., 1972).

Grail Psalms Inclusive Language Version (text only) (Chicago: GIA Publications, Inc., 1983).

ICEL Lectionary Music. Psalms and alleluia and gospel acclamations for the liturgy of the word. Various composers (Chicago: GIA Publications, Inc., 1982).

Psalms and Selected Canticles. Robert Kreutz (Portland: Oregon Catholic Press, 1983).

Psalms for All Seasons: From the ICEL Liturgical Psalter Project. Various composers (Washington, DC: NPM Publications, 1987).

Psalms for the Cantor, Volumes I–VII. Various composers (Schiller Park IL: World Library Publications, 1985-1987).

Psalms for the Church Year. Marty Haugen and David Haas (Chicago: GIA, 1983).

Psalms for the Church Year, Volume II. Marty Haugen (Chicago: GIA Publications, Inc., 1988).

Psalms for the Church Year, Volume III. David Haas and Jeanne Cotter (Chicago: GIA Publications, Inc., 1989).

Psalms for the Church Year. David Clark Isele (Chicago: GIA Publications, Inc., 1979).

Psalms for Feasts and Seasons. Christopher Willcock, SJ. Liturgical Press.

Psalms for Singing. Stephen Somerville. (Schiller Park: World Library Publications, 1976).

Psalms for Sundays and Seasons. Twelve psalms for soloist, choir and congregation. Jim Hansen (Waco: Chancel Music, 1984; distributed by Oregon Catholic Press).

Psaltery. Steven Warner (Chicago: GIA Publications, Inc., 1990).

Respond and Acclaim. Owen Alstott (Portland: Oregon Catholic Press, 1991).

Salmos. Manuel F. Garcia (Portland: Oregon Catholic Press, 1984).

Service Music for the Mass, Volumes 1–5. Various composers (Schiller Park IL: J.S. Paluch Company, Inc., 1988–1989).

PERIODICALS

Assembly (Notre Dame: Center for Pastoral Liturgy). Five times a year. Each issue explores the tradition, meaning and practice of some aspect of the liturgical event in order to help the community and its ministers enter more deeply into the spirit of the liturgy.

Bishops' Committee on the Liturgy Newsletter (USCC). Ten times a year.

Catechumenate: A Journal of Christian Initiation (LTP). Six times a year. Each issue contains pastoral and scholarly writing on topics concerning initiation.

Environment & Art Letter (LTP). Twelve times a year. Explores issues concerning the environment for worship, both permanent and seasonal.

Liturgical Ministry (Liturgical Press). Quarterly. Each issue focuses on a single topic, aiming to bridge the academic and pastoral approaches to liturgical ministry.

Liturgy (Washington DC: The Liturgical Conference). Quarterly. The Journal of The Liturgical Conference, an ecumenical organization. Each issue explores a single aspect of liturgy, usually taking in many disciplines and many church traditions. Back issues are available and are often excellent resources.

Liturgy 90 (LTP). Eight times a year. Features articles on the seasons and sacraments, regular columns on music, environment and art, questions and answers.

National Bulletin on Liturgy (Ottawa: National Liturgical Office, Canadian Catholic Conference). Four times a year. Each issue explores one topic in detail, often with extensive bibliographies. Many of the "thematic" back issues of this fine journal are still available.

Pastoral Music (Washington DC: National Association of Pastoral Musicians). Six times a year. Often contains several major articles on a single theme together with reviews and announcements. Centers on music but touches on all areas of liturgy.

Worship (Collegeville: The Order of St. Benedict). Six times a year. Scholarly journal which, since 1926, has been the primary support of liturgical renewal throughout the English-speaking world. Order from The Liturgical Press.

Addresses of Publishers

Augsburg Publishing House/Fortress Press
Box 1209
Minneapolis MN 55440

Canadian Conference of Catholic Bishops
90 Parent Avenue
Ottawa, Ontario K1N 7B1, Canada

Canon Law Society of America
Catholic University of America
Washington DC 20064

Catholic Book Publishing Company
257 West 17th Street
New York NY 10011

Center for Pastoral Liturgy
PO Box 81
Notre Dame IN 46556

Church Hymnal Corporation
800 Second Avenue
New York NY 10017

Cokesbury
Post Office Box 801
Nashville, TN 37202

Crossroad Publishing Company
575 Lexington Avenue
New York NY 10022

Daughters of St. Paul
50 St. Paul's Avenue
Boston MA 02130

Farrar, Straus & Giroux, Inc.
19 Union Square, West
New York NY 10003

GIA Publications
7404 South Mason Avenue
Chicago IL 60638

Michael Glazier, Inc.
(now part of Liturgical Press)

HarperCollins Publishers
10 East 53rd Street
New York NY 10022

William J. Hirten Company
6100 17th Avenue
Brooklyn NY 11204

ICEL (International Committee
on English in the Liturgy)
1275 K Street NW
Suite 1202
Washington DC 20005-4097

The Liturgical Conference
8750 Georgia Avenue – Suite 123
Silver Spring MD 20910-3621

The Liturgical Press
P. O. Box 7500
Collegeville MN 56321-7500

National Association of Pastoral Musicians
225 Sheridan Street NW
Washington DC 20011

New Dawn Press
P. O. Box 13248
Portland, OR 97213-0248

OCP (Oregon Catholic Press)
5536 NE Hassalo
Portland OR 97213

Oxford University Press
200 Madison Avenue
New York NY 10016

Pastoral Press
5640-D Sunnyside Avenue
Beltsville MD 20705

Paulist Press
992 Macarthur Boulevard
Mahwah NJ 07430

Prentice-Hall
1230 Avenue of the Americas
New York NY 10020

Pueblo Publishing Company
(Now part of Liturgical Press)

St. Vladimir's Seminary Press
575 Scarsdale Road
Crestwood NY 10707

The Seabury Press
C/O Harper and Row Publishers, Inc.
10 East 53rd Street
New York NY 10022

USCC (United States Catholic Conference)
3211 Fourth Street, NE
Washington DC 20017-1194

World Library Publications
3815 North Willow Road
Schiller Park IL 60176

ADVENT

Introduction to the Season

As a season of preparation, Advent is oriented toward Christmas, and the historical development of Advent flows from the development of the Christmas feast. Various theories have arisen to explain the placement of Christmas on December 25 (see page 33). Whatever the reason for that date, however, the result is that Christmas is celebrated near the winter solstice, the shortest day of the year. This time of year has been a focus for ritual and celebration in many ancient cultures. It may well be that Christmas was placed at this time because of scriptural evidence, but it inevitably was affected by the connection with the solstice.

Thus both Advent and Christmas have acquired a variety of symbols and themes that revolve around darkness and light. During this time of year darkness seems to be dominant. Even though we are less attuned to the changes of seasons because of our ability to create artificial daylight in our homes and workplaces, there is still a strong awareness at this time of year that the days are shortening and the nights are lengthening.

This decrease in daylight affects people in varying degrees. Recent studies have given the name "Seasonal Affective Disorder" (SAD) to the symptoms manifested by some people who seem especially sensitive to the absence of daylight. But even among those less drastically affected, almost no one is oblivious to the changing of the seasons and the shortening of the days.

The dominant theme of Advent–Christmas is the coming of the Light of the World. While we generally focus during Christmas on the historical coming of Jesus to Bethlehem, Advent makes it clear that this cycle celebrates more than just that historical event, important though it is. The *General Norms for the Liturgical Year and Calendar* puts it succinctly:

> Advent has a twofold character: as a season to prepare for Christmas when Christ's first coming to us is remembered; as a season when that remembrance directs the mind and the heart to await Christ's second coming at the end of time. Advent is thus a period for devout and joyful expectation. (#39)

Advent not only recalls the first coming of Christ in history, it looks for his Second Coming at the end of time. And if this is true of Advent, it must also be true of Christmas. Both seasons are part of the way Christians celebrate the mystery of Christ's presence in the world.

Thus, Advent and Christmas should always be seen as encompassing the full scope of Christ's comings. This festal cycle celebrates the Incarnation — the presence of God in our world — with all the effects that this presence creates. The celebration encompasses Jesus' birth at Bethlehem, his manifestation to the world at Epiphany and at his baptism in the Jordan, and his victorious return at the end of the world. While different aspects of the Incarnation will receive greater focus on various days, planners should never lose sight of the breadth of the mystery that is being celebrated.

The Light of the World has come into the world, and nothing will ever be the same. Yet the darkness seems to retain great power. Sin and evil still run rampant through our lives and our society. The powers of darkness may have been conquered by Christ's resurrection, but they act like they don't know it yet!

■ LONGING FOR A SAVIOR: The continued presence of sin and evil in our world is the basis for Advent's longing and expectation. We still yearn for a savior, not because we pretend that Christ has not yet been born but because the work of redemption is not yet complete. While we know that the final victory is assured, there is much that remains to be brought under the rule of God. The kingdom is present in our midst but has not yet come in its fullness. It is for that fullness that we long.

The full experience of the power of this festal cycle requires that we celebrate each section of it fully. Advent must not anticipate Christmas, nor should Christmas be truncated by ending its celebration too soon. A balance must be maintained that allows the emphasis of each part of the cycle to be fully experienced while still linking each part to the others. So Advent is a season of longing, but it also recognizes the reasons we have for joy in the fact that Christ has already come. Christmas celebrates the presence of God in our world, but does not pretend that evil has been completely vanquished and sin does not exist.

Within the overall ambiance of the cycle, then, Advent focuses more on the darkness that still reigns in our world. Advent is a time for lament, for crying out to God about the evils that surround and oppress us. It is a season when the physical darkness that grows with each passing day reminds us of the powers of darkness that seem to reign in our world. They do not reign ultimately, of course, for "the earth is the Lord's and the fullness thereof." But they exist and affect our lives and the lives of millions for the worse. Evil is real, and we do ourselves no favors by pretending that it is not.

■ NAMING EVIL: It is a sad fact that many church members today are unwilling to talk about sin and evil. We have become uncomfortable naming or confronting evil. This may be partially a result of our recent past, when so much emphasis was put on sin that it overshadowed the grace of Christ in our awareness. It may also be a result, in part, of our accommodation to a culture that has largely abandoned any attempt to articulate common values and standards of behavior.

If we have no shared values, no standards of right and wrong, then it is hard to speak of good and evil, sin and virtue. Many in our culture, which prides itself on being pluralistic, have concluded falsely that respect for the rights and opinions of others means we can never challenge or confront evil in our midst. In recent years, talk of right and wrong has given way to concerns about political correctness and social graciousness, both of which change as the popular winds blow.

While the church certainly needs to be open to our culture, it cannot capitulate to this abandonment of values. Though we must respect the rights of others to see things differently, we cannot conclude that every opinion is correct and every position is valid. The church must call into question any position or behavior that is contrary to the gospel.

■ RESPONDING TO EVIL: Various responses arise when people recognize the disparity between the standards of the gospel and the reality of life. Some people try to deny the gap and to live in a Pollyanna world where everything is wonderful and evil does not exist. Others despair of coping with the powers of darkness and retreat into a safe enclave, associating only with like-minded people in some kind of psychological (or even physical) ghetto or commune. Others become overwhelmed by the darkness and become depressed and negative. Still others rail against the night, ranting and raving against all who do not measure up to their standards.

These varied responses shape the way a community worships. Some approaches to worship insist that all must be goodness and light, that no darkness exists, and that everyone should feel great about life when they leave church. In this approach, there is no room for any prophetic confrontation or gospel challenge to evil. It is considered impolite to speak of anything that might disturb the worshipers.

Another faction takes the stance that the world is so evil and popular culture is so depraved that worship must have nothing to do with it. It is better to retreat into the old Latin Mass or some other arcane form of worship that is totally "other-worldly." Those who find the darkness overwhelming may shape a worship that is continually negative, focused almost exclusively on the sins of the members and/or the evils outside.

Our biblical and worship tradition suggests a different response and a different style of worship. It begins with an honest recognition that evil does exist and that sin is a reality of human life. It does not attempt to cover over or explain away the painful fact that evil continues to exert its influence in our world and even in our individual lives. It faces the darkness honestly.

■ LAMENT: Several scholars have noted that the first biblical response to such recognition of evil is the lament. (For more in-depth discussion of this topic, see Gordon Lathrop's "A Rebirth of Images" in *Worship,* volume 58, number 4 [July 1984], page 291ff. and Gail Ramshaw's "The Place of Lament Within Praise: Theses for Discussion," in *Worship,* volume 61, number 4 [July 1987], page 317ff.) The psalms and the prophets are filled with examples of God's people crying out in lament about their fate or the fate of their nation. There is frequent reference to the apparent absence of God, to the evil that threatens to (and sometimes does) overwhelm God's people, and to the sins of the people that often bring on such tragedy.

Lament does not wallow in negativity, however, but leads naturally to prayer and to hope. The biblical lament calls God's attention to the evil facing the individual or the nation and then seeks God's help in overcoming that evil. It does this with a confidence that relies on God's promises and God's example in the past. Lament and thanksgiving are linked, as the *anamnesis* recalling God's past wonders in praise and thanksgiving is joined to a confident prayer that God will continue to act on our behalf in the present and the future.

Thus lament offers a way of praying that avoids the naive pretense that evil does not exist and that all is well with the world, without falling into a negative view of life or of the world "outside." It is a prayer of hope, grounded both in the reality of life with its mixture of good and evil and in the promise and power of God, whose ultimate victory over evil is certain. Lament is thus a fundamental style of prayer for those who live in this "time between," this age of "the already and the not yet." We live in hope, a confident hope based on God's promise, but a hope which recognizes that all is not well, that there is still more for which we long.

Advent as a time of hope and longing is an ideal time to seek the recovery of the prayer of lament. The need is not to compose new prayer forms or texts; our liturgies for Advent already contain many such expressions of longing and expectation. The issue is how to help our communities recognize both the need for lament and also the reason for our hope. The challenge is to make the texts come alive in the present by linking the longing of the ages to the yearnings of our own hearts.

For many people, however, the first step must be learning to speak again of sin and evil. We speak in Advent of the coming of the Savior, but many people have no clear sense of why we need a savior. From what are we to be saved? If sin and evil are not real, who needs a savior? Advent longings only begin to make sense when we recognize the continuing existence and power of evil around us. Then we know why we need a redeemer. Facing the darkness makes us long for the Light.

■ RECONCILIATION: Most parishes, of course, have some focus on sin during Advent, celebrating one or more penance services and scheduling extra times for individual reconciliation. Too often, however, this is perceived (and presented?) in exclusively individual terms, urging people to prepare their hearts for Christmas by having their sins forgiven. Rather than being fully integrated into Advent lament and longing, it is understood primarily as a pre-Christmas cleansing to be suitably prepared for the feast. While this perspective is not invalid, there is much more to Advent. Not only the penance services but all our Advent gatherings might well include a strong cry of lament, expressing clearly our need for a savior and our longing for the kingdom.

It has often been stressed that Advent and Lent are different in character, though both are preparatory seasons and both have penitential aspects. Perhaps one way of understanding the difference is to see Lent as having a greater focus on individual repentance and renewal leading to the baptismal recommitment at

Easter, while Advent focuses more on the broader reality of evil and sin in our world, stressing the social and institutional evils that oppose the values of the kingdom and the rule of the Prince of Peace.

This cannot be exclusive, of course, for much of the social and institutional evil around us results from individual choices and decisions that are sinful; and institutions and cultures are changed only through the conversion of hearts. But there is much in our world that stands in stark contrast to the values of the gospel, much that makes it all too evident that the kingdom has not yet arrived in all its fullness. These are the things that should lead us both to lament and to longing, to crying out for the Savior and to hope in God's promise.

The particular expression of these evils will vary from year to year. Despite the end of the Cold War and signs of increasing freedom, suffering is still widespread in many parts of our world, and conflict is still a common fact of life. Wars continue to cause death and destruction, refugees number in the millions, disease continues to run rampant, poverty still oppresses multitudes, hunger and starvation stalk the globe, family violence and sexual abuse scar both children and adults for life, crime flourishes at home and abroad, environmental destruction continues to devastate the planet, abortion and euthanasia are still common around the world, too many marriages end in divorce and too many children lack stable homes, sexism and racism still fuel discrimination, unemployment and homelessness still afflict untold numbers, and on and on. There is no dearth of themes for lament, no lack of reasons to yearn for a savior. There is much darkness about.

It is important that these forces of evil be named and made concrete. Where does war rage this year? What natural disasters have afflicted peoples and nations lately? What local evils need to be faced and opposed? What longings and yearnings are real in the hearts of our people this year? Often the longings are there, but they go unnamed and unarticulated. Naming them and speaking them in worship can relieve our often vague anxieties while focusing our energies to oppose evil and pray for redemption.

The roots of some of these evils are to be found in our own lives and hearts, and thus confronting them will require some personal conversion of attitudes, habits, and lifestyles. There is darkness within us as well as around

us. Other evils we can name may not be the result of our own actions but are nevertheless able to be influenced by our efforts; confronting these will challenge us to work for change through social protests, political action or concrete efforts to help. Some of the evils we lament may seem beyond our influence or control; these should evoke in us in a special way the awareness that we need a savior and should prompt us to sincere prayer for God's redemptive power to heal us and our world. These may remind us that ultimately all the efforts we can make to bring about the kingdom are dependent on God's power at work in us and that the fullness of the kingdom cannot be accomplished by human effort alone. Only God can offer redemption; only God can conquer the darkness.

The parish's observance of Advent, then, should be a time in which the community looks honestly at life from the perspective of the gospel, cries out in lament over the evils that afflict God's people, yearns in hope for the power of God to set us free, and reaches out to share that hope by taking concrete steps to confront evil and foster change wherever possible. We recognize the darkness but we do not give in to it, for we live in hope based on the power of the Light who has come into the world. "The light shines on in the darkness, darkness that did not overcome it" (John 1:5, from the Mass during the Day on Christmas).

This perspective on Advent can also help the parish deal with the perennial conflict between society's insistence on celebrating Christmas in advance and the church's observation of Advent. Certainly one of the evils that besets the world is the excessive consumerism that defines our culture. There is no honest way for a sincere Christian to celebrate Advent or Christmas without rejecting the constant pressure to buy love by purchasing gifts and to celebrate solely by spending and consuming. Parishes should provide assistance to help parishioners develop an approach to both Advent and Christmas that emphasizes the true meaning of the season.

This is not accomplished by strident condemnation of merchants, advertisers or the culture. The more effective approach is to help people see the deeper meaning beneath the holiday customs of society and then help them find ways to express that deeper truth in action. The spirit of giving that is stressed by the advertisers, for example, can remind us of the need to give especially to the poor, with whom Christ identified himself. The Christmas lighting displays can remind us of the Light of the World. The songs about peace on earth can prompt action to foster peace. The parties and feasting can remind us to share God's gifts not only with friends and family but with all who are hungry. A delicate balance is needed to find a path that effectively confronts the false or distorted values of the culture while still recognizing and building on the deeper truth from which our holiday customs arose. Helping parishioners to adopt a simpler and more focused celebration can do much to relieve the pressure and stress that so many people experience in the December frenzy of activity. Many people in our culture sense the need to turn back to the basic meaning of Christmas; the church should offer practical and gentle guidance in how to do that.

Images of Advent

THE most powerful images of Advent are the comings of Christ at Bethlehem and at the end of time. These two events remind us that we live in that "in-between" time when the kingdom is present but not yet fulfilled. Along with the symbols of light and darkness, the prophets in Advent remind us of the need to repent and also remind us of God's promises. We hear from the great prophet Isaiah every Sunday in Advent this year; he also appears on the first eleven weekdays as well as on December 20. In the final days of the season we hear from Jeremiah, Zephaniah and Malachi. The Sunday gospel passages from Matthew present us with the image of the coming of the Son of Man in judgment (first Sunday), the call to repentance from John the Baptist (second and third Sunday) and the struggle of Joseph to cope with Mary's unusual pregnancy (fourth Sunday). St. Paul urges continued conversion (first Sunday) and harmony in the community (second Sunday). James counsels patience and perseverance (third Sunday), and then Paul gives us a summary of the whole gospel (fourth Sunday), reminding us of the full scope of the Advent–Christmas celebration.

Besides the Blessed Virgin, who is celebrated on December 8 under the title of the Immaculate Conception, on December 12 as Our Lady of Guadalupe and on the fourth Sunday, Advent saints celebrated this year include John Damascene, Nicholas, Ambrose, Blessed Juan Diego, Pope Damasus I, Lucy (whose name means light), John of the Cross, Peter Canisius and John of Kanty.

Other important images of Advent include the kingdom of God (some prefer the "reign of God" as less patriarchal language), the Advent wreath (light shining in the darkness) and the colors of purple and rose, which can speak of our longing and our hopes.

An African American Perspective

THE *General Norms for the Liturgical Year and the Calendar* state that Advent is a period for "devout and joyful expectation." It is a time of preparation for the remembrance of the incarnation of the Lord and a waiting for his return. Spirituals express this reality well. James Cone says that spirituals communicate the idea of both a transcendent present and a transcendent future (*The Spirituals and the Blues,* New York: Seabury, 1972).

■ TRANSCENDENT PRESENT: One spiritual trumpets: "If anybody asks me who I am, I tell 'em I'm a child of God." To be a child of God means to live in the present in hope, because God has broken into human history in the event of Jesus Christ and has defeated evil in every form. We are free.

> Oh, freedom, oh, freedom, oh, freedom over me,
> And before I'd be a slave, I'll be buried in my grave,
> And go home to my Lord, and be free. (*Lead Me, Guide Me,* #298)

This radical freedom demands action. No free person could possibly accept the status quo if it is ensnared in injustice and oppression. The present situation must be changed. So slaves were always on the move to a future of promise. They sang:

> De gospel train's a comin',
> I hear it jus' at han',
> I hear de car wheels rumblin',
> An' rollin' thro' de lan'.

De fare is cheap an' all can go,
De rich an' poor are dere,
No second class aboard dis train,
No diff'rence in de fare. (*Songs of Zion,* #116)

Cone further suggests, "Because black slaves believed that the gospel was a message about the future of God breaking into the reality of their present, they were liberated *from* the bondage of the present and free to be *for* God's future." This hope was not a denial of the present. On the contrary, because of this hope the enslaved could accept history and trust that their history was moving to a radically new reality. This trust in God even against the will of the slave master led to what Delores Williams calls a biblical appropriation of survival and a quality of life (*Sisters in the Wilderness* [Orbis, 1993]). While our ancestors survived, they worked. They worked for the freedom of all God's children. They worked believing that

There is a balm in Gilead
To make the wounded whole,
There is a balm in Gilead
To heal the sin-sick soul.
        (*Lead Me, Guide Me,* #157)

■ TRANSCENDENT FUTURE: Our ancestors also believed in the transcendent future: heaven. For them heaven was a "true home," a "gettin' up morning," a "New Jerusalem." It was a place of golden streets, pearly gates and long white robes. It was place where

Soon-a will be done-a with the troubles
    of the world . . . (*Songs of Zion,* #158).

■ IN JOYFUL HOPE: Make no mistake about it, these songs are not simply palliative. They are great theological statements about the divine future—a reality that we cannot here contain. They were a source of survival and hope then. They are to be sung now as we "wait in joyful hope for the coming of our Savior, Jesus Christ."

The Hispanic Mística and the Liturgy

THE season of Advent poses challenges to those responsible for liturgical preparation in multicultural parishes, especially communities with Hispanic parishioners. In parishes with Mexican Americans, for example, in addition to the standard four weeks of Advent prescribed in the *General Calendar,* the preparation for Christmas is enriched by two nine-day celebrations, or *novenarios,* that in many ways are more deeply rooted in their cultural celebration of the faith. The first is the nine days beginning on December 3 in preparation for the feast of Our Lady of Guadalupe on December 12. The second is the custom of *Las Posadas,* beginning on December 16 and running to Christmas eve, that reenacts the search of Mary and Joseph for lodging in Bethlehem prior to the birth of Jesus.

■ NOVENARIO OF OUR LADY OF GUADALUPE: Some may find it hard to reconcile a focus on a Marian feast during the early part of Advent with the rest of the liturgical season. In the eyes of many who are not Hispanic, Guadalupe seems to usurp the place of devotions more in keeping with the nature of the season, such as the Advent wreath. The seeming conflict becomes very pronounced when the feast falls on one of the Advent Sundays. Before arriving at determinations about the way in which the parish will celebrate this season, however, it is important for non-Hispanics not only to understand the importance that Mary of Guadalupe represents for Mexican Americans and many other Latino groups in the United States, but also to understand that she can be celebrated in a manner in harmony with the liturgical year.

Being able to "read the image" is necessary in order to appreciate the points of contact between Guadalupe and Advent, and to understand the profound emotional attachment many Hispanics have toward Mary under this title. The image appeared on the *tilma,* or cloak, of Blessed Juan Diego after he used it to gather roses out of season—a miraculous sign of Mary's appearance on the hill of Tepeyac outside of Mexico City. This event took place during the first brutal years of Spanish rule in Mexico, when the world of the native peoples seemed to be coming to an end.

Mary appears on the *tilma* as a young *mestiza,* a woman of Amerindian and European heritage. For that reason she is affectionately called *La Morenita,* "the little brown one." Because she appears as a *mestiza,* Guadalupe presents God's "yes" to the native people of the Americas. She is an image of holiness and dignity with which the native and mestizo peoples of the Americas can identify.

La Morenita is pregnant, for she wears the blue band traditionally worn by Aztec women who were with child. And on her womb appears a flower, the Aztec symbol for new life and a new era. Like the church during Advent, she is waiting for the birth of Christ, who will usher in an era of peace and justice for those long oppressed by the arbitrary power of the strong.

Space prevents a more detailed discussion of the image, but this brief description points to some of the reasons why Guadalupe is so important for Hispanic peoples and is an appropriate icon for Advent.

The *Novena Guadalupana* is celebrated with joy and culminates at dawn on December 12 with processions to the church, the singing of *las mañanitas* (the traditional Mexican birthday song) and other songs to her image, the eucharistic celebration and the special food associated with festivity: *pan dulce* (sweet rolls) and *menudo* (tripe soup). Red roses are distributed, and in some parishes *danzas* are held. These *danzas,* a form of prayer as well as entertainment, are performed by adults or children dressed in Aztec garb and are sometimes performed in the church as well as in the social hall of the parish.

■ LAS POSADAS: The second of the novenas is called *Las Posadas,* the inns. This communal devotion, brought to the New World by the Spanish missionaries, dramatically reenacts Mary and Joseph's search for lodging in Bethlehem and takes place in the homes of parishioners. Accompanying a couple dressed as Mary and Joseph or bearing their statues, each evening of the novena the community visits three to five homes where a ritual dialogue takes place denying the holy couple *posada* (lodging).

Finally they come to the house chosen to offer hospitality, often indicated by the *luminaria,* lighted candles set inside paper bags that line the paths leading to the door. The ritual dialogue and song take place. Finally all are invited in for a warm drink, and treats are given to the children. For many Hispanics in the United States the *posadas* celebration is not only a commemoration of Mary and Joseph's search for lodging in Bethlehem, but is also reflective of their own lives as people coming as strangers to a country where hospitality has not always been offered freely.

■ BRIDGING THE GAP: Both of these celebrations, dear to the ancestral traditions of many His-

panics, offer a way of bridging the gap that is often perceived between church and the rest of life. They bring prayer and the community closer to the home with the Hispanic gift of emphasizing the heart as well as the head. And both novenas appropriately help every heart prepare room for the Messiah.

Preparing the Parish

FOR Advent planning, as for any liturgical planning, worship leaders should seek to work in cooperation with other parish groups, such as the school, religious education staff, adult education team, parish social clubs and the St. Vincent de Paul society. Together, they can develop a coordinated approach to the season that is reflected in all parish activities. Such cooperation is essential for a consistent and effective observance of the season. A school Christmas pageant or an Altar Society Christmas party right in the middle of Advent will not help the parish maintain the needed perspective on the season. Changes in "traditional" schedules may take time, but the effort is worthwhile. A "red-and-green" dress-up day at the elementary school can become a "purple-and-rose" day. A children's Christmas pageant can become an Advent pageant that prepares for Christmas, or it can be scheduled after school resumes around Epiphany and thus help the parish maintain the Christmas spirit throughout that season. Christmas parties can be scheduled during the Twelve Days of Christmas instead of in early December. Gradually, the parish staff can help people learn to celebrate both Advent and Christmas well.

Seeing Advent as a season for lament and longing requires a raising of awareness of the evils that confront us. Religious education classes, bulletin and newsletter articles, and pulpit announcements can invite parishioners to recognize and name the forces of evil that the community needs to lament and from which we need to be freed. Scripture study groups, prayer groups and other small community groups might be encouraged to discuss what evils currently afflict our world and the local community. Such input from the community can help those who prepare the liturgies tap into the real yearnings that live deep in the hearts of the parishioners.

Some focus on light and darkness during this season can help parishioners link their natural feelings with the liturgy. Bulletin items and Advent materials might call attention to the solstice itself (December 22 this year) and the decreasing daylight as it approaches. Then the beginnings of the recovery of daylight after the solstice can be linked to the celebration of Christmas. Encouraging the use of *luminaria* at Christmas, both at church and at home, can also be linked to this theme of darkness and light. Plans and perhaps materials might be made available early in Advent for preparing the *luminaria,* and prayers might be suggested for families to use when they light them. Prayers might also be offered when people put up and first illuminate Christmas lights in their homes.

Taking It Home

ADVENT provides excellent opportunities to link parish worship with home activities and devotions. Some parishes have been successful with "Family Advent Day" on the First Sunday of Advent. With activities planned for adults, teens, elementary students and toddlers, such a program might provide some education about Advent and its themes of lament and expectation, the singing of Advent songs, the making of family Advent wreaths and the sharing of suggestions for family Advent prayers and rituals. It might also allow participants to name some of the evils that afflict them and others in the world.

At a minimum, parishes should provide easy access to the materials for home Advent wreaths at reasonable cost, to encourage this custom and thus keep Advent visible at home. Advent calendars of various types can also be made available for purchase for home use; this is often an effective way to help children catch the spirit of waiting and anticipation. LTP's *Fling Wide the Doors* is an exceptionally beautiful Advent calendar that continues throughout the Christmas season. Saints of the season appear on their proper days, a scripture passage appears on the back of each door, and a pamphlet with prayer for each day is included.

Other possibilities for linking church and home include blessing home Advent-wreath candles along with the wreath in church and providing blessing prayers to accompany seasonal activities such as shopping for gifts, making cookies, wrapping presents and decorating. Simple prayers that link these activities to spiritual preparation for Christmas will help parishioners to keep Advent at home and will make these activities resonate more easily with Advent themes on Sunday. Booklets like *Keeping Advent and Christmastime* or the Sunday handouts called *Welcome, Yule!* might also be provided for home use. *Take Me Home* has pages for children and families for the beginning of Advent, St. Nicholas, Our Lady of Guadalupe, St. Lucy and the final week of Advent. All three resources are from LTP.

■ THE GIVING TREE: Many parishes have developed the custom of a "Giving Tree" during Advent. Cards listing gifts needed for the poor are hung on the tree, to be taken by parish members at the beginning of Advent. The gifts are then returned near the end of the season for distribution at Christmas. This custom can be linked to the broader themes of lament and longing to help people realize the meaning of the season and the deeper purpose of gift giving. This charitable program can also link Christmas shopping to the Christian love that should mark all those who follow the one born at Bethlehem. Such a Giving Tree would be best placed in the entryway or at some other convenient location rather than in the sanctuary area, so that the simplicity of Advent decor is not compromised.

Other efforts at social outreach (e.g. food collection, Christmas baskets, etc.) could include a brief prayer service that would link these concrete efforts to spread God's love with our need for a savior. Particular emphasis might be given to the need for broader changes in economic systems and international relations, or whatever other structures give rise to poverty, unemployment and homelessness.

The Mass

ESTABLISHING the proper tone for Advent liturgies requires a blend of lament and hope, of longing and joy. Advent should be marked not by the austerity of Lent but as a preparatory season leading up to a major feast; it should be somewhat subdued so that it does not make the feast itself anti-climactic. For example, the Gloria is not omitted as a sign of penitence but in order that the angels' song will be fresh and powerful on the night of Christmas. The proper tone for Advent is a combination of lament, expectation and gradually increasing joy as the great feast approaches.

INTRODUCTORY RITES

The omission of the Gloria already makes the entrance rites different, but various other options are possible to mark the season as special. The opening hymn should be a text that speaks clearly of Advent longing; the same well-chosen hymn could be used for each of the Sundays of Advent to unify the season. Explore the possibility of using Bernadette Farrell's "Litany of the Word" (OCP, 7162) as the gathering music for the season. Its rhythmic flow and accessibility make it a possible treasure for the parish. Music for Advent should be somewhat restrained; singing an opening hymn with no accompaniment or with a single wind instrument guiding the melody line could lend a simple dignity that would mark the season as special while also distinguishing it from the following festal period.

The Advent liturgy might begin with the usual procession to and reverencing of the altar. The altar and Advent wreath could be incensed, though if incense seems unusually festive in your parish, it might best to reserved for Christmas. If the Advent wreath is in the entrance-way or is hanging over the assembly, the liturgy might begin with a call to face the wreath (with the ministers standing near the wreath, perhaps with the processional cross held underneath it). Then the sign of the cross, the greeting and introductory words, and even the penitential rite are sung or said, followed by the procession to the chair, which is accompanied by the entrance psalm or hymn. The penitential rite might be modified to include a prayer as the wreath is lighted (see page 18). At the chair, the presider proclaims the opening prayer.

■ SELECTING TEXTS: Advance planning is important in choosing the texts for Advent's Sundays and feasts. One greeting, selected from the sacramentary or from the *Book of Blessings* (#1549

or #1577), might be used at all major assemblies during the season. The second set of invocations (C*ii*) of the penitential rite in the sacramentary are appropriate for the Sundays of Advent and might be chanted throughout the season. Richard Proulx's *Three Plainsong Kyries with Tropes for the Sacramentary* (GIA, G-3162) works well. Particularly recommended is the music of set II, which is adapted from chant Mass IX (also found in *Worship*, #274). This edition is set for cantor and congregation. There is also a compatible choral edition (GIA, G-3161). The Kyrie from Marty Haugen's *Mass of Remembrance* (*Gather*, #96), with its beautiful melodic line reminiscent of longing and lamenting, would be an appropriate alternative. The invocations from John Schiavone's "Advent Wreath Service" (OCP, 8968) are fitting, using either the choral arrangement or cantor line. Other ideas for these texts are found on page 14.

LITURGY OF THE WORD

The lectionary readings for Advent are powerful passages, but familiarity may make them hard to hear clearly. Lectors should practice well to proclaim these selections richly and fully. The words of Isaiah should ring in our ears long after the service is ended. The pericopes from Paul and James should be a clear call to conversion of life. And the gospels are rich passages ranging from eschatological warnings to the preaching of the Baptist to the touching story of Joseph's dream. Priests and deacons should prepare as well as the lectors!

THE PSALM

Three options are available for the responsorial psalm during Advent as during any season of the liturgical year: 1) the proper psalm assigned to the day in the lectionary; 2) the seasonal psalms assigned to the season, which are listed in #175 in the lectionary; or 3) a common responsorial refrain, which is found in #174, with the verses of the proper psalm for the day. The seasonal responsorial psalms and the seasonal psalm responses often capture the central meaning of the season. Advent's seasonal psalm response sounds a cry of lament, "Come, O Lord, and set us free." Sung with each Sunday's proper psalm, this refrain would express well our longing for salvation. Even when other options are selected for the psalms, this sentence could be used for the response to the petitions of the prayer of the faithful. (Be careful to word the petitions in a way that makes grammatical sense with this or any other special response, and remember to include prayers concerning the evils that the local community has identified.)

The two seasonal psalms listed are both strong choices. Psalms 25 and 85 call on the Lord with sure confidence; taken together, they attune our hearts to the message of expectant hope. Planners might select one of these psalms to be used throughout Advent so that the repetition can gradually shape the assembly's hopes.

Recommended musical settings for Psalm 25 include:

- Marty Haugen, "To you, O Lord" in *Psalms for the Church Year* (GIA, G-2664)

- Rawn Harbor, "Psalm for Advent" in *Lead Me, Guide Me,* #500 (GIA)

- Howard Hughes, "To you I lift up my soul" in *Psalms for Advent* (GIA, G-1905) or *Lead Me, Guide Me,* #499 (GIA)

- David Isele, "To you, O Lord" in *Psalms for the Church Year* (GIA, G-2662)

- Robert E. Kreutz, "Come, O Lord" in *Psalms and Selected Canticles* (OCP)

- Scott Soper, "To you, O Lord" (OCP, 8979-CC)

- Christopher Willcock, "To You, O Lord" in *Psalms for Feasts and Seasons* (Liturgical Press)

Recommended settings of Psalm 85 are:

- J. Robert Carroll/J. Gelineau, "Lord, let us see your kindness" *Worship Lectionary/Accompaniment/Cantor Book,* #770 (GIA)

- Michael Connolly, "I Will Hear What God Proclaims" (GIA, G-2401)

- Marty Haugen, "Let us see your kindness" in *Psalms for the Church Year* (GIA, G-2664)

- Christopher Willcock, "Lord, let us see your kindness" in *Psalms for Feasts and Seasons* (Liturgical Press)

■ GOSPEL ACCLAMATIONS: At #193 and #202, the lectionary offers marvelous jewels for catechists, liturgical planners and anyone who wants to enter into the spirit of Advent. Twenty-one verses from the scriptures and from our ancient traditions are listed as gospel acclamations for the weekdays of Advent. They provide a summary of themes of the season, gems for meditation and sources for daily prayer. The seven listed for late Advent are the revered O Antiphons, borrowed (and abridged) from the evening

prayer celebrations of the week before Christmas. These antiphons express powerfully the church's Advent longings and suggest various themes of lament and hope. A parish might select a few of these for this Advent, repeating them often to facilitate a true "learning by heart." Three suggested settings of music for the gospel acclamation verses for Advent are:

- John Schiavone, *Gospel Acclamation Verses for Advent* (GIA, G-2110)

- *ICEL Lectionary Music* (GIA, G-2626)

- David Haas, Advent Gospel Acclamation (OCP, 8732)

■ SUNDAY GOSPELS IN ADVENT: Year A is the year of Matthew. As explained in the introduction to the lectionary (#93):

Each gospel reading has a distinctive theme: the Lord's coming at the end of time (First Sunday of Advent), John the Baptist (Second and Third Sunday) and the events that prepared immediately for the Lord's birth (Fourth Sunday).

■ THE PRESENTATION OF JEWS AND JUDAISM IN ADVENT: Our lectionary often presents the first readings as a prelude to the gospel, but the Jewish scriptures should not be understood only as preparation. These ancient words still speak important messages to us today. In 1988, the United States Bishops' Committee on the Liturgy issued a helpful booklet on the presentation of Jews and Judaism in Catholic preaching, *God's Mercy Endures Forever.* Available from the United States Catholic Conference (USCC) Publications Office, this document draws from earlier statements from the Holy See's Commission for Religious Relations with the Jews. Its remarks about Advent (#11) are worth quoting here:

The lectionary readings from the prophets are selected to bring out the ancient Christian theme that Jesus is the "fulfillment" of the biblical message of hope and promise, the inauguration of the "days to come" described, for example, by the daily Advent Masses, and on Sundays by Isaiah in Cycle A and Jeremiah in Cycle C for the First Sunday of Advent. This truth needs to be framed very carefully. Christians believe that Jesus is the promised Messiah who has come (see Luke 4:22), but also know that his messianic kingdom is not yet fully realized. The ancient messianic prophecies are not merely temporal predictions but profound expressions of eschatological hope. Since this dimension can be misunderstood or even missed altogether, the homilist needs to raise clearly the hope found in the prophets and heightened in the proclamation of Christ. This hope includes trust in what is promised but not yet seen. While the biblical prophecies of an age of universal "shalom" are "fulfilled" (i.e., irreversibly inaugurated) in Christ's coming, that fulfillment is not yet completely worked out in each person's life or perfected in the world at large (*Guidelines and Suggestions for Implementing the Conciliar Declaration "Nostra Aetate,"* no. 4, II, 1974 no. 2). It is the mission of the church, as also that of the Jewish people, to proclaim and to work to prepare the world for the full flowering of God's reign, which is, but is "not yet" (cf. 1974 *Guidelines* II). Both the Christian "Our Father" and the Jewish "Kaddish" exemplify this message. Thus, both Christianity and Judaism seal their worship with a common hope: "Thy kingdom come!"

■ DISMISSAL OF THE CATECHUMENS: If catechumens are present in the assembly, they should be sent forth with words of dismissal that allude to the hopes and longings of the community which they increasingly share. (See the sample text on page 27.)

■ GENERAL INTERCESSIONS: A set of intercessions for Advent is given on page 27, and a set for Advent is printed in appendix I of the sacramentary. Both texts are simply patterns. They must be adapted to each community; they are seasonal skeletons that need to be fleshed out with local concerns and images. Some intercessions might be repeated each week of Advent, with new ones added for current needs. The intercessions offer an ideal place to give voice to our lament, our longing to be set free from all sin and oppression.

LITURGY OF THE EUCHARIST

■ EUCHARISTIC PRAYER: The preface during most of the season (until December 16) is Advent Preface I. As the season moves toward the birth of Christ (December 17–24), the more urgent words of Advent Preface II are used. Because Advent is short this year, each preface will be used on two of the Sundays of the season. Acclamations for the eucharistic prayer ought to be consistent throughout the season, again helping to mark the time as a unified period. The same acclamations might also be continued through Christmas to suggest the integral connection of the two seasons. If this option is employed, consider singing the acclamations in unison during Advent with no added instrumental or choral parts, adding these embellishments during the Christmas season. A more festive set of acclamations may also be appropriate for Christmas. Highly recommended are the acclamations from Richard Proulx's *Missa Emmanuel* (GIA, G-3489). This new Mass setting is based upon the familiar "O come, O come, Emmanuel" and employs cantor, choir and congregation. The assembly participation is spontaneous because the melody lines are so well known. Christopher Walker's "Glastonbury Eucharistic Acclamations" (OCP, 7165) are another option for the Advent/Christmas cycle. Anticipating the fact that many Christmas worshipers will be visitors and some only occasional worshipers, these acclamations are fitting. Designed so that the assembly repeats each line after the cantor, the use of these acclamations may prove to be an important vehicle of hospitality for the parish visitors. Save the wonderful descants in this arrangement for the Christmas season!

■ COMMUNION RITE: During Advent, this rite can take on a seasonal tone, explicitly expressing the church's longings. See page 29 for examples: an introduction to the Lord's Prayer, a prayer at the peace greeting and an invitation to communion.

The Simple Gradual lists Psalm 85 for Advent communion processions. Marty Haugen's setting, "Lord, make us turn to you" (*Gather,* #37), effectively captures the spirit of this season. Other refrain-style choices should include Haugen's "My soul in stillness waits" (GIA, G-3331), based on the "O Antiphons," or Jacques Berthier's "Wait for the Lord" (Taizé; GIA, G-2778). Also appropriate for the communion processional are responsorial-style settings of the Magnificat. James Chepponis's setting of the Magnificat (GIA, #2302) provides an easy assembly refrain with verses that can be sung by one or two cantors. Working the Magnificat into the assembly's repertoire also provides the musician with an alternate Marian song for the Marian feasts during the year. The assembly's familiarity with a Magnificat may also assist in the planning and celebration of Evening Prayer during the year.

■ CONCLUDING RITE: The dismissal of ministers bearing the eucharist for the homebound can take on a seasonal form as noted in the texts for the eucharistic assembly, page 29.

■ BLESSING AND DISMISSAL: One Advent blessing and one dismissal might be memorized by the presider and deacon for all the Sunday Masses of the season. Solemn Blessing 1 from the sacramentary would be appropriate throughout the season. A shorter blessing is found at #1534 of the *Book of Blessings,* and another is given on page 29 of this book.

MUSIC

What is the sound that surrounds us as we enter this season? The music of Advent can assist in drawing the assembly into the spirit of lament and expectant longing characteristic of the season. Supportive of this spirit, the music of the season tugs at the assembly's heartstrings, drawing them into the mystery of the incarnation of Christ. Musical intervals of perfect fifths and suspended seconds and fourths should support the sound of this season, particularly for musicians whose improvisational skills are keen. The sound of the season enters the ear of the assembly, enticing the mind and heart toward a realization of the many presences of Christ in our lives and an expectancy as we move toward the feast of Christmas. A good mix of major and minor keys expresses well the many movements and feelings of the season. Just as we are struck by an environment that signals a multivalency of Advent meaning, so should the music strike our hearts on many levels.

There is a wide array of music written for the Advent season. Because of the season's brevity, musicians may be tempted to overload the season with every latest Advent composition while still striving to maintain music from the tradition. Simplicity should guide the musician's search for the sound of the season for his or her assembly. Smaller parishes where the musical resources may be more or less restricted need not feel that due to a lack of SATB choirs, pipe organs or symphonic instruments, their experience of the season is diminished. A small rural assembly simply led by a single guitar, singing "O Come, O Come, Emmanuel" in a small church set in the darkness of the encroaching winter solstice can beautifully and profoundly express the sound of the season. Those musicians with more or even unlimited resources could serve their assemblies well by scaling back the musical embellishments and truly allowing the assembly's song to well up deeply from its heart.

With this in mind, consider again great Advent hymn, "Conditor alme siderum." Several translations are available; see "Creator of the stars of night" in *Worship* (GIA), *The Music Issue* and *Breaking Bread* (OCP) or in the *Hymnal for the Hours* (GIA). The text is poetic and displays for us the images and dual nature of this season. The tune is simple, part of our collective memory, and can be sung without accompaniment. Chant-style hymns (e.g. "Creator of the stars of night") work particularly well sung unaccompanied. A simple addition of handbells playing chord clusters at the end of each phrase in these hymns can be most effective while also helping the assembly stay on pitch. The text and its tune are uniquely Advent music. Including a hymn such as this each year can be an important reminder of the generations of Christians who sang this hymn each Advent and the heritage of faith that they pass on to us.

Assemblies respond well to the familiar, yet are open to new musical offerings, in moderation. Musicians often become "tired" of a particular piece long before an assembly even begins to get used to it. Remember that the musicians have spent hours practicing the given piece and often may hear the piece at four or five different liturgies on a given weekend, while the assembly may hear it once and sing it once or twice! The more that a particular selection of music is sung, the better the assembly tends to sing it. We should certainly work to improve the parish repertoire by replacing music of questionable quality, but constant introduction to new music is of little benefit. During the short season of Advent we should carefully and actively strive to help our people build their musical "library."

Musical instruments should lead and accompany gently during Advent. This is not the season to pull out all the stops. Musicians could do well during this season to explore the more subtle aspects of their instruments. New colors, timbres, articulations and performance practices could be a revelation for musicians and assemblies.

There is a wealth of fine hymnody for the season of Advent, and we should explore the possibilities. Some unique examples would include Haugen's "Awake! Awake, and greet the new morn," and the traditional French carols, "People look east" and "O come, Divine Messiah," all of which are set in a gentle 6/8 meter. "Wake, O wake and sleep no longer" (OCP resources and GIA's *Worship*), while admittedly challenging to an assembly, is a worthy addition to the Advent repertoire. Perhaps the choir or cantor could sing it the first week and the assembly be taught it in the ensuing weeks. It may take a few years for this piece to become the assembly's own, but the addition is well worth the work. Organists could sharpen their skills by playing the Bach arrangement for this chorale, "Wachet Auf," as a prelude or solo played during the preparation of the gifts.

Other hymns for the season would include "Each winter as the year grows colder," Haas's "People of the night" and "God of all people," all contemporary selections from *Gather*. OCP's resources offer many worthy choices for the season, including "The King shall come when morning dawns" *(Kentucky Harmony)*. This hymn tune presents a haunting melodic line which could be introduced by a solo instrument (flute or oboe are fitting) or a single solo organ stop. Other hymns from Oregon Catholic Press include "You clouds of heaven, open wide," a reworking of the ancient *Rorate Coeli* text. *The Collegeville Hymnal* (GIA) offers a chant setting of the *Rorate Coeli*, with the text in English or Latin. Effective use could be made of this chant, perhaps using a few select men's voices (or women's voices, or alternating voices). Again, these ancient texts not only support the sound of the season, but connect present-day assemblies to the rich heritage of the past.

Other offerings from the OCP resources include Bernadette Farrell's "Come to set us free"; Ernest Sands's "Alleluia! Hurry the Lord is near," a particularly appropriate piece for children's choir; Bob Hurd's "Ready the way"; and Bernadette Farrell's "Litany of the Word" (OCP, 7162). Combining any of these with the parish's vast body of more traditional hymns should offer us a very nice variety of music. Any new music should be intended to become a permanent part of the assembly's repertoire.

In choosing pieces to add to the repertoire, look especially for those that reflect well Advent's lament and longing. Lament psalms form the largest category in the whole psalter; many are individual laments for sin (which may be more appropriate for Lent) but a number are communal laments that would be useful in Advent. Some examples of good repertoire choices for Advent include:

- Psalm 146, "Lord, come and save us" by Marty Haugen (*Gather*, #60)

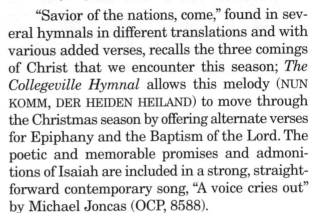

- Psalm 80, "Lord, make us turn to you" by Marty Haugen (*Gather*, #37)
- "Come, O long-expected Jesus" (*Worship*, #364)
- "O holy city seen of John" (*Worship*, #685)

"Savior of the nations, come," found in several hymnals in different translations and with various added verses, recalls the three comings of Christ that we encounter this season; *The Collegeville Hymnal* allows this melody (NUN KOMM, DER HEIDEN HEILAND) to move through the Christmas season by offering alternate verses for Epiphany and the Baptism of the Lord. The poetic and memorable promises and admonitions of Isaiah are included in a strong, straightforward contemporary song, "A voice cries out" by Michael Joncas (OCP, 8588).

Perhaps the most familiar Advent hymn is "O come, O come, Emmanuel." It certainly should remain one of the sounds of Advent, but not the only sound! It does not need to be sung every Sunday and is probably best reserved for the final week, when the "O Antiphons" are properly used as a final preparation for the great feast of Christmas. Consider Katherine Crosier's arrangement of this familiar hymn (GIA). Intended as a processional, this arrangement for choir, assembly and handbells works well and may provide a good introductory piece later to a pre-Mass program of carols at the parish's midnight Mass at Christmas.

Some choral gems would include Paul Manz's beloved *a capella* anthem "E'en so, Lord Jesus, quickly come" (Morning Star), John Ferguson's two-part "Comfort, comfort" (Augsburg), Leland Sateren's "Come, thou long-expected Jesus" (Augsburg), and "O Holy Mary" by Owen Alstott (OCP). Consider adding the traditional spiritual "Soon and very soon" to your choir's Advent repertoire. Two very fine Advent and Christmas choral collection resources are GIA's *A Choir Book for Advent* and *A Choir Book for Christmas*. Both contain settings for unison, two, three and four parts for both accompanied and *a capella* singing.

Cantors are an important liaison with our assemblies during the season of Advent. The cantor must prayerfully sing the texts and graciously invite the assembly to join in the musical experience. If the cantor is unsure of the music or is self-absorbed in the process of singing, the congregation is the loser. The cantor must work and prepare to make the text that is being sung so much his or her own prayer that the congregation joyfully will anticipate making it theirs also. This requires a great deal of preparation on the part of the cantor and the music director.

Whatever musical choices are made, each musician must remember that the sound of the assembly singing is the preeminent sound of the Advent season (and every other season as well!). What works well in one parish may not in another. Given the wide variety of resources from parish to parish, the sound of the season inevitably will vary. Each musician must carefully review the Advent music that a particular parish music resource offers. An informal "sing-in," by the cantors or members of the choir and some assembly members, of the Advent offerings in the current missalette, hymnal, music supplement or choral offerings by the publishers, done in a prayerful preparation session for the season, might prove invaluable. Musicians must be open to the varying tastes within our communities, gently guiding our assemblies using the judgments offered to us by our bishops in *Music in Catholic Worship* (USCC). A rereading of this document may once again be timely for all of us.

Other Ritual Prayer and Sacraments

Advent is a season with great richness and spiritual potential. Parishes should offer other opportunities to celebrate the season beyond the Sunday Mass. Even though people are usually very busy at this time of year, many would welcome such opportunities for a respite from all the shopping and partying.

LITURGY OF THE HOURS

Many parishes have begun to recover the church's daily prayer by scheduling Vespers (Evening Prayer) during Advent and Lent. Celebrated as day breaks and as darkness falls, Morning and Evening Prayer highlight the season's emphasis on light and darkness. Parishes that have been celebrating Vespers or Morning Prayer for several years during Advent should plan to make this daily prayer a part of every

season. Those who have not yet begun will find Advent an ideal time to start. Note, too, that the great gospel canticles, the Benedictus at Morning Prayer and the Magnificat at Evening Prayer, are Advent texts from the Gospel of Luke.

■ BLESSING THE ADVENT WREATH: The *Book of Blessings* (BB), in chapter 47, suggests Evening Prayer I of the First Sunday of Advent as an appropriate setting for the blessing of the Advent wreath and the lighting of the first candle. The liturgy of Evening Prayer, modified to include these elements, looks like this:

- introduction (but not a lucernarium), hymn, psalmody, reading (perhaps of Isaiah as in BB, #1526), homily, silence, responsory, gospel canticle (Magnificat), all as usual

- intercessions (BB, #1530)

- Lord's Prayer (as introduced in BB, #1531)

- prayer of blessing (BB, #1532 or #1533)

- lighting of the first candle

- concluding rite (BB, #1534)

Parishes that regularly begin the celebration of Evening Prayer with a service of light (lucernarium) might use the prayer of blessing from the *Book of Blessings* and light the first candle at the start of the celebration. Then the first Advent candle will be the light praised in hymn and thanksgiving. In subsequent weeks, the Advent candles would be used at Evening Prayer for this lucernarium.

■ OFFICE OF READINGS—VIGILS: The practice of keeping vigil together has much to offer a parish. People who join in worship on the eve of great feasts or on Saturday nights during the seasons can be formed in the spirit of the church. The calendar need not be filled with these vigils. A season's Saturdays or a few solemnities can be selected at first. Bible-study groups or other groups of parishioners may want to move their meetings to Saturday or to the eves of solemnities on these occasions. The *Liturgy of the Hours* gives this description:

As with the Easter Vigil, it was customary to begin certain solemnities (different in different churches) with a vigil. Among these solemnities, Christmas and Pentecost are preeminent. This custom should be maintained and fostered, according to the particular usage of each church. Where it seems good to celebrate other solemnities or occasions of pilgrimage with a vigil, the general norms for celebrations of the word should be observed (#71, #73).

Again, since in the Roman rite the Office of Readings is always of uniform brevity, especially for the sake of those engaged in apostolic work, those who desire to extend the celebration of the vigils of Sundays, solemnities and feasts in accordance with tradition should do as follows.

First, the Office of Readings is to be celebrated as in the *Liturgy of the Hours* up to the end of the readings. After the two readings, and before the "Te Deum," a canticle should be added from the special appendix in the *Liturgy of the Hours*. Then the gospel should be read; a homily on the gospel may be added. After this, the "Te Deum" is sung and then the prayer.

On solemnities and feasts the gospel should be taken from the lectionary for Mass; on Sundays it should be taken from the series of gospels on the paschal mystery in the appendix to the *Liturgy of the Hours*.

Those unfamiliar with the format of a vigil can review appendix I of the *Liturgy of the Hours*. Canticles and paschal gospels are given for each of Advent's four Sundays, for the Immaculate Conception and for the commons of saints whose memorials fall in Advent. Consider gathering part of the parish for Saturday nights in Advent or for the eve of the local solemnity if the parish is named after Francis Xavier or Ambrose or one of the other saints of Advent.

If there are musicians in the parish available to assist in the celebration of the hours, this will add a further dimension to the richness of this tradition. The hymns and psalmody take on even greater meaning where they are sung and accompanied well.

■ LESSONS AND CAROLS: This traditional service is actually a vigil service, like the extended Office of Readings just described above. Services of lessons and carols should not be mere concerts with a few readings interspersed. The assembly can be involved with the addition of psalmody and perhaps a *lucernarium*, along with the "concert music" selections. During this season, the scriptures and songs of Advent should be used, with Christmas carols reserved for their proper season. *The Book of Occasional Services* (Episcopalian liturgical book, from the Church Hymnal Corporation) has a fine "Advent Festival of Lessons and Music."

COMMUNAL PENANCE

John the Baptist's call to conversion rings through Advent. While not officially described

as a penitential season (which distinguishes it from Lent), it is still a season for ongoing conversion. If you schedule a communal celebration of reconciliation, appendix II of the *Rite of Penance* provides a complete service for Advent. Careful use of darkness and lighting can bring such a service into the mood of the season in a powerful, nonverbal way.

COMMUNAL ANOINTING OF THE SICK

Parish communal anointing services should be scheduled periodically throughout the year. Sundays in Ordinary Time, especially those with pericopes about healing, would seem to be the best Sundays for this. If the need arises for anointing within Mass on an Advent Sunday, the special ritual Mass is not permitted, though one of the scripture passages from the *Pastoral Care of the Sick* can be used, perhaps as a second reading. Other prayer texts can be found on page 30 for the reception of the sick and for the prayer after anointing.

At anointings outside Sunday Mass in Advent, there are several readings listed in #297 that are appropriate in Advent. In the Old Testament section, the Isaiah passages at G and I are Advent pericopes. The passage from Revelation at W in the New Testament section and from Luke at O in the gospels are also especially appropriate for Advent.

FUNERALS

Funeral Masses are not allowed on the Sundays of Advent or on December 8. When funerals are celebrated, the spirit of Advent should clearly mark our worship. What better way to console the grieving than to draw on the Advent themes of lament and eschatological hope. Psalm 25, one of the common psalms for Advent, also may be chosen for funerals during these days. The readings of the Advent weekday, with their words of hope and expectation, may be used for funerals. There is also a strong passage from Isaiah in the funeral lectionary.

While the *Order of Christian Funerals* multiplies our available opening prayers, we still need more options for the prayer over the gifts and the prayer after communion. The Advent prayers from the sacramentary often work for this purpose. In a similar way, the traditional music for Advent, generally known to many of the faithful, expresses well the intensity of human longing at funerals. "O come, O come, Emmanuel" is particularly appropriate and familiar. Its lyrics are a plea for God to save us from the power of death.

MARRIAGE

"When a marriage is celebrated during Advent or Lent or on other days of penance, the parish priest should advise the couple to take into consideration the special nature of these times" (*Rite of Marriage*, #11). This directive is too often ignored. On Advent Sundays and on December 8, it means that all the Mass texts must be from the current day. It also means that the parish's Advent decor should determine the visual environment. It must not be removed or overshadowed by wedding flowers and banners. Those who do not want violet and rose colors for their wedding should not plan to be married in Advent. Be sure to light the appropriate number of candles in the Advent wreath for all gatherings, including weddings and funerals.

The readings of the day, especially if they reflect on the prophetic images of God marrying God's people, should be considered for days other than Sunday as well. The reading from the Song of Songs is traditionally associated with Advent. Intercessions and music also must be arranged with an awareness of Advent's character: Christmas carols do not belong at an Advent Saturday wedding any more than they belong at an Advent Sunday Mass.

RITE OF CHRISTIAN INITIATION OF ADULTS

Contrary to the recent custom of many parishes, the rite of acceptance into the order of catechumens and the rite of welcoming candidates are not prescribed for the First Sunday of Advent. The tendency to schedule these rituals at Advent usually flows from the attempt to compress a multiyear catechumenate into a nine-month school year, which is largely ineffective for proper formation of catechumens. A review of the liturgical and parish calendars will suggest other times as more appropriate for the rite of acceptance. These powerful rites are better celebrated on Sundays in Ordinary Time. Liturgies of the word and other prayers celebrated with catechumens and candidates outside the Sunday assembly should be prepared with Advent in mind.

The Worship Environment

During Advent, the playing of the organ and other musical instruments as well as the floral decoration of the altar should be marked by a moderation that reflects the character of this season but does not anticipate the full joy of Christmas itself. (*Ceremonial of Bishops*, #236)

THIS moderation is achieved only with careful sensitivity. It is not Lenten austerity, but it shouldn't anticipate the evergreens and flowers of Christmas, either. Since the season is one of growing anticipation, visual elements might be added each week, building to the feast, but this should be restrained and subtle, like the small change of lighting one more candle on the wreath each week.

■ THE ADVENT WREATH: It is customary in most parishes to have an Advent wreath in church. Such a wreath should be large enough to be visible to all, but it should not overshadow the altar, lectern or presider's chair. It may be suspended overhead or placed on a stand. This circle of greens with four candles is meant to be a simple foretaste of the evergreens of Christmas—and this means not using evergreens anywhere else during Advent. Chapter 47 of the *Book of Blessings* places the blessing and lighting of the Advent wreath on the First Sunday of Advent, either after the general intercessions at Mass or in a separate celebration of the word or during Evening Prayer. This source notes that the candles are traditionally three violet and one rose (which is lit for the third week), but that four violet or four white candles may be used. The text also notes that

When the Advent wreath is used in church, on the Second and succeeding Sundays of Advent, the candles are lighted either before Mass begins or immediately before the opening prayer; no additional rites or prayers are used. (#1513)

This instruction seems to indicate a concern that too much attention may be given to the wreath, and it is a concern that should be taken seriously. At the same time, it seems possible that creative use of the wreath could be made in connection with the penitential rite in a way that does not overemphasize the wreath but still links it to home use of a different prayer each week. See page 26 for an example.

Alternatively, lighting the wreath just before the opening prayer might suggest a creative invitation to prayer, one that links the thrust of the prayer with the lighting of the wreath (see pages 26–27). Lighting the candles during the silence for prayer and chanting the oration might give adequate solemnity to the rite without unnecessary wordiness. Then the same prayer invitation and oration might be provided in the bulletin that week for home use with the wreath.

■ OTHER IMAGES: The season of Advent has given rise to many images: statues or windows of John the Baptist, images of Isaiah or one of the other prophets, or the "Jesse Tree." (The most ancient renderings of this Christian interpretation of the Hebrew Scriptures show pictures of the various offspring of Jesse, though symbols of various ancestors of Christ are often used today.) If your church has these images or any others appropriate to the season, attention can be given to them with candles or by reproductions of them on Advent handouts. If not, local artists may create one for the entranceway this year.

■ OUTDOORS: Our Catholic tradition of celebrating Advent as distinct from Christmas should be expressed in the face we show our neighbors. Outdoor mangers and Christmas lights should be set up or illuminated only on the last day or two before Christmas. The importance of allowing Advent to have its own time needs creative adaptation in each community—how can our longings and readiness be expressed in color and other embellishments? Purple strips of cloth? An outdoor tree with "Jesse" figures?

■ VESTURE: Chasubles, dalmatics, copes and stoles for Advent are customarily made of violet and purple, with trims and ornament in silvers, whites, dark blues and grays—the colors of winter. The use of blue as a predominant color for vesture, though now common in some Christian denominations, is not traditional in the Roman Catholic church. Care should be taken to ensure that the vesture used in Advent is different from that used during Lent, and that this vesture returns year after year. Avoid vesture with passion symbols.

December

◯3 Lectionary #1   Violet
First Sunday of Advent

■ ADVENT EVE: To emphasize the theme of light and darkness, parishes might begin the season with first Vespers of Sunday on Saturday evening. This could include the first lighting of the Advent wreath (see page 16 regarding an outline). Another way to begin is with a vigil of Advent readings and psalms (See lessons and carols, page 17).

■ THE END-TIME: Advent always begins with a gospel proclamation about the end of time. Today we turn to Matthew and hear part of his eschatological discourse. Matthew's description of the judgment will be proclaimed at the end of the current liturgical year, on the Feast of Christ the King. Thus the liturgical year begins and ends with awareness of the promised return of the Lord.

As the end of the millennium approaches, we will likely see more and more written about the imminent end of the world. Matthew's words remind us that the Son of Man will come when we least expect it: Christ came in history in the most unlikely of circumstances, and it is a safe bet that he will come to us again with a similar disregard for our sense of respectability and appropriateness. We are called to be on guard, lest we miss the master's coming.

The first reading paints a beautiful picture of the peace and harmony that the Lord's coming will bring. The second reading urges us to "cast off deeds of darkness and put on the armor of light," reflecting well a fundamental Advent theme.

■ BLESSING THE WREATH: See the *Book of Blessings,* #1517ff., if the Advent wreath was not blessed at Evening Prayer I. Familiar Advent psalm antiphons or other refrains, such as "Prepare the way of the Lord" (Taizé, GIA), "My soul in stillness waits" (Haugen, GIA) or "A voice cries out in the wilderness" (Joncas, OCP), effectively add assembly participation to rituals such as this. One song written specifically for the lighting of the Advent wreath (and which doesn't assign some artificial significance to each candle) is "Wait for Messiah" from the *Hymnal for Catholic Students* (GIA/LTP).

■ THE WEEK AHEAD: The readings for the first weekdays of Advent are described in the introduction to the lectionary (#94):

> In the first part of Advent there are readings from Isaiah, distributed in accord with the sequence of the book itself and including salient texts that are also read on the Sundays. For the choice of the weekday gospel, the first reading has been taken into consideration.

Friday's feast will interrupt these readings. If planners do not wish to miss Isaiah's wonderful description of the coming day of the Lord, it could be used in place of the pericope assigned to Thursday, which has similar themes of justice and God's power. Wednesday is the optional memorial of St. Nicholas, a special day in many families. The parish might want to give a small gift to children after Mass on Sunday to connect with home observances of St. Nicholas and to remind children of the true origin of Santa Claus.

Note that the first preface for Advent (P-1) is to be used until December 16; the second preface is reserved for the final eight days (December 17–24).

MON 4 #176   violet
Advent Weekday

John of Damascus, presbyter, religious, doctor of the church, optional memorial/white. ▪ A monk at the monastery of Saint Sabbas near Jerusalem in the eighth century, John wrote many doctrinal works, especially arguments against the iconoclasts. Known as the last of the Greek Fathers, he also composed a number of hymns and other texts used in the Byzantine liturgy. Today's readings and psalm all speak of the nations coming to Jerusalem from east and west to take their place in the kingdom.

TUE 5 #177   violet
Advent Weekday

Today's readings present the powerful image of the peaceable kingdom in Isaiah (which expresses a basic longing of people all over the world), while the gospel reminds us how blessed we are to live in the time of partial fulfillment of that vision.

WED 6 #178   violet
Advent Weekday

Nicholas, bishop, optional memorial/white. ▪ Christian tradition has immortalized this fourth-century bishop of Myra (Turkey) as a symbol of generosity. He's the patron of children, brides, sailors and pawnbrokers, as well as of Greece, Sicily and Russia.

Nicholas has had and continues to have an important place in many Eastern churches, but this feast has not had a high ranking in the Roman church. The cultural practices carry on nonetheless. A marvelous book on the whole phenomenon of Saint Nick is *Saint Nicholas of Myra, Bari, and Manhattan: Biography of a Legend* by Charles Jones (University of Chicago Press, 1978).

The readings are from the weekday. Today's passage from Isaiah is also found in the funeral lectionary and might well be the preferred first reading at funerals in Advent. The vision of the banquet in both readings and in the psalm suggests our longing for the heavenly banquet, which the eucharist anticipates. The proper collect can conclude the general intercessions if the weekday collect is used for the opening prayer.

THU 7 #179 violet
Ambrose, bishop, doctor of the church
MEMORIAL

Elected bishop of Milan by popular acclaim while he was still a catechumen, Ambrose became a gifted liturgical reformer, a brilliant preacher, a wise doctor of the church, the "Father of Western hymnody" and a model bishop. Although he died on Holy Saturday (397), his memory is kept on the anniversary of his ordination as bishop in 374.

One of the other rites of the Catholic church, the Ambrosian rite, has taken its name from him. Similar in many ways to the Roman rite, it remains one of the few other Western rites to survive the medieval and post-Tridentine efforts to bring about ritual uniformity. A few of its notable differences from the Roman rite are its calendar (for example, six Sundays in Advent and the beginning of Lent with ashes on the First Sunday of Lent) and its order of Mass (for example, a proper hymn after each day's gospel and the peace greeting at the conclusion of the liturgy of the word). The Ambrosian rite is celebrated in the dioceses around Milan.

Intercessions for this day might include the Catholics of that rite. Since the prayers for Ambrose are proper, they should be used—with their fitting allusions to Advent (light, glory, preparation for the feast of eternal life). As is almost always the case, the readings should be those of the season. The first pericope assigned to Friday might be used today. Thursday's texts focus on what is required of those who would enter into the kingdom. Only the nation that is just, those who keep faith and those who put Christ's words into practice will enter the kingdom. Prayers of lament for our nation may be appropriate today.

#689 white

FRI 8 The Immaculate Conception of the Virgin Mary
SOLEMNITY

Though this is the patronal feast of the United States, it is not one that fosters easy understanding on the part of the faithful. There is often confusion between the Immaculate Conception of Mary and the virgin birth of Jesus. This feast celebrates Mary's preservation from sin from the first moment of her conception in the womb of St. Ann. Yet the gospel of the day speaks of Jesus' conception in Mary's womb, which contributes to the popular confusion. A few words of introduction after the sign of the cross and greeting would be helpful today to clarify the question. One possibility:

Today we honor holy Mary,
and celebrate her conception in
the womb of Saint Ann.

As we praise God,
who kept her sinless from the
first moment of her life,
let us remember God's mercy
which has freed *us* from sin
in baptism.

■ HISTORY OF THE MARIAN FESTIVALS: The dogma of the Immaculate Conception was officially proclaimed by Pope Pius IX in 1854, but the feast has a much longer history. From the earliest centuries of Christianity, popular religious imagination ascribed many qualities to the life of Mary—about the special relationship of Joachim and Ann, her marvelous conception and birth, her dedication in the Temple, the annunciation, her espousal to Joseph, the wondrous birth of the Lord, her relationship to Jesus at home and in his ministry, her place with the apostles at Pentecost, and her sleep in the Lord ("dormition," later to be drawn into belief in her assumption).

Pious devotions and beliefs were sometimes quite fantastic, based only on apocryphal writings (such as the tradition that from the age of three Mary was brought up by virgins in the Temple). Our calendar, with more than a dozen Marian observances, shows the richness and diversity flowing from this devout attention to every aspect of the blessed Virgin. This is in addition to the optional practice of remembering her on many Saturdays in Ordinary Time and the attention she receives on many other days, such as the Presentation and Christmas. Her centrality to the Catholic tradition should be obvious.

■ HISTORY OF THIS SOLEMNITY: By about the fourth and fifth centuries, Augustine of Hippo and other writers began to reflect on the possibility that Mary was preserved from sin. While some speculated that this may have even been from the moment of conception,

> Great saints in the early and middle ages of church history denied an immaculate conception of the Virgin Mary—not out of any dishonor or lack of love for the Mother of God, but because it was incomprehensible to them that "any" human being could not be born in sin or inherit the sin of the first parents. Theologians such as St. John Chrysostom, St. Bernard of Clairvaux, and St. Thomas Aquinas believed that Mary's sinlessness would have detracted from the dignity of Christ as Savior of all men and women. It would be as though Mary did not need Christ's redemptive death and resurrection. (Secretariat, Bishops' Committee on the Liturgy, *Holy Days in the United States*, page 74)

Meanwhile, monasteries and then various dioceses (around the year 700) began liturgical commemorations of the maternity of Ann. This feast of conception was easily transformed into a celebration of Mary's sinlessness as that belief matured. Wise theologians noted that this was not a denial of the paschal mystery—rather, that Mary benefitted from the grace of Christ in advance. By the time Europeans brought Catholicism to the Americas, it was a popular feast. Father Marquette is especially famous for his devotion to this doctrine. Eight years before the papal proclamation of the dogma, the bishops of the United States declared Mary under this title the patron of the nation.

■ MAINTAIN THE ADVENT SPIRIT: Because the angel's message and Mary's response match the expectancy of the season, let almost everything stay the same as worship on Sunday. The alternative opening prayer links the feast to the season ("Prepare once again a world for your Son"). Some possible adaptations to the seasonal order include: a sung Gloria, a petition for the rights and dignity of all the people of the United States, floral and candle arrangements near the image of Mary (although attention to this image is fitting throughout the season) and some Marian music appropriate to Advent ("She will show us the Promised One," for example). "The angel Gabriel from heaven came" (*Worship*, #695) and Owen Alstott's "O holy Mary" (OCP, 8724) are two other good hymns for this feast. Be sure also to use some Advent hymns along with the Marian music. See page 29 for inserts for eucharistic prayers used in France. The solemn blessing printed with today's texts in most editions of the sacramentary has been updated in the *Book of Blessings* (where it is listed as solemn blessing #20 in appendix II); note that the language has been made more inclusive. The seasonal blessing used on other Advent days would also be appropriate today.

9 #181 violet
S A T
Advent Weekday

Blessed Juan Diego (Cuatitlatoatzin), hermit, optional memorial/white. ▪ This Native Mexican is now honored as more than just the one who saw Our Lady of Guadalupe. Recognition of his own holiness led to his recent beatification. If the optional memorial will be observed locally (and it certainly should be if the parish has a significant Hispanic presence), care should be taken to use the correct texts. The scriptures, as usual, are from the season; those assigned for today fit well with this memorial, speaking of the gifts of God and especially the gift of healing. The opening prayer for Mass is proper, but was released after the current sacramentary. It and other propers published since the last sacramentary can be found in *Sacramentary Supplement* (Catholic Book Publishing Company). If you do not yet have it, an opening prayer (and Liturgy of the Hours texts) from the Common of Holy Men and Women should be used. In line with the summary of norms found at the beginning of the "Commons" section of the sacramentary, the prayer over the gifts and the prayer after communion may be taken from the seasonal weekday.

10 #4 violet
Second Sunday of Advent

The appearance of John the Baptist is central to Advent. His prophetic preaching calls us to repent and reform our lives. Isaiah proclaims a beautiful vision of God's peace where the wolf will be the guest of the lamb. And St. Paul exhorts us to live in harmony with one another. This dual call to reform and to peace offers an ideal time for issuing an invitation to an Advent penance service. Some communal reflection on what reform John would demand in our own time might give voice to our need for salvation in the homily.

■ THE WEEK AHEAD: Tuesday's feast of Our Lady of Guadalupe will displace the Advent weekday readings. Those readings might be used on Wednesday if you don't want to skip Isaiah's words of comfort.

11 #182 violet
M O N
Advent Weekday

Damasus I, Pope, optional memorial/white. ▪ Damasus, pope from 366 to 384, fostered devotion to martyrs, composing epitaphs for many of their tombs. It was during his pontificate that Christianity was declared the official religion of Rome. Damasus also encouraged Jerome to translate the Bible into Latin, as it was becoming the principal language of the liturgy. The readings today can remind us of our need both for forgiveness and healing and for God's power to meet that need.

TUE 12 — #707–712 white — Our Lady of Guadalupe
FEAST

This feast is growing in importance in our country as a larger percentage of the church in the United States is made up of persons with Hispanic backgrounds. This is a feast for all the Americas that focuses on a wonderful image of Mary and a marvelous story of its origins. See page 8 for a discussion of the image and its meanings.

■ LECTIONARY: The scriptures of this day are to be drawn from the Common of the Blessed Virgin Mary. One of the passages from the prophetic books (there are three from Isaiah, one from Micah and one from Zechariah) would help link this day to the Advent season. Either of the passages from Luke 1 are traditional for Advent.

■ SACRAMENTARY: The presidential prayers for Mass, issued too recently to be part of the 1985 edition of the sacramentary, can be found in *Sacramentary Supplement* (Catholic Book Publishing Company). The solemn blessing of the Blessed Virgin Mary (the inclusive-language translation of it is at #20 of appendix II in the *Book of Blessings*) may be used at any celebrations this day, eucharistic or otherwise.

WED 13 — #184 red — Lucy, virgin, martyr
MEMORIAL

Lucy is the perfect Advent saint; her name means "light." Although she was martyred in Sicily, she is often associated with Sweden, mainly because a Stockholm department store, capitalizing on a rural folk custom, began promoting a December "Lucy Queen" much the same way American department stores hire Santas to sell their wares. Despite the commercialism, Christians everywhere have found reason to honor Lucy. The rich traditions that surround St. Lucy's Day take as their jumping off point the beautiful Advent gospel of the wise and foolish bridesmaids, Matthew 25:1–13. Tuesday's weekday readings might be used today, though Wednesday's assigned texts have their own beauty. The first reading concludes with the wonderful promise of God's strength for endurance, an important gift in the face of the evils we lament. Either first reading could be linked to Lucy's martyrdom, and the gospel for either day gives similar assurance of God's care.

THU 14 — #185 white — John of the Cross, presybyter, religious, doctor of the church
MEMORIAL

John's *The Dark Night of the Soul* gives us at least one clue as to how to celebrate his memory in Advent: In darkness, in the pain of the cross, we find light. John's commitment to seeking God's will even in the darkness and to trusting in God's wisdom even when it is not apparent fits well with today's readings. The first reading emphasizes God's powerful help and guidance, while the gospel reminds us of our favored status as those born into the kingdom.

FRI 15 — #186 violet — Advent Weekday

Today's readings challenge our response to the Word of God addressed to us. Too often we are like the children in the gospel, obstinate in our unwillingness to cooperate with God.

SAT 16 — #187 violet — Advent Weekday

The readings today speak of Elijah and suggest that John the Baptizer was Elijah returned. The prediction of the passion in the gospel offers an opportunity to link the Advent season with Lent–Easter. The one whose incarnation we celebrate in Advent–Christmas is the Crucified and Risen One.

■ LAS POSADAS: Tonight the Advent novena (called *Las Posadas*—"lodgings") begins. This novena, commemorating the journey of Mary and Joseph from Nazareth to Bethlehem, is popular in much of Latin America and the Philippines. The customs of this novena, especially the nighttime or early dawn processions, if observed according to their original significance, weave together Advent vigilance, hospitality and social justice. It can be a good way to focus on the need for redemption of both our social structures and individual lives. See page 9 for a fuller description of *Las Posadas*.

17 — #7 violet or rose — Third Sunday of Advent

This is Gaudete Sunday, the day traditionally called "rejoice." This title comes from the first word of the Latin entrance antiphon. Both the first reading and the gospel give the reasons for joy; it flows from God's saving action. The second reading from James is less clearly joyful than the Pauline passages in Years B and C; it counsels patience as we continue to wait.

■ PRAYER TEXTS: The first opening prayer and the prayer after communion both offer the imprecise word "birthday" as a translation for the Latin "day of birth." There is a difference. A birthday is simply the remembrance of a past event; but what we celebrate is his presence, his "birth" in our own lives. In both prayers, "birthday" would more correctly read "birth." What is at stake here is an understanding of a Christian festival as something far more than a historical commemoration. At Christmas we celebrate Christ's presence in our own time, so that we can declare: Today is born our Savior, Christ the Lord. The preface for the rest of Advent is the second Advent preface (P-2).

For the liturgy of the hours today, the readings, the antiphons for the Benedictus and Magnificat and the intercessions are taken from December 17 rather than from the Third Sunday of Advent. This would also suggest that the gospel acclamation (which is based on the Magnificat antiphon) should come from December 17, the first O Antiphon; it invokes Christ as Wisdom of God, guiding creation with power and love and teaching us to walk in the paths of knowledge.

■ THE WEEK AHEAD: Today begins the final section of Advent, marked by the "O Antiphons." They are each day's antiphons for the Magnificat at Evening Prayer, as well as the gospel acclamation verses at Mass (see lectionary #202). They are set metrically in the hymn "O come, O come, Emmanuel." Appropriate verses may be sung during the gospel acclamation at Mass or at any gathering this week. Two other settings are Marty Haugen's "My soul in stillness waits" (GIA 2652) and "Let the King of Glory come" by Michael Joncas.

■ THE READINGS: The introduction to the lectionary (#94) gives an overview of this week:

In the last week before Christmas the events that immediately prepared for the Lord's birth are presented from Matthew (chapter 1) and Luke (chapter 1). The texts in the first reading, chosen in view of the gospel reading, are from different Old Testament books and include important messianic prophecies.

MON 18 #195 violet
Advent Weekday

Today's first reading recalls God's promise to raise up a righteous shoot to David, and the gospel recounts the Annunciation to Joseph, son of David. Since this is also the beginning of Hanukkah, this might be a good day to focus on the correct understanding of the relationship between Christianity and Judaism. For further reading on this issue, see *God's Mercy Endures Forever*, #13, by the Bishops' Committee on the Liturgy and Gabe Huck's comments on page 49 of Pawlikowski and Wilde's *When Catholics Speak about Jews* (LTP). The O Antiphon today invokes the Leader of ancient Israel, the giver of the law to Moses on Sinai, who will rescue us with God's mighty power.

■ HANUKKAH: Our Jewish neighbors begin celebrating this feast today. Hanukkah, the eight-day festival of lights, brings all religious peoples a message of light and fidelity. It also invites us to pray for our sisters and brothers in the covenant. The story can be read in 1 and 2 Maccabees—it is about resistance to tyranny, the renewal of the Jewish people and the cleansing and rededication of the Temple. In this festival there are remarkable lessons about the dangers of cultural assimilation and the abandonment of religious tradition. Later traditions tell of

the lamps that burned for eight days at the rededication even though only one day's oil had been supplied.

TUE 19 #189 violet
Advent Weekday

The story of the conception of Samson is presented here as a model for the conception of John the Baptizer. Both were gifts to a barren couple, and both were consecrated to the Lord's service. The O Antiphon today invokes Christ as the flower of Jesse's stem and a sign of God's love for all people, and begs him to come and save us without delay.

WED 20 #190 violet
Advent Weekday

The word for today is "Immanuel." The gospel account of the Annunciation to Mary stands as the fulfillment of God's promise to dwell with us. Once again, we are reminded that Advent celebrates the continuing Incarnation, the present dwelling of God with us, not just the historical commemoration of Christ's birth. The O Antiphon for today calls upon the Key of David, opening the gates of God's eternal kingdom and freeing the prisoners of darkness.

THU 21 #191 violet
Advent Weekday

Peter Canisius, presbyter, religious, doctor of the church, optional memorial. ▪ Whether commemorating Peter or not, every parish should consider reading the Song of Solomon passage instead of Zephaniah. This is a rare opportunity to hear it and to recognize the presence of God in sexual love. This could easily be linked to the gospel's image of two pregnant women rejoicing in God's favor. The O Antiphon for the day calls upon the Radiant Dawn, splendor of eternal light, the sun of justice, who will shine on those lost in the darkness of death.

F
R **22** #192   violet
I   **Advent Weekday**

Today's gospel presents us with the beautiful canticle of Mary— the Magnificat. The first reading reveals the ancestry of this Marian text in the canticle of Anna, which forms the responsorial for the day. There are numerous musical settings of the Magnificat that could be sung. The O Antiphon invokes the King of all nations, source of the church's unity and faith, who comes to save all humanity, God's own creation. Today is also the winter solstice, the shortest day of the year in the Northern Hemisphere.

S
A **23** #200   violet
T   **Advent Weekday**

John Kanty, presbyter, optional memorial. ▪ Once again, these late Advent days allow for only brief commemorations, today of this Polish priest and professor. In the intercessions today, pray for Poland and for universities.

The readings present different perspectives on the coming of the Lord: Malachi reminds us of the judgment of the Lord, while the gospel shows Zachariah praising God after the birth of the Baptizer. The O Antiphon calls upon Emmanuel, God present among us, our King and our Judge, to come and save us.

✳ **24** #10   violet
        **Fourth Sunday
        of Advent**

The first opening prayer is a rewrite of the old Angelus collect, which links the incarnation and the paschal mystery of Christ. Both opening prayers remind us

of the usual Marian focus of this Sunday, though the second one is clearer on that score; this year's gospel might suggest using the first prayer, with its reference to angelic revelation. The readings of the day focus on the virgin birth, foreshadowed in the prophet's words to Ahaz and explained by the angel's words to Joseph. Homilists might want to give some attention to Joseph this year, since he is so seldom mentioned in the readings. There is no O Antiphon assigned to today, because Evening Prayer tonight will be First Vespers of Christmas.

INTRODUCTORY RITES

Greeting

From the Christ who was, who is, and who
    is to come:
grace, light and peace be with you all.

Penitential Rite with Lighting of the Advent Wreath

FIRST SUNDAY OF ADVENT
As we begin our celebration, let us call to mind
our need for salvation.

Lord Jesus, you came to offer salvation to all
people: Lord, come and save us.

Christ Jesus, you come in word and sacrament to strengthen your people: Christ, come
and save us.

Lord Jesus, you will come at the end of time to
establish God's kingdom in its fullness: Lord
come and save us.

The first candle is lit.

Almighty God, as we begin this Advent season, we ask you to continue the work of our
salvation begun in your Son, Jesus. Let your
blessing come upon us as we light this wreath;
turn our hearts to you and grant us the peace
and joy for which we long. We ask this through
Christ our Lord.

SECOND SUNDAY OF ADVENT
As we enter into this Advent liturgy, let us call
to mind God's promise of mercy and healing:

Lord Jesus, you came to proclaim God's justice for all: Lord, come and save us.

Christ Jesus, you come with God's comfort for
the poor and oppressed: Christ, come and
save us.

Lord Jesus, you are the savior the Baptist
proclaimed: Lord, come and save us.

Two candles are lit.

Lord God, we long for the new heavens and
new earth you have promised. May the light
of this wreath be a sign of hope to all people,
and especially to those who are oppressed by
injustice. Let the word of your truth lead us

all toward your kingdom for which we long.
We ask this through Christ our Lord.

THIRD SUNDAY OF ADVENT
As we begin our celebration, let us recall with
joy the salvation God has prepared for us.

You came to bring us joy and hope: Lord, come
and save us.

You bring glad tidings to the poor and healing
for the brokenhearted: Christ, come and save
us.

You proclaim liberty to captives and release
to prisoners: Lord, come and save us.

Three candles are lit.

Almighty God, your promise of salvation fills
us with joy and hope. We long for its fulfillment in our own time. Hear the cries of your
people and let your power be evident in our
world, that we and all people may have ever
new reasons to rejoice in your love. We ask
this through Christ our Lord.

FOURTH SUNDAY OF ADVENT
As we gather on this final Sunday of Advent,
let us open our hearts to God's merciful grace.

Lord Jesus, you are Son of God and Son of
Mary: Lord, come and save us.

Christ Jesus, you came to establish God's
kingdom: Christ, come and save us.

Lord Jesus, Son of David, your reign over us
will be without end: Lord, come and save us.
All four candles are lit.

Lord God, the brightness of our wreath reflects
the glory of your Son, whose coming we soon
will celebrate. Yet darkness still reigns in so
many parts of our world and of our lives. May
the coming celebration of Jesus' birth bring
us closer to the kingdom you promise. We ask
this through Christ, our Lord.

or

FIRST SUNDAY OF ADVENT
*After the homily, use the blessing for the wreath found in
the Book of Blessings, #1517.*

SECOND SUNDAY OF ADVENT

As we light our Advent wreath, let us pray that God's power will be at work in our world, to bring healing and joy to all who long for God's coming.

Two candles are lit in silence. Presider then proclaims the opening prayer.

THIRD SUNDAY OF ADVENT

As we light the candles of our Advent wreath, let us pray that the joy of Christ's coming may spread throughout our world, especially to those who are oppressed and suffer injustice.

Three candles are lit in silence. Presider then proclaims the opening prayer.

FOURTH SUNDAY OF ADVENT

As we light our wreath on this final Sunday of Advent, let us pray that we, like Mary, may be open to the coming of Christ into our lives so that we may be instruments of the coming of God's kingdom in its fullness.

Four candles are lit in silence. Presider then proclaims the opening prayer.

Invitation to Penitence

[My brothers and sisters:]
coming together to the table of word
    and eucharist,
let us be alert to the advent of our God
and prepare the Lord's way by turning
    from our sins,
embracing justice and truth,
and finding comfort in the Christ who
    promises peace.

Penitential Rite

You came as redeemer to announce glad
    tidings of salvation:
Lord, have mercy.

You come as shepherd to gather
    and feed us:
Christ, have mercy.

You will come as judge to establish a new
    heaven and earth:
Lord, have mercy.

LITURGY OF THE WORD

Dismissal of Catechumens

My dear friends: With the assurance of our loving support, this community sends you forth to reflect more deeply on the word of God we have shared. Our Advent prayer is that God may bless you with every spiritual gift and strengthen you with the comfort of glad tidings, so that in due time you may share fully at the Lord's table and be found blameless on the day when Christ comes in glory.

General Intercessions

Invitation to prayer

The Lord comes to save us and to establish the kingdom: let us give voice in our prayer to the longings of all the human race, especially those who are poor and forgotten.

For the church

For the church throughout the world,
that we faithfully announce peace
and work for justice
until the Lord comes in glory:
let us pray to the Lord.

For all people of faith
who proclaim the Good News of Christ
and serve the needs of the poor:
let us pray to the Lord.

For the world

That God's peace may come,
and the violence of this world pass away:
let us pray to the Lord.

For a spirit of wisdom and mercy
to guide the leaders of all nations:
let us pray to the Lord.

For various needs

That God who is comfort
may hear the cries of all who are in need:
let us pray to the Lord.

For all who seek healing
in their lives and in their hearts,
that in Christ's name they be raised
    to new life:
let us pray to the Lord.

For the local community

For those awaiting the birth of a child,
that their hearts be filled with peace
and their fears be turned to joy:
let us pray to the Lord.

For our benefactors
and those who have asked to be
remembered in prayer:
let us pray to the Lord.

Attuned to the Sunday readings

For all peoples of the Middle East,
that their nations and leaders
seek the ways of peace together:
let us pray to the Lord.

For catechumens, candidates and inquirers

For the inquirers and catechumens,
that God will grace them
with the fullness of faith:
let us pray to the Lord.

For the catechumens and candidates,
that God will make them
honorable members of the holy church:
let us pray to the Lord.

For the departed

For those who have died in the peace
of Christ,
and for all the dead whose faith is known
to God alone:
let us pray to the Lord.

Concluding Prayers for the General Intercessions

FIRST SUNDAY OF ADVENT
God of majesty and power,
amid the clamor of our violence
your Word of truth resounds;
upon a world made dark by sin
the Sun of Justice casts his dawning rays.

Keep your household watchful
and aware of the hour in which we live.
Hasten the advent of that day
when the sounds of war will be
    for ever stilled,
the darkness of evil scattered,
and all your children gathered into one.

We ask this through him whose coming
    is certain,
whose day draws near:
your Son, our Lord Jesus Christ,
who lives and reigns with you in the unity
    of the Holy Spirit,
God for ever and ever.

SECOND SUNDAY OF ADVENT
Your kingdom is at hand,
O God of justice and peace;
you made John the Baptist its herald
to announce the coming of your Christ,
who baptizes with the Holy Spirit and
    with fire.

Give us a spirit of repentance
to make us worthy of the kingdom.
Let complacency yield to conviction,
that in our day justice will flourish
and conflict give way
to the peace you bestow in Christ.

Grant this through him whose coming
    is certain,
whose day draws near:
your Son, our Lord Jesus Christ,
who lives and reigns with you in the unity
    of the Holy Spirit,
God for ever and ever.

THIRD SUNDAY OF ADVENT
God of glory and compassion,
at your touch the wilderness blossoms,
broken lives are made whole,
and fearful hearts grow strong in faith.

Open our eyes to your presence
and awaken our hearts to sing your praise.
To all who long for your Son's return
grant perseverance and patience,
that we may announce in word and deed
the good news of the kingdom.

We ask this through him whose coming
    is certain,
whose day draws near:
your Son, our Lord Jesus Christ,
who lives and reigns with you in the unity
    of the Holy Spirit,
God for ever and ever.

FOURTH SUNDAY OF ADVENT
Eternal God,
in the psalms of David,
in the words of the prophets,
in the dream of Joseph
your promise is spoken.
At last, in the womb of the Virgin Mary,
your Word takes flesh.

Teach us to welcome Jesus, the promised
    Emmanuel,
and to preach the good news of his coming,
that every age may know him
as the source of redemption and grace.

Grant this through him whose coming
    is certain,
whose day draws near:
your Son, our Lord Jesus Christ,
who lives and reigns with you in the unity
    of the Holy Spirit,
God for ever and ever.

LITURGY OF THE EUCHARIST

Eucharistic Prayer Inserts

SUNDAYS IN EUCHARISTIC PRAYERS II AND III:
    See page 84.

DECEMBER 8 IN EUCHARISTIC PRAYER II:
    Lord, you are holy indeed,
    the fountain of all holiness.
    We gather here before you
    and in communion with the
        whole church
    we celebrate the day the Virgin Mary
    was conceived without original fault,
    because you chose her to be the Savior's
        mother.
    Through him, who took away the sin
        of the world,
    we pray:
    Let your Spirit come upon

DECEMBER 8 IN EUCHARISTIC PRAYER III:
    . . . a perfect offering may be made
    to the glory of your name.
    This is why we gather before you,
    and in communion with the whole
        church
    we celebrate the day the Virgin Mary
    was conceived without original fault,

because you chose her to be the Savior's
    mother.
Through him, who took away the sin
    of the world,
we bring you these gifts.
We ask you to make them holy

Introduction to the Lord's Prayer

God so loved the world that he sent his only
Son to be our Savior: let us, therefore pray
with confidence for the coming of the kingdom, as Jesus taught us:

Prayer for Peace

Lord Jesus Christ, whose first coming we
bless and whose final coming we long for as
the advent of perfect peace: Look not on our
sins, but on the faith of your church, and
grant us the peace and unity of your kingdom where you live for ever and ever.

Invitation to Communion

This is the Lamb of God who takes away the
sins of the world: the Savior who is to come.
Happy are those who are called to his supper.

CONCLUDING RITE

Dismissal of Eucharistic Ministers

Go forth in peace to the sick and homebound
of our community, bearing the word of life
and the Body of Christ together with the
assurance of our love and concern. Be to our
brothers and sisters heralds of glad tidings
and ministers of Christ's abiding presence.

Blessing

May the Sun of Righteousness shine upon
you and scatter the darkness from before
your path; and may almighty God bless you

Dismissal

Go in peace to prepare the way of the Lord.

Opening Prayer

Lord,
you have given us a mind to think,
the strength to love,
and the joy to give.
Help us to be always ready and eager
to welcome Jesus every day
until at last he comes to call us home
    to himself.
We ask this through Christ our Lord.

Prayer over the Gifts

Accept, O Lord, this bread and wine,
our precious gifts to you.
Change them for us
into your most precious gift of all:
Jesus Christ our Lord,
who lives and reigns for ever and ever.

Prayer after Communion

Let your bread of life, O Lord,
strengthen us for our journey
until we come to the happiness
of our heavenly home.
We ask this through Christ our Lord.

—*Italian sacramentary*

TEXTS FOR THE ANOINTING OF THE SICK WITHIN MASS

Introduction/Reception of the Sick

We have come together in this Advent season to celebrate the sacraments of anointing and eucharist. The prophet Isaiah sang of a day when the desert would blossom and the parched land exult, a day when weary bodies and frightened hearts would find fresh strength and new courage, a day when the Lord, like a shepherd, would gather the lambs in his arms and speak tender words of healing and comfort. May Christ draw near to us now in these sacraments, as once he came among us, the good physician of souls. May Christ ever be the health and strength of all who look forward to the day when he will come again in glory.

Prayer after Anointing

Strong and gentle God,
with justice for the afflicted
you come to save us;
with healing for the weary
you draw near to comfort us.
To those whom we have anointed
grant courage and strength.
Preserve them whole and entire,
spirit, soul and body,
irreproachable for the coming
of our Lord Jesus Christ,
who lives and reigns for ever and ever.

CHRISTMAS

Introduction to the Season

THE development of the feast we call Christmas occurred around the fourth century after Christ's birth. The early church celebrated only one annual feast, the paschal celebration that we now call Easter. This single feast encompassed the whole mystery of Christ's birth, life, death and resurrection. The same mystery was celebrated each Sunday as a "little Easter," though in fact the Sunday itself seems to have been the original feast, with the annual paschal feast developing second.

This annual feast, then, originally included what we now celebrate at Christmas. The incarnation was the beginning of our redemption. This ancient perspective is an important one for us today. The liturgical year spreads out the various aspects of the one mystery of redemption, but every feast is linked to every other. Easter is the core, and every other celebration is oriented toward and connected to that great festival.

After several centuries, various Christian communities began to celebrate a separate feast of the Incarnation. These celebrations evolved over time, with differences between the East and West, into the celebration cycle we now call Advent – Christmas – Epiphany. Two theories try to explain this evolution.

Perhaps the most popular theory says that the date of Christmas was chosen to counteract pagan celebrations of the winter solstice. Because no one had any idea when Jesus was born, the incarnation of the Sun/Son of Righteousness was commemorated at the same time that the pagans celebrated the rebirth of the sun. The celebrations were marked by lights and evergreens, copying and transforming Roman customs. An adaptation of this hypothesis sees the Christian festival as a complement, not as a contradiction; the great syncretist emperor, Constantine, favored the new cult of Christianity gathering its adherents on the same day as the pagans and for what seemed to be a similar veneration of the Sun/Son.

The other thesis suggests that the date of Christmas was set by calculations internal to the scriptures. The revelation regarding the conception of a son to Zechariah during his priestly duties at Yom Kippur places the conception of John the Baptist in September and his birth in June. Gabriel told Mary that Elizabeth was "in her sixth month"; this places the conception of Jesus in March and his birth in December. This also complemented a theory that understood Jesus' death to have been on the anniversary of his conception. Based on Passover dates, this was calculated to have been March 25, thus placing his birth on December 25. In many Eastern areas, the date for Passover (and the Lord's death and conception) was calculated to be April 6, thus making January 6 the festival of Christ's birth.

■ THE COMING OF THE LIGHT: However the date was first set, the proximity of the pagan festivals of light helped these feasts become marked by solar symbolism. Christmas celebrates the dawn of the Light of the World. The powers of darkness are overcome by his coming to share our life. The long reign of sin is ended and grace has been poured out upon the earth. The Sun of Justice has arisen, and evil is vanquished.

Even using such language reminds us of the connection between Christmas and Easter, for Easter celebrates Christ's victory over sin and evil. Christmas is like a preview of Easter, for it celebrates the same mystery at its beginning. The Byzantine rite makes this clearer than our Western liturgy, for its celebration of the Christmas cycle is modeled on the paschal celebration and frequently uses some of the same texts for both festivals. The great Orthodox theologian and liturgist Alexander Schmemann called Christmas–Epiphany the "winter Pascha" (see Thomas Hopko, *The Winter Pascha*, St. Vladimir's Seminary Press, 1984).

Both these seasons were shaped by preparation for baptism, which for centuries in East and West was celebrated both at the Easter Vigil and at Epiphany. This is why the feast of the Baptism of the Lord is part of our Christmas cycle today, having once been part of the focus of Epiphany. And Advent in some areas had preparation for baptism as its primary purpose, just as Lent did. Thus both Christmas and Easter are festivals that celebrate our own birth, through baptism, to new life.

This is perhaps the hardest thing to remember about Christmas. It celebrates the incarnation, not just the nativity. The incarnation is an ongoing process of salvation, while the nativity is the once-for-all historical event of Bethlehem. We do not really celebrate Christ's "birthday," remembering something that happened long ago. We celebrate the stupendous fact of the incarnation, God entering our world so thoroughly that nothing has been the same since. And God continues to take flesh in our midst, in the men, women and children who form his body today. And the birth we celebrate is not just the past historical event but Christ's continuing birth in his members, accomplished by the power of the Spirit through the waters of baptism.

Generally in the West, we now focus on the Easter Vigil as the premier time for baptism, especially for adults, so Epiphany no longer has the same baptismal character. But the meaning of the Christmas–Epiphany celebration should never be reduced to a mere historical reenactment. What we celebrate is our redemption in Christ and the transformation of all creation by the presence of the divine in our midst. The birth that truly touches our life is our own birth by water and the Spirit, by which we share Christ's life. A "birthday cake for the baby Jesus" just does not begin to suggest the richness of this festival, and the use of such approaches may actually prevent people from appreciating the full meaning of Christmas.

The celebration of the coming of Light into the world, however, does not pretend that *all* is sweetness and light. The inbreaking of the kingdom is celebrated as the victory that it is, but the Christmas cycle also recognizes the darkness that still exists. The three feasts that immediately follow Christmas, the feasts of St. Stephen, St. John and the Holy Innocents, remind us that following Christ requires a willingness to embrace suffering and even death. Here again, Christmas manifests its paschal links. The one born at Bethlehem is the one who dies on Calvary and rises to new life. And this is baptismal, too, since we share in Christ's death and resurrection through baptism.

The readings and images of Christmas are full of paschal echoes, though they often go unnoticed by parishioners. And if they are noticed, they are thought to be inappropriate. Slowly and gently, we must learn again as a community the intimate connection between Christmas and Easter. Then it will become obvious that Christmas is not a time for dramatic pretending. It is, rather, a time to celebrate and embrace all the implications of the fact that God took on our flesh and dwelled among us, a time to celebrate the eternal gift of God to us that came to its fullness in the death and resurrection of Christ.

If Advent has been observed with bracing honesty about the darkness that surrounds us, then the community will recognize the Christmas feast as a time for deeply celebrating the presence of the kingdom. The star of Bethlehem shines in the darkness of the night, but it shines brightly and foretells the ultimate victory. If in Advent we admit that the kingdom has not come in its fullness, Christmas is a time to rejoice in the fact that the kingdom is being born in our midst. If Advent is a time to face the reality of evil in our world, Christmas is a time to rejoice in the reality of grace poured out on the earth. If Advent is a time to lament the continuing power of darkness around us, Christmas is a time to celebrate the light of the world born at Bethlehem. If Advent is a time to face honestly the sin that still dwells in us, Christmas is a time to celebrate the forgiveness of God revealed in Jesus. If Advent is a time to lament the seeming absence of God in the midst of our broken world, Christmas is a time to celebrate the presence of God among us. Advent and Christmas are linked, like two sides of the same coin.

The challenge, then, is to link Advent lament and Christmas celebration. Christmas presents God's resounding answer to all our cries and longings during Advent. This can be expressed in various ways in the celebrations of the Christmas season. A song such as "Proclaim the joyful message/Cry out with joy and gladness," which uses the same tune and similar but different words for Advent and for Christmas, expresses clearly the fulfillment of Isaiah's hope. Words of greeting and introduction at the liturgy can speak of our joy that the light has come and the darkness has been pushed back. Homilies during Christmas can recall our Advent longings as they proclaim their fulfillment in the newborn Savior. Our intercessions can speak of our joy in the presence of the Redeemer while we continue to pray that the kingdom will be advanced more and more. In numerous ways it should be evident that our honest facing of evil during Advent has deepened our joy as we contemplate the wonder of Christmas. With the birth of the Savior, we know that our redemption is at hand, and if Advent has been observed strongly, we know the joy of the sinner redeemed, the slave freed, the lost one found and the victim saved.

■ STRUCTURE OF THE SEASON: The many aspects of the Christmas story and the sharing of dates between Eastern and Western churches led our ancestors to shape an entire season, now extending from December 25 until the Baptism of the Lord. The progression of the liturgical texts allows us to identify three phases to the season.

1. December 25 to January 1 forms an octave of Christmas.

2. The days from January 1 to Epiphany are marked by liturgical texts continuing the motifs of Christmas. John 1 is the prominent gospel for this period. Since Epiphany is now on the Sunday after January 1, this phase of Christmastime is a full week this year. The continuation of our liturgical "holiday season" after New Year's Day should inform our domestic and parish customs. Our homes and daily prayer should reflect the liturgical riches still being celebrated.

3. The Roman Rite continues the season from Epiphany to the Baptism of the Lord, which again is only one day this year. The texts of the liturgy can help us appreciate the relationship between Christmas and Christ's baptism. The connection is not obvious if Christmas is seen as simply the birthday celebration of an infant—Jesus was not baptized as an infant! But if Christmas celebrates the manifestation of the Incarnate One, then his baptism in the Jordan continues that celebration by commemorating the manifestation of his role and mission.

Images of the Season

THE dominant image of the season is clearly the crèche, or manger scene. One finds it on Christmas cards, in most homes and churches, and frequently even in living tableaux. Popularized by St. Francis of Assisi, it has become the central symbol of the season for many, so much so that people are often surprised to learn that the "stable" was probably a cave, not a wooden structure (a cave at Bethlehem has been venerated by Christians since before the destruction of Jerusalem in AD 70). While the crèche may foster the historical pretending noted above, it also offers the possibility of seeing beyond the sentimental to deeper meanings.

Artistic depictions of the nativity at least as far back as the fourth century give the ox and ass center stage, almost always picturing their heads on either side of the Lord in the manger.

The earliest Christians knew why: In Isaiah 1:3, God laments, "An ox knows its owner, and an ass, its master's [Lord's] manger; but Israel does not know, my people has not understood." An old manuscript of Habakkuk said, "In the midst of two animals, thou shalt become known." Thus the ox and the ass came to be emblems of paradise and fulfillment.

The animals might also remind us of the great visions of Isaiah, particularly the great passage from chapter 11 (see Tuesday of the First Week of Advent). The lion and the lamb and all others will live in harmony.

Because the evangelists wrote their birth and infancy narratives as summaries of the meaning of Jesus' life and redemptive work, it is certainly legitimate to see in them hints of what is to come. The savior is placed in a manger, a feed-box; he is to become our spiritual food. He is wrapped in bands of cloth and laid in the manger; after the crucifixion, he is wrapped in linen cloth and laid in the tomb. The Magi came seeking the newborn "King of the Jews"; on the cross Pilate put an inscription that read, "Jesus of Nazareth, the King of the Jews." He was born in a stable; "the Son of Man has nowhere to lay his head." His birth was heralded by a star, a light shining in the darkness; "the light came into the world, but people loved darkness rather than light." His birth was announced first to shepherds, among the lowliest of their society; he was to be the Good Shepherd and one "spurned, and we held him in no esteem."

All these hints remind us that Christmas draws its true meaning from Easter, from the paschal mystery we celebrate in every liturgy. Other aspects of the Christmas story remind us of the dimensions of Christ's mission. The proclamation of his birth to the shepherds recalls his mission to proclaim good news to the poor. The visit of the Magi points to the universal scope of his mission, to the Gentiles as well as to the Jews. The gold, frankincense and myrrh they brought point to his kingship, his divinity and his coming death. The words of Simeon at his presentation in the Temple and his flight into Egypt to escape Herod remind us that his coming overturns the established order and challenges all power structures, as does Mary's great Magnificat ("He has cast down the mighty from their thrones and lifted up the lowly") proclaimed on December 22 and sung every evening at Vespers.

Other symbols of the season also point to Easter. The Christmas tree began as a reminder of the tree of life and of the life-giving cross. Some parishes use the trunk of the parish Christmas tree to form the limbs of the cross for Good Friday. Holly is a Christmas symbol because its thorns and red berries remind us of the suffering of Christ; so, too, the red poinsettia was adopted as a Christmas flower. The wreath was an ancient symbol of victory that here reminds us of Christ's victory over death at Easter.

Numerous Christmas carols also make very clear the connection of Christmas with the mission of Jesus and with the paschal mystery.

■ THE SAINTS IN CHRISTMASTIME: During the days of Christmas, Mary is seen as the glorious mother, the Seat of Wisdom presenting the redeemer to all nations. The saints of these weeks should take on a similarly seasonal cast—with joy we remember holy ones who shined with the light of Christ, who paid the price of discipleship. Throughout its history, the church has kept the memory of the earliest martyrs on the days right after Christmas. The incarnation exacts a price through the centuries. Besides Stephen, John and the Holy Innocents, this season includes celebrations of Thomas Becket, Basil the Great, Gregory Nazianzen, Elizabeth Ann Seton, John Neumann, Blessed Andre Bessette and Hilary. However fully these saints are celebrated, it should be clear that these feasts and memorials are part of our Christmas celebration.

An African American Perspective

SEARCHING the songs of black folk looking specifically for the "Christmas spirituality" can create real disappointment. There are significantly few. James Cone, in citing Howard Thurman, posits that white masters, overseers and preachers intentionally overlooked the birth of Christ because of its significance for political liberation of the oppressed:

It was dangerous to let the slave understand that the life and teachings of Jesus meant freedom for the captive and release for these held in economic, social, and political bondage. (*The Spirituals and the Blues: An Interpretation.* New York: Seabury, 1972, p. 50)

Be that as it may, enslaved African peoples did sing some songs about this wondrous event. Perhaps the most celebrated, "Go tell it on the mountain," should be sung throughout the Christmas season.

The readings, prayers, antiphons, acclamations and psalms of this entire season proclaim the beginning of our salvation, the revelation of God's glory to the whole world, the ministry of the one "who went about doing good works and healing all in the grip of the devil" (Acts 10:38) and "bringing the good news of salvation to the poor" (Preface of the Baptism of the Lord). Surely here is something to shout from the highest mountaintops. Here is something that must be shared with all who even today find themselves struggling with sin, senseless violence, poverty, rejection and death.

Those who were shackled by a heavy burden knew that the birth of Mary's boy child was the inaugurating event of their freedom. Their bodies may have been owned, but not their souls and spirits. They knew that this baby in a crib was the conquering king destined to restore peace and justice, destined to be the source of the rise *and fall* of many nations. They knew of this liberation and they sang of it boldly as a reminder to themselves and to their "owners." Some realized that this same Jesus Christ who was the Sun of Justice then would certainly shine on them, or they who were caught in the shadow of death. So they sang. And the very brave sang in the direction of the big house, reminding "the masters" that freedom could come through personal conversion and that it also could come through revolution. They told it on the mountain and everywhere.

We would do well—all of us—to sing this song. Perhaps it could serve as a reminder to us as the living body of Christ. We live in an age when people all too easily are oppressed by meaninglessness, hopelessness and despair. Our conversion to a life of loving care and service is urgent. Our sisters and brothers hunger still. Our active work on behalf of the poor is a revolution still sought. In our singing, in our praying and in our deeds might all the world know "that Jesus Christ is born."

The world should also know something else: that this Son of God was also son of Mary. In commenting on the spiritual "Sister Mary had-a but one child," Arthur C. Jones relates this story and its equally compelling comment:

'Sixteen children I've had, first and last; and twelve I've nursed for my mistress. I always set my heart upon buying freedom for some of my children. . . . But mistress McKinley wouldn't let me have my children. One after another—one after another—she sold 'em from me. Oh, how many times that woman broke my heart!'

Charity Bowery's testimony, typical of the personal accounts of African women in bondage, calls out directly for spiritual allegiance with Sister Mary, whose love and whose fear for the child are of equal magnitude to those of enslaved women. The symbolic story of Sister Mary's triumph over the evil forces in her environment provides an opening for the emergence of hope in circumstances where hope would otherwise be impossible. (*Wade in the Water: The Wisdom of the Spirituals,* Maryknoll: Orbis, 1993, pp. 27–28).

In an age when so many of *all* our children are prey to abuse, kidnapping, divorce, drugs, gang violence, sexual diseases, poverty, despair and death, it might behoove all of us to sing of Mary. Better yet, we might be inspired by this song to do what she said: protect her child. We might do what she did all his life and even at his death: "rock [them] in a weary land."

The Hispanic Mística and the Liturgy

ALTHOUGH more and more Hispanic families are adopting the Nordic custom of the Christmas tree, a characteristic Latin decoration for both home and church during the Christmas season is the crèche, or *pesebre.* The custom of creating a *Belén,* or Bethlehem scene, was brought to the new world by the Friars Minor in imitation of their founder, St. Francis, who built the first crèche to teach the humble people of his day about the real humanity of Christ. While many European groups have also maintained the use of the manger scene, the Latin American (and Italian) *pesebres* can be very elaborate, unlike our usually sober North American versions. It would seem somehow incomplete in the Latin religious imagination if the baby Jesus were flanked only by Mary and Joseph, the shepherds and a few animals.

The *pesebre* is not meant to be a strictly historic representation. It is a statement of faith in the continuing relevance of Christ's birth among us; even today, one will often see Bethlehem depicted as a small village or even a big city *barrio*, full of trucks and buses and contemporary people—all living their daily lives in the presence of the Christ child. For this reason, the construction of the crèche every year can be an important parish activity of Christmas preparation. Each year the Belén can be changed to incorporate new elements from the life of the community into the scene. As seasonal art it can also involve members of the community in preparing the *ambiente* of the church for the celebration of Christmas, helping to make people feel more *en su casa,* especially if the church happens to be inherited from another ethnic group.

The *pesebre* is not only elaborate; it is also interactive. It is dedicated by the simplest but most human of all rites: *la acostada del niño*—literally, "putting the (Christ) child to bed." At home, this is usually done at the *Noche Buena* (Christmas Eve) by the youngest child of the family, who gently places the figure of the baby Jesus in the manger as prayers are said by the family. The *acostada* is also sometimes practiced in church in conjunction with the introductory rites of the *Misa del Gallo* (Midnight Mass at Christmas). Two parishioners are honored by being named *padrinos,* or sponsors, and have the privilege of carrying the Christ child in the procession from the door of the church to the crib. Thus, the act of putting a child to bed, an experience shared by all, becomes the life reference for this celebration of the incarnation.

Fittingly, the end of the Christmas season is marked by a rite called *la levantada del niño*—the lifting up of the (Christ) child. In much the same way that the baby Jesus was placed in the *pesebre,* special representatives from the community are chosen to pick up the statue and carry away the other easily portable fixtures of the manger scene so that they can then be stored until next year. Traditionally, this happened the evening of the Feast of the Epiphany, January 6. But with the 1956 reform of the calendar that makes the Baptism of the Lord a feast separate from Epiphany (placing it on the Sunday after Epiphany and using it to mark the end of the Christmas season), it would make better sense

to schedule *la levantada* for this, the last Monday of the Christmas season.

Preparing the Parish

AS always, planners need to find ways to help parishioners celebrate the season fully in the midst of a culture that celebrates Christmas before December 25 and then assumes that it's all over before the sun rises on the 26th. Our liturgical calendar has a Christmas season that extends from Christmas Day until the feast of the Baptism of the Lord, which is January 18 this year. Enabling the Christian community to maintain the spirit of celebration through the festal season is a major challenge, but one worth attempting.

Catholics need to learn from one another ways to keep the festival through Epiphany and on to the Baptism of the Lord. They do not need to be told that they are "doing it all wrong," nor do they need extensive written notes on the "real length" of Christmas. Positive encouragement is much more fruitful in helping people keep these days. A parish can support the keeping of the season, for example, by scheduling its traditional Christmastime parties during Christmas rather than during Advent. Older parishioners can share with youngsters the remembered customs of Epiphany, when people from places such as Puerto Rico would sing their songs of the Three Kings, when a carol-sing or pageant would unfold in the week between Christmas and New Year's Day, or when local churches would offer "First Night" gatherings of their own. This is education through scheduling and peer support.

An even more difficult issue is the question of just what it is we are celebrating. Most Christians recognize that the feast is supposed to be about Christ and not just about excessive consumerism. But that is only the most obvious of the questions about the meaning of Christmas. More subtle but no less important is the problem of the over-sentimentalized and limited view of Christmas that makes it into a dramatic reenactment of the events of the past, a time to pretend that we are at Bethlehem, where the Christ child lies in a manger.

This sentimental view of Christmas is strong both within and outside the church. It is supported by some carols, by numerous Christmas cards, by stories and television shows, by many sermons on Christmas, and even by the crèche sets in churches and in homes. It is comforting and enjoyable to imagine oneself in the peace and joy of that night in Bethlehem, with the star overhead and the angels singing on high. The image of the mother with her newborn son evokes powerful emotional responses in almost every human being. It is not hard to understand why this sentimental, historical time-warp approach has taken a firm hold in the minds of many Christians.

The strength of that approach suggests two basic principles for planners who seek to challenge it. One is that there is much in this perspective that is good, that has value and that should be maintained somehow. The second is that attempts to deepen the community's understanding and celebration of Christmas will not succeed by direct assault on the popular mentality. It will be much more effective if efforts are directed to broadening and deepening people's perspective while encouraging and strengthening what is solid in the popular approach.

Before planners can begin to face these challenges, they must examine their own assumptions about Christmas. Is Christmas a birthday celebration for the baby Jesus, or is it a celebration of the continuing incarnation of God in our world? Is a birthday cake for baby Jesus an appropriate Christmas symbol? Is Christmas really for children, or is it an adult feast? Is Christmas just a time of "comfort and joy," or does it challenge us to mission? Does Christmas stand on its own, or is it intimately related to Easter? Does it seem odd to celebrate the "death and resurrection of the Lord" on Christmas morning? Would it jar us to see a cross over the crèche instead of the usual star? Planners might find it helpful to discuss at length the introduction to the season at the beginning of this section.

Because January 1 falls on a Monday this year, the Solemnity of Mary, the Mother of God, will not be observed as a holy day of obligation in the United States. Planners should find ways to make it clear that the absence of the obligation does not mean that we are ignoring the feast. This might be a good day to plan only one or two strong celebrations rather than a full schedule, focusing parish resources on celebrating the day well. An evening Mass on New Year's Eve has become very popular in many parishes; some have it early in the evening, others near midnight to greet the new year. Another Mass might be celebrated in mid-morning for those engaged in other celebrations the night before. This ancient feast of Mary, the beginning of the new year and the annual day of prayer for peace are too important to be skipped simply because the legal obligation is lifted.

Taking It Home

ALMOST all Christian families have religious symbols and customs with which they mark this feast. Parishes might encourage the use of the crib scene in the home by making worthy but inexpensive sets available for purchase during Advent. Parishes should encourage families to maintain the decor and the celebration throughout the season. Texts from *Catholic Household Blessings and Prayers* could be shared with all, and perhaps the parish can make it available for purchase (it comes in both hardcover and paperback versions). The blessing of a Christmas tree, the blessing of a manger, table prayers for Christmas, the blessing of a new year and the blessing of homes at Epiphany all provide a rich treasury for every parish home. LTP's *Welcome, Yule!* also provides blessings for the home.

Catechists might provide reflections on Christmas carols for home prayer, making clear the deeper meanings of the feast. Suggestions should also be given for observing the traditional Twelve Days of Christmas at home (see the next section). Parishes with African American members might want to link the Kwanzaa celebration to Christmas, offering support and affirmation of this family-oriented observance which begins on December 26. LTP's *Take Me Home* resource has pages for children and families for Christmastime, Epiphany, and the Baptism of the Lord.

■ THE TWELVE DAYS OF CHRISTMAS: The first mention of this period dates to Ephrem Syrus at the end of the fourth century; in 567, the Council of Tours declared these twelve days a festal period. Parishes can offer a variety of things to families and individuals to help keep the festal spirit alive during this time.

There are different ways of counting the days; in England, December 25 is not included, so that January 6 is the Twelfth Day. In Germany, Belgium and Holland, December 25 is included, making Epiphany the Thirteenth Day. Whichever pattern one adopts, the key is to keep the days from Christmas to Epiphany as a special, festive time. Though certain customs are associated with the feast days in this period, there is no standard list of activities for each of the Twelve Days. Parishes might explain various customs and traditions and let parishioners devise their own schedule for using them. What is given here is meant to be suggestive, not prescriptive; local creativity is to be encouraged.

Days that do have special customs include:

- December 26: The Feast of St. Stephen has been marked by various ceremonies involving horses, probably because of confusion with a different St. Stephen, a missionary to Sweden who loved horses. It was also a day for blessing water and salt in the Tyrol. In England this is Boxing Day, a term that refers to the custom of workers carrying clay boxes from house to house to collect donations for Christmas feasting. It is customary in England to give employees gifts on this day.

- December 27: The Feast of St. John has a special blessing of wine (St. John's Wine) in Germany and Austria.

- December 28: The Feast of the Holy Innocents, which is also known as Childermas, was usually a day to avoid work. It was considered an unlucky day to start any project, perhaps because King Herod was unsuccessful in his efforts. It also has often been observed as a Fool's Day (like April 1) because Herod was fooled and Jesus escaped. In some places a choir boy took the role of bishop and was attended by other youths, presiding over the festivities and the prayers that did not require an ordained priest.

- December 29: The Memorial of St. Thomas Becket has been a day of special celebration in England since his martyrdom on this date in 1170. In Poland, this is also a day for a winter sleigh party called *Kulig,* with a fire in the woods, a hearty meal and a dance around the fire.

- December 31: Many New Year's Eve customs are familiar from contemporary New Year's Eve parties. In Ecuador, families make an *Año Viejo,* a figure of the old year, from an old shirt and trousers stuffed with straw. They then display it in the front window, and people walk through the town to see their neighbors' creations. At midnight the figure is set on fire, while the *Año Viejo's* last will and testament is read and children who play his "widow" scream in grief. Then all join in a festive dance for the new year.

- January 1: New Year's Day is often observed with special foods, including newly baked bread, to mark the freshness of the new year.

- January 5: The eve of Epiphany has been a traditional time for wassailing, for drinking toasts of wassail.

- January 6: The Feast of Epiphany is traditionally a day for blessing homes. It is also Twelfth Day and often a day for special parties for Twelfth Night, which is sometimes celebrated the evening before. It is a day for gifts in Italy and among Eastern Christians in commemoration of the gifts of the Magi. In France it is customary to bake a cake with a coin (or a bean or pea) in it; whoever gets that piece is king/queen for the day. In New Orleans, a tiny figure of the Christ Child is baked into the cake; whoever gets it has to plan the Mardi Gras party. In Greek coastal towns, water is blessed: A procession forms from the church to the water, where the priest blesses a cross and throws it in the water. People dive for the cross, and whoever finds it gets gifts and carries the cross through the town all day.

Other customs observed at various times during this period include the Feast of Fools (often January 1, 6 or 13 in the Middle Ages, especially in France but also in Germany and Bohemia), eating mincemeat pie each of the Twelve Days (to bring twelve happy months in the new year), and the staging of plays by mummers and maskers.

The song "The Twelve Days of Christmas" speaks only of gifts for each day. Some families have spread out the Christmas gift-giving to span the Twelve Days, much like the gift-giving at Hanukkah spans eight days. Creative thinking can find small gifts for each day appropriate to the feast: for example, a gift of jewelry (gemstone) or rock candy on St. Stephen's Day (he was stoned to death), wine or something involving birds on St. John's Day (John is represented by the eagle), a silly gift on Holy Innocents (Fool's Day), or a family game on Holy Family Sunday.

It seems that this song actually began with Catholics in England as one of the ways they taught the faith to their children during the period (1558–1829) they were forbidden to practice their religion. Several schemas link doctrines to the twelve days:

- The partridge stands for Christ, who gathers his own under his wings—God's first gift.

- Two turtle doves represent the sacrifice of the Jewish family at the birth of a son, or the two Testaments of the Bible.

- Three French hens symbolize the gifts of the Magi; the persons of the Trinity; or faith, hope and love.

- Four calling birds remind us of the four evangelists.

- Five golden rings suggest the first five books of the Old Testament, the Torah.

- Six geese suggest the six days of the week when humanity labors.

- Seven swans remind us of the seven gifts of the Holy Spirit.

- Eight maids represent the people saved in the Ark or the eight beatitudes.

- Nine ladies represent the fruits of the Spirit (Galatians 5:22) or the nine ranks of angels.

- Ten lords stand for the Ten Commandments.

- Eleven pipers represent the eleven apostles who were faithful.

- Twelve drummers remind us of the articles of the Apostles Creed, the gates of heaven or the tribes of Israel.

Families and individuals might also look for ways to reach out to others during these twelve days. For example, St. John's day is a good day to talk about Christ's continuing presence as God's greatest gift to us. It might also be a good day to look through our possessions for items that can be given to others in light of the new gifts we have already received. Children might pick out a toy today to give to less fortunate children. Holy Innocents day might involve prayer for abused children and for the unborn, along with a reading of the story of the Innocents, Matthew 2:13–18. This might be a good day to make a gift to an agency that deals with children's needs or with problem pregnancies.

The Mass

INTRODUCTORY RITES

THE texts for Christmastime, beginning on page 55, include a greeting and penitential invocations. The greetings from the *Book of Blessings* (#1549, #1577) also are appropriate for these 15 days. Other invocations for the penitential rite are found at form C*iii* in the sacramentary. The rite of sprinkling can be used on the Sundays and feasts, which would resonate with the practice in Eastern churches of blessing baptismal water on Epiphany. A seasonal text for this appears on page 55.

■ GLORY TO GOD: This is the season to highlight this song of the angels. A setting of the Gloria should be chosen for its strength and attractiveness, and enhanced in performance with vocal harmonies, handbells, flute or whatever is available at a particular celebration.

The familiar "Gloria in excelsis Deo" refrain from "Angels we have heard on high" becomes the assembly's refrain in three settings: "A Christmas Gloria" by Paul Gibson (OCP 9551) is the most recent. Written for assembly, cantor, SATB choir, organ and trumpet in C, it makes imaginative use of the carol's melodic material for the unison verses and employs varied harmonics for the SATB refrains. Other worthy choices include "Christmas Gloria" by Daniel Laginya (GIA, G-2971), for cantor and congregation; "Gloria for Christmastime" by Richard Proulx (GIA, G-3085) for two-part mixed voices, cantor and congregation (and flute/oboe obligato); and "Chant Style Gloria" with optional Christmas refrain by Howard Hughes (WLP, 8534). Two settings by Benedictine composers are, like the Laginya, effective for cantor and congregation alone but invite creativity when used with choir and/or instruments: the Gloria by Columba Kelly in *The Collegeville Hymnal* (The Liturgical Press) and the "Glory to God" from Becket Senchur's "Mass of Hope," found in *People's Mass Book* (World Library Publications). "Glory to God" by Peter Jones (OCP) is another fitting, festive Gloria for the day and the season, particularly if brass is available. These settings can be made more festive by the imaginative use of handbells and by dividing the verses between the men and women of the choir.

LITURGY OF THE WORD

■ THE PSALM: Psalm 98 is the seasonal psalm for Christmas and can be used for all fifteen days. A few suggested arrangements:

- David Haas and Marty Haugen, "All the ends of the earth" (GIA, G-2703)

- Rawn Harbor, "Psalm for Christmas" (GIA, *Lead Me, Guide Me*, #504)

- David Isele, "All the ends of the earth," in *Psalms for the Church Year* (GIA, G-2262)

- Richard Proulx and John Hirten, "Psalm for Christmas Day" (GIA, G-3631)

- Michael Joncas, "All the ends of the earth" (GIA, G-3431)

■ GOSPEL ACCLAMATIONS: Eight verses (lectionary #212 and #219) supplement the proper verses listed with the several solemnities and feasts of this season. One of them might be featured in seasonal handouts, allowing everyone to become familiar with a concise expression of the season's meaning. Using a different one each year for this purpose will gradually expose parishioners to more of the richness of the feast.

■ AFTER THE HOMILY: When catechumens are dismissed, an appropriate seasonal dismissal text may be used. See the example on page 55. The profession of faith, highlighted on Christmas by genuflecting at the remembrance of the incarnation, should be said or sung in the most solemn way known by the parish. For general intercessions, see the suggestions in appendix I of the sacramentary (#4 for the Christmas season) and also on page 56 in this book.

LITURGY OF THE EUCHARIST

■ EUCHARISTIC PRAYER: Six prefaces are designated for these days—some specific to a day and four others evoking general themes of the season. Eucharistic Prayer I has special inserts for Christmas Day and its octave, as well as for Epiphany. See page 58 for a translation of the inserts the French use on these same days in Eucharistic Prayers II and III.

If the eucharistic acclamations during Advent have been sung very simply, consider dressing them up for the Christmas season. Festive settings that employ a call and response between the cantor and assembly, such as Howard Hughes's "Mass of the Divine Word" (GIA, G-2415), facilitate participation and are a sign of hospitality to visitors during this season. Christopher Walker's "Glastonbury Eucharistic Acclamations" (OCP, 7165) also fit into this category and offer a refreshing set of lively acclamations. Written for cantor and unison choir, any group of musicians could effectively lead these settings. The descants add beauty and solemnity to the simple assembly response lines. The Vermulst "People's Mass" is widely known;

consider the fine arrangement by Richard Proulx of this Holy, Holy and the "Danish Mass" memorial acclamation and Amen (World Library Publications). The acclamations from Richard Proulx's "Community Mass" (GIA) are also well known and can be dressed up with the optional instrumental parts.

■ COMMUNION RITE: Sample texts for the introduction to the Lord's Prayer, the prayer for peace and the invitation to communion are given on page 59. Christmas is a good time to teach congregations to sing *during* the communion procession, since the music is usually well known. Carols, particularly those with refrains, are appropriate throughout this season. "What child is this" and "We three kings" are good Epiphany choices.

CONCLUDING RITE

■ BLESSING AND DISMISSAL: A seasonal text for sending eucharistic ministers to the homebound and sick may be found on page 59.

Planners might select one blessing text for use throughout the season. See #2 in the sacramentary, page 59 in this book, and #1559 or #1589 in the *Book of Blessings*. Two days suggest other possibilities (or the same seasonal text can be kept): On January 1, see #3 and #10 in the sacramentary, or #20 in the *Book of Blessings*; on January 7, see #4 in the sacramentary.

MUSIC

Most, if not all, members of the assembly have been listening to Christmas music for as long as seven weeks (since Halloween in many department stores and malls). Radio, television and MUZAK in shopping malls, grocery stores and elevators have all been bombarding the consumer with the "sounds of Christmas." While the intent of most of these music media is to put us into the holiday shopping spirit, the parish's sound of Christmas finally brings the texts and music of the carols into dialogue with the incarnation event in the context of the assembly of believers. As Christians, we sing of the coming of Jesus in human history as the Christ child/God-man sent for our redemption. The hymns, carols and service music of this season, while familiar, challenge us anew because we are essentially not the same people who heard and sang them last year. Many members of our assemblies have experienced significant events since their last Christmas celebration. Christmas has a way of crystallizing our past experiences, bringing them once again to the fore. New children or grandchildren, new jobs, significant moves, loss, pain, death, serious illness, a promotion or a job loss all present themselves once again to the human family as we approach the Christmas feast. The music of Christmas often serves as a catalyst. As we gather to sing our "Joy to the world, the Lord is come," our song is in conversation with these many life events and should offer the kind of joy and consolation that come only in and through Christ.

■ FAMILIARITY: Beginning with the Christmas Masses and continuing through the Feasts of the Holy Family and Epiphany, the assembly should be singing the same settings of the Gloria, the responsorial psalm, the acclamations and the Lamb of God to underscore the unity of the season. The service music should express the joy and delight of this season of incarnation and manifestation.

■ HYMNODY: Christmas carols form the basic repertoire of this short season. Musicians should trust that their assemblies know a wide array of carols; after all, they have been listening to a vast number of them for the last several weeks in stores, in shopping malls and at holiday parties. Musicians often find themselves simply duplicating the previous year's selection of carols, which is often a duplicate of the year before that. Perhaps this year could see the use of a wider variety of carols over the season. Any carols not previously sung by the assembly could be introduced gradually and combined with those that are favorites among assembly members. Paying attention to the ethnic makeup of the assembly might yield some new music. Ask members of the assembly for samples of their ethnic Christmas music and consider using some of these selections.

Every parish has its own favorite selections of choral music for Christmas. Simply rehashing every piece sung for the past twenty years might make the preparation time less stressful, but Christmas offers an opportune time to expand the repertoire with more challenging vocal selections. Choirs generally tend to dedicate themselves more to their art during the intense preparation periods before Christmas and Easter and to work harder at perfecting their choral sound. Early September is not too

soon to begin working on a few new Christmas pieces. It may be time to give some of the old favorites a rest for a while!

Because the size and musical capabilities of choirs vary so greatly, general suggestions are difficult to make. But the following recommendations might be worth considering. "Gaudete," a Renaissance piece published by GIA (G-3056) offers a bright, simple option. (This arrangement can be enhanced with percussion instruments and works well as a processional.) Consider challenging the choir with Handel's "Hallelujah Amen!" from *Judas Maccabeus* or "Gloria in excelsis" from Antonio Vivaldi's *Gloria*. Both take some time and effort, but choirs will benefit from the works of such masters. Oxford University Press's *Carols for Choirs* series offers some real gems and imaginative arrangements. Try "Ding-dong merrily on high" or "Infant holy, infant lowly" from Book One. The carol arrangements by David Willcocks in this collection are among the finest. Instrumental parts are also available from the publisher. Katherine Crozier's arrangement of "Of the Father's love begotten" (GIA, G-2837) is a worthy setting of this traditional chant, with effective choral and handbell parts. If you are looking for a "different" and refreshing arrangement of "O holy night" that does not rely on a soloist, try Craig Courtney's arrangement of this popular Christmas hymn (Beckenhorst Press, BP-1332). Other recommendations include: John Rutter's "Candlelight Carol" (Hinshaw), David Hurd's "A stable lamp is lighted" (GIA, G-2754); "A maiden most gentle," a French carol arranged by Andrew Carter (Oxford); Anthony Prower's "Sing lullaby" (Concordia); and Gerald Near's setting of "What is this lovely fragrance?" (Areole/Paraclete Press). A change of pace and style would be the West Indian Carol, "The Virgin Mary had a baby boy," arranged by John Leavitt (Augsburg). This last composition could include rhythm instruments and other percussion.

Other Ritual Prayer and Sacraments

LITURGY OF THE HOURS

MORNING and Evening Prayer are appropriate settings for the blessing of the parish Christmas tree or manger on Christmas itself. If a small group gathers for these celebrations over the following days, they might gather near one of these symbols of the season.

Appendix I of the *Liturgy of the Hours* includes material for extended vigils on the eves of Christmas Day, Holy Family, January 1, Epiphany and the Baptism of the Lord. See the notes on page 48 for a Christmas Eve vigil. As noted under Advent (page 16), the service of lessons and carols is actually a vigil service. Additional texts for such a service in Christmastime are available in the Episcopal *Book of Occasional Services* on page 36.

COMMUNAL ANOINTING OF THE SICK

The ritual Mass for the anointing of the sick is not permitted on Christmas Day, on January 1 or on Epiphany. Throughout the Christmas season, however, celebrations with the sick, both in small groups and in the parish assembly, can draw on the season's messianic and manifestation images. The three scripture passages from Isaiah in the rite are appropriate, as they were in Advent. The reading from 1 John fits with the others from this letter throughout the season. The passage about Jesus and John the Baptist (Luke 7:18–23) brings the sick into the image-world of Christmas—their health and the providence of God are as central to the season as crèches are, for the sick and the suffering are living icons of the epiphany of God. See page 64 for a seasonal introduction and a prayer after anointing.

FUNERALS

Funeral Masses are not permitted on Christmas Day, on January 1 or on Epiphany. When mourners gather with the parish for Christmastime funerals, the rite's readings from Isaiah and 1 John are appropriate. The readings of the day, often vividly presenting the paschal mystery, also can be used. "Hark the herald angels sing" is a fitting carol for inclusion in the funeral liturgy, as is "Good Christian friends." Pretending it is not Christmastime at a funeral is impossible in a church full of poinsettias—homilists must face this and speak of the paschal mystery revealed in the images of Christmastime.

MARRIAGES

The ritual Mass for marriage cannot be used on Christmas Day, on January 1 or on Epiphany. As noted in #11 of the introduction to the marriage rite, one of the proper readings from the rite of marriage can be integrated into the day's texts on Holy Family and the Baptism of the Lord. On these same two days, nuptial Masses that are not parish Masses can use the full set of marriage texts. This notation presumes that at least some marriages are celebrated at parish Masses!

Within the marriage lectionary, the Song of Songs, 1 John (2 options) and the wedding feast at Cana (John 2:1–11) are traditional and beautiful both for weddings and for this time of year. The Cana event is central to the celebration of Epiphany. This "first miracle" is one of the great manifestation stories. It expresses well the messianic fullness entered into at Christmas—and at weddings.

ORDERS OF BLESSING

The *Book of Blessings* has helped many communities rediscover the joy of praising God while gathered around the traditional symbols of this season.

■ BLESSING OF A CHRISTMAS MANGER: The *Book of Blessings* (chapter 48) has an order for gathering by the manger, listening to the word of God, singing carols and blessing the manger. It is described in this *Sourcebook's* entry for Christmas Day.

■ BLESSING OF A CHRISTMAS TREE: The same *Book of Blessings* (chapter 49) provides an outline and texts for a parish assembly to bless and light a Christmas tree. This might also be an opportunity for parish members to gather in prayer with those who are associated with the parish but who do not usually share in its liturgical life (day-care workers and their families, or self-help programs that rent space, for example). If the parish has a large outdoor tree lit for the season, gather around it for this blessing.

The Worship Environment

GREAT care should be given to the proper times for decorating (the Fourth Sunday of Advent should not look like Christmas) and taking down (right after January 18). Because the Fourth Sunday falls on December 24 this year, Christmas decorating will be more of a challenge than usual, but careful planning and preparation should enable it to happen quickly that afternoon. Enlisting many parish volunteers can be a fitting way to conclude Advent.

■ MANGER: The manger should not be set up in front of or under the altar. As the *Book of Blessings* envisions it, the manger may be set up outdoors. "If the manger is set up in the church, it must not be placed in the presbyterium [sanctuary]. A place should be chosen that is suitable for prayer and devotion and is easily accessible by the faithful" (#1544).

Planners should look into the traditions of all cultures represented in the parish and allow the display to express the real faith of a given place, not the "ideal" of some catalog. Christ is to be born now in us, not in the stable again.

■ CHRISTMAS TREES, GREENS AND FLOWERS: These items must never obscure the altar, the ambo, the presider's chair or the font. No matter how beautiful a garland of greens or a pyramid of poinsettias may be, it must not obscure the focal points in our worship.

■ CIVIL RESPONSIBILITY: The local fire marshal or civic regulations may have to be consulted. What space is needed for the safe evacuation of the assembly? Are cut trees and real greens allowed? How do we place lit candles in relationship to these and to straw? Even if we were not caught up in an overly litigious society, we would not want our liturgy to bring with it the potential for danger.

If we do not like the answers we receive from the fire marshal and if we are sure that other answers respect both the liturgy and public safety, then it is time for representatives of the parish or the diocesan liturgical commission to see the boards or officials responsible.

■ OUTDOORS: What are you putting outdoors to announce the good news to all your neighbors? A weatherproof banner? Lights on a large evergreen tree? A manger? Garlands over the entries? Luminarias along the parish walkways, lit at night on Christmas and on Epiphany? Words of greeting on the parish sign? Lights on the steeple or tower? One huge wreath on the tower or around a rose window?

December

#13–16 (LMC, #13)
white

M O N 25 **Christmas Day**
SOLEMNITY

GENERAL NOTES FOR ALL MASSES OF CHRISTMAS

■ HOSPITALITY: This is a day of opportunity for outreach to infrequent churchgoers as well as a day to enjoy those who consistently form the assembly for worship. Hospitality should be obvious to both groups.

Begin worship with a word of welcome to all, and especially to visitors, college students home for the holidays and those who have been away for a while, with a warm invitation to join the community often. (See page 55 for an example.)

Hospitality for the whole assembly is a challenge on such a busy day. Perhaps simple refreshments after Mass are possible. If refreshments are offered, be sure to offer some variety in beverages; having only coffee eliminates those who have other tastes. Or perhaps a brass ensemble playing outside before and after Mass would be a way to set a festive mood.

■ MUSIC: Our assemblies on this day often include many visitors, both relatives in town for the holidays and those who live nearby but come to worship only on special feasts. Familiar Christmas carols will be known even by visitors, but service music may not. A special Christmas worship bulletin would be very helpful; we cannot assume that visitors will know where to find the service music or a particular acclamation.

Our longing and lament in Advent find fulfillment in this feast of new birth. Our songs and the way we sing them should be bright, familiar, fresh and lively. On this feast, worship deserves the very best that the music ministers can produce (and here we include the presider and the assembly). The goal, as always, is full participation by the whole assembly; be sure to choose music that everyone can participate in comfortably. That in itself will almost assure success, enjoyment and inspiration.

When you have a tentative plan for the Christmas music, it is helpful to review all the texts together, making sure that the historical representation of Christmas is not the overwhelming focus of what we will sing at this celebration.

■ CHANTING THE GOSPEL: Chanting the gospel can add to the festivity if it is sung well and with clarity. Two sources are "Chants for the Readings" by Joseph T. Kush (GIA, G-2114) and Columba Kelly's setting in "Liturgical Music for the Priest and Deacon," published at St. Meinrad's Archabbey.

■ THE PROFESSION OF FAITH: A genuflection is made today during the profession of faith at the line that begins, "by the power of the Holy Spirit." Introduce the creed in a way that cues the community to this change, then slow the recitation (or singing) to allow a reverent genuflection.

■ EUCHARISTIC PRAYER: The sacramentary has a proper insert for Eucharistic Prayer I. See page 58 for samples used elsewhere in prayers II and III.

■ ANNOUNCEMENTS: Major celebrations like Christmas often prompt words of gratitude to all who made the arrangements. These words should be chosen carefully: Who is thanking whom? Certainly the impression should never be created that the laity helped the pastor conduct his parish. Pastoral leaders should voice such thanks in the name of the entire assembly. The assembly itself might also be acknowledged, especially if participation has been exemplary.

SCHEDULING

There appears to be a growing trend across the country to celebrate Christmas at church on Christmas Eve rather than on Christmas morning. This trend has been growing since evening Masses were permitted and anticipated Masses for Sundays and holy days became common. It has perhaps been fostered by the widespread practice of focusing an early Christmas Eve Mass on children, a decision popular with many families. In some communities, 90 percent of the worshipers come to Mass on the Eve. The difficulties are created in two directions: overcrowding at Christmas Eve Masses and half-empty churches on Christmas morning. History may offer us some perspective on the situation.

■ HISTORY OF THE MASSES ON CHRISTMAS: As early as the sixth century, multiple Masses existed on Christmas in the city of Rome (cf. Jounel in Martimort, *The Liturgy and Time*). Beginning about AD 330, a Christmas Day Mass was celebrated at St. Peter's. Around 500, a replica of Bethlehem's manger was built under the basilica of St. Mary Major. Residents as well as visiting pilgrims asked for a liturgy during the night like the one in Bethlehem, which was celebrated at the time it was said that Jesus was born. Thus Christians have long had a strong desire to celebrate this mystery during the night.

The Mass at Dawn originated at the fourth-century church of St. Anastasia. This church had been founded in the home of a Roman woman named Anastasia, and the Romans, wishing to honor both the person who founded the church as well as the custom of naming a church after a saint, looked for a saint named Anastasia. They discovered the stories of this fourth-century martyr who spent her life strengthening the Christians at Aquileia. They had no difficulty saying that she was born in Rome, 400 miles from Aquileia. Worshipers at that church (especially the Byzantine authorities who lived nearby) remembered their patron saint on December 25. Out of respect for the Byzantine authorities, the popes began stopping there for a Mass commemorating Anastasia before continuing to the Vatican for the Christmas Day Mass. A reference to her remained in the Dawn Mass of Christmas until just a few decades ago.

For centuries, Christmas Eve day had a penitential Mass, and the first eucharist of the feast was celebrated at Midnight. The most recent reforms provide two Masses—one for the last Advent morning on December 24 and the other for the first hours of the feast itself. Describing this festive Mass, the Vatican commentary on the Roman Calendar notes:

> The medieval notion of a vigil as a day of penance before a feast has been completely abolished. With the exception of the Easter Vigil which is celebrated sometime during the

night, the term "Mass of the Vigil" now refers to the Mass which can be celebrated in a festive way in the evening, before or after Evening Prayer I of certain solemnities. (page 23)

The current liturgical title of the first Mass of Christmas in Latin is "Night," not "Midnight." The liturgical day of Christmas begins at Vespers, as do all our principal festivals. Certainly some people come for Mass on Christmas Eve for reasons of convenience, but many may be responding to the desire to celebrate the birth of the Light of the World during the darkness of night. This resonates with all the solstice connections of this feast as well as with the perception that Christ was born during the night.

In recent centuries, this desire has led to packed midnight Masses, but this is not usually feasible for families with small children. Many senior citizens also find an earlier time more suitable. Those who prefer to celebrate after dark, whether early in the evening or toward midnight, may well be holding to a tradition as ancient as the feast itself.

The challenge for the parish staff is to arrange the schedule in a way that allows full celebration both on the Eve and on Christmas itself. This may mean scheduling only one or two Masses on Christmas morning with several planned for the Eve. Even if the eucharist is celebrated by most on the Eve, domestic prayer and parish gatherings for the liturgy of the hours can help parishioners keep the whole feast holy. Planners can set up Evening Prayer I, the Office of Readings, Morning Prayer, Evening Prayer II as well as the various celebrations of the eucharist. Announcements of these liturgies may include suggestions on how they may be part of keeping the

feast. Resources should be provided to households to assist them in shaping domestic prayer for the feast. (See "Taking It Home" at the end of today's section.)

EVENING PRAYER I

Large parishes or parishes that have implemented the liturgy of the hours might consider at least a simple celebration of Evening Prayer on the Eve and/or on the feast itself. If the regular ministers are overwhelmed by preparing for the Masses, then the leadership of this liturgy might be performed by a community of religious living in the parish or by a few households who will take on this responsibility. On the eve, this celebration could include the blessing and lighting of the parish's Christmas tree.

MASS IN THE EARLY EVENING

All the available texts from the lectionary and the sacramentary should be evaluated for appropriateness to this evening. All the readings for the Vigil Mass presume that the assembly is awaiting Christmas, implying that the assembly will reconvene later at night or in the morning. Yet for many this will be the only liturgical event of the festival, so a strong pastoral case can be made for proclaiming the story as found in Luke 2. If there are many children in the assembly, texts should be selected with the norms of the *Directory for Masses with Children* in mind; its principles for children often provide a beautiful and fully liturgical celebration for all ages in the assembly. Readings from the *Lectionary for Masses with Children,* however, may only be used for a liturgy of the word with children apart from the main assembly.

■ BLESSING THE MANGER: Blessing of the parish's manger may fit well into this Mass. Consider having the assembly or perhaps the children process there with joyful song.

VIGIL/OFFICE OF READINGS

This is not the Vigil Mass but the Office of Readings extended into a vigil service. Based on the norms from the *Liturgy of the Hours* (#71, #73 and the Christmas Office of Readings) and recent specifications (*Ceremonial of Bishops*, #238), this vigil may take one of these forms before the late-night Mass.

■ TRADITIONAL ROMAN OPTION: For communities familiar with the liturgy of the hours, and for those who want to use the customary Roman form, this option might be considered. Unless specified, everything that follows is from the Office of Readings on Christmas:

▪ Opening procession

▪ Greeting and opening dialogue (from the ordinary)

▪ Hymn

▪ Psalmody, sung

▪ Verse

▪ Reading: Isaiah 11:1–10

▪ Responsory, sung

▪ Sermon of St. Leo the Great

▪ Responsory, sung

▪ Antiphon for Christmas, sung (from appendix I)

▪ One, two or three canticles, sung (from appendix I)

▪ The antiphon is repeated.

▪ Gospel: Matthew 1:1–25 or 1:18–25 (from the Vigil Mass in the lectionary), proclaimed by the deacon or assisting presbyter, with candles and incense

▪ Gloria, sung by all in its Christmastime setting

▪ Opening prayer (sacramentary)

▪ The liturgy of the word continues as usual.

■ OPTION WITH SERVICE OF LIGHT AND CAROLS: For other parishes, especially those that have been holding a concert before the late-night Mass, this option may be considered. The pattern here is similar to the Easter Vigil.

▪ Entrance procession: During it, the invitatory from the *Liturgy of the Hours* may be sung ("Christ is born for us; come let us adore him"). The church is in darkness, and those in the procession carry lit candles. Use the large candles from the Advent wreath to lead the procession if these candles can be detached. The procession pauses a few times so that the ministers can pass their light to members of the assembly near them. When the procession arrives at the altar, there and throughout the space candles are lit, including perhaps pew candles or the consecration candles on the walls.

▪ Greeting: A sung dialogue on light (e.g., "Light and peace in Jesus Christ our Lord." "Thanks be to God.") may be found in many liturgical resource books (for example, *Worship*).

▪ Hymn with references to light such as "O little town of Bethlehem" or "O come, divine Messiah."

▪ Thanksgiving for the light is sung by cantor, deacon or priest. As the community sings its Amen, a few lights may be turned on and the assembly may extinguish its candles.

▪ Introduction or welcome (page 55)

▪ Readings and carols: Several may be chosen from this list of traditional readings.

  • Reading I: Genesis 15:1–12, 17–18 (lectionary #373)

  • Psalm or carol

  • Prayer (prayers for each of these five readings are on page 64)

  • Reading II: 1 Samuel 1:9–20 (lectionary #306)

  • Psalm or carol

  • Prayer

  • Reading III: Isaiah 7:1–9 (lectionary #390) or 7:10–14 (lectionary #10)

  • Psalm or carol

  • Prayer

  • Reading IV: Judges 13:2–7, 24–25 (lectionary #196)

  • Psalm or carol

  • Prayer

  • Reading V: Christmas homily by St. Leo the Great (Office of Readings)

  • The Proclamation of the Birth of Christ, sung by the cantor (pages 60–61). As the proclamation concludes, the rest of the lights in the space may be turned on.

  • Gloria, sung by all in its Christmastime setting

  • Opening prayer

  • The liturgy of the word continues as usual.

MASS IN THE NIGHT

This Mass might be preceded by a vigil rather than by musical selections from the choir. Beginning with music by the choir can diminish the assembly's participation in the Mass because it prepares them to be spectators. If the choir is to do more than provide glorious music for the Mass itself, then at least include carols for all before Mass so that everyone knows they are expected to take part.

■ THE PROCLAMATION OF THE BIRTH OF CHRIST: If one of the forms of vigil has not preceded the Mass, this chant (pages 60–61) could be used just before the processional hymn—a prayerful way to begin.

MASS AT DAWN

Since this will probably be the only Mass of the feast for many in the assembly, the gospel from Midnight Mass might be read before the verses assigned to the Dawn Mass. Many times this early Mass is attended by older people or those whose children are grown and have moved away and whose grandchildren are far away. Their needs and hopes might make this morning's homily quite different from last evening's. The inaccurate word "birthday" appears in the prayer after communion: "birth" is the more precise translation.

If a number of people who live alone participate in this early morning Mass, a breakfast gathering immediately after Mass may be welcome.

MORNING PRAYER

This liturgical prayer might be welcomed by those who make the parish gathering the high point of their Christmas. The schedule could be Mass, then breakfast and Morning Prayer; or Morning Prayer could precede breakfast and Mass, with appropriate dispensation from the full one-hour fast. Those who celebrated the eucharist in the evening might also appreciate this liturgy to begin the festival day. A starting time of 9:00 AM might work well for families with small children who have been up since dawn!

MASS DURING THE DAY

"Humankind" and "us" are more inclusive than "man" and "him" in the first opening prayer. Although rubrics permit the interchangeable use of the four sets of Christmas readings, the proclamation of the prologue to John's gospel is a venerable tradition at this Mass during the Day. This reading is an important reminder that the feast is much broader than the manger scene; it links

us again to the light-darkness theme of the season.

MIDDAY PRAYER AND CHRISTMAS DINNER

Parishes might consider sponsoring a festive dinner on holidays like this. The guests could include those who would otherwise eat alone, those who wish to share with a wider community, and the homeless of the area. Let the meal include some time for singing carols as well as at least a brief liturgical prayer. For this liturgy, there are at least three options:

- If the parish nativity scene was not blessed earlier, the full form of this rite (*Book of Blessings*, #1547–1561), with carols added, can be led by a deacon or by a lay minister, either male or female.

- A full rite for table prayer might seem too daunting in some households, but at this gathering it can be expanded with carols and a Christmas reading or two (*Book of Blessings*, #1038–1045, 1048).

- Christmas Midday Prayer from the *Liturgy of the Hours* can be used with familiar musical settings of the assigned psalms or adapted with carols and a fuller passage from the New Testament. This, too, may be led by a deacon or lay minister.

CHRISTMAS DAY AFTERNOON

If possible, leave the church open throughout the day and announce it at all Masses with an invitation to return. Some people may want to come with their guests to show off their parish home and spend a few moments in prayer at the manger.

EVENING PRAYER II

Many people seem to welcome an opportunity to go out this evening. Long lines of cars can often be seen on those streets with large light displays, and movies and sports events draw large crowds. The parish can offer an opportunity for communal prayer through the celebration of Evening Prayer on Christmas Day. The canticle from Colossians and the reading from 1 John help put the assembly in touch with the many levels of meaning of Christmas — in ways far more poetic than most sermons.

TAKING IT HOME

Most people will participate in only one public liturgy at church. Pastoral leaders should share resources for domestic prayer — ideas for keeping the whole day sacred. Parishioners who come to church only once might sense a need for some domestic prayer at other times during the feast. If the household goes to church for Mass early on the Eve, the manger or the tree can be blessed later that night. The prayers at table on the day itself should be more extensive than usual. In *Catholic Household Blessings and Prayers*, see the table prayer (page 70), the blessing of a Christmas tree (page 113), and the blessing of a manger scene (page 117).

Every parish should find ways to include the homebound. Providing transportation and assistance at church may enable some to join the parish assembly. Those who cannot come should be visited with communion, with gifts and with Christmas prayers. Even if the parish does not yet have a regular network of visitors and eucharistic ministers, plenty of volunteers should come forward for this day (if asked with plenty of notice).

TUE 26 #696 (LMC, #437 and 456–459) red
Stephen, first martyr
FEAST

Some people are surprised by the celebration of the feasts of Stephen, John and the Holy Innocents right after Christmas. They seem to intrude on the feeling of "comfort and joy" that the carols lead us to expect at this season. Historically, these feasts were celebrated on these dates even before Christmas appeared on the 25th, and so they originally had no connection to Christmas. Nevertheless, we now experience them as part of the Christmas cycle, so it is important to recognize the connections between the birth of Christ and these saints' days.

Stephen is known as the protomartyr, the first follower of Jesus to die for his faith. Stephen is said to have died with a prayer of forgiveness for his killers on his lips, in clear imitation of his master.

Celebrating this feast the day after Christmas reminds us of the implications of Christ's birth. Stephen was killed because he was preaching the Good News of Jesus. We are also called to spread the good news to others, and we must be willing to imitate the Lord even to the point of death if that is necessary.

WED 27 #697 (LMC, #438 and 452–454) white
John, apostle, evangelist
FEAST

Like John's gospel on Christmas Day, this apostle's feast calls us to a different view of Christmas. John reminds us that Christmas is much more than the babe in the manger: It is the wedding of the human and the divine forever. Today's feast offers us an opportunity to reflect on the implications of the incarnation and the enduring joy of "God with us," no longer as the babe in the manger but as the risen one who lives and reigns forever.

The First Letter of John provides a succinct expression of both the fact and the meaning of the incarnation. The gospel reading of the resurrection also reminds us that Christmas does not stand on its own but is the prelude to the greater feast of Easter, the beginning of the redemption Christ won for us by his death and resurrection.

The hymn "By all your saints still striving" (*Worship*, #706) includes a verse for this saint.

THU 28 #698 (LMC, #439 and 456–459) red
The Holy Innocents, martyrs
FEAST

This feast seems more naturally related to Christmas because it commemorates those infants who died when Herod tried to destroy the newborn king. Yet it, too, reminds us that Christmas is not all "Silent night" and "Joy to the world." The coming of Jesus into the world was a sign of contradiction. Though he came to bring us fullness of joy, he also brought conflict and suffering.

While the gospel recounts the story of the slaughter, the first reading from John speaks of light and darkness and calls us to admit our own sinfulness and trust in the one who died for our sins.

FRI 29 #203 white
Fifth Day in the Octave of Christmas

Thomas Becket, bishop, martyr, optional commemoration / white. ▪ Because this memorial falls during the Octave of Christmas, the texts are from the season, except for the optional use of the collect of the saint for the opening prayer or with the intercessions.

Becket was a twelfth-century chancellor of England who became the bishop of Canterbury and had to decide whom he would serve when the king opposed the church. After many struggles, including six years of exile in France, Becket was murdered in his cathedral by agents of the king. He witnesses again, therefore, to the conflict the gospel often involves, which dovetails with the gospel account of Simeon's prediction that the child will be a "sign that will be opposed." His imitation of Christ also fulfills 1 John's call to conduct oneself just as Jesus did. This day, however, is primarily a day of celebration within the octave, so attention to Becket should not overshadow the season.

SAT 30 #204 white
Sixth Day in the Octave of Christmas

Today's gospel continues the account of the presentation of the child in the Temple, shifting from the meeting with Simeon to the encounter with the prophetess Anna. Besides reminding us of the role women have played in salvation history from the beginning, Anna can challenge us to imitate her role as an evangelizer: She "talked about the child to all who looked forward to the deliverance of Jerusalem." The reading from the First Letter of John promises that those who do the will of God will live forever. It is rather difficult to avoid the masculine focus of this passage; this might prompt some to substitute the passage assigned to December 31, which will otherwise be omitted this year.

⊛**31** #17   white
The Holy Family
FEAST

The main thing to remember about this feast is that it is part of Christmas. It is placed here because it celebrates the incarnation, making it clear that Jesus was born into the human condition in all its fullness. This is a day to celebrate his identity with us rather than focusing narrowly on family life. A blessing of families or renewal of vows by all married couples is not appropriate today. Such rituals should be planned in Ordinary Time, perhaps on Trinity Sunday or the Twenty-third Sunday in Ordinary Time, with Paul's words on love fulfilling the law and the gospel's promise that Christ is present when two or three gather in his name, or on the Twenty-eighth Sunday with its gospel of the wedding feast as an image of salvation.

Traditional hymns on this day would include "Once in royal David's city," "Sing of Mary, pure and lowly," "Our Father, by whose name," and "What child is this?"

"Human family" and "people" would be more inclusive than "family of man" and "men" in the alternative opening prayer.

Note that the American bishops approved a shorter version of today's second reading, using just verses 12 to 17; the decision was confirmed by Rome in June 1992.

In some parishes people bring devotional objects to church today to be blessed. After the recessional, those who bring such Christmas gifts may gather by the manger and a priest or deacon can use chapter 44 of the *Book of Blessings* (the shorter form is for use after Mass). If this is not a local custom, it might be a good one to start. We need to learn that blessings are to be celebrated as communal prayer, and parishes should offer periodic opportunities for such gatherings.

January

M
O   #18 (LMC, #15)   white
N   **Octave of Christmas/**
    Mary, Mother of God
    SOLEMNITY

This solemnity is not a day of obligation this year because it falls on Monday. Nevertheless, it is a day of significance for both the church and the culture. The dispensation from obligation is not intended to suggest that the feast be ignored. Rather, it offers us an opportunity to recover the original meaning of holy days as days of true celebration.

■ NEW YEAR'S EVE: This is a night that leads some people instinctively to prayer. Parishes might consider an evening vigil service to welcome in the new year or an evening Mass for the feast, either early before the parties begin or perhaps timed just before or at midnight to welcome the new year. Resources for a vigil service include the following: *The Book of Occasional Services* offers "A Service for New Year's Eve." The *Liturgy of the Hours,* in appendix I, gives canticles and a gospel to form a full vigil. *Catholic Household Blessings and Prayers* (page 121) has a brief service for blessing the new year.

■ MASS ON THE DAY: Perhaps only one Mass should be scheduled today, in late morning, so that a full assembly might be possible. This date combines a multitude of themes and images; it is the Octave Day of Christmas, the feast of Mary's maternity, the day of Jesus' circumcision, the name day of Jesus, the beginning of the civil year and the world day of prayer for peace! No parish can properly celebrate all those themes in any given year, though several can be integrated with careful planning.

With the permission of the bishop of the diocese, the votive Mass for Justice and Peace may be used on this day. However, unless there are significant current world developments that call for placing special emphasis on prayer for peace, it seems best to celebrate the Marian feast while including prayer for peace as a secondary theme. This is not hard to do: Mary is the Queen of Peace, the newborn child is the Prince of Peace, and the first reading for the day is the Aaronic blessing that asks God to "look upon you kindly and give you peace."

The celebration of Mary as the Mother of God is a natural theme of the Christmas season, and this is the oldest Marian feast. It should be celebrated as a Christmas feast, however, with music and prayers that suggest the connection. Several Christmas carols highlight mother and child ("Silent night," "What child is this," "O little town of Bethlehem," "Of the Father's love begotten," and "Lo, how a rose e'er blooming"), and the alternate opening prayer weaves together various aspects of the feast. The intercessions should include peace and justice throughout the world; their collect prayer could be taken from the "Masses and Prayers for Various Needs and Occasions, 24, Beginning of the Civil Year." The special blessing for the Beginning of the New Year seems appropriate; repeating the Aaronic blessing might also be fitting, but this is the only day to use the New Year blessing, and people do expect some attention to the New Year. A hymn that links Christmas and peace (e.g. "Hark! The herald angels sing") would be an appropriate concluding song.

#206   white
T 2 Basil the Great and Gregory Nazianzen, bishops, doctors U of the church
E
MEMORIAL

The gospel passages for this week, drawn mostly from the first chapter of the Gospel of John, recount the baptism of Jesus and the beginnings of his public ministry. Thus they continue the Christmas celebration, reminding us that we are celebrating God's presence among us, not just the babe at Bethlehem. Today's gospel recalls the testimony of John the Baptizer about Jesus. The first reading speaks of the promise of eternal life for those who remain faithful to Jesus, the Anointed One.

Basil and Gregory, who lived in the fourth century in what is now Turkey, became friends in school in Caesarea. Basil was bishop of Caesarea, a reformer of the liturgy and the father of Eastern monasticism, influencing Benedict, Cassian and others in both East and West. Gregory was bishop at Nazianzen and archbishop at Constantinople, but he preferred monastic solitude. These two friends, together with Basil's younger brother, Gregory of Nyssa, formed an effective trio of teachers of the faith in a time of great theological development. While the readings and prayers should be from the Christmas season, the saints' prayer can be used as the opening prayer or as the collect for the intercessions.

#207   white
W 3 Christmas Weekday
E
D

In today's gospel, John continues giving witness to Jesus, making it clear that Jesus is greater than John; he is the "Lamb of God who takes away the sins of the world." The first reading speaks of our position as children of God and calls us to live up to that status by avoiding sin.

#208   white
T 4 Elizabeth Ann Seton, married woman, religious founder, educator
H
U
MEMORIAL

Elizabeth was the first native-born American to be canonized. A widow and the mother of ten children, she founded the first U. S. religious community, the first Catholic parish school and the first Catholic orphanage in the former British colonies. Elizabeth died on this date in 1821 and was canonized in 1976. Thousands of women religious trace their history to Elizabeth.

The readings listed in the sacramentary are to be used only in those communities where her memorial is celebrated as a solemnity (for example, in a parish that carries her title). Otherwise, use the proper presidential prayers for her day and Christmastime texts at all other points. Today's gospel recounts how two of John's disciples come to follow Jesus and how Andrew brings Peter to discipleship. The first reading continues yesterday's point that those who belong to God cannot sin.

■ SCHOOL LITURGY: This might be the best day for celebrating the Christmas season with school students. (See the resources starting on page 74 in the *Leader's Manual of the Hymnal for Catholic Students*). Be sure the school's Christmas decorations are still up when the children return. A school celebration during Christmastime is far better than a "Christmas" Mass the day before school vacation begins, when the liturgy should be drawing us into the O Antiphons and the growing expectation of the feast.

#209   white
F 5 John Neumann, bishop, religious, missionary, educator
R
I
MEMORIAL

Known for his holiness, his learning, his writing and his preaching, John, an immigrant from Bohemia, became bishop of Philadelphia in 1852 and died on this date in 1860. In 1977, he became the first American bishop to be canonized.

Mass prayers are proper to the memorial, but once again the readings listed in the sacramentary are only for those parishes named after him or for those in the archdiocese of Philadelphia. Otherwise, use the seasonal readings. Today's gospel recounts the call of Philip and Nathaniel. The first reading calls us to love one another and to show that love in concrete actions. This provides a good opportunity to reflect on our obligation to give to others the love we have received through Christ's coming into the world.

SAT 6 #210 white
Christmas Weekday

Blessed André Bessette, religious, optional memorial/white. ▪ The dioceses of the United States share this observance with Canada. Born near Montreal in 1845, André worked as a young adult in the French-Canadian communities of Rhode Island and Connecticut. On returning to the province of Quebec, he became a Holy Cross brother in 1870 and became famous as the "man of prayer on the mountain." He inspired many with a love of St. Joseph and became renowned for his healings and his special commitment to the poor and afflicted. He instigated the building of a magnificent shrine to Joseph in Montreal. He died on this date in 1937 and was beatified in 1982. An opening prayer is provided in the sacramentary; the other orations can be from the day or from the Common of Holy Men and Women.

The gospel for the day is Mark's account of Jesus' baptism by John. The first reading reminds us of the other "baptism" Jesus experienced, his death and resurrection ("not in water only, but in water and in blood").

7 #20 (LMC, #16) white
The Epiphany of the Lord
SOLEMNITY

IMAGES OF THE DAY

This great feast celebrates the appearance of the divine in human history. This manifestation took place in a variety of events, and this day has commemorated many of them. Over the centuries, three of these events have been the focus of the liturgy: the visit of the Magi, the baptism of the Lord and the wedding feast at Cana (see the antiphons for the gospel canticles at Morning and Evening Prayer). These themes may have come to the fore because various local churches began the year's cycle of gospel readings on this feast. Each of the three (in the order listed above) forms the early part of the gospel of Matthew, John and Mark.

Differences in calculating dates of Jewish feasts between East and West led to the East celebrating January 6 as the date of Christ's birth. In both East and West, the winter solstice and the returning sun filled both feasts of the incarnation with solar symbolism. In the East, there were also pagan beliefs that on this day the rivers run red with wine. Thus, the manifestation stories of the baptism of the Lord making the Jordan sacred and the turning of water into wine at Cana picked up ancient themes and gave new meaning to them.

Even these three ancient mysteries—the Magi, Cana and the baptism of Jesus—do not come close to exhausting the ways in which God's presence in Jesus was revealed. Our celebration of the feast might also focus on ways that the Incarnation continues to reveal God to the world today.

LITURGY OF THE DAY

Ritual Masses are forbidden for marriages, funerals and communal anointings. The Christmastime environment remains. The *Ceremonial of Bishops,* #240, calls for "a suitable and increased display of lights"—a reminder that this is a season of light.

The music of Epiphany offers the opportunity to sing about the Magi, the gifts that they carried, the star and the long journey. Consult the topical or liturgical index in your hymnal for the appropriate hymns and sing them well. There are few things worse than a bogged-down rendition of "We three kings"! A fine choral selection for this day is the Mendelssohn "There shall a star from Jacob come forth" (Addington Press, Hinshaw Music).

MASS

▪ INTRODUCTORY RITES: Children could be invited to take part in the entrance procession, perhaps carrying silver stars on sticks and wearing halos of garland in their hair. At every Mass with children present, they need to be drawn into the celebration in a variety of ways. Presiders and planners need to think in terms of the entire assembly.

The official entrance antiphon summarizes much of the significance of the feast. Thought it is generally replaced by an entrance hymn, these words might be used in the presider's comments after the greeting. Both today and tomorrow, the rite of blessing and sprinkling with water is appropriate (See the text on page 55). In the alternative opening prayer, "people" would be more inclusive than "men."

■ LITURGY OF THE WORD: *The Ceremonial of Bishops* (#240) assumes a tradition long advocated in this *Sourcebook:*

> After the singing of the gospel reading, depending on local custom, one of the deacons . . . or someone else, vested in cope, will go to the lectern (ambo) and there announce to the people the movable feasts of the current year.

For a sung text, see pages 62–63. Homily and intercession ideas for today can be found on pages 35 and 44 in *When Catholics Speak about Jews.*

■ LITURGY OF THE EUCHARIST: There is a proper insert to Eucharistic Prayer I. See pages 58–59 for the inserts used in France for Prayers II and III.

LITURGY OF THE HOURS

See appendix I of the *Liturgy of the Hours* for texts to extend the Office of Readings into a vigil on Saturday night. This Sunday is also a grand night for the parish Christmas choir concert. Precede it with Evening Prayer and carols for everyone to sing; conclude it with a festive parish supper or open house.

TAKING IT HOME

Seasonal materials can provide households with texts for table prayer (*Catholic Household Blessings and Prayers,* page 70). The same book (page 126) offers a blessing of the home and household for Epiphany, a traditional custom in various ethnic groups. (An alternative order for this is in the *Book of Blessings,* chapter 50.) This blessing reminds us that Christ is manifest in our homes and in daily life, too. Stars cut from foil wrapping paper (by children and adults off from school and work) could be distributed to all who come for worship, to be taken home as decorations that also serve as reminders of the feast. If something like this is done, homilists should integrate the symbol into the worship.

M O N **8** #21 (LMC, #17)   white
The Baptism of the Lord
FEAST

Once part of the Epiphany celebration in the West, it became a separate feast in 1956, assigned to January 13. In the recent reforms it was assigned to the Sunday after Epiphany, but this year (with Epiphany celebrated later than January 6) it is moved to Monday. Consider an evening Mass and encourage all to come

to conclude the Christmas season. It should be clear that this feast is part of Christmas–Epiphany, a manifestation of Christ to the Jewish people. Keep the Christmas decorations up and use the Christmas order of rites and prayer texts. This is the end of the Christmas season and the "last hurrah" for carols. Other appropriate hymns are: "On Jordan's bank," "When John baptized in Jordan's river," "Songs of thankfulness and praise," and "I bind unto myself today."

The rite of sprinkling should be used at Mass today, perhaps (see the text on page 55) with water from the font.

Homilists should consider the distinct treatment each evangelist gives to this story of Christ's baptism. The use of the three synoptic accounts allows the assembly to hear the varying approaches over time. They should not be simply harmonized into a general picture.

Evening Prayer II (followed by more carols and perhaps an "undecorating party") can bring Christmastime to a close. Ordinary Time begins tomorrow.

INTRODUCTORY RITES

A Christmas Welcome

As we begin the celebration of this great feast, I wish to welcome all of you who have come to celebrate here at _____ parish.

We welcome those of you who are guests from out of town or from other parishes. It is good to have you with us.

We extend a special word of welcome to our college students and other young adults home for the holidays. It is a joy to see your bright and shining faces among us.

And, of course, we rejoice in all those here whose faces we see each week. It is good for all of us to be here together to celebrate the love of God revealed in the gift of the Word Incarnate.

Greeting

The peace and love of God our Father, manifested in Christ who was born for our salvation, be with you all.

Rite of Blessing and Sprinkling of Holy Water

Dear brothers and sisters: let us implore the blessing of God our Father that this rite of sprinkling water may revive in us the grace of baptism through which we have been immersed in the redeeming death of the Lord, the Word made flesh and the Son of Mary, that we might rise with him to new life.

O God our Father,
by your voice thundering over the waters
    of the Jordan,
you proclaimed Christ as your beloved Son
and summoned us to place our faith in him.
R. *Cleanse and bless your church, O Lord!*
[Or: *Glory and praise to you, O Lord!*]
[Or: *Glory to God in the highest!*]

O Christ, beloved Son,
by your baptism you sanctified the waters
    of the Jordan
and unsealed for your church the fountain
    of baptism,
the cleansing flood of health and
    holiness. [R]

O Holy Spirit,
you descended upon Christ in the form
    of a dove,
confirming the Father's witness,
anointing Jesus with the oil of gladness,
and inviting us to become his disciples. [R]

Great are you, Lord God, enthroned above
    the flood forever,
yet choosing to make your dwelling
    in our midst
through Christ, your Word made flesh.
Bless this water as you did the waters
    of the Jordan,
and let the power of baptism so inundate
    our souls
that by the witness of our words and deeds
your saving power may be proclaimed
    to the ends of the earth.

We ask this through Christ our Lord.
—*text adapted from the Byzantine Rite*

Invitation to Penitence

In these shining days of Christmas,
as we celebrate the mystery of God with us,
let us turn to the Lord
and ask God's gracious mercy.

Penitential Rite

Eternal Word, through whom all things were made: Lord, have mercy.

True Light, enlightening everyone born into the world: Christ, have mercy.

Son of God, made flesh in the womb of the Virgin Mother: Lord, have mercy.

LITURGY OF THE WORD

Dismissal of Catechumens

Dear catechumens: with the assurance of our loving support, this community sends you forth to reflect more deeply on the word of God we have shared. Our prayer for you in this season of Christmas joy is that the mystery of the Word made flesh may strengthen your resolve to embrace Christ as your Savior and lead you to share fully with us at the Lord's table as children of God and heirs, in hope, of eternal life.

General Intercessions

Invitation to Prayer

In Christ, Emmanuel, the Word made flesh,
we have beheld God's love for us; let us draw
near to God in prayer, therefore, with joy and
hope of all who trust in God's saving power.

For the church

For the church in all nations,
made holy by the living word
and the power of the Spirit:
let us pray to the Lord.

For all the ministers of the holy church,
and for all who serve in the name of Christ:
let us pray to the Lord.

For the world

For peace among the nations,
that war may cease
and the needs of the poor be served:
let us pray to the Lord.

For the rulers and leaders of every land,
that they serve with humble hearts
and seek the common good:
let us pray to the Lord.

For various needs

For the refugees and exiles in every land,
the foreigners and strangers in our midst,
and all separated from their families
       and homes:
let us pray to the Lord.

For this nation and all its people,
and for those who work in its service:
let us pray to the Lord.

For the local community

That the homeless ones in our town
       be welcomed as Christ
who has come to be with us:
let us pray to the Lord.

For the families and friends who gather
       in these days,
that Christ's peace reign in our hearts
       and homes:
let us pray to the Lord.

Attuned to the Sunday readings

For those who have not heard the good news
       of salvation,
those who have heard but have not believed,
and those who have forsaken their faith:
let us pray to the Lord.

For catechumens, candidates and inquirers

For the catechumens of the church,
that they be counted among those God
       has chosen:
let us pray to the Lord.

For the catechumens and candidates,
that Christ fill them with the light of faith:
let us pray to the Lord.

For the dead

For all who have fallen asleep in the faith,
and for all who have pleased the Lord from
       the beginning:
let us pray to the Lord.

Concluding Prayers for the General Intercessions

25 DECEMBER
THE BIRTH OF THE LORD
Vigil Mass
God of Abraham and Sarah,
of David and his descendants,
unwearied is your love for us
and steadfast your covenant;
wonderful beyond words
is your gift of the Savior,
born of the Virgin Mary.

Count us among the people
       in whom you delight,
and by this night's marriage of earth
       and heaven
draw all generations into the embrace
       of your love.

We ask this through Jesus Christ,
       your Word made flesh,
who lives and reigns with you in the unity
       of the Holy Spirit,
in the splendor of eternal light,
God for ever and ever.
—© ICEL

Mass at Midnight
Good and gracious God,
on this holy night you gave us your Son,
the Lord of the universe, wrapped in
　　swaddling clothes,
the Savior of all, lying in a manger.

On this holy night
draw us into the mystery of your love.
Join our voices with the heavenly host,
that we may sing your glory on high.
Give us a place among the shepherds,
that we may find the one for whom
　　we have waited,
Jesus Christ, your Word made flesh,
who lives and reigns with you in the unity
　　of the Holy Spirit,
in the splendor of eternal light,
God for ever and ever.
—© ICEL

Mass at Dawn
Today, O God of light,
your loving kindness dawns,
your tender compassion shines upon us,
for in our Savior, born of human flesh,
you reveal your gracious gift
of our birth to life eternal.

Fill us with wonder on this holy day:
let us treasure in our hearts
what we have been told,
that our lives may proclaim
your great and gentle mercy.

We ask this through Jesus Christ,
　　your Word made flesh,
who lives and reigns with you in the unity
　　of the Holy Spirit,
in the splendor of eternal light,
God for ever and ever.
—© ICEL

Mass during the Day
We praise you, gracious God,
for the glad tidings of peace,
the good news of salvation:
your Word became flesh,
and we have seen his glory.

Let the radiance of that glory
enlighten the lives
of those who celebrate his birth.
—© ICEL

Reveal to all the world
the light no darkness can extinguish,
our Lord Jesus Christ,
who lives and reigns with you in the unity
　　of the Holy Spirit,
in the splendor of eternal light,
God for ever and ever.

THE HOLY FAMILY
SUNDAY WITHIN THE OCTAVE OF CHRISTMAS
Loving God,
guardian of our homes,
when you entrusted your Son
to the care of Mary and Joseph,
you did not spare them the pains
that touch the life of every family.

Teach us to rely on your word,
that in our trials as in our joys
we may be clothed in gentleness
　　and patience
and united in love.
Make us ever thankful
for the blessings you give us
through Jesus Christ, your Word made flesh,
who lives and reigns with you in the unity
　　of the Holy Spirit,
in the splendor of eternal light,
God for ever and ever.
—© ICEL

MARY, MOTHER OF GOD
Most high God,
you come near to us this Christmas season
in the child born of the Virgin Mary.
In the depths of darkness, she gave birth
　　to light;
in the depths of silence, she brought forth
　　the Word.

Grant that we who ponder these things
　　in our hearts
may recognize in her child
our Lord and Savior, Jesus Christ,
who lives and reigns [with you in the unity
　　of the Holy Spirit,
in the splendor of eternal light,
God,] for ever and ever.
—© ICEL

6 JANUARY

THE EPIPHANY OF THE LORD
Lord God of the nations,
we have seen the star of your glory
rising in splendor.
The radiance of your incarnate Word
pierces the darkness that covers the earth
and signals the dawn of peace and justice.

Make radiant the lives of your people
with that same brightness,
and beckon all the nations
to walk as one in your light.

We ask this through Jesus Christ,
        your Word made flesh,
who lives and reigns with you in the unity
        of the Holy Spirit,
in the splendor of eternal light,
God for ever and ever.
—© ICEL

THE BAPTISM OF THE LORD
God of the covenant,
you anointed your beloved Son
with the power of the Holy Spirit,
to be light for the nations
and release for captives.

Grant that we who are born again
of water and the Spirit
may proclaim with our lips the good news
        of his peace
and show forth in our lives the victory
        of his justice.

We make our prayer through Jesus Christ,
        your Word made flesh,
who lives and reigns with you in the unity
        of the Holy Spirit,
in the splendor of eternal light,
God for ever and ever.
—© ICEL

LITURGY OF THE EUCHARIST

Eucharistic Prayer Inserts

SUNDAY IN EUCHARISTIC PRAYERS II AND III:
        See page 84.

CHRISTMAS AND ITS OCTAVE IN EUCHARISTIC PRAYER II:
Lord, you are holy indeed,
the fountain of all holiness.
We gather here before you
and in communion with the whole
        church,
we celebrate the most holy night
        (the most holy day)
when Mary, in her glorious virginity,
gave birth to the Savior of the world.
Through him, our Redeemer and
        our Lord,
we pray:
Let your Spirit come upon . . .

CHRISTMAS AND ITS OCTAVE IN EUCHARISTIC PRAYER III:
. . . a perfect offering may be made
to the glory of your name.
This is why we gather here before you,
and in communion with the whole
        church
we celebrate the most holy night
        (the most holy day)
when Mary, in her glorious virginity,
gave birth to the Savior of the world.
Through him, our Redeemer and
        our Lord,
we bring you these gifts.
We ask you to make them holy . . .

EPIPHANY IN EUCHARISTIC PRAYER II:
Lord, you are holy indeed,
the fountain of all holiness.
We gather here before you.
and in communion with the whole
        church
we celebrate the most holy day
on which your only Son
who shares your own eternal glory
appeared before us
in a true body of our own flesh.
Through him, our Redeemer and
        our Savior,
we pray:
Let your Spirit come upon . . .

EPIPHANY IN EUCHARISTIC PRAYER III:

> *. . . a perfect offering may be made*
> *to the glory of your name.*
> This is why we gather here before you,
> and in communion with the whole
> church
> we celebrate the most holy day
> on which your only Son,
> who shares your own eternal glory,
> appeared before us
> in a true body of our own flesh.
> Through him, our Redeemer and
> our Savior,
> *we bring you these gifts.*
> *We ask you to make them holy . . .*

Introduction to the Lord's Prayer

The Son of God took flesh among us as a child that we might become in spirit and truth the children of God; therefore with gratitude and joy we pray:

Prayer for Peace

Lord Jesus Christ,
at whose holy birth the choirs of angels
announced the glad tidings of peace
to the world:
Look not on our sins, but on the faith
of your church . . .

Invitation to Communion

This is the lamb of God, who takes away
the sins of the world:
Emmanuel, God-with-us, born of Mary to be
the Savior of all nations. Happy are
those who are called to his supper.

CONCLUDING RITE

Dismissal of Eucharistic Ministers

Go forth in peace to the sick and homebound of our community, bearing the word of life and the Body of Christ, together with the assurance of our love and concern. Join their voices to our hymn in praise of God's glory and in the name of this community share God's peace with them in the gift of Emmanuel.

Blessing

May the God of infinite goodness, who in the Word made flesh wedded earth to heaven and heaven to earth, fill your hearts with joy at the glad tidings of salvation and make you a light to those who long to behold the beauty of the Savior's face:
And may almighty God bless you...

Dismissal

As witnesses of God's glory and heralds of God's peace, go forth in joy and gladness to love and serve the Lord.

PROCLAMATION OF THE BIRTH OF CHRIST

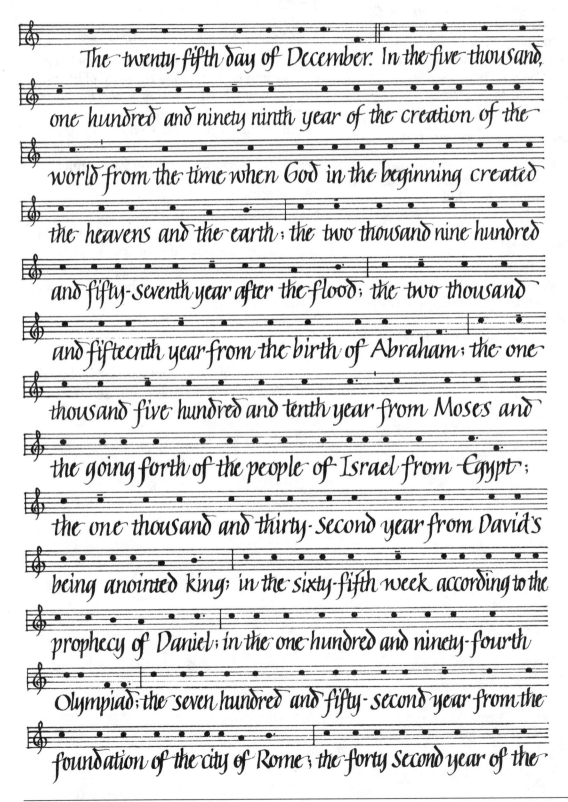

The twenty-fifth day of December. In the five thousand,
one hundred and ninety ninth year of the creation of the
world from the time when God in the beginning created
the heavens and the earth; the two thousand nine hundred
and fifty-seventh year after the flood; the two thousand
and fifteenth year from the birth of Abraham; the one
thousand five hundred and tenth year from Moses and
the going forth of the people of Israel from Egypt;
the one thousand and thirty-second year from David's
being anointed king; in the sixty-fifth week according to the
prophecy of Daniel; in the one hundred and ninety-fourth
Olympiad; the seven hundred and fifty-second year from the
foundation of the city of Rome; the forty second year of the

reign of Octavian Augustus; the whole world being at peace,
in the sixth age of the world, Jesus Christ, the eternal God
and Son of the eternal Father, desiring to sanctify the world
by his most merciful coming, being conceived by the Holy
Spirit, and nine months having passed since his conception,
was born in Bethlehem of Judea of the Virgin Mary, being
made flesh.　The Nativity of our Lord Jesus Christ
according to the flesh.

Suggestions for using the Christmas proclamation:

This proclamation, taken from the entry for December 25 in the ancient martyrology, could be sung at the beginning of the Midnight Mass. It should be done without explanation, with great simplicity and reverence in the silence and darkness as the assembly keeps vigil.

Acolytes with lighted candles might accompany the cantor to the ambo or another appropriate place in front of the assembly. The cantor may indicate with a gesture that the assembly is to stand; when all are standing, the proclamation begins. The tradition calls for the assembly to kneel after the words "having passed since his conception . . ." and to rise before "The Nativity of our Lord . . ." The cantor should stop at both times to allow this to take place. The acolytes and other ministers should know beforehand so that they can model for the assembly the kneeling and the rising.

When the proclamation is concluded, the entrance rites of Midnight Mass—which have truly begun with this chant—can continue with song.

Text copyright © 1989, United States Catholic Conference (USCC), 3211 Fourth Street NE, Washington DC 20017-1194. All rights reserved. Text was prepared by Rev. Richard Wojcik. Chant based on an adaptation of the original chant by Msgr. J. T. Kush. Calligraphy by Rosie Kelly.

PROCLAMATION OF THE DATE OF EASTER

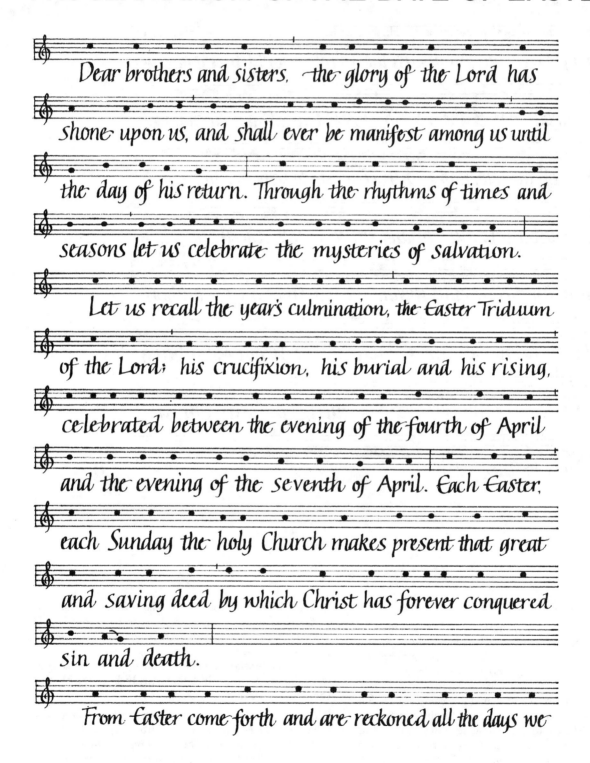

Dear brothers and sisters, the glory of the Lord has

shone upon us, and shall ever be manifest among us until

the day of his return. Through the rhythms of times and

seasons let us celebrate the mysteries of salvation.

Let us recall the year's culmination, the Easter Triduum

of the Lord; his crucifixion, his burial and his rising,

celebrated between the evening of the fourth of April

and the evening of the seventh of April. Each Easter,

each Sunday the holy Church makes present that great

and saving deed by which Christ has forever conquered

sin and death.

From Easter come forth and are reckoned all the days we

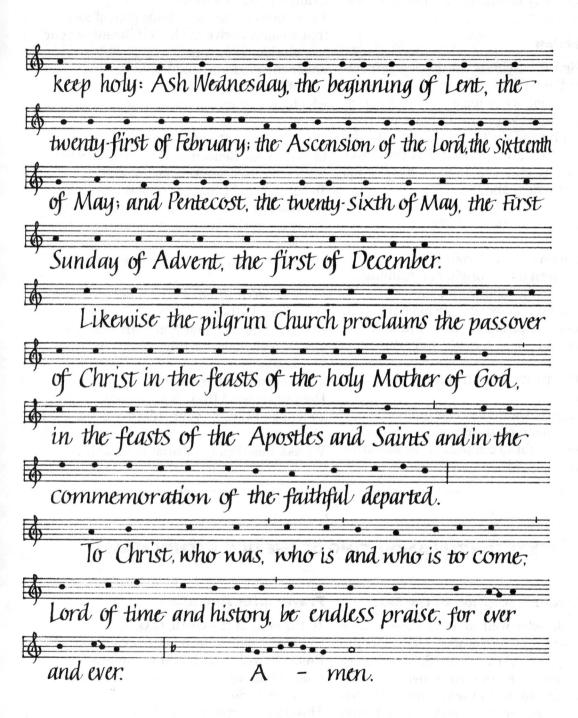

keep holy: Ash Wednesday, the beginning of Lent, the twenty-first of February; the Ascension of the Lord, the sixteenth of May; and Pentecost, the twenty-sixth of May, the First Sunday of Advent, the first of December.

Likewise the pilgrim Church proclaims the passover of Christ in the feasts of the holy Mother of God, in the feasts of the Apostles and Saints and in the commemoration of the faithful departed.

To Christ, who was, who is and who is to come, Lord of time and history, be endless praise, for ever and ever. A - men.

Suggestions for using the Epiphany proclamation:

This proclamation, announcing the date of Easter and the various dates that depend on Easter, is chanted by a cantor after the gospel reading or homily on the solemnity of the Epiphany. The proclamation can be sung from the ambo with lights and incense as at the gospel. The line, "Each Easter, each Sunday, . . ." may sound like an error when chanted. The Italian sacramentary reads: "Every

Sunday, as in a weekly Easter, . . ." Cantors, take note of the key change in the final lines. After a brief pause, this section should take on a different character, as the proclamation concludes with an acclamation of praise.

These prayers may be used with the Christmas vigil outlined on page 48.

Introduction

In this vigil we celebrate the dawn of our salvation in the birth of our Lord Jesus Christ, the Father's only-begotten Son, born for us of the Virgin Mary. With gratitude let us recall his humanity and the life he shared with the children of the earth, praying that the power of his divinity may enable us to answer his call to forgiveness and life.

FOR USE WITH READING I (GENESIS):
O God,
in the human nature of your Son
you have given us the origin and fulfillment
    of our relationship with you.
Keep us faithful to this gift we have received,
for our every hope of salvation is in him,
who lives and reigns for ever and ever.

FOR USE WITH READING II (1 SAMUEL):
Merciful God,
by the birth of your only-begotten Son
and by his death on the cross,
you have brought to completion the salvation
    of your people.

Grant us, your servants,
a firm faith in this wondrous plan of love,
that we may arrive at the fulfillment of your
    glorious promises
under the guidance and by the grace
    of Christ your Son,
who lives and reigns for ever and ever.

FOR USE WITH READING III (ISAIAH):
Listen, O our Redeemer, to the supplication
of all who celebrate this joyful night.
To save us and bring us immortality,
you entered and renewed our human nature:
Bring us on the final day to your heavenly
    feast,
where you live and reign for ever and ever.

FOR USE WITH READING IV (JUDGES):
O God our Father,
In the mystery of your Son's birth among us,
you help us to understand your wondrous
    kindness
and your desire to save us.
Help us respond to such generosity
by living always as your children, doing good
    to all.
We ask this through Christ our Lord.

TEXTS FOR THE ANOINTING OF THE SICK WITHIN MASS

Introduction/Reception of the Sick

The people who walked in darkness have seen a great light. As the angels sang glory to God and peace on earth, the Sun of Justice dawned with healing rays over a land shrouded in gloom. In these days of Christmas joy, we gather in the name of that child born for us of the Virgin Mary, Jesus, the Prince of Peace, Emmanuel: God with us. Let us ask him to be among us now as we celebrate his healing presence in the sacraments of anointing and eucharist.

Prayer after Anointing

To the ends of the earth, O God,
you have made known your saving power.
Embrace with health and wholeness
those whom we have anointed in the name
    of your Son.
Through him whom we acknowledge as
    the Word made flesh,
grant our brothers and sisters the comfort
    they seek
and that peace which is your will for all of us
through Christ our Lord.

WINTER
ORDINARY TIME

Introduction to Ordinary Time

WINTER Ordinary Time comes as a break between high seasons, a pause between the two major cycles of the year. Advent – Christmas is over, and Lent – Easter has not yet begun. This year we have just over six weeks in this period, which seems all too short for those preparing for Lent and the Triduum!

The name "Ordinary Time" is a bit of a misnomer. The term in Latin is really more accurately translated "ordinal," which is to say, counted. "Ordinal Time" is simply the period marked by counting the Sundays of the year that do not fall in the two great cycles. Some parishes prefer to speak of "Sundays of the Year," though that is also confusing since the Twentieth Sunday of the Year liturgically is not the Twentieth Sunday in the annual calendar.

What we call these weeks, however, is not as important as how we think of them. There is a real sense in which no time is "ordinary." At the Easter Vigil we proclaim that "all time belongs to Christ and all the ages." Every minute of every day is sacred time for the Christian, and any day can be a day to encounter the Lord and celebrate God's love. And no Sunday is really ordinary, because every Sunday is a celebration of the resurrection of the Lord.

■ THE SUNDAY: Sunday is the original Christian feast. It was the church's day of celebration even before there was an Easter celebration and thus long before there was Christmas. Ordinary Time is, therefore, the season of Sundays. Ordinary Time is an ideal time to focus on the Sunday and its meaning in our lives.

By a tradition handed down from the apostles and having its origin from the very day of Christ's resurrection, the church celebrates the paschal mystery every eighth day, which, with good reason, bears the name of the Lord's Day or Sunday. For on this day Christ's faithful must gather together so that, by hearing the word of God and taking part in the eucharist, they may call to mind the passion, the resurrection, and the glorification of the Lord Jesus and may thank God, who "has begotten them again unto a living hope through the resurrection of Jesus Christ from the dead" (1 Peter 1:3). Hence the Lord's Day is the first holy day of all and should be proposed to the devotion of the faithful and taught to them in such a way that it may become in fact a day of joy and of freedom from work. Other celebrations, unless they be truly of greatest importance, shall not have precedence over the Sunday, the foundation and core of the whole liturgical year. (*Constitution on the Sacred Liturgy,* #106)

The reform of the calendar after the Second Vatican Council sought to reestablish the primacy of the Sunday. Many feasts that had come to eclipse it over the centuries were either suppressed or ranked lower than the Sunday. Thus only rarely today is the Sunday replaced by a feast; only nine festivals are important enough to displace the celebration of the Sunday itself.

Despite this clear intention of the reform, however, the Sunday frequently gets overshadowed by themes promoting various causes. Some of these come from Vatican congregations, others from the national bishops' conference, some from the local diocese, and still more from varied parish groups and local associations. National or diocesan offices often send out books with liturgical adaptations for such Sundays; some of those suggestions are appropriate, but some are poorly composed and liturgically unsound.

Mission Sunday, Vocation Sunday, Right to Life Sunday or any other "cause Sunday" should be integrated into the parish's worship in such a way that the primacy of the Sunday and the Sunday readings is maintained. The *Ceremonial of Bishops* gives a clear guideline on this matter. After repeating the conciliar statement on Sunday and its precedence, it decrees:

> This has particular application to the practice, frequently involving a Sunday, of assigning a special theme to a particular day, for example, dedicating a day to the promotion of peace and justice, vocations, or the missions. In such cases the liturgy to be celebrated is the Sunday liturgy, but the theme proposed may be brought out in the songs chosen or in the introductions, the homily, or the general intercessions. (#229)

Thus the readings and orations are from the Sunday (and the homily should flow from the readings), but the theme may be integrated into the celebration in the homily, the intercessions, and perhaps in a song or two, so long as the celebration of the Sunday itself remains primary.

Sunday Rest

MANY older Catholics in this country remember when Sunday was observed stringently as a day of rest. In many states, civil law kept most businesses closed, and Catholics were taught to avoid "unnecessary servile work" under pain of sin. This was not the way the early Christians observed Sunday, but the Pilgrims and Puritans and the Jansenists did link Sunday and the Sabbath rest, leading to the establishment of the "blue laws" forbidding the conduct of business on Sundays.

Recent years have seen much change in the culture's approach to Sunday. Most retail businesses now have Sunday hours; even some banks are open on Sunday. Some Christians react very negatively to such changes, while many others obviously accept them with no difficulty. The key to a healthy approach to the observance of Sunday is to see it as a day of freedom. As the "eighth day," the first day of the new creation, Christians have come to see Sunday as a day of freedom from the demands of ordinary life. The first value of this freedom from work is that it enables the community to gather for worship on Sunday. Early Christians did not have this freedom; Sunday was a workday like any other day. It was only after Christianity became the official religion that Sunday gradually became a day devoted primarily to worship. The 1983 *Code of Canon Law* (canon 1247) expresses this tradition:

> On Sundays and other holy days of obligation the faithful are bound to participate in the Mass; they are also to abstain from those labors and business concerns which impede the worship to be rendered to God, the joy which is proper to the Lord's Day, or the proper relaxation of mind and body.

The core of Sunday is our public worship. We are to keep ourselves free from anything that would prevent joining the assembly for the praise of God. Beyond that, Sunday invites us to enter into the joy of the day of the Lord and to experience the freedom of the children of God. Our observance of the Sunday is intended to help us experience the presence of the kingdom of God in our lives. We may not be able to live fully in the kingdom; the demands of daily life remind us that the kingdom has not yet fully arrived. But on Sunday, on the eighth day, the day of the new creation, we praise God in union with the heavenly hosts, we celebrate the redemption Christ has won for us through his death and resurrection, and we experience the freedom of the children of God as we leave the work of the week behind for a day.

Ordinary Time offers the parish an opportunity to recover the significance of Sunday, both by careful preparation of worship and by encouraging full observance of Sunday as a day of worship, prayer, family life and re-creative activities. Celebrating such a special day every week keeps this time from being merely "ordinary."

■ THE GOSPEL OF MATTHEW: This is the year of Matthew in the lectionary, Year A. We have already heard from Matthew on all four Sundays of Advent, at the Christmas Vigil Mass, and on Epiphany and the Baptism of the Lord. Matthew has about 400 more verses than Mark, and we will hear most of them during this liturgical year, either on Sundays or on weekdays.

Matthew's gospel was written about AD 85–90 for a Christian community, probably in present-day Syria. The writer of Matthew evidently knew Mark's gospel and uses much of Mark in his own work. About 200 verses (out of 1068) are not found in Mark but are found in Luke; it is generally assumed these come from a source of sayings of Jesus, called "Q" (from *Quelle,* "source" in German). Beyond the verses based on Mark and on Q, Matthew also has some material that is unique to this gospel.

It is possible that this gospel is rooted in a collection of sayings of Jesus compiled by the apostle Matthew, but the mature work evidently was written by a later author. The writer was probably an early Christian teacher and church leader. The gospel was written after the fall of Jerusalem in AD 70 and reflects a Jewish-Christian perspective. But it also seems to reflect the conflict with Judaism, probably flowing from the exclusion of the Christians from the synagogue after AD 80.

Matthew's gospel stresses the teaching of Jesus, in contrast to Mark, who seems to focus more on Jesus' actions and miracles. Matthew's gospel is structured into five major sections of teachings, with narrative material between each section, the infancy narratives at the beginning and the passion and resurrection material at the end. The following outline results:

chapters 1–4	Narrative: Birth and beginnings
5–7	First section of teaching: Sermon on the Mount
8–9	Authority and invitation: Jesus' miracles of healing
10	Second section of teaching: Mission discourse
11–12	The rejection of the Baptist and Jesus by the Jews
13	Third section of teaching: Seven parables of the kingdom
14–17	Acknowledgment by the disciples
18	Fourth section of teaching: Community discourse
19–22	Authority and invitation: Journey to Jerusalem and teaching in the Temple
23–25	Fifth section of teaching: Woes, coming of the kingdom
26–28	The last days of Jesus in or near Jerusalem, crucifixion, resurrection and appearances in Galilee

C. H. Lohr has noted that the sections of this outline are linked in pairs around the central section in Chapter 13: The rejection by the Jews is paralleled by the acknowledgment by the disciples, the mission discourse by the community discourse, the section on miracles by the section on teaching in the Temple, the sermon on the Mount by the woes and teaching on the coming of the kingdom, and the birth and beginnings narrative by the death and resurrection narrative. The symmetry of the narrative sections is not as clear as with the teaching sections, but this insight reminds us how carefully the author of this gospel arranged his material.

Many scholars have seen the five sections of teaching in this gospel as Matthew's "Torah," a deliberate imitation of the first five books of the Bible, presenting Jesus as the giver of the new "Torah" or "Law." The term "law" here refers not just to legal prescriptions but to a whole pattern for living according to God's will. Matthew presents Jesus as the new Moses, who was traditionally viewed as the author of the Torah.

Benedict Viviano, OP, in the *New Jerome Biblical Commentary,* concludes that

> Matthew's primary intent was to write a handbook for church leaders to assist them in preaching, teaching, worship, mission and polemic. But he has inserted this handbook into the story of a living person, Jesus Christ, to keep it from becoming merely an academic or a gnostic doctrine and to keep it focused on Christ and his kingdom as the good news of salvation. (p. 631)

Several characteristic concerns mark Matthew's gospel. The author is concerned with showing clearly that Jesus is the Christ, the expected Messiah. He puts great emphasis on the kingdom of God, which Jesus proclaimed and inaugurated. This emphasis on the kingdom leads to a focus on justice and the law. More than any other gospel, Matthew expresses a concern for the church community and its ongoing life and structure. Finally, this gospel presents Jesus as forming a new covenant, which is reflected in his "Torah" structure and in frequent use of the fulfillment of the Old Testament as explanation for events in the life of Jesus. Matthew frequently presents Old Testament texts as foretelling or foreshadowing things that Jesus did or things that happened to him.

■ MATTHEW IN ORDINARY TIME 1996: In Winter Ordinary Time, the Sunday pericopes are from chapters 4 and 5, the beginning of Jesus' preaching and the first part of the Sermon on the Mount. The Second Sunday of Ordinary Time draws from John rather than from Matthew. After Pentecost, we will begin in chapter 9 and continue basically in order through chapter 25. It is important to note, however, that much of the gospel is omitted from the Sunday readings, while the weekday readings from Monday of the Tenth Week in Ordinary Time through Saturday of the Twenty-first Week give a more thorough exposure to the whole text. Planners and preachers might find it helpful to study the index of readings in the back of the lectionary to understand how much is skipped on Sundays and seek ways to help Sunday worshipers understand the selected verses in context of the larger story.

■ THE SAINTS IN WINTER: Because Ordinary Time lasts more than six weeks this winter, we have a number of saints to celebrate before Lent. The Conversion of Paul and the Presentation of the Lord are the two feasts of this period. These feasts are joined by eight obligatory memorials and nine optional ones. Parishes should choose from among the optional memorials in light of the community's devotion to various saints, as well as in view of the importance of developing a world-wide awareness of God's holy people.

Taking It Home

CATHOLIC *Household Blessings and Prayers* has prayers for the Week of Prayer for Christian Unity (page 160), prayers for Martin Luther King Day (page 195) and Washington's Birthday (page 196), and a ritual for Receiving Blessed Candles at Home on Candlemas Day (pages 161–64).

LTP's *Take Me Home* resource has pages for Martin Luther King day, St. Anthony of Egypt (the patron of pets, January 17), Presentation, Valentine's Day and Mardi Gras.

This would also be a good time of year to encourage parishioners to read the readings for Sunday Mass during the week prior to the cele-

bration. Printing the citations in the bulletin the previous Sunday enables the assembly to prepare to hear the word more fully. Bible-study groups might use a resource like *Share the Word* (Paulist Evangelization Office), which provides commentary on the three readings and the psalm for each week, or LTP's *At Home with the Word,* which offers each week's readings and reflections on how they might be lived out. The liturgy of the word will never reach its full potential in our assemblies until we become a people of the word, using the Bible as a constant source of study and prayer. This wintertime, with its fewer outdoor activities than other seasons, might be the best time of year to encourage people to develop a habit of regular use of the Bible. Offering Bible-study programs or organizing groups for regular Bible study is an important support to individual Bible reading.

The Mass

INTRODUCTORY RITES

THOSE who prepare the liturgy need to be aware of the options for prayer texts, a familiarity that comes only with study and practice. The norms for weekdays in Ordinary Time can be found in the *General Instruction of the Roman Missal* (#313–316, #323).

■ TEXTS FOR SAINTS' DAYS IN ORDINARY TIME: For memorials, the prayers are taken from each saint's day. Sometimes only an opening prayer is given at the date; other texts are to be filled in from the "commons" texts in the sacramentary. The readings are almost always from the seasonal progression. Only on rare and high-ranking days should the semi-continuous flow of scriptures be interrupted by other readings.

■ TEXTS FOR OTHER WEEKDAYS IN ORDINARY TIME: The scriptures are always from the proper weekday. There are many options for the sacramentary prayers. Those who choose the texts should adopt one or more of the traditional systems for this selection:

- *Use prayers from the previous Sunday.* When a feast falls on Sunday (e.g., Baptism of the Lord or Christ the King), the prayers printed for the current week in Ordinary Time are used even though they were not prayed on the preceding Sunday.

- *Use votive Masses.* The assigning of certain votive Masses to particular weekdays has been abandoned, but the fifteen sets of prayers listed as votive Masses can be used on any "open" day.

- *Use "Masses and Prayers for Various Needs and Occasions."* Planners might consider some progression through the sets of prayers that have significance for the whole year and the entire parish—such as "For the Universal Church" (#1)—and then some specific choices for particular times of the year (for example, "For Peace and Justice" [#22] near civil holidays).

- *Select texts from "Masses and Prayers for Various Needs and Occasions" according to the readings of the day.* Despite its merits, this method must be used carefully to avoid becoming too didactic.

As indicated in the *General Instruction* (#316c), texts from the Masses for the Dead are to be used sparingly. The Mass intentions can be included in the intercessions with other prayers.

■ SIMPLER RITES FOR ORDINARY TIME: Keep the introductory rites simple, with a concise introduction and a short penitential rite. The sacramentary texts B, C*i* and C*viii* seem best for this time of year. In some parishes, the singing of the Gloria is reserved for holy days and other special occasions. It may seem reasonable to recite the Gloria during Ordinary Time, but the Gloria is an ancient hymn. There are many beautiful but simple settings for the Gloria; perhaps one can be used throughout Ordinary Time until it becomes familiar and easy to sing well. Carrol Thomas Andrews's Gloria ("A New Mass for Congregations") in *Worship* (#234) is a solid and straight-forward setting of this hymn. It is a very melodic setting with a repeated opening and closing section and a contrasting middle section. Consider the chant setting of the Gloria from John Lee's "Congregational Mass." Found in GIA's *Worship* hymnal, this Gloria offers possibilities for alternating sections between cantor and assembly or between men and women. A simple setting for Ordinary Time, this Gloria also works well sung through by the entire assembly.

LITURGY OF THE WORD

■ THE LECTIONARY, CATECHUMENS AND CHILDREN: A healthy sign of the growing integration of our worship with other areas of parish life is the trend of basing catechetical and catechumenal sessions on the lectionary. Care should be taken, however, not to see the liturgy as a lesson plan. The liturgy of the word is not a lesson on a theme. Rather, the liturgy (readings, psalm, gospel acclamation, homily and silence) is an opportunity to encounter the living Lord who speaks to us. The catechetical sessions flow from this encounter as a time to reflect on what we have experienced. This is especially important to remember when a parish offers a separate liturgy of the word for children. Great care must be taken so that it is truly a liturgy, a time of prayer and celebration, not another religious education class. (The bishops of the United States have provided a lectionary for use in Masses with children and in separate liturgies of the word. LTP's ritual edition of the *Lectionary for Masses with Children* is beautiful enough to convey to both children and adults the power and dignity of the word of God. Study editions are also available.)

Even when the liturgy of the word for children is well done, many have questioned the advisability of removing the children from the assembly regularly. Our worship assembly should be inclusive of all members of the body of Christ. Children belong there as much as adults do. And the assembly needs the enthusiasm and freshness that children bring to any group. If you have been taking the children out every week, consider doing it only once a month or every other week. Then take a good look at the assembly's worship; if children are bored there, it is likely the adults are, too. Preparing liturgy that is good for children (not childish, but alive) will be a gift to the adults as well!

■ SUNDAY RESPONSORIAL PSALM: Eight common psalms for Ordinary Time are listed in the lectionary (#175). Music ministers may select one or two of these for the winter Sundays. This provides a repetition by which the psalms can sink into people's consciousness and eventually become their own. Yet some liturgists question whether the use of common psalmody should be a permanent situation or a transitional technique, employed to build familiarity with psalmody but designed to lead a community to a more complete experience of the psalter through the singing of the proper psalm for each Sunday and feast. Many publishers provide settings of the proper psalms in their hymnals, worship aids and supplemental publications.

If common psalmody is your choice, consider Psalm 27 for the Second, Third and Fifth Sundays; it is the assigned psalm for the Third

Sunday and echoes the theme of light in all three first readings. For the Fourth, Sixth and Seventh Sundays, Psalm 19 responds well to the words about the law and commandments.

The following are some suggested settings of Psalms 27 and 19:

- Richard Proulx, Ps. 27: The Lord is my light *(Worship Lectionary Accompaniment, Cantor Book)*

- Christopher Willcock, Ps. 27: The Lord is my light *(Psalms for Feasts and Seasons,* Liturgical Press)

- David Haas, Ps. 27: The Lord is my light *(Gather)*

- Psalms for Ordinary Time, #527 (Leon C. Roberts) and #528 (Anthony E. Jackson) in *Lead Me, Guide Me* (GIA)

- David Haas, Psalm 19: Lord, you have the words *(Gather)*

- Robert Kreutz, Psalm 19: Lord you have the words (OCP, *Music Issue)*

- Christopher Willcock, Psalm 19: Lord, you have the words *(Psalms for Feasts and Seasons,* Liturgical Press)

- Ralph C. Verdi, Psalm 19 *(Psalms for Cantors Series,* World Library)

■ SUNDAY GOSPELS: When we turn to the Gospel of Matthew on the Third Sunday, we hear the beginning of Jesus' Sermon on the Mount. For five weeks, we hear from the fifth chapter of Matthew, offering homilists an opportunity to lead the assembly in a prolonged consideration of the demands the gospel makes on the followers of Christ.

LITURGY OF THE EUCHARIST

We have nine approved eucharistic prayers in the United States. Too many assemblies never hear most of the approved prayers, with numbers two and three being repeated too often. Though there are eight prefaces available for the Sundays in Ordinary Time (and six for weekdays), these weeks, with the absence of festal prefaces, are good opportunities to use the fourth prayer and/or the prayers for reconciliation, which have their own prefaces. If prayers II and III are used, see the sample inserts on page 84.

■ ACCLAMATIONS: The eucharistic acclamations during this time should return to one of the "standard sets" of the parish. With publishers still offering new settings in every catalog and workshop, it is easy to assume that newer is better and that we do our people a disservice if we do not keep abreast of the latest offerings. A few high-quality sets of responses, acclamations and litanies are all that is needed to let people know them well and sing them as prayer. If it is time to reconsider the quality and long-term effectiveness of your parish's settings, look for one that can be equally successful with or without a choir and additional instruments, and that everyone can look forward to singing again after it has been set aside for some time.

■ COMMUNION PROCESSIONAL: This is a good time to rely on your established communion antiphons and to continue to build that repertoire. Settings of Psalm 34, "O taste and see," are always appropriate. Two others to consider adding are Richard Proulx's arrangement of "I received the living God" *(Worship)* and James Chepponis's "Life-giving bread" *(Gather)*.

CONCLUDING RITE

The *Book of Blessings,* in appendix II, reprints the solemn blessings found in the sacramentary and adds four more. Copy these four and add them to the others in the sacramentary until a new edition groups them all together.

As we consider the life of discipleship this season, a strong "sending forth" song is in order. Some pieces composed for this purpose include "Take Christ to the world" by Paul Inwood; the John Raphael Peacey text "Go forth for God; go to the world in peace," which is set to Erik Routley's challenging tune LITTON in the *Collegeville Hymnal* (#603) but is also compatible with the more familiar Genevan Psalter tune TOULON and with NATIONAL HYMN; and the strong setting of the gospel mandates to "teach all nations" and "feed my sheep" found in Leon Patillo's "Go" *(Lead Me, Guide Me,* #66). David Haas's "Go out to all the world" found in *(Who Calls You By Name, Volume II)* is also appropriate.

MUSIC

Other songs worth exploring for this time include "Give me a clean heart" by Margaret J. Douroux *(Lead Me, Guide Me,* #279); "Go, make of all disciples" in *Worship* (GIA) set to the ELLACOMBE tune; "Sing of the Lord's goodness" in *Gather* (GIA), a strong faith statement in 5/4 time; "Church of God" *(In Perfect Charity,* OCP, 8405), Margaret Daly's lilting gathering hymn with refrain; and Christopher Walker's noble processional "Out of darkness" (OCP, 9232), which is at its best when the angular, syncopated verses are sung by the choir and the assembly joins in the refrain. For evening services, Marty Haugen's "God of day and God of darkness" (*Gather,* #319) is appropriate.

Now might be a good time to look ahead at and review your plans for music at the Triduum. Is there a hymn or psalm, presently unfamiliar to your assembly, that you would like to work into the music for Triduum? Consider familiarizing the assembly with this new piece during this period of Ordinary Time. A careful review of your musical resources at this time might yield some new discoveries.

Other Ritual Prayer and Sacraments

LITURGY OF THE HOURS

THOUGH many parishes have learned to celebrate Morning Prayer and/or Evening Prayer during Advent and Lent, the liturgy of the hours should form the rhythm of daily life throughout the year. Ancient customs and canons, recent councils and all the contemporary liturgical books highlight Sunday Evening Prayer as the most important of the hours for all the faithful to celebrate.

Some parishes have found it easier, however, to begin with regular weekday evening prayer, on one day a week or even on a daily basis. Such a prayer might be scheduled to precede the usual starting time for parish meetings so that parishioners can gather for prayer before business. Another approach is to highlight special feasts (as well as Sundays) by celebrating evening prayer on those days. If daily Mass is not celebrated on some weekdays, consider using morning and/or evening prayer rather than having a communion service.

■ VIGILS: Appendix I of the *Liturgy of the Hours* offers canticles and gospel references for expanding the Saturday night Office of Readings into an extended vigil. It also gives similar texts for the eve of February 2 and for the commons if

your titular solemnity or dedication anniversary occurs during these weeks.

CHRISTIAN UNITY

The days from January 18–25 are designated the Week of Prayer for Christian Unity. Material for this observance is available each year from the Graymoor Ecumenical Institute, Garrison NY 10524. The "Order for the Blessing of Ecumenical Groups" in the *Book of Blessings* (#553–569) may also be useful if your parish is joining other Christian communities for a service during this week.

The Worship Environment

EACH season of the year offers challenges to good worship, but for much of this country, the winter is perhaps the most difficult time for those who gather for worship on Sunday. Besides the frequent challenge of even getting to church through ice and snow and freezing cold, conditions once people arrive are often less than hospitable. The building may be cold, floors may be wet and slippery, the atmosphere may be dark because the sun is often hidden, and the assembly gathers in heavy coats, sweaters, hats, gloves and scarves—all of which can make "feeling at home" difficult.

Parishes should consider turning an unused space near the entrance into a coatroom or perhaps setting up coat racks in the vestibule; it may not look great, but it is hospitable. Or have everyone use another entry (perhaps one through the rectory or hall) and leave coats there. Or leave enough space in every pew to allow for a coat pile. No matter what solution works best, leave the heat on high enough for comfort, increase the number and training of the ushers (coat racks may need to be watched), and make inviting announcements about this.

January

TUE 9
#306 (LMC, #193–231)   green
Weekday

■ THE READINGS: The first readings assigned to weekdays in the first five weeks in Year II of Ordinary Time are taken from 1 and 2 Samuel, followed by 1 Kings. We are given a semi-continuous progression through these three books, which recount the beginning and early years of the Israelite monarchy. This period extends from before the birth of Samuel, through the kingships of Saul, David and Solomon, until the split in the kingdom shortly after the death of King Solomon. For the last two weeks of the season, we switch to the Letter of James.

The books of Samuel and Kings form a unified work of religious history that illustrates the faithfulness and unfaithfulness of Israel. The sections we read in this winter Ordinary Time concern mostly the early days and the glory days of Israel's monarchy. The establishment of the monarchy itself is regarded as a challenge to God's rule, but the Lord eventually accepts the king, who is seen to rule in God's stead. Faithfulness to the Lord thus becomes the touchstone for evaluating the reign of any king. Saul, David and Solomon, the first three kings of Israel, are shown as both faithful and sinful, with their virtue and sin affecting the lives of all in the kingdom. There is much material here for reflection on our own faithfulness and sinfulness.

The weekday gospels for this winter Ordinary Time are taken from the first nine chapters of Mark. The introduction to the lectionary notes that the weekday gospels each year "are arranged so that Mark is read first (weeks 1–9), then Matthew (weeks 10–21) and finally Luke (weeks 22–34). The first twelve chapters of Mark are read in their entirety, omitting only those two passages from the sixth chapter which are read on weekdays at other times of the year." Because they are taken first from Mark's earliest chapters, the gospels of these first days continue the manifestation themes emphasized in the Christmas season.

The first reading assigned to Monday of this week might be prefixed to today's passage because it begins the story. Today's reading recounts the conception and birth of Samuel, and the responsorial is the canticle Hannah sang when she brought him to the Temple and dedicated him to the Lord. The gospel presents Jesus teaching "in a spirit of authority," an authority that even unclean spirits acknowledged. Here, too, the previous day's pericope easily could be used with this passage, because they are continuous verses.

For the texts from the sacramentary, see "First Week in Ordinary Time."

WED 10
#307 (LMC, #193–231)   green
Weekday

1 Samuel today recounts the wonderful story of Samuel's call by God, matched perfectly by the psalm response. The gospel presents Jesus as a healer, but also notes that he is called principally to "proclaim the good news." It's a good day to reflect on our own call to serve God.

THU 11
#308 (LMC, #193–231)   green
Weekday

The readings for today present an interesting contrast. The Israelites lost the Ark of the Covenant by taking it into battle as a kind of miraculous talisman—a misplaced trust. The leper in the gospel, on the other hand, is cured through his trust in Jesus.

FRI 12
#309 (LMC, #193–231)   green
Weekday

When there is a free choice of prayer texts, presiders and planners may choose texts that reflect the penitential nature of Fridays. Readings, as always, should be from the weekday. Appropriate Masses include:

- From the Masses and Prayers for Various Needs and Occasions: #13, For Unity of Christians; #15, For Persecuted Christians; #22, For Peace and Justice; #28, For Those Who Suffer from Famine; #29, For Refugees and Exiles; #30, For Those Unjustly Deprived of Liberty; #32, For the Sick.

- From the Votive Masses: #2, Holy Cross; #5, Precious Blood; #6, Sacred Heart.

Today's first reading recalls the struggle over whether Israel should have a king; choosing a king was regarded as a rejection of God's direct rule, though eventually the king was seen as God's servant. The gospel reveals the authority of Jesus to forgive sins, an authority greater than a king's.

SAT 13
#310 (LMC, #193–231)   green
Weekday

Hilary, bishop, doctor of the church, optional memorial/white. ■ *Blessed Virgin Mary, optional memorial/white.* ■ Hilary converted from paganism through the study of the scriptures. A married man, he was elected bishop of Poitiers, France, in about 350. He spent the rest of his life combating Arianism, which denied the divinity of Christ (see the opening prayer). His vigorous defense of Christ's divinity led to his exile to Phrygia by Emperor Constantius II in 356, but he was such an effective defender of orthodoxy in the East that the Emperor decided he'd be less trouble back in Gaul. So he was returned to his see in 360. One of his greatest theological works was a treatise on the Holy Trinity.

Issued in the United States in 1987, the *Collection of Masses of the Blessed Virgin Mary* provides parishes with 12 sets of presidential prayers and prefaces from a much larger Latin edition. The fuller edition has also been published in English. The Saturdays of Ordinary Time not already devoted to another saint can serve as an introduction to the Lord's Day. As the weekly remembrance of the Lord's resurrection is prepared, she who watched by the tomb can be commemorated. The scriptures included in the collection are meant only for pilgrimages and local solemnities. Parishes dedicated to Mary without specifying her image or title may adopt one of these Mass titles for use at solemn local gatherings.

Today's first reading introduces Israel's first king, Saul, called by God to lead Israel. The gospel reading recounts the call of Levi the tax collector and makes clear that the mission of Jesus is to call sinners to repentance and salvation.

⊕**14** #65 (LMC, #59)   green
Second Sunday in Ordinary Time

■ MARTIN LUTHER KING JR.: This weekend, the United States observes his birthday. Prepare well ahead of time by ordering the packet of materials for bulletin inserts and ecumenical prayer services (available also in Spanish and Vietnamese) distributed by the National Catholic Conference for Interracial Justice (NCCIJ), 1200 Varnum Street NE, Washington DC 20017; 202-529-6480. The prayer marking Martin Luther King Jr. Day found in

Catholic Household Blessings and Prayers (page 195) might be used to conclude the general intercessions. LTP offers two resources for commemorating Dr. King: *Evening Prayer Commemorating the Birthday of Dr. Martin Luther King Jr.,* a special edition of LTP's periodical on black Catholic liturgy, *Plenty Good Room;* and *Amazing Days: Martin Luther King Birthday,* a handout with quotations, prayers and commentaries that can be used as a bulletin insert.

The readings today speak clearly of the call to servanthood: for Isaiah, for the psalmist, for Paul, for the Baptist and for Jesus. This could easily lead to reflection on the ministry of Martin Luther King Jr. and God's call to us today.

15 #311 (LMC, #193–231)   green
M O N   **Weekday**

■ MARTIN LUTHER KING JR.: Today is an excellent day for using prayers from the Masses and Prayers for Various Occasions: #21, For the Progress of Peoples; #22, For Peace and Justice; or from appendix X in the sacramentary, #6 (Independence Day and Other Civic Observances). The second Eucharistic Prayer for Masses of Reconciliation is especially appropriate today, too. The readings should be taken from the weekday; the first reading shows Samuel chastising the king for disobeying the Lord (much as Dr. King did), and the gospel addresses the question of fasting and the newness of the kingdom, which can prompt us to ask how open we are to new ways of thinking and acting toward other races.

16 #312 (LMC, #193–231)   green
T U E   **Weekday**

The readings of the day recount the anointing of David as king of Israel and Jesus' insistence that he is Lord even of the Sabbath.

David was chosen to become Israel's king, even though as the youngest he was thought least likely to be a leader. God often chooses the weak of the world to do great things. The gospel reminds us that all human institutions, even the church, must be subject to the will of Christ.

17 #313 (LMC, #193–231)   white
W E D   **Anthony, abbot**
MEMORIAL

Anthony was born in Egypt in 251 and died in 356. St. Athanasius wrote about Anthony's life soon after his death, presenting a model of a life consecrated to God. At age 20, Anthony gave away his rich inheritance and became a hermit, living an austere life of prayer for the next 85 years. At age 54, he responded to many requests and organized a monastery of scattered cells; he is thus known as the Father of Monasticism. In the twelfth century, the Hospital Brothers of St. Anthony were famous for their works of charity and also for raising swine; this led to their patron becoming the patron of domestic animals in the late Middle Ages. Chapter 25 in the *Book of Blessings* has an order for blessing animals, which might be used in homes today to bless pets.

Today's gospel reminds us that our religious traditions can get in the way of God's will, while the story of David and Goliath shows us how those who serve the Lord can overcome great obstacles.

18 #314 (LMC, #193–231)   green
T H U   **Weekday**

■ THE WEEK OF PRAYER FOR CHRISTIAN UNITY is observed throughout the world from January 18 to 25. Intercessions every day should include prayer for unity. If any gathering in Unity Week includes children from the school or religious education program, see page 77 of LTP's *Leader's Manual of the Hymnal for Catholic Students* for prayer service ideas. The Mass for Christian Unity prayers (#13 in the Various Needs section) could be used.

The first reading recalls Saul's unfair resentment of David and Jonathan's role as reconciler between the two; the gospel shows Jesus mobbed by a great crowd seeking healing. May the Spirit raise up those today who can reconcile the churches and heal our divisions.

F R I 19 #315 (LMC, #193–231)   green
Weekday

The first reading today shows Saul again seeking David's death, while David refuses to seek vengeance. The gospel recounts the choice of the Twelve. Both could be related to the quest for unity: Ecumenism requires the tolerance and forgiveness David showed, and the church built on the Twelve should be one church.

S A T 20 #316 (LMC, #193–231)   green
Weekday

Fabian, pope, martyr, optional memorial/red. Sebastian, martyr, optional memorial/red. ▪ *Blessed Virgin Mary, optional memorial/white.* ▪ Sebastian, a soldier from Milan who was martyred in Rome, is the better-known of today's two saints because of the numerous images of his body pierced by arrows. Fabian, a layman elected pope, was martyred in the persecution of Decius in 250 and is remembered for his courage facing death, which edified the Romans.

The first reading recounts the death of Saul and Jonathan, and expresses David's grief, not only for his best friend Jonathan but also for Saul, despite Saul's continual rejection of David. The very short gospel reminds us that Jesus

was also misunderstood, even by his family.

During this Week of Prayer for Christian Unity, see Mass #25, "Image and Mother of the Church" in the *Collection of Masses of the Blessed Virgin Mary*. It is also printed in the sacramentary, at appendix X.4 (note the error in line 6 of the prayer after communion; it should read, "*to* all nations").

21 #68 (LMC, #62)   green
Third Sunday in Ordinary Time

Today's prophecy from Isaiah is interpreted as having been fulfilled by the coming of Jesus. Both the psalm and Paul's words to the Corinthians remind us to put our trust in the Lord. Jesus' call to reform and Paul's words about factions give an easy basis for preaching about the importance of seeking reunion among Christians. Remember to include prayer for Christian unity in the intercessions.

■ BLESSING LITURGICAL MINISTERS: Each parish must find an appropriate time to prepare new ministers for the liturgy, to provide opportunities of renewal for current ministers and to bless or commission new and old ministers. A regular schedule for such training and blessing might follow one of these patterns:

▪ Preparation in the fall with blessings in early Advent, although this tends to burden an already full time of year.

▪ Preparation in the fall with blessings on one of these wintertime Sundays.

▪ Preparation during the Easter season with blessings on Pentecost. This model has caught on in many areas and has much to recommend it; however, care must be taken not to transform Pentecost into a day that focuses just on the liturgical ministers.

▪ Preparation through the summer, with blessings in September, perhaps along with the religious education ministers. This may focus too much on a school-year model of ecclesial life.

Each model has its adherents, and local traditions should be changed only with great caution; yet Sundays in late January and early February seem to provide the most suitable time for this blessing. For 1996, Matthew's account of the call of the first disciples suggests this Sunday as a possibility.

The *Book of Blessings,* in chapters 61 and 62, provides orders for blessing readers, servers, sacristans, musicians and ushers. The term "commissioning" is used only in chapter 63, "Order for Commissioning Extraordinary Ministers of Holy Communion." Planners who wish to bless all the liturgical ministers at the same liturgy can add sections from chapters 61 and 63 of the *Book of Blessings* into the more inclusive chapter 62.

■ THE WEEK AHEAD: The readings for the Conversion of Paul on Thursday will come from the sanctoral lectionary, as will Friday's first reading. The "lost" seasonal passages on Thursday do not need to be added to other days, but Friday's passage from 2 Samuel should be prefixed to Saturday's since it explains Nathan's parable.

Today is the first day of Ramadan for our Muslim neighbors, a month of complete fasting from sunrise to sunset each day. In the Islamic calendar, this is the year 1415 AH (after the Hegira, Muhammad's migration from Mecca to Medina).

MON 22 — Weekday
#317 (LMC, #193–231)
green

Vincent, deacon, martyr, optional memorial / red. ▪ Vincent, a deacon at Saragossa, Spain, was imprisoned and tortured with his bishop in 303; after bishop Valerius was exiled, Vincent endured more torture, from which he died. This is an important feast in many areas of the world, especially in French wine and champagne regions. Some say that his name at one time in history was confused with the word for vine. Others say that vine-tenders favor deacons, the ministers who pour the wine at Mass.

▪ PRO-LIFE: This anniversary of the Roe *v.* Wade Supreme Court decision needs some recognition, but it should not take over the Mass. Whenever a group uses the eucharist as a way to get their point across, liturgy suffers. Let the readings of the day subtly but powerfully shape our response to all issues of justice. In the first reading, David begins his reign over all the tribes of Israel, and in the gospel, Jesus insists that a divided kingdom cannot stand. Both offer an opportunity to preach about life issues in a country divided about abortion, euthanasia and other life questions. Both readings also remind us to continue to pray for unity among Christians.

TUE 23 — Weekday
#318 (LMC, #193–231)
green

In today's first reading, the Ark of the Covenant is brought to Jerusalem amid great festivity. The presence of the ark, symbolizing God's presence, helped to unify the nation. Jesus insists that those who do God's will are his family, a good point to remember in our search for unity in the Christian family.

WED 24 — Francis de Sales, bishop, religious founder, doctor of the church
#319 (LMC, #193–231)
green
MEMORIAL

Francis was bishop of Geneva around the time of John Calvin. Known for his compassion and for his writings on the spiritual life, he also labored diligently for the restoration of Catholicism, always being gentle and sensitive even to his opponents. He thus serves as a good model for our quest for unity. His axiom was, "A spoonful of honey attracts more flies than a barrelful of vinegar."

The Lord's promise to sustain David's house in the first reading invites the kind of trust in God that Francis had, and the gospel parable of the sower and seed can also be related to the preaching and writing of Francis de Sales.

THU 25 — The Conversion of Paul, apostle
#519 (LMC, #247) white
FEAST

This feast marks the conclusion of the week of prayer for unity. Several saints have a secondary feast to commemorate the transfer or "translation" of the saint's remains from one place to another. This feast began as such a remembrance, but because the Latin *translatio* also can mean "conversion," it came to be a celebration of that famous moment on the road to Damascus.

The first reading (either option) tells the story and the gospel gives the goal of Paul's conversion. Pray today for Christian unity and for all those on conversion journeys, especially catechumens.

FRI 26 — Timothy and Titus, bishops
#520 and #321
(LMC, #193–231)   white
MEMORIAL

Both disciples and assistants of Paul, Timothy was bishop of Ephesus and Titus of Crete. Portions of the letters addressed to each of them are the options for the first reading (#520). The gospel parables of the kingdom (#321) are appropriate for these early bishops and sowers of the word. The prayers should be from the saints. Petitions might include the Christians of Ephesus and Crete, as well as all who serve as bishops today.

SAT 27 — Weekday
#322 (LMC, #193–231)
green

Angela Merici, virgin, religious founder, educator, optional memorial / white. ▪ *Blessed Virgin Mary, optional memorial / white.* ▪ In the sixteenth century, Angela Merici founded the first teaching order of women in the church, the Company of St. Ursula, dedicated to the religious education of poor girls. The order was started as a "secular institute" and only after her death did it become an order of nuns. Angela was convinced that "disorder in society is a result of disorder in the family" and sought to improve social conditions by educating future wives and mothers.

Today's first reading is a powerful story of God's response to David's sin (described in yesterday's pericope, which could be combined with today's). Nathan's words to David, "You are the man!" can apply to all of us in various ways. The obedience of the wind and sea in the gospel story provides a sharp contrast to human disobedience.

☀28 #71 (LMC, #65) green
Fourth Sunday in Ordinary Time

Today's gospel of the beatitudes begins the Sermon on the Mount, which we will hear from the next four Sundays as well. Zephaniah's promise of the humble remnant sets the stage for Christ's call to poverty of spirit. Paul's words to the Corinthians also call us to humility.

■ CATHOLIC SCHOOLS WEEK: This week, which includes the memorial of St. John Bosco, is usually designated Catholic Schools week. The National Catholic Education Association provides preaching and worship suggestions for this Sunday and next, as well as a prayer service for January 31. Care should be taken to respect the integrity of the Sunday itself if either Sunday (certainly not both!) is chosen as a day to celebrate the role of the school in the local community. See the comments on the primacy of Sunday on page 68 in this *Sourcebook*.

■ THE WEEK AHEAD: The feast on Friday will replace the weekday readings that day. The readings assigned to that day may be omitted without violence to the progression, but the gospel might be combined with Saturday's in order not to skip the story of the Baptist's beheading.

29 #323 (LMC, #193–231) green
Weekday
M O N

The first reading today occurs during a revolt led by David's son Absolom. David's response to being cursed might make us question how open we are to God's word when it doesn't affirm or please us. The gospel raises a similar issue

as the Gerasenes beg Jesus to leave their district.

30 #324 (LMC, #193–231) green
Weekday
T U E

The readings recount two deaths and the reactions of the parents: David grieves over the death of his rebellious son, Absolom, and Jairus trusts in the power of Jesus to raise his daughter from death. Remember to pray for parents who have lost children in death.

31 #325 (LMC, #193–231) white
John Bosco, presbyter, religious founder, educator
W E D
MEMORIAL

This nineteenth-century Italian priest cared for and educated orphan boys, eventually founding the Society of St. Francis de Sales, dedicated to the education of boys, and the Daughters of Our Lady, Help of Christians to educate girls. He died on this date in 1888 and was canonized in 1934. This is a good day to celebrate Catholic Schools Week with students and families.

The first reading views David's census as sinful, perhaps because he was relying on the power of his army (the census was a military survey) instead of trusting in God. The neighbors of Jesus also evidence a lack of faith, limiting his ability to work wonders there.

February

1 #326 (LMC, #193–231) green
Weekday
T H U

Black History Month begins today. Communities wishing to mark this in the liturgy may do so in the intercessions and homilies. This observance, like so many others, expresses genuine human dreams and sentiments, but the

timing is difficult to mesh with the liturgy. The saints especially revered in black Catholic communities (for example, Peter Claver on September 9 or Martin de Porres on November 3) would be good days for parishes to reflect on the histories of black Americans.

The first reading recalls the death of David and the accession of Solomon to the throne. David's final words are a wonderful example of a final testament or witness to faith. The gospel speaks of the rejection that often accompanies the preaching of God's word.

2 #524 (LMC, #252) white
The Presentation of the Lord
F R I
FEAST

■ FROM THE MANGER TO JERUSALEM: This feast stands both logically and in the calendar between the nativity and the death and resurrection of the Lord. The baby of Bethlehem is presented in Jerusalem, the place where the paschal mystery will be fulfilled. Thus we are led toward the core of salvation history as we celebrate some of the most beautiful rites of the year.

■ HISTORY: This feast celebrates Christ as the light of nations and the meetings with Simeon and Anna. It is an echo of both Christmas and Epiphany, celebrating again Christ's manifestation. At one time, it was the end of the Christmas season. In Jerusalem, the festival was reported at least as early as the year 386 to be on February 14, the fortieth day after Epiphany. A little later, the commemoration of this event began to be observed in Rome on February 2, the fortieth day after Christmas. A procession with lights was included at an early date, giving rise to the name "Candlemas" or "Light Mass."

■ GROUNDHOG DAY: Today residents in the northeast watch Punxsutawney Phil stick his head up from his burrow 90 miles from Pittsburgh. Local residents say that their custom goes back to the German *Lichtmesse* ("Light Mass") tales, which held that if an animal casts a shadow on February 2, there will be six more weeks of winter. In the Midwest, folks turn to a wild groundhog in Sun Prairie, Wisconsin. This folklore reminds us of the power that light and darkness hold over us. Today marks a turning point from winter to spring, from Christmas to Easter.

■ SUMMON THE ASSEMBLY: To celebrate the rites with candles most effectively, an evening Mass should be considered. Meetings scheduled tonight might be delayed or abbreviated and religious education groups and parish societies might be encouraged to place this evening on their winter schedule—whatever will let this feast shine in the lives of the community. If the parish has a school, see LTP's *Leader's Manual of the Hymnal for Catholic Students* (page 78) for curricular and liturgical ideas. Whatever Masses are celebrated today should include the opening blessing and should be celebrated as fully as possible.

■ HYMNODY: Consider the hymns from the *Liturgy of the Hours* that are specific to this feast; also fitting are "I want to walk as a child of the light" (*Worship* and *Hymnal for Catholic Students*) and "How brightly beams the morning star," which celebrates Christ as "sudden radiance" and "Lord and master," echoing the sacramentary texts for this day.

■ BLESSING OF CANDLES AND PROCESSION: The ritual action is described in the sacramentary and more fully in the *Ceremonial of Bishops:*

* All gather (each with an unlit candle—not a taper) in some place outside the hall of the eucharistic celebration. Ushers can assist the assembly as the ministers, vested for Mass, go there for the opening.

  If weather or lack of space prevents the gathering in a separate place, use the "solemn procession" option in the sacramentary and find a way to fill your worship place with candlelight. The procession should be an action of the whole assembly—not just a few people moving from the ambo to the altar.

* The candles are lit, and a song is sung.

* The sign of the cross and the greeting follow.

* The deacon or presider speaks or chants the invitation, using the text in the sacramentary.

* The blessing over the candles is prayed.

* The candles are sprinkled with water in silence.

* Incense is placed in the censer.

* The deacon or presider announces the procession, as in the sacramentary.

* The procession moves to the site of the eucharist, with all bearing lit candles and singing. A simple chant setting by Richard Proulx of the sacramentary texts for the "Blessing of Candles and Procession" is found in *Worship*. Other possibilities include singing one of the hymns suggested above as the candles are lit or having a solo instrument play (and perhaps improvise around) the melody which will be sung in procession. Although the rite suggests a processional canticle or hymn and an entrance hymn for the Mass, two different pieces of music followed by a sung Gloria makes this rite unwieldy. The Canticle of Simeon (*Nunc dimittis*) can be sung for the procession. A metrical setting is given in *Worship*. The translation "Lord, bid your servant go in peace" is set to the lovely hymn tune MORNING SONG, #691. An alternative is to sing a setting of the Gloria for the procession. Look at the Taizé setting, "Gloria III Canon with the Glory to God verses" (GIA, G-3262), which uses the refrain given in *Worship,* #401.

* The presider venerates (and incenses) the altar while the hymn continues.

* The Gloria is sung, unless it was used during the procession.

* The opening prayer is said.

■ THE MASS: For inspiration, homilists may study the homily found in the Office of Readings. The candles may be lit again as the assembly stands for the eucharistic prayer. See the sample inserts for the eucharistic prayer on page 85.

SAT **3** #328 (LMC, #193–231)   green
Weekday

Blase, bishop, martyr, optional memorial / red. ▪ *Ansgar, bishop, religious, missionary, optional memorial / white.* ▪ *Blessed Virgin Mary, optional memorial / white.* ▪ Many parishes use the optional memorial of St. Blase, bishop of Sebaste (Armenia) and martyr of the fourth century. The "Order for the Blessing of Throats on the Feast of St. Blase" (*Book of Blessings,* chapter 51) is proper to this memorial. The blessing may be presided over by a priest or deacon, or by a layperson, male or female. The blessing can be celebrated during Mass, at its own liturgy of the word, or as part of Morning or Evening Prayer (before the gospel canticle). There is no provision mentioned for celebrating this blessing on any other day. The texts for the blessing make clear that it is intended to be part of the celebration of the feast of Saint Blase. "Pastoral reasons" do not warrant offering the blessing at Sunday Mass this weekend; the pastoral response is to urge people to celebrate the memorial with devotion, within which the blessing finds its proper place as prayer rather than quasi-magical protection.

If there is a local Scandinavian heritage, the memorial of Ansgar, the great missionary to Denmark and Sweden in the ninth century, might be selected instead of Blase.

The first reading with Solomon's prayer for wisdom might be linked to Blase's wisdom in preferring even death to denying his faith; the gospel's emphasis on Jesus' concern for the flock might be linked to the church's care for people today, expressed in many ways, including blessings.

⊛**4** #74 (LMC, #68) green
**Fifth Sunday
in Ordinary Time**

Today's readings are a clear call to discipleship, to letting our light shine before all (gospel) by our service to those in need (Isaiah) and by our preaching the Good News (Paul). This would be another good day for blessing parish ministers, who help the light of Christ shine brightly in our midst.

▪ THE WEEK AHEAD: Tuesday's memorial has special readings at #528. If these are used, the assigned weekday gospel might be prefixed to Wednesday's selec-

tion, since it is part of the same discourse.

M
O**5** #329 (LMC, #193–231) red
Agatha, virgin, martyr
N MEMORIAL

Agatha was martyred in Sicily in 251 after much torture, including cutting off her breasts. The proper and common prayers of the saint should be used. The first reading's evident reverence for the ark of the covenant might be linked to the reverence Jesus showed toward the sick. In the new covenant, we believe God dwells not in the ark but in each person. Agatha's tortures might lead us to pray for all those temples of God who suffer the indignity of torture in our own day. Agatha is also the patron of nurses, whose ministry might also be the focus of intercession.

J. Frank Henderson, a prominent liturgist and cancer-research scientist in Canada, has frequently suggested (page 35 in *Canadian Studies in Liturgy: No. 1, Holy Days: Opportunities and Challenges*, 1985) that Agatha could assume a vital role as patron of women with breast cancer. Today the concerns of these women can also be part of the intercessions. This would also be an appropriate day for the communal anointing of the sick (whatever their disease) or a blessing of the sick (*Book of Blessings*, chapter 2, an order which can also be led by either an ordained or a lay minister). The latter blessing might be scheduled this day for any support group of women or cancer patients in the parish.

T
U**6** #330 (LMC, #193–231) green
Weekday
E

Paul Miki, religious, missionary, martyr, and his companions, martyrs. ▪ Twenty-six Japanese and European Jesuits, Franciscans and laymen were martyred at Nagasaki on February 5, 1597. They

were martyred as a result of a Spanish captain's boast that the missionaries were preparing the way for the conquest of Japan by Spain. An excerpt from the account of their martyrdom is found in the Office of Readings. On his cross, Paul Miki, a Jesuit brother and eloquent preacher, prayed: "I hope my blood will fall on my fellow men as fruitful rain." Others would be martyred at Nagasaki during the next century (see Lawrence Ruiz and companions on September 28).

Solomon's prayer asks God to always watch over God's people and hear their prayers. Jesus challenges the Pharisees for putting human rules ahead of God's word. Both passages could be related to those who need God's protection from persecution today and to those who violate God's laws in pursuit of their own goals.

W
E**7** #331 (LMC, #193–231) green
Weekday
D

The visit of the Queen of Sheba emphasizes Solomon's wisdom in serving God; Jesus teaches the wisdom of attending to interior motives and not just external observances.

T
H**8** #332 (LMC, #193–231) green
Weekday
U

Jerome Emiliani, presbyter, religious founder, optional memorial/ white. ▪ A sixteenth-century Venetian soldier, Jerome was captured and imprisoned, which led him to reform his life. Ordained at age 37, he devoted himself to the care of orphans and the poor. If the community wishes to celebrate Jerome's memorial, the proper and common prayers of the saint evoke the spirit of his life.

Today's readings contrast the unfaithfulness of Solomon and the faith of the Syro-Phoenician woman; faith is lacking in the one chosen by God and found in the outsider.

F R I 9 #333 (LMC, #193–231)   green
Weekday

In the first reading, the prophet Ahijah dramatically expresses the split between the northern kingdom of Israel and the southern kingdom of Judah. In the gospel, Jesus cures the deaf man with a speech impediment.

S A T 10 #334 (LMC, #193–231)   white
Scholastica, virgin, religious founder
MEMORIAL

Scholastica was the twin sister of St. Benedict, and soon after he founded his monastery at Monte Cassino, she established a community of women nearby. This is a day to pray for all monastic men and women, especially for members of the Benedictine family and for the learning and good liturgy that marks their history and present work.

King Jeroboam uses religion to strengthen his kingdom, setting up false idols and abandoning the true God. Jesus feeds the crowds. Some reflections on the importance of good national leaders and their obligation to care for the poor and hungry might be in order today.

11 #77 (LMC, #71)   green
Sixth Sunday in Ordinary Time

Today's readings suggest reflection on the Christian approach to God's law and commandments. The wisdom of which Paul speaks leads us to go beyond mere literal observance, as the Sermon on the Mount makes clear.

M O N 12 #335 (LMC, #193–231)   green
Weekday

Today we begin the Letter of James, which will provide our first readings until Lent begins. This is known as the first of the "Catholic Epistles," a group of seven that apparently were given that title because they were accepted as canonical in "all" the churches (cf. *New Jerome Biblical Commentary,* page 771). This letter consists of a series of exhortations revolving around a concern that the faith of the recipients be expressed in action in every aspect of life.

Today's passage sums up several of the themes of the letter: joy, wisdom, faith and humility. Jesus is distressed because instead of trusting in faith, the Pharisees wanted a sign for proof.

T U E 13 #336 (LMC, #193–231)   green
Weekday

Both of today's readings caution us to resist temptation, but James also stresses the positive reality of God's gifts to us here and hereafter.

W E D 14 #337 (LMC, #193–231)   white
Cyril, religious, missionary, and Methodius, bishop, missionary
MEMORIAL

These two brothers were ninth-century missionaries, liturgical reformers and translators among the Slavic peoples. Petitions for the peoples of Eastern Europe, for liturgical reformers and translators and for missionaries are in order today. The first reading from James could be applied to Cyril, Methodius and even Valentine. Jesus' cure of the blind man in the gospel speaks symbolically about the gradual process of believers coming to see as God sees.

■ VALENTINE'S DAY: The only thing that we can say with certainty about Valentine is that someone by that name was buried on the Flaminian Way outside of Rome on February 14. He was probably a priest, martyred about the year 270. A basilica was built in his memory, and devotion to him spread. Because all we know is his burial place, we can only speculate on his connection with love. One theory is that the custom of choosing a "valentine" on this day is linked to an old belief that birds choose their mates on February 14. A more likely basis is the ancient celebration in the East on this day, 40 days after Epiphany, of the feast of the "Meeting"—what we in the West have come to call the Presentation. Perhaps the intercessions should include issues of friendship and love.

T H U 15 #338 (LMC, #193–231)   green
Weekday

The gospel account of the incident at Caesarea Philippi presents us with a fundamental issue of faith: Do we judge by God's standards or by human ones? James raises the same issue in how we react to wealth and status.

F R I 16 #339 (LMC, #193–231)   green
Weekday

Today's passage from James is the classic treatment of faith and works; our lives must reflect our faith in practice. The gospel calls us to self-denial if we truly believe.

S A T 17 #340 (LMC, #193–231)   green
Weekday

Seven Founders of the Order of Servites, religious, optional memorial/white. ▪ *Blessed Virgin Mary, optional memorial/white.* ▪ Seven men from prominent families in thirteenth-century Florence joined together in a life of prayer, sharing a devotion to the Blessed Virgin. Six were later ordained priests; Alexis, who died on this date in 1310, humbly declined. The Servites were among the mendicant orders who helped revitalize the church after the Fourth Lateran Council (1215).

James today urges control of our tongue, which can do so much evil but also can do much good. The gospel account of the Transfiguration leads to questions about resurrection, about Elijah and about the coming suffering of the Son of Man.

⚙**18** #80 (LMC, #74)   green
Seventh Sunday in Ordinary Time

Today's readings call us to love as God loves, not only our compatriots (Leviticus) but even our enemies (gospel). This kind of loving may be foolishness to the world, but it is wisdom in Christ (Corinthians).

■ LENTEN ANNOUNCEMENTS AND HANDOUTS: Masses on this last Sunday before Lent probably will include many announcements. If you are handing out many papers, booklets and Catholic Relief Service's "rice bowls," consider providing them all in one convenient bag for each household. Many parishes provide materials for Lenten prayer, penance and service. Using a written covenant, some parishes ask all members to pledge toward common Lenten disciplines, such as praying a daily mealtime grace, fasting, helping out at a community clean-up day or contributing to one or two specific charities. Any such common observances must be chosen with care, avoiding anything that would make them appear to be this year's gimmick. These covenants might be collected on Ash Wednesday or on the First Sunday of Lent.

If such materials are provided for the season of Lent, parishes should be sure to provide similar helps for Easter. LTP's *Paschal Mission* is one good example of commercially available materials that include the whole Lent – Triduum – Easter cycle.

■ PREPARING ASHES: Another custom that prepares for Lent is burning last year's palms outdoors after the recessional. Everyone might have been asked over the last few Sundays to bring old palms on this day. Sing a good hymn during the fire, such as "All creatures of our God and King" with its verse about "Thou fire, so masterful and bright."

M
O **19** #341 (LMC, #193 – 231)   green
N **Weekday**

■ PRESIDENTS' DAY: This might be a day to use prayers from Appendix X, #6 in the sacramentary (Independence Day and Other Civic Observances). Other options for the opening prayer are found under Masses and Prayers for Various Needs and Occasions, #17 – 21. The prayer found in *Catholic Household Blessings and Prayers* for this day (page 196) could be used as part of the general intercessions.

James gives good advice about jealousy and ambition today. The last sentence of the reading is a pregnant one that formed the basis for one of John Paul II's themes for the World Day of Prayer for Peace — not a bad theme for this civil holiday. The gospel story of the boy the disciples couldn't cure gives us a line that we all can make our own: "I do believe! Help my lack of trust!"

T #342 (LMC, #193 – 231)
U **20** green
E **Weekday**

It is a coincidence of the calendar that both readings fit well this day before Lent begins. James calls us

to look within for the source of dissension and violence. Jesus predicts the trials he will undergo and calls his disciples to be servants of all.

■ MARDI GRAS: "Fat Tuesday" developed as a day of feasting on the last of the winter's meat before Lent began. Celebrating it well can be a good reminder to take lenten fasting seriously. The current excesses of New Orleans are sometimes unworthy of Christians, but we can celebrate without immorality. A pancake supper or doughnut fry today is a traditional fund-raiser and a traditional part of carnival. A potluck supper on this day can help the parish begin Lent.

On or about this day, our Muslim neighbors celebrate Id al-Fitr, a day of feasting to mark the end of the 30-day fast of Ramadan.

LITURGY OF THE WORD

Concluding Prayers for the General Intercessions

SECOND SUNDAY IN ORDINARY TIME
Merciful God,
you sent your Son, the spotless Lamb,
to bear the sin of the world.

Make our lives holy,
that your church may bear witness
    to your purpose
of reconciling all things in Christ,
who lives and reigns with you in the unity
    of the Holy Spirit,
God for ever and ever.
—© ICEL

THIRD SUNDAY IN ORDINARY TIME
God of salvation,
the splendor of your glory
dispels the darkness of earth,
for in Christ we behold
the nearness of your kingdom.

Now make us quick to follow where
    he beckons,
eager to embrace the tasks of the gospel.
We ask this through our Lord Jesus Christ,
    your Son,
who lives and reigns with you in the unity
    of the Holy Spirit,
God for ever and ever.
—© ICEL

FOURTH SUNDAY IN ORDINARY TIME
O God,
teach us the hidden wisdom of the gospel,
so that we may hunger and thirst
    for holiness,
work tirelessly for peace,
and be counted among those
who seek first the blessedness
    of your kingdom.

We ask this through our Lord Jesus Christ,
    your Son,
who lives and reigns with you in the unity
    of the Holy Spirit,
God for ever and ever.
—© ICEL

FIFTH SUNDAY IN ORDINARY TIME
Heavenly Father,
you have called your Church
to be the salt of the earth and the light
    of the world.

Give us vigorous faith and a love that
    is genuine,
so that all may see our works
and give you the glory.

We make our prayer through our Lord
    Jesus Christ, your Son,
who lives and reigns with you in the unity
    of the Holy Spirit,
God for ever and ever.
—© ICEL

SIXTH SUNDAY IN ORDINARY TIME
All-seeing God,
you alone judge rightly our inmost
    thoughts.

Teach us to observe your law from the heart
even as we keep it outwardly.
Purify our desires,
calm every anger,
and reconcile us to one another.
Then will our worship at your altar
render you perfect praise.

We make our prayer through our Lord
    Jesus Christ, your Son,
who lives and reigns with you in the unity
    of the Holy Spirit,
God for ever and ever.
—© ICEL

SEVENTH SUNDAY IN ORDINARY TIME
Heavenly Father,
in Christ Jesus
you challenge us to renounce violence
and to forsake revenge.

Teach us to recognize as your children
even our enemies and persecutors
and to love them without measure
    or discrimination.

We ask this through our Lord Jesus Christ,
    your Son,
who lives and reigns with you in the unity
    of the Holy Spirit,
God for ever and ever.
—© *ICEL*

LITURGY OF THE EUCHARIST

Eucharistic Prayer Inserts

SUNDAYS IN EUCHARISTIC PRAYER II:
>*Lord, you are holy indeed,*
>*the fountain of all holiness.*
>We gather here before you
>and in communion with
>   the whole church
>on this first day of the week,
>we celebrate the day
>Christ rose from the dead.
>Through him, whom you raised to your
>   right hand,
>we pray:
>*Let your Spirit come upon . . .*

SUNDAYS IN EUCHARISTIC PRAYER III:
>*. . . a perfect offering may be made*
>*to the glory of your name.*
>This is why we gather here before you,
>and in communion with the whole
>   church
>on this first day of the week
>we celebrate the day
>Christ rose from the dead.
>Through him, whom you raised to your
>   right hand,
>*we bring you these gifts.*
>*We ask you to make them holy . . .*

PRESENTATION OF THE LORD IN EUCHARISTIC
PRAYER II:
>*Lord, you are holy indeed,*
>*the fountain of all holiness.*
>We gather here before you,
>and in communion with the whole
>   church
>we celebrate the day
>the Virgin Mary presented in the temple
>her newborn child,
>your only Son, our Lord.
>Through him, light born from your light,
>we pray:
>*Let your Spirit come upon . . .*

PRESENTATION OF THE LORD IN EUCHARISTIC
PRAYER III:
>*. . . a perfect offering may be made*
>*to the glory of your name.*
>This is why we gather before you,
>and in communion with the whole
>   church
>we celebrate the day
>the Virgin Mary presented in the temple
>her newborn child,
>your only Son, our Lord.
>Through him, light born from your light,
>*we bring you these gifts.*
>*We ask you to make them holy . . .*

LENT

Introduction to the Season

It is early morning. I am walking a sand bed that once was the bottom of a great inland sea. I stop and listen to the seagulls and surf far above me, and I understand that dimension of prayer which is a thirst and a pleading for water. Flash floods visit this desert flat from time to time like those moments of inspiration, those visitations of the spirit that vanish as suddenly as they come, leaving the ground dry again thirsting for the sea that once was everywhere.

The desert, like the sea, is a leveler of differences between [people]. The elements are all larger than you are and you strain across vast empty spaces to other human beings, all of you brothers [and sisters] in the elemental predicament of place. (Murray Bodo, *Walk in Beauty: Meditations from the Desert*)

THE Lent – Triduum – Easter cycle can be imaged as a journey from the water, into the desert and back to the water. Immediately after his baptism, Matthew says, Jesus went into the desert wilderness, led by the Spirit. For forty days he was alone there, fasting, praying and confronting temptation. It is in conscious imitation of their master that Christians go into the desert, too, keeping a fast of forty days.

Like Jesus, most of us enter the desert of Lent after baptism. But the memory of that encounter with the water of life sustains us in the dryness of the wilderness. And we go forward in the company of the catechumens who thirst for that living water as they prepare for the Easter sacraments. We go into the desert with them to renew our own thirst, to intensify our own longing for the living water that only God can give us.

Thirst is used in the psalms as an image of human desire for the divine.

As a deer longs for flowing streams,
so my soul longs for you, O God.
My soul thirsts for God, for the living God
(Psalm 42:1 – 2)

O God, you are my God, I seek you,
my flesh thirsts for you;
my flesh faints for you,
as in a dry and weary land
where there is no water. (Psalm 63:1)

I stretch out my hands to you,
my soul thirsts for you like a parched land.
(Psalm 143:6)

If we do not thirst, or if we do not recognize our thirst, we will not be drawn to the water that sustains our life. The purpose of Lent, then, is to awaken our thirst again, to help us recognize not only that we are thirsty but also what it is for which we thirst. For we spend much of our lives striving after a variety of experiences and possessions that we think will satisfy us. We keep ingesting all sorts of things that do not satisfy our real thirst and leave us with the taste of ashes in our mouths.

Lent begins with ashes on our brows, reminding us of fundamental truths about ourselves. The dust of the ashes reminds us that death is inevitable for each of us. The ashes speak of repentance and of our need to convert our lives. The words at the imposition of ashes call us to reform and to believe in the Good News. The ashes speak of a fire that has grown cold, a fire that needs to be rekindled within us by the time we gather around the new fire at the Vigil. Like a phoenix rising from the ashes, we seek to rise from our sinfulness to a fuller life with Christ.

But before we can embrace the new life of the resurrection, we must embrace the cross. Before coming to the font, we must travel the desert. To embrace new life, we must be willing to embrace death. To become our true selves, we must slay the false selves behind which we have been hiding.

Though it sounds negative, the dying to self to which we are called is the only way to fullness of life, and thus it is a profoundly positive step in our spiritual life. When we live our lives on false principles, when we try to have life without embracing death, when we refuse to face ourselves with desert honesty, we gradually become more dead than alive. Like Lot's wife turning into a pillar of salt, our hearts turn into stone. Shaking off the powers of death is not easy, but it is essential if we are to be fully alive with the joy of the resurrection.

We make our Lenten journey through the desert in the company of the catechumens and candidates preparing for the initiation sacraments at Easter. This is the origin of Lent (see "History of Lent" in this section), and it is not only the origin but the core meaning of the season. The whole church seeks to accompany the catechumens not only to offer them support but to share in their conversion journey. All members of the church seek to renew their own commitment and deepen their own conversion by sharing the journey of those on the way to the font for the first time.

We perhaps have not paid sufficient attention to the full implications of this shared journey. It is important to remember that the readings and prayers of the Lenten season, especially for the Sundays and even more especially in the current cycle (Year A), have been chosen to speak to the catechumens quite directly about the journey they are experiencing. Since we all hear the same texts, they are also intended to call us back to sharing that same journey. All members of the church are expected to be walking in the footsteps of the catechumens, to be sharing their struggles and their growth toward fuller identity with Christ.

It might help us to understand this season, then, if we looked carefully at the readings and prayers of the season from the vantage point of the catechumens. What do these texts have to say about their experience on the way to the font? How do these texts foster the conversion that they are seeking? How do they affirm and how do they challenge various aspects of their lives? With whom would they identify in the scripture stories and why? Answers to these kinds of questions can reveal the spiritual power of these Lenten texts to touch and change lives, not only those of the catechumens but of all who journey with them.

It must be admitted that the way these readings and prayers will touch the catechumens will vary from person to person and from year to year. Yet there are some basics that undoubtedly will recur often, and these have led the church to use these texts repeatedly for this intensive spiritual phase of the catechumenal journey. Pamela Jackson provides a number of examples of reflections on the readings for the catechumenate rituals, including four of the Sundays of Lent, in her wonderful little book, *Journeybread for the Shadowlands* (see "Resources"). The same approach can give us insights into all the readings and texts of the season.

We are to journey through Lent, then, as though we were all catechumens. We are to listen to the readings and pray the prayers as though we were approaching the waters of life for the first time. We seek to understand and thus to enter into the experience of the elect, those called to enter into the paschal mystery of Christ Jesus through the waters of the font. Thus we all prepare to come to the water again, to be more deeply converted to Christ and to renew our baptismal promises with conviction.

This is in accord with fundamental principles of anthropology and sociology, which remind us that the way any community initiates new members both reflects and shapes the community's identity. Thus, sharing in the initiation of new members provides an opportunity for the whole community to reaffirm their identity and their purpose or mission. This is certainly the intent of the re-establishment of the catechumenate as the premier mode of initiation for the church today. It makes both the process and the rituals of initiation communal once again, so that the whole community will be formed by continual recourse to this primal stage of Christian life.

So those who prepare the celebrations of Lent (and of Triduum and Easter as well) should envision these liturgies from the vantage point of the catechumens. For example, how would catechumens relate to the story of Jesus' temptations on the First Sunday of Lent? What are the similarities between the struggles Jesus experienced and the struggles of people in our own time? How might the other readings of that Sunday touch the catechumens? On the Second Sunday of Lent, how would catechumens hear Abram's call to go forth to an unknown land, and how does that same call apply to the whole assembly? What does the story of the Transfiguration say about the transforming power of God's grace for catechumens and for us all?

On the Third Sunday, how can the catechumens quench their thirst? Where do they find living water and how much does the whole assembly long for the water of life? On the Fourth Sunday, what blindness affects the catechumens, and how can their eyes be opened to see as God sees? How much blindness exists throughout our community of faith that still needs healing? Such questions can help planners shape prayers, music and ritual decisions in a way that will invite the whole assembly into the conversion journey.

Understanding the close connection between the conversion experience of the catechumens and the ongoing conversion of the whole assembly should make it obvious that liturgy planners need to be in close communication with those who are guiding the catechumenate. How catechumens hear these readings and prayers need not be answered only in theory. Let the catechumens share their struggles, and let planners listen carefully to how these texts speak to those who are seeking the Lord. This can then become the basis for preparing the liturgy in a way that might speak to all members of the assembly.

Planning Lent, of course, is only part of a larger planning effort to deal with the Lent–Triduum–Easter cycle as a whole. The cycle does not end at the Vigil but continues until Pentecost, which reminds us that the purpose of our initiation and annual renewal is mission. Our liturgy becomes unhealthy if the church turns in on itself; the point of efforts to renew ourselves and celebrate well must be found beyond the church walls and beyond the membership. We are called to mission, and Lent–Easter is a time to renew ourselves for that mission. Though we deal with Lent in this *Sourcebook* separately from Triduum and Easter, planners are urged to read all three sections before beginning Lenten planning. In order to properly plan any part of this cycle, it is necessary to have an overall sense of the whole 90 days (actually, it's 96 days) and the issues that need to be addressed in the local community.

History of Lent

WHAT we have come to call Lent developed in the fourth century, when three intersecting movements coalesced. The first was a paschal fast that gradually developed from two days into a forty-day observance. The second was the pattern of initiation that gradually developed into a full catechumenate with an intense period of spiritual formation leading to the sacraments at Easter. The third was the order of penitents, which sought a second conversion for those who sinned seriously after baptism. Modeled on the catechumenate, this process culminated with reconciliation just before Easter.

Thus the forty-day fast was understood as the final stage of preparation for those called to baptism and also as a time for reconversion for the already baptized. As the whole community accompanied the elect and the penitents through this season, it came to be seen as a time for baptismal renewal for all the members of the church.

In subsequent centuries, however, both the catechumenate and the order of penitents gradually disintegrated. Lent was still seen as a penitential season, but the emphasis was on individual works of self-denial and on personal identification with the passion and cross of Christ. Lent was still a prepartion for Easter, but the baptismal focus was largely lost, and the communal nature of conversion was ignored. Prayer, fasting and almsgiving were held up as Lenten activities, but they became private rather than corporate.

The *Constitution on the Sacred Liturgy* of the Second Vatican Council called for a recovery of the ancient tradition:

Lent is marked by two themes, the baptismal and the penitential. By recalling or preparing for baptism and by repentance, this season disposes the faithful, as they more diligently listen to the word of God and devote themselves to prayer, to celebrate the paschal mystery. The baptismal and penitential aspects of Lent are to be given greater prominence in both the liturgy and liturgical catechesis. Hence:

a. More use is to be made of the baptismal features proper to the Lenten liturgy; some of those from an earlier era are to be restored as may seem advisable.

b. The same is to apply to the penitential elements. As regards catechesis, it is important to impress on the minds of the faithful not only the social consequences of sin but also the essence of the virtue of penance, namely, detestation of sin as an offense against God; the role of the church in penitential practices is not to be neglected and the people are to be exhorted to pray for sinners.

During Lent, penance should be not only inward and individual, but also outward and social. The practice of penance should be fostered, however, in ways that are possible in our own times and in different regions and according to the circumstances of the faithful. (#109–110)

For more than thirty years now, we have been in the process of the liturgical renewal, including the renewal of Lent and the Triduum. The gradual re-establishment of the catechumenate across the country is having a salutary effect on the revitalization of these seasons. Yet there is still much to be done. Too often the catechumenate itself is largely isolated from other areas of parish life, with the result that many Catholics still have only a vague understanding of the initiation process, at best.

The effort needed to continue this renewal will be energy well spent. What is at stake is no less than the very identity of the church. Initiation establishes that identity, and the Lent–Triduum–Easter cycle is the time of year when the whole community has regular access to the initiation process. It is in this way that the church is continually recalled to her roots and to the Lord she claims to follow.

Sometimes people seem to think of the liturgical seasons as a kind of play-acting and thus view efforts to improve worship as the somewhat esoteric concern of a few who enjoy ritual and music. But it is in the liturgical life of the church community that the whole life of the church is nourished. If the community is fed pablum, it will be weak and immature. Only if it is fed with the strong nourishment of deep engagement in the mystery of Christ's own death and resurrection will it be strong enough to carry on Christ's work. And only a community committed to carrying on that mission deserves the name "church."

■ THE STRUCTURE OF LENT: Most people know that Lent is 40 days long, but they think that the 40 days are the six weeks plus the four days of the week of Ash Wednesday (which totals 46 days), minus six Sundays, which equals 40 days.

But Lent does not end on Holy Saturday; it ends on Holy Thursday evening. Lent brings us to the Triduum, not to Easter Sunday. The span from Ash Wednesday to Holy Thursday is 44 days. The "forty" are now calculated thus:

From the time of the Fathers, as the sermons of St. Leo the Great mention, the 40 days of Lent were counted from the First Sunday of Lent until Holy Thursday. The Roman Missal and Breviary have kept this practice to the present time. (Commentary on the *General Norms for the Liturgical Year and Calendar,* 1969)

Thus at least four phases of the season of Lent can be discerned:

1. Ash Wednesday and the next three days: These four days form a preview of the season. In some regions of the world early in Christian history, the fasting began on Ash Wednesday while the Forty Days began on Sunday. Over these days, the scriptures and other liturgical texts announced the major aspects of the season and called all to enter in. The first Sunday of Lent still stands as a "beginning" day with the rite of election and the penitential procession.

2. First Sunday until the Saturday of the Fourth Week: These 28 days receive much of their direction from the flow of scripture readings and from penitential rites, including penance services, the penitential rite ordinarily celebrated on the Second Sunday for candidates for reception into the full communion of the church, and the first two scrutiny rites for the elect. Only one feast, St. Joseph, breaks this penitential period in 1996, though the Fourth or "Laetare" Sunday brings its own nuances of mid-Lent joy.

3. From the Fifth Sunday on, attention becomes focused on the passion of Christ.

4. Passion Sunday to Triduum: These last days are an intensification of the third phase of Lent. They are given high liturgical precedence so that

the church will not be distracted from its final preparations for the Triduum.

■ THE SAINTS IN LENT: In our current calendar, only a few saints' days occur during Lent. In addition to the solemnities of Joseph and the Annunciation, the calendar this year includes one feast, the Chair of Peter, plus two obligatory commemorations and five optional ones. Those who prepare the liturgy should take an overall look at Lent and chart out which of these five will be observed. They should be celebrated only if they have a special relationship with the local church. When saints are commemorated in Lent, the opening prayer for the memorial may be used at that point in the liturgy or as a conclusion to the intercessions; elements of the homily and some petitions of the general intercessions also can rise from the memorial. Otherwise, the celebration remains a Lenten liturgy; the vesture is violet and all other Lenten texts are used (See *General Instruction of the Roman Missal*, #316a).

Images of the Season

IN addition to the image of the desert discussed earlier, the great scripture stories long associated with Lent provide a wealth of other images for Lenten prayer and reflection. The skein of images which follows is drawn from the long history of Lent, from the Sunday readings of Year A and from the daily readings for Lent:

Noah, flood, ark, dove, olive branch, rainbow
Abraham, stars and sand on the seashore, animals cut in half, smoking brazier and flaming torch, promised land
Samaritan woman, well, drink, spirit and truth, prophet
Man born blind, whose sin?, thrown out of synagogue
Lazarus, tomb, stench, winding cloths, untie him, go free
Roses, spring, rose vestments
Desert, Satan, stones into bread, temple parapet, kingdoms of the world, angels ministering
Elijah, raven, bread and water, 40-day hike, Mt. Horeb
Transfiguration, three booths, clothes dazzling white, Moses and Elijah, cloud, voice

Moses, burning bush, take off your shoes, holy ground, land of milk and honey, I am who am
Fig tree in vineyard, no fruit, manure, another year
Joshua, promised land, unleavened bread
New creation, ministry of reconciliation, ambassadors for Christ
Tax collectors, sinners, prodigal son, loose women, famine, pigs, fodder, embrace, kiss, robe, ring, shoes, fatted calf, music, dancing, elder brother, lost—found, dead—back to life
Rivers in the wasteland, water in the desert, something new
All as loss, rubbish, wealth of Christ, racing, prize, finish line
Woman caught in adultery, stones, sand writing, woman alone with Jesus
Ass, palms, cloaks, Hosanna, stones crying out
Well-trained tongue, back beaten, face spit on, beard plucked, face like flint
Form of a slave, human estate, death on a cross, highly exalted, name above every name, Jesus is Lord
Bread, wine, betrayer, Gethsemani, drops of blood, kiss of Judas, swords and clubs, courtyard fire, denials, cock crow, Sanhedrin, Pilate, Herod, Barabbas, cross, Simon of Cyrene, daughters of Jerusalem, Skull Place, two criminals, divided garments, dice, sour wine, darkness, sanctuary curtain, centurion, Joseph of Arimathea, linen cloth, tomb, rock
Sheep and goats, judgment, least of my brothers and sisters
Jonah, Nineveh, ship, storm, fish, shore, conversion of city
Esther, Mordecai, pogrom, Haaman
Barren bush in desert, tree beside running water
Jeremiah in the pits
James, John, mother, cup to drink, baptism to share
Rich man, Lazarus, bosom of Abraham, great gulf, finger in water, rise from dead
Joseph and his brothers, slavery, Pharaoh
Vineyard, tenants, servants, son
Wandering Arameans, Exodus, Red Sea, dry land, desert wanderings, manna, water from the rock
Naaman, Elisha, widow of Zaraphath
Unforgiving servant
Casting out by Beelzebul
Pharisee, tax collector
New heavens, new earth, new Jerusalem
Cure of royal official's son
Water flowing from the temple
Pool at Bethesda
Moses, Sinai, commandments, golden calf
Lamb to slaughter

Susanna, two men, trial, Daniel
Seraph serpents, uplifted pole
Nebuchadnezzar, Shadrach, Meshach and
   Abednego
Caiaphas, one die for many
Suffering servant
Mary, perfume, drying feet with hair, Judas

An African American Perspective

REPENTANCE and baptism are the two great realities we celebrate in Lent. The images and rhythms of many of the spirituals, along with our fasting, prayer, and good works, can lead us into a deeper experience of these realities. "I shall not be moved," "Lord, I want to be a Christian," "I want Jesus to walk with me," "Balm in Gilead," "Steal away," "Hush, hush, somebody's calling my name" and "Somebody's knocking at the door" are just seven powerful examples. But to this list I should like to add three more that bear further focus: "Standing in the need of prayer," "Scandalize' my name" and "Sinner please."

■ STANDING IN THE NEED OF PRAYER: The spirituals call *all* people to conversion and accountability. "Standing in the need of prayer" is paradigmatic in this regard.

> Not my brother nor my sister . . .
> Not the preacher nor the deacon . . .
> Not my father nor my mother . . .
> Not the stranger nor my neighbor . . .
> It's me, O Lord,
> Standin' in the need of prayer . . .
>   (*Songs of Zion*, #110)

Arthur C. Jones notes that

> Although singers understood the importance of calling others on their transgressions, they also knew the ultimate responsibility for transforming their lives rested entirely on their own shoulders. They could not depend on others to change them; they had to do it themselves. However, in such an enormous undertaking, they needed everything they could get in the way of help from the Almighty. (*Wade in the Water: The Wisdom of the Spirituals.* Maryknoll: Orbis, 1993, page 105).

With Lent's emphasis on repentance, this song seems most fitting. Surely none of us could cast the first stone.

But what of this spiritual's emphasis on "I"? Here John Lovell in his book *Black Song: The Forge and the Flame: The Story of How the Afro-American Spiritual Was Hammered Out* could be instructive:

> The theory of the spiritual poet is that, if one person can be transformed . . . why cannot the same thing work for a whole crowd or nation of people? This theory is very little different, in the poetic sense, from a doctrine of implied revolution; only the method needs working out. . . . The spiritual poet often initiates the revolution in himself. The "I" of the spiritual, however, is not a single person. It is every person who sings, every one who has been oppressed and, therefore, every slave everywhere. (New York: Paragon House edition, 1986, page 226).

Even if one were not comfortable with this notion, this spiritual still has power for our age. We live in a culture where many are tempted to blame their sinful actions solely on their alcoholism, on their early mistreatment at the hands of cruel parents or on any other of a number of psychological and social factors. These factors might indeed be such that they diminish or even nullify some sinful actions (see *Catechism of the Catholic Church*, 1735). But for the vast majority this is not the case. Many would rather forego any personal responsibility for sin. In these situations it is important for us to remember that it is not my mother's, sister's, brother's, deacon's or preacher's fault, but "me standing in the need of prayer."

■ SCANDALIZE' MY NAME: Lent is a time of reconciliation. This spiritual provides a wonderful context in which to call attention to our need for forgiveness of one another.

> Well, I met my sister (brother, preacher)
>   de other day,
> Gave her (him) my right han',
> Jes' as soon as ever my back was turned
> She (he) took 'n' scandalize' my name.
>
> Do you call dat a sister (brother, 'ligion)? No! No!
> You call dat a sister (brother, 'ligion)? No! No!
> You call dat a sister (brother, 'ligion)? No! No!
> Scandalize' my name. (*Songs of Zion*, #159)

In Christ's name we grant forgiveness to those who have caused us hurt and harm. We likewise ask for forgiveness of those whom we have offended. In writing on this powerful spiritual, Jones notes that in such a song,

> singers highlighted a truth that we as heirs of the songs have sometimes attempted to avoid: Race by itself does not determine morality. Immoral and

offensive actions, regardless of the color of the offender, are simply wrong. (Jones, 108)

One can be hurt by a member of this Christian community whether that person be "brother, sister, neighbor, preacher," black or white. We must acknowledge the "scandal" and grant forgiveness. It is one of the great realities of Lent.

■ SINNER PLEASE: During Lent we baptized people celebrate in a special way with those seeking the water of life. At several points in this journey we celebrate the scrutinies. These are times that compel the elect to deep soul searching. These are times when the baptized recall the pervasive presence of evil. As a way of framing the intercessory prayers in these rites, the assembly might sing "Sinner, please." It is a song that recalls for all, but particularly for the elect, the need for conversion. But even more, this song assures us all of God's liberating power — a God who wages war on sin and death and, in is Christ Jesus, is victorious.

> Sinner, please don't let this harvest pass . . .
>
> I know that my redeemer lives . . .
> Sinner, please don't let this harvest pass . . .
>
> Sinner, O see the cruel tree, cruel tree . . .
> Sinner, please don't let this harvest pass . . .
>
> My God is a mighty man of war . . .
> Sinner, please don't let this harvest pass . . .

The Hispanic Mística and the Liturgy

OF all the celebrations of the official liturgical year, perhaps none is so well attended by Hispanics as Ash Wednesday (*Miércoles de Ceniza*). Non-Hispanic pastoral agents are sometimes puzzled by the fact that even those who do not regularly come to church on Sunday will make a special effort to be marked with ashes on this, the beginning of the penitential season of Lent. Several reasons have been advanced that try to describe why this sacramental is so important in the Latino community, but there is little doubt that it touches on a very important part of the *mística,* or Hispanic cultural world view (see page xvii).

The Christian custom of imposing ashes originated in the early centuries of the church as a signal of the entrance of an individual into the order of public penitents. Nevertheless, some scholars have speculated that the importance attached to this observance also partially reflects values deeply held by the peoples of the Americas even before the coming of Columbus.

The spirituality of the native peoples, with its emphasis on equilibrium and harmony in humanity's relationship between the divine and the world of nature, seems to be reflected by Ash Wednesday and the penitential season of Lent. Aztec spirituality, for example, insisted that right relationship between humanity and the gods was maintained by reciprocal sacrifice. Miguel León-Portilla, a noted scholar of Nahua (Aztec) culture, describes how the duality present in their concept of *tlamacehua* — to do penance, to deserve blessing — was basic to their view of the world and was the primary reason why Aztecs engaged in ascetic and ritual practices such as personal bloodletting and even human sacrifice. Although this concept is distinct from the Christian view of penance, some scholars have speculated that this background has something to do with the power of ashes and of the other ascetic and penitential practices introduced by the Spanish missionaries and embraced by the native and mestizo peoples of the Americas.

Among many Hispanics, as with other Catholics, Ash Wednesday is also a way of proclaiming one's belonging to the church community, of being *Católico* even if not *practicante* (practicing). The reception of ashes also evokes facing the fact of death squarely in the face. The traditional phrase spoken at the imposition of ashes, "Remember that you are dust and to dust you shall return," is a sober reminder to many of the need for repentance in the context of our creatureliness and mortality. Ashes also speaks of the wholeness of all creation, the organic relationship of human beings with *la tierra* (the earth) and the fact that death is an inevitable part of life (see the discussion on *El Día de los Muertos* in November, page 220). It takes courage and self-possession to face death with faith and honesty; both these virtues are especially prized among Hispanics. The ashes, traced in the sign of the cross, dramatically mark all members of the community and speak of their radical equality before God as people with limitations and imperfections.

In many Latin American countries it is common to see a more dramatic means of marking the forehead with ashes. Rather than using dry ashes, the ashes are mixed with water, creating a kind of thick paste resembling earth. This mud-like substance is then conferred in the usual manner with the hand or by being stamped on the forehead with a wooden or rubber stamp etched with an elaborate cross. Unlike marks made with dry ashes, this sign does not easily wear off, and it is worn proudly during the day. While we may never be able to explain satisfactorily from history the great importance that *Miércoles de Ceniza* enjoys among Latinos, it is a moment when the liturgical year and the popular religious imagination come together and offer to Hispanic parishes a wonderful possibility for reaching out to many who describe themselves as *"Católico, pero no practicante"* (Catholic, but not practicing).

Preparing the Parish

IF Lent is about baptismal preparation and conversion, then obviously Lent will be best celebrated if the community is fully involved with the journey of the catechumens and candidates toward the Easter sacraments. A fully developed catechumenate is the most important way to prepare the parish for Lent. This is a time to be sure that the catechumens are known and recognized; putting their pictures and short biographies in the bulletin and/or on parish bulletin boards can help (See "Worship Environment" in this section). Individuals and groups can be invited to "adopt" a catechumen as a special focus of prayer and fasting during Lent; don't forget to involve shut-ins in this ministry, too.

Parishes and other communities who have no catechumens this year (convents and hospitals, for example) still need to celebrate the journey of catechumens. Such communities might contact neighboring parishes and obtain the names and pictures of area catechumens who could be "adopted" with prayer, fasting and letters from their neighbors.

Parishioners might be invited through the bulletin in the weeks prior to Lent to imagine themselves as approaching the waters of the font for the first time. What would they need to change in order to prepare for the Vigil? What areas of their lives still need conversion? And

what kind of penance would foster conversion, a true change of behavior on a permanent basis? Those are the best penances for Lent. Suggestions might even be offered of penances appropriate for various areas of sinfulness: fasting for those inclined to overeat or overdrink, service opportunities for those too focused on self, daily scripture reading for those who think of God only on Sundays, acts of charity toward those one finds it difficult to forgive, etc.

Parishes would do well to "fast" from baptisms during Lent so that Easter might take its proper place as the baptismal season *par excellence*. This will require advance notice to expectant families so that they know to plan for baptisms during Easter. Preparation for first eucharist should also be clearly linked to the Easter season; it is best to schedule it in that context (it's not really a Mother's Day celebration!), and preparation sessions for parents and students should make clear the link between Easter and this initiation sacrament.

Parish organizations also need to observe Lent; this is not a time for "business as usual." Every committee and organization should be encouraged to plan its gatherings and activities for the year in a way that respects the liturgical seasons. Lent might be the ideal time for a group evening of recollection, efforts at greater care for the needy, reexamination of group goals, etc. It is certainly not the time for parties, gambling fund-raisers, school dances and the like. Let Easter clearly become the season for celebration.

Taking It Home

LENT must be lived throughout all the Forty Days, at home as well as at church. Many parishes produce collections of prayers, meditations and domestic rites to complement the more public events of the season. Such local publications can link domestic prayers of penitence to the days when communal penance is celebrated and can make prayers for the elect, candidates and catechumens specific. Also, people can be encouraged to use *Catholic Household Blessings and Prayers*. It includes:

- Table prayers for days of fasting and almsgiving (page 62) and for the weekdays of Lent (page 76)

- An "Ash Wednesday Blessing of the Season and of a Place of Prayer" (page 132)

- Blessings of Lenten disciplines: fasting, almsgiving (page 137)

- Prayers for St. Joseph Day (pages 165 and 346)

- A "Passion Sunday placing of branches in the home" (page 140)

- A renunciation of sin, a profession of faith and a renewal of baptismal vows (pages 371 and 372) to prepare for the Easter Vigil

It is also important to help people link Lent with the Triduum and Easter. Prayers and devotions given to parishioners for home use should extend from the beginning of Lent until Pentecost (See LTP's *Paschal Mission* materials as a model). Suggestions might also be given for linking Lent and Easter visually at home: A cross on the table during Lent can be draped in white for Easter, a bare branch for Lent can be replaced by a sprouting branch or spring flowers for Easter, etc. Palms from last year might be brought from home to church to be burned for ashes to begin the season; then new palm can be given a prominent return on Passion Sunday with the prayers in *Catholic Household Blessings and Prayers,* which speak of the palm as a sign of Christ's victory. Money saved at home by fasting and other forms of penance can be used during the Easter season for local outreach and service projects; if families are directly involved, the connection between Lenten renewal and Easter mission will be more obvious.

LTP's *Take Me Home* resource has pages for children and families for Mardi Gras, Ash Wednesday, each week of Lent, St. Joseph, Annunciation, Palm Sunday and the Triduum.

The Mass

INTRODUCTORY RITES

THE key point to remember in preparing Lenten liturgies is desert simplicity. During this season, we strip down to the bare essentials. Decoration should be minimal. Musical instruments are used only as necessary to accompany singing—no preludes, postludes or instrumental background music. The liturgy itself is simplified by the absence of the Gloria and the

Alleluia. Planners might discuss other ways that this tone of simplicity and desert emptiness can shape the celebration. Some parishes, for example, dispense with the entrance procession during Lent or begin in silence instead of using an opening hymn.

■ GATHERING MUSIC: Since instrumental preludes are to be avoided during the Lenten season, the gathering music will rise up out of the quiet desert simplicity that marks the 40-day journey. Struck by the new emptiness of the arena for worship, the assembly's "fast" creates a hunger that is first sated by the sound that enters the mind and heart. Musicians may choose to opt for a common musical way to gather during the entire season. Perhaps a setting of the classic chant "Attende Domine," taken from the parish's hymnal or Lenten missalette, could help mark these Lenten beginnings. As the sound of this familiar chant fills the space, many worshipers will hearken back to earlier Lents, perhaps from childhood. Although the music is familiar and has been sung through the years, the hearts of the assembly have experienced conversion through decades of Lents. Once again, standing before the God of compassion and mercy, worshipers are drawn into the reality of sin and, not in any hopeless way, cry for mercy and consolation.

Other options for gathering music could be drawn from the Taizé repertoire. Consider using "Adoramus Te Domine II" (*Music from Taizé,* Volume II; GIA G-2433). Liturgy planners with a poetic gift could be enlisted to write verses for each of the Lenten Sundays. Examples of verse texts for the first week, for instance, could include: "In the desert of repentance . . . adoramus te domine"; "In a land parched dry and lifeless . . . adoramus te domine." Creative verses, particular to the third, fourth and fifth Sundays, could draw upon the rich scriptural images of water/ thirst, darkness/light and death/life. The music in each case is the same, but the varied texts could draw the assembly deeper into the Lenten desert of repentance as the season unfolds.

Another option for gathering music is Rory Cooney's "Jerusalem, my destiny" (GIA, G-3413). This music presents a strikingly different timbre than the previous examples. With its driving refrain, "I have fixed my eyes on your hills, Jerusalem, my destiny . . . " the assembly is, in a sense, forced out of complacency and pulled into the Lenten journey toward the cross, toward Jerusalem. Verses for each Lenten Sunday express the various stages of the journey. This piece is particularly appropriate for parishes journeying with the elect, with its refrain's concluding phrase, "the journey makes us one."

■ PENITENTIAL RITE: In choosing music for the penitential rite, consider using "Three Plainsong Kyries," with tropes from the sacramentary as arranged by Richard Proulx (GIA, G-3162). A choral companion edition is also available (G-3161).

One way of approaching the penitential rite is to use a sung setting of the "Lord, have mercy," with invocations recited by the deacon or presider. In this case, after all have been invited to kneel, the cantor would intone the text and then invite the assembly to repeat it. As soft instrumental music continues, the invocation is recited, then the cantor cues the assembly again. For a strikingly different arrangement, consider using Avon Gillespie's "Lord, have mercy" from "Mass No. 1 in G," found in GIA's *Lead Me, Guide Me* hymnal (#455). With its African American flavor and interesting choral arrangement, this setting captures the penitential cry characteristic of the season. Another option is "Kyrie 3" from *Music from Taizé* (Volume I, GIA, G-2433); the invocations could be chanted as the choir (or an instrument) sustains the final F-sharp major chord. The deacon, presider or cantor could sing the invocations, freely moving through the intervals within the chord structure. This type of free chanting could provide a way for a presider or deacon who is a hesitant singer to become more comfortable with his musical role.

LITURGY OF THE WORD

■ SCRIPTURES OF THE SEASON: As in every Lent, we hear accounts of Jesus in the desert and of the Transfiguration on the first two Sundays; this year we hear Matthew's versions. In this cycle the assigned readings for the next three Sundays are the ones to be used if the scrutinies are being celebrated with the elect, so there is no need this year to make decisions about which pericopes to use. This is a good opportunity to make full use of these powerful stories from John's gospel and their rich baptismal nuances. Some time spent studying commentaries on these pericopes will be helpful for both preachers and planners.

The lectionary also bids us pay attention to the first readings of Sunday:

The Old Testament readings are about the history of salvation, which is one of the themes proper to the catechesis of Lent. The series of texts for each year presents the main elements of salvation history from its beginning until the promise of the New Covenant.

The readings from the letters of the apostles have been selected to fit the gospel and the Old Testament readings and, to the extent possible, to provide a connection between them. (1981 *Introduction to the Lectionary*, #97)

■ PSALM: The seasonal psalms for Lent are Psalms 51, 91 and 130. Psalm 51 is appointed for Ash Wednesday and at least three other times in the Lenten weekday lectionary. It is also used each Friday at Morning Prayer in the Liturgy of the Hours. Settings of Psalm 51 appear in every major hymnal. If the parish has a "standard" setting of Psalm 51, which helps identify the season for the assembly, retain it. Three newer settings in contrasting styles worth investigating are:

- Psalm 51: "Be merciful, O Lord" by John Karl Kirten (GIA, G-3318)
- Psalm 51: "Be merciful, O Lord" by Steven Janco (GIA, G-3518)
- Psalm 51: "Be merciful, O Lord" by Joseph B. Smith (GIA, G-3494)

■ GOSPEL ACCLAMATION: During Lent the alleluia is excluded completely, even for solemnities or ritual Masses that happen to fall in Lent. No hymns with it. No acclamations with it. No antiphons with it. No alleluias!

The traditional substitute acclamations for the alleluia are found in many hymnals and in the lectionary's introduction (#9 in the 1969 edition, #91 in the 1981 edition). Many fine settings of the four acclamations are available in every hymnal. Choose one or two settings and use them for the entire season. Number 223 in the lectionary provides 17 verses for singing with this acclamation on weekdays. These verses capture well the spirit of the season; some of them might be used on program covers or on Lenten booklets.

■ DISMISSAL OF THE CATECHUMENS AND THE ELECT: All year long, the catechumens are to be dismissed each Sunday after the homily. In Lent, both the catechumens and those of their number who have become the elect are dismissed. Alternative forms of the dismissal are given in the *Rite of Christian Initiation of Adults* for particular moments in Lent: #116 for the First Sunday if catechumens are being sent to the cathedral; #136 to conclude the rite of election (if this is celebrated at your parish); #155, #169, #176 for each of the scrutinies.

The rite provides two texts for dismissing catechumens (RCIA, #67) that make the spirit of the dismissal clear. Other words may be used, but any dismissal should convey concern and affection. A Lenten seasonal formula is proposed here on page 115.

■ PROFESSION OF FAITH: The profession of faith is called for on Sundays, on March 19 and on March 25. The rites of initiation during Lent change the conclusion of the liturgy of the word. On the First Sunday (at either the rite of sending or the rite of election), on the Second Sunday (at the penitential rite for the candidates for reception into the church) and then on the Third, Fourth and Fifth Sundays (at the scrutinies of the elect), the dismissal of the catechumens and the elect is followed by the general intercessions and then the creed. This order is present in many of the rituals integrated into the eucharistic assembly, reflecting a more ancient ritual sequence by ending the liturgy of the word with the great profession of faith.

■ GENERAL INTERCESSIONS: The intercessions should take on a seasonal cast; for examples, see page 115. Appendix I of the sacramentary also has two sample forms for the season. All parishes, even if they have no elect in the local community, should pray for the elect throughout the diocese and the world.

On the Sundays when catechumenal rituals are celebrated, there are two different kinds of intercessions close together in the liturgy. It is helpful to keep them distinct. The intercessions for the elect might be chanted with a sung "Lord have mercy" or "Kyrie" response. In bilingual communities, perhaps the intercessions for the elect could be done in various languages, with a sung refrain following each intention. The assembly then may use a familiar format for the general intercessions after the dismissal of the catechumens and elect.

The rubrics in the RCIA say that the general intercessions and the creed can be omitted on these Sundays "for pastoral reasons." If so, then prayers for the church and the world can be added to the prayers for the elect. This option,

however, violates the meaning of the general intercessions as "prayers of the faithful." It makes sense only in parishes where the dismissal is omitted and the faithful are joined by the catechumens for the eucharist—which should be the rare exception by now, because the RCIA clearly calls for regular dismissal of catechumens.

LITURGY OF THE EUCHARIST

Excluding the preface for the Chrism Mass, there are 12 Lenten prefaces in the sacramentary (P 8 – P 19). Some are linked to the scriptures for a particular Sunday, and some are more suited for the latter part of Lent when our focus turns more and more toward the passion of Christ. Two other prefaces are used for St. Joseph on March 19 and for the Annunciation on March 25. Read through all of them and also through the two eucharistic prayers for reconciliation. Note also the inserts available here (page 117 for Eucharistic Prayers II and III on the Annunciation) and in the sacramentary (for the elect in Eucharistic Prayer I at Masses with scrutinies; for the deceased in Eucharistic Prayers II and III). Then schedule eucharistic prayers and prefaces for the season.

Eucharistic prayer acclamations should remain constant for the Lenten season, at least for Ash Wednesday and the first four Sundays. Pick a set that will help carry over the "Lenten" sound. Chant-style settings work well. Some parishes use the same eucharistic prayer acclamations for the entire 90-day Lent/Easter cycle, adding choral and instrumental embellishments during the Triduum and into the Easter season.

■ COMMUNION RITE: The third introduction to the Lord's Prayer in the sacramentary seems particularly appropriate for Lent. Another sample (as well as texts for the peace prayer, the introduction to communion and the sending forth of eucharistic ministers) can be found on page 118.

The communion procession provides an opportunity to sing the appointed psalms for the Sundays of Lent when a common psalm is used consistently during the liturgy of the word. Some of the appointed psalms may already be in your parish's repertoire. The singing style is easy for the congregation, who only have to be responsible for the refrain while the verses are sung by the cantor or choir. The psalms for Year

A (Psalms 51, 33, 95, 23 and 130) contain a wide variety of themes: repentance, trust, openness to God, protection, supplication and hope. Refrain-style settings of these psalms can be found in the *Worship* and *Gather* hymnals. Particularly useful are the settings by Marty Haugen found in *Gather*.

CONCLUDING RITE

Before the council, the prayers over the people were commonly used during Lent. Today these prayers may be used throughout the year, but several are especially appropriate for this season (See, for example, # 4, 5, 6, 7, 10, 12, 15, 16, 17, 18, 21 and 24). Appropriate three-part blessing texts include solemn blessing #5 in the sacramentary and #2047.5 ("Lent"), #1417 ("Blessing of Stations of the Cross") and #1676 ("Blessing of Ashes") in the *Book of Blessings*.

See the *Leader's Manual of the Hymnal for Catholic Students* (pages 81–92) for models of weekday liturgy with children.

MUSIC

This season of "penitential" sounds and images should provide the worshiping community with a strong reminder of God's continual mercy and forgiveness. The music should be strong yet simple; simplicity and austerity are the hallmarks of the Lenten season. In the tradition of the Roman Rite, the use of musical instruments is discouraged other than to accompany congregational song (see *Musicam Sacram,* #66). This might be the time to again consider unaccompanied singing, a time of "fasting," if you will, from the joyful sounds of musical instruments so that when they return at Easter, the "feasting" might take on a heightened and renewed sense of joy and delight. The *Ceremonial of Bishops* (#252) puts it this way: "In Lent, the altar should not be decorated with flowers, and musical instruments may be played only to give necessary support to the singing."

Conversion is at the core of the Lenten season. Therefore the function of music in the liturgy during Lent is primarily to support this conversion journey of the assembly. Perhaps nowhere else in the liturgical year is music so crucial. For the hard-hearted assembly member, music can often provide the only way "in." As is often the case, no amount of spoken words can penetrate a heart hardened by years of transgression and guilt. A simple chant or cry for mercy characteristic of the season might penetrate and begin to soften the most hardened of hearts. Musicians ought never underestimate the power of their gift. Music's language speaks like no other. Musicians could make it their aim to spend some personal time with one or all of the main characters of this season: the Samaritan woman at the well, the man born blind, or one of the siblings in the Lazarus story. When a musician is deeply in touch with the faces of these characters within him- or herself, the music reaches a level that words fail to describe.

When looking at the musical shape of the gathering rites for Lent, consider their purpose. As noted in *Music in Catholic Worship,* "the purpose of these rites is to help the assembled people become a worshiping community and to prepare them for listening to God's word and celebrating the eucharist." As a worshiping community, we join with one another and travel the road of conversion together. The gathering rites form us as a people "on the way." Disposing us to careful, attentive listening to God's word is an important function of the gathering music, particularly in this season.

The gospels of the Third, Fourth and Fifth Sundays are at the core of the season and are the basis for the scrutinies celebrated with the elect on those days. These texts are long and consideration should be given to their proclamation. David Haas and Victoria Tufano have teamed together to offer arrangements of these gospels faithful to the biblical texts (GIA, G-3662). The narrative line is kept intact but is punctuated with acclamations sung by the assembly at appropriate places in the narrative. Musicians could also search their own repertoire of well-known hymns to find a musical fragment that could also serve as an acclamation in place of those composed by Haas. For instance, the first line of John Foley's "Come to the water" ("O let all who thirst, let them come to the water.") works well for the gospel of the Third Sunday. Playing an A-flat chord in place of the prescribed F chord at the end of this line is effective. The second line of Margaret Daly's "Church of God" ("He has called you out of darkness into his marvelous light!") is an appropriate acclamation for the Fourth Sunday's gospel. Beginning this acclamation in the key of E and progressing up chromatically each time it is sung supports the movement and intensity of the gospel. Consider the refrain form Suzanne Toolan's "I am the Bread of Life" as an acclamation for the Fifth Sunday.

In each of these examples, the goal to be reached is a drawing of the assembly into the gospel story. In a sense, a musician should aim to invite, through music, each assembly member to *become* the woman at the well, or the man born blind, or one of the characters in the Lazarus story. In this way, the kind of conversion called for in the Lenten journey can become a reality. We cannot underestimate the power of these gospels to effect salvation. And music can assist in helping this occur in our very midst!

The scrutiny rites themselves, celebrated on these Sundays, flow from the strong proclamation of the gospels. When done mechanically, straight from the text of the *Rite of Christian Initiation of Adults,* these rites often fall flat. For a rite that is intended to "uncover, then heal all that is weak, defective or sinful in the hearts of the elect; to bring out, then strengthen all that is upright, strong and good," (RCIA, 141) the scrutinies often are "wimpy" rituals lacking any flavor of real conversion.

An important component of the scrutinies are the intercessions for the elect. The RCIA says that "both the introduction and the intentions may be adapted to fit various circumstances" (#153). A well-planned preparation session for each of the scrutinies, including the elect, their sponsors, the catechumenate team and members of the assembly, could yield a list of weaknesses and evils present in the world, in society and in our personal lives that reflection on the scriptures has helped uncover. These could then be chanted in place of the intercessions as found in the text. A strong musical setting of the Kyrie could be chanted alongside these named evils, underscoring the belief that even in the midst of weakness and sin's destructive potential, Jesus Christ is the power that triumphs. The impact that this type of litany of deliverance has on an assembly is far-reaching. When the exorcism prayer, with its accompanying gesture of laying on of hands is then prayed, the scrutiny takes on a power of its own and effectively draws the entire worshiping community into a deeper level of conversion. Creativity and cooperation among those involved in the order of Christian initiation of adults is crucial in approaching the scrutinies.

A search of the parish's standard Lenten repertoire will reveal some classic Lenten hym-

nody such as "Lord, who throughout these forty days," "Again we keep this solemn fast," "O Sun of Justice," and "Jesus, remember me." Consider "By the Babylonian rivers" (found in GIA's *Worship* hymnal), a haunting tune that speaks to the heart of freedom and captivity. More contemporary Lenten hymns, such as Marty Haugen's "Tree of Life" and Rory Cooney's "Jerusalem my destiny" offer fine tunes and texts.

A solid choral setting of Psalm 51, "Create in me" by Nancy and Bruce Muskrat (Concordia) is worth considering. Michael Joncas's arrangement of the traditional Baptist hymn "O Healing River" (GIA, G-2594) warrants attention, especially for the Third Sunday of Lent.

David Haas's two-volume collection from GIA, *Who Calls You By Name,* contains singable, pastorally appropriate music for the season. The Lenten gospel acclamation, with verses for the Sundays of Lent in Year A, is a gem. The other acclamations, psalms and songs in these volumes can be taught easily and help support the sound of the season. Haas's work with the implementation of the RCIA is evident throughout as he offers some ground-breaking music for the rites. Reprintable music for the assembly is included in each volume.

A musical setting of 12 acclamations by Lynn Trapp, "Rite of Christian Initiation of Adults" (Morning Star, MSM-80-907) provides a wealth of material faithful to the texts of the rite, including a simple and effective chant formula and response for the signing of the senses, a litany of the saints, and a blessing of water and acclamation during baptism. An assembly score is also available.

Other Ritual Prayer and Sacraments

LITURGY OF THE HOURS

MANY parishes have developed a tradition of celebrating Evening Prayer on at least one day each week during Lent. This practice provides a good base for developing a regular celebration of the liturgy of the hours throughout the year. Perhaps your parish might try celebrating Evening Prayer or Morning Prayer every day during Lent, when people are normally more open to additional opportunities for prayer.

The patristic readings in each day's Office of Readings offer good complements to the brief pieces of scripture found in Evening Prayer.

■ VIGILS: The possibilities of Saturday night vigils can be explored for this season. For each week, appendix I of the *Liturgy of the Hours* provides canticles and gospels to be added to the Office of Readings to produce an extended vigil. The gospels listed there are particularly evocative of Lent. Texts also are included for the solemnities of Joseph and the Annunciation (especially fitting for communities that bear one of these titles).

COMMUNAL PENANCE

Most parishes schedule penance services during this season. For resources in planning an order of service, see the two Lenten services in appendix II of the *Rite of Penance*. For parish schools and for catechetical programs for children, see GIA/LTP's *Leader's Manual of the Hymnal for Catholic Students* (page 87). Many parishes have learned to schedule more than one penance service during Lent, offering multiple opportunities for the community to gather and experience God's mercy. A service early in Lent also can offer the possibility for people to confess their sins, accept a penance to be carried out through the weeks of Lent, and then come back for absolution near Easter.

COMMUNAL ANOINTING OF THE SICK

While the ritual Mass texts for anointing are forbidden on the Sundays of Lent and on March 19 and 25, the rite can be celebrated at Mass even on those days. Sickness knows no season, and the Lenten prayer texts plunge the anointing of the sick deep into the paschal mystery. One of the ritual readings may be substituted for a Lenten scripture passage. The passages of the ritual Mass from Isaiah 52, from Romans 8 and from Colossians are particularly appropriate to Lent. See page 118 for Lenten texts for the reception of the sick and for the prayer after anointing.

FUNERALS

Funerals may not take place at Mass on the Sundays of Lent. On weekdays, consider using the day's scriptures, which are often rich in the imagery of the paschal mystery. If the day's scriptures seem inappropriate, consider the funeral readings from Job or Lamentations, the Passion narratives, or the two parts of the raising of Lazarus linked together as on the Fifth Sunday of Lent this year.

MARRIAGES

Even though the Roman rite permits marriages to occur in Lent, because of the nature of Lent, weddings really should be scheduled outside this season. If any wedding does occur in Lent, the liturgical committee, pastoral ministers and the couple preparing for marriage must take account of the nature of the season (*Rite of Marriage*, #11; see also the *Ceremonial of Bishops*, #604). This "taking account" includes the same ban on flowers and instrumental music as at every other Lenten liturgy.

STATIONS OF THE CROSS

Many parishes continue the tradition of Stations of the Cross on Fridays. Many recent publications offer a variety of formats and emphases for this devotion. Some are traditional in style, while others focus on contemporary issues that reflect the passion of Christ today. While venerable and fitting, the "Stabat Mater" is not mandatory at stations. Consider using one of the readily available translations of "Vexilla regis" (e.g. *Worship*, #435), a powerful hymn celebrating the triumph of the cross. Another option is the chanted Agnus Dei (Mass XVIII). This provides a fine opportunity to blend some of our rich heritage of Latin chant into the liturgy. The first invocation, with its "miserere nobis," speaks well to this Lenten devotion. Remember, too, that the procession is central to this devotion. If at all possible, everyone should walk to each station with the cross, with the candle and incense bearers, and with the leader. For further texts, see the "Order for the Blessing of Stations of the Cross," chapter 42 in the *Book of Blessings*.

BAPTISMS AND CONFIRMATIONS

The Vatican has emphasized the inappropriateness of baptism and confirmation during all of Holy Week. See the *Circular Letter Concerning the Preparation and Celebration of the Easter Feasts*, #27. A strong case can be made for extending that insight to all of Lent. A pastorally sensitive policy that would defer baptisms and confirmations from Lent to the Easter season can help people to enter more fully into the desert spirit of Lent and to see the link between initiation and the Easter season.

The Worship Environment

AS with everything else in Lent, the key to the Lenten environment is simplicity and barrenness, reflecting the desert experience. Some parishes use sand and cacti to express the desert theme, but the main point is the emptiness of the desert. In contemporary churches with warmer and more hospitable architecture, it may take creative ideas to make the space less festive than usual. Perhaps the old custom of removing statues and images or covering them with purple cloth would be effective in many settings. The stripped-down worship environment allows us to focus on what is most important: the assembly, the elect, the candidates and the penitents.

■ NO FLOWERS: The Roman rite is specific about flowers this season—none are allowed. The only exceptions this year are March 17, 19, and 25. This means a stripped-down sanctuary and nave for weddings and funerals, too.

■ NO CROSS: Lent is not focused primarily on the passion. The cross becomes our focus on Good Friday, when it is unveiled or presented. That is why many parishes keep the tradition of veiling or removing the cross throughout Lent. In ancient times, the cross, gilded and jeweled as a sign of victory, would be veiled during penitential seasons. Like giving up the alleluia during Lent to sing it with gusto at Easter, the cross was veiled during Lent to be restored during the Triduum.

■ ART IN LENT: Once the church is stripped, appropriate art and a few restrained decorations still have a place. Designs for bulletins or participation booklets, for artifacts and for book covers should imitate art of the era when Lent was clearly a time for catechumens and penitents. Christian art before the year 800 shows Lent as

we once more know it to be—baptismal, penitential and communal in nature. Most local churches even used the same scriptural passages that we use today.

Communities might consult area residents who have studied early Christian art or get *Clip Art of the Christian World: Christian Art from Its Origins to the Fifteenth Century* (Collegeville: The Liturgical Press, 1990). See also the fuller work from which this was derived: *Art of the Christian World, AD 200-1500: A Handbook of Styles and Forms* (New York: Rizzoli International Publications, 1982). Here one will find several composite pieces depicting the death or resurrection of Jesus, framed by images from the gospels we read in Lent and Eastertime. LTP publishes a series of clip-art books by Steve Erspamer. These are filled with contemporary images, based on traditional forms and symbols.

Where can this art go? See the following notes on the catechumeneon, alms box, Book of the Elect, entranceway, outdoors and other buildings. Also lift the level of booklet and bulletin art by portraying the real Lent experienced in today's liturgy.

■ CATECHUMENEON: This is the term used to designate spaces that may have been the rooms to which catechumens were dismissed, the rooms through which they passed on their way to the baptistry on Easter. Where is yours? Give it special attention this season. Let everyone in the parish know which room is used by the elect and the catechumens.

■ ALMS BOX: If the parish has pledged its alms to a particular charity, a large vessel for collecting that money could be placed prominently in church—perhaps in the entranceway or at the side of the nave.

■ BOOK OF THE ELECT: The parish should place the Book of the Elect in a place that signals its importance. People should be able to see the signatures of those to be initiated, for whom they are praying. Many parishes with elect or with candidates for full communion display pictures of those preparing for the sacraments. Those preparing for infant baptism, first eucharist and confirmation during Eastertime might be represented with photographs or lists of names as well. These might be on the regular bulletin board but could be situated in some other well-traveled space.

■ ENTRANCEWAY: The gathering for the penitential procession on the First Sunday of Lent and for the blessing of palms on Passion Sunday requires a large space where all can at least stand. In much of the United States, the weather prevents using an outdoor plaza. If such a place is available, be sure that it is ready for these Lenten gatherings, outfitted in shades of purple and cleared of crosses and images of the saints.

■ OUTDOORS AND OTHER BUILDINGS: In Lent, as in every season, parishes should express the liturgical year to the neighborhood. An array of purple strips of fabric hung outside the building would be a simple but elegant way to announce that this community is preparing for Easter. Other buildings should not be overlooked, either. All the buildings of the parish should contribute to the season. Parish centers, schools, rectories and convents can and should be decorated with images of the season. A parade of Easter bunnies decorating the windows of the school as people walk past in the procession of palms creates a jarring clash of symbols. This kind of seasonal focus will take negotiation among the adults, but the children will not mind drawing eggs and bunnies during the Easter octave.

■ VESTURE: While customarily purple, the vesture of Lent should ideally be different from the vesture of Advent—though just what that difference should be is less clear. Some argue that royal purple (a deep, bloody purple) is especially appropriate as the color of the *vexilla regis,* the banner of the king who "reigns from the tree." Others argue that traditional Lenten vesture was a somber blue-violet, almost black. Both traditions suggest nothing gaudy. In any case, avoid appliquéed Lenten symbols. Plainness and simplicity are as important as color.

On Laetare Sunday, rose vestments may be worn. This color is a dusky "old rose," not a hot pink. White vestments will be worn for March 19 and 25, and for funerals if purple is not worn.

February

■ DAY OF FAST AND ABSTINENCE. There are only two days in the year when Catholics are obliged to fast and abstain: today and Good Friday. So this is the only required fast day of Lent. This fasting can help us be aware all day long that Lent is beginning; all are encouraged to embrace fasting according to their own ability throughout Lent. *Catholic Household Blessings and Prayers* (page 132) offers an "Ash Wednesday Blessing of the Season and of a Place of Prayer," which might be used for morning prayer or when the family gathers after work and school.

■ DAY OF ASHES: The ashes used today come from burning the palm branches blessed the preceding Palm Sunday. (Be sure to make and use fresh ashes; using ashes from earlier years misses the connection with last year's celebration.) Some parishes make a ritual of burning palms on Tuesday or the preceding weekend. Burning the palms as a part of today's liturgy, however, is not our tradition. Today's symbol is ashes, not fire.

The wearing of ashes is a pre-Christian expression found in Judith 9:11, Daniel 9:3 and Jonah 3:6. Jesus was familiar with the practice (Matthew 11:21), and the early church made it a sign of public penance. Ashes were sprinkled on penitents' heads. Around the year 1000, ashes came to be used by all the faithful. In 1091, Pope Urban II recommended the custom to all churches in communion with Rome.

The rubrics call for foreheads to be signed with ashes, and traditionally this is done in the form of a cross. Thus we are "branded" again with the sign of our baptism, reminding us of the purpose of Lent as a time of baptismal renewal.

■ DAY OF PUBLIC CATHOLICISM: Today Catholics will be visible at work, at the store, in school. This is about the only day when Catholics stand out, when conversations may naturally turn to religion, to Catholic traditions, and to the meaning of Lent. Parishes might offer their members some catechesis on the meaning of ashes and of Lent to help prepare them to give a simple explanation to those who ask. In 1994 a policeman in Georgia was suspended for the day when he refused to remove his ashes at work; while most do not face such injustice, wearing the ashes does allow us to proclaim our faith.

■ DISTRIBUTION OF ASHES OUTSIDE THE PARISH MASS: The rubric printed at the end of the day's texts in the sacramentary notes the possibility of ashes being distributed at a service outside Mass. A full order for the blessing and distribution of ashes is included in the *Book of Blessings* (chapter 52). This celebration can take place in the church or with a gathering of the sick (such as in a nursing home). This service may be led by a priest, deacon or layperson, male or female. When a layperson celebrates the rite, the ashes are blessed earlier. When a liturgy is scheduled with children, review the resources in the *Leader's Manual of the Hymnal for Catholic Students* (page 81).

■ ENVIRONMENT FOR WORSHIP: Because the ashes are the focus for today's worship, it is appropriate to give them some visual prominence. A pedestal placed in the sanctuary or in the midst of the assembly (or near the font or the entrance if all can turn and face it there) could hold the ashes in a dignified ceramic or glass bowl. Smaller vessels for distributing the ashes can be arranged around the bowl and filled after the blessing. The ashes could remain visible for the whole season, or at least until Sunday. In any event, ashes should not be placed on the altar or ambo, nor should they be just one more item on the credence table.

■ INTRODUCTORY RITES: The gathering rite today is simple—no penitential rite (the ritual with ashes is today's penitential rite) and no Gloria. Singing a litany for the opening procession using "Kyrie eleison" is somewhat of a lost tradition in our liturgical history. Look at the various Taizé settings of the "Kyries" as possibilities; however, you will need to compose invocations (model them after penitential rite C and keep them brief). James Hansen has a complete book of litanies for processionals, *Litany: When the Church Gathers,* published by OCP.

■ BLESSING AND GIVING OF ASHES: No formal introduction is provided in the sacramentary for this rite, but presiders could use the brief words found in the *Book of Blessings* (#1663), followed by the invitation to prayer found in the sacramentary.

The music to be used for the distribution of ashes should be chosen to accompany a procession of all those gathered, without requiring a hymnal or worship aid.

Hymns generally are not good choices here. Two Lucien Deiss pieces (World Library, *People's Mass Book*) would accompany this action well: "My soul is longing for your peace" (Psalm 131) and "Grant to us, O Lord," based on Ezekiel and Jeremiah. The refrain of "Give us, Lord, a new heart" by Bernadette Farrell (OCP, #7104) is quite lovely. It is easily coupled with the verses of any psalm that speaks of trust and conversion (such as Psalms 25, 62 and 130) and can be chanted to Tone 14 by Joseph Smith, found in the *Lead Me, Guide Me* hymnal. Tom Conry's "I will lift up my eyes," found in both *Gather* and the OCP resources, is also a good choice. This would also be an ideal place to use the "Attende Domine" tune.

The processional singing could continue until after the ministers wash their hands. The distribution of ashes is followed by the general intercessions.

■ LITURGY OF THE EUCHARIST: In addition to the suggested preface for this day (Lent IV), consider Lent III, which speaks of self-denial as a form of expressing thanks and of the social dimension of Lent.

T
H **22** #535 (LMC, #263)   white
U   **The Chair of Peter, apostle**
     FEAST

This is an ancient feast, dating to the fourth century, which really celebrates the unity of the church expressed in the role of Peter's successors. The chair of Peter, the *cathedra* of *ex cathedra* pronouncements, stands for the teaching role of the pope. By pure coincidence, it falls on the birthday of George Washington, the "father" of the United States.

The hymn "By all your saints still striving" provides a verse for this occasion. The readings speak of the papal ministry of shepherding the flock. Intercessions today

could include the pope, parishioners of the Lateran basilica (where the Pope's *cathedra* is located) and bishops. The hymn "Lord, you give the great commission" (*Worship*, #470) could link this feast with the ministry shared by all believers.

F
R **23** #222 (LMC, #176–184)   violet
I   **Friday after Ash Wednesday**

Day of abstinence. ▪ *Polycarp, bishop, martyr; optional commemoration.* ▪ Polycarp, bishop of Smyrna (Ismir, Turkey, today), is known as one of the apostolic fathers because he was an immediate disciple of the apostle John. Polycarp wrote:

> When it is in your power to do good, withhold not, because alms deliver from death. All of you be subject to one another, having your behavior blameless among the Gentiles, that by your good works both you may receive praise and the Lord may not be blasphemed in you.

The readings today talk of fasting, but Isaiah makes clear that we are called to fast from apathy, injustice and sin, which fits nicely with Polycarp's witness.

■ DAY OF ABSTINENCE: Every Friday is a day of penance, but the Fridays of Lent claim special status as days of abstinence. Penitential practices are mirrored in the liturgical texts of Fridays, such as Psalm 51 at Morning Prayer and at the eucharist.

S
A **24** #223 (LMC, #176–184)   violet
T   **Saturday after Ash Wednesday**

Today's passage from Isaiah again issues a call to conversion, to go God's way rather than our own. The gospel presents the call as an invitation; Jesus calls us to respond to him as completely as Matthew (Levi) did.

☀ **25** #22 (LMC, #18)   violet
    First Sunday of Lent

According to ancient tradition, this is the first day of the Forty Days. It features a special penitential procession, the gospel about Jesus' 40-day fast in the desert and the rite of election.

■ PENITENTIAL PROCESSION: The *Circular Letter* on the Easter feasts (#23) suggests that the penitential procession envisioned in the *Ceremonial of Bishops* (#261) be held in all parishes this day. See page 120 for an outline. While it is a new practice for most areas of the United States, this tradition is quite ancient. The procession signals clearly the call to repentance, perhaps especially important for those who did not gather on Ash Wednesday.

■ THE MASS: See page 115 for ideas for the texts of this day and of all Lenten Sundays.

■ THE READINGS: Today's readings contrast the disobedience of our first ancestors with the obedience of Christ in the face of temptation. Paul's comments in Romans remind us that despite original sin, grace abounds even more than sin. Remember to ask how the elect will hear these readings and base the homiletic and liturgical preparation on the answer.

■ RITE OF SENDING OR RITE OF ELECTION: If your diocese celebrates a rite of election at the cathedral, you probably will use the rite of sending the catechumens for election. The texts for catechumens (adults and children) begin at #111 of the *Rite of Christian Initiation of Adults*. The order for parishes with baptized candidates for reception into full communion but without catechumens begins at #438 of that rite. The order to use if a parish is blessed with both appears at #536. Appropriate music for this parish celebration can be found in David Haas's collection *Who Calls You By Name.*

Planners should keep in mind that the testimony given by the godparents at the rite of sending should communicate to the assembly what God has done in the lives of the elect. If the godparents are to give individual testimony rather than use the formulary given in the rite, they should be instructed to avoid communicating a list of achievements of the individual catechumen or candidate. Remember that this rite is not a "merit badge" awards ceremony. The inquiry of all the assembly is concerned with *God's* action in the lives of the elect during their long initiation journey. Consider singing "We praise you, O Lord" (Mike Balhoff, Darryl Ducote, Gary Daigle) as an acclamation following the testimonies. The text appropriately draws attention to "all *God's* works" being wonderful—wonderful in the lives of the elect whom we send to the diocesan celebration.

Musicians might consider contacting the planners for the diocesan celebration of the rite of election. Using some of the same music at the parish rite of sending that will be used at the diocesan rite might help connect the two celebrations.

#225 (LMC, #176 – 184)
violet

MON 26 Lenten Weekday

In contrast to the practice for weekdays in other seasons, the lectionary passages for the gospel and for the first reading in Lent were selected because of their relationship to each other. Today's readings link the second section of the commandments, which refers to relations with other people, with the Last Judgment in Matthew, which hinges on our care of those in need.

#226 (LMC, #176 – 184)
violet

TUE 27 Lenten Weekday

Isaiah today speaks of God's word doing God's will, as we pray in the Lord's Prayer, "your will be done." This is the core of conversion, aligning our will with God's.

#227 (LMC, #176 – 184)
violet

WED 28 Lenten Weekday

Both readings invite us into the story of Jonah. In the early days of the church, Jonah was central to Lenten liturgies, to art for the paschal season and to the curriculum for the catechumenate. The entire story, from the first call of Jonah to his brooding under the gourd plant, can be seen in countless illuminated liturgical books and on many mosaic pavements. The most extensive of these, in Aquileia (northeast Italy), graces the floor of what modern scholars consider to be a fourth-century *catechumeneon,* a room for the meeting of catechumens, which could hold well over a thousand people. Jonah can form part of our private reading and meditation for Lent.

#228 (LMC, #176 – 184)
violet

THU 29 Lenten Weekday

The first reading at Mass is from Esther, the only time it is read publicly from our weekday and Sunday lectionary. The story of Esther forms the basis of the Jewish holiday of Purim. The book of Esther would make good spiritual reading before Purim, which is celebrated by our Jewish neighbors next Tuesday. The gospel today re-emphasizes the importance of trusting God as Esther did.

March

#229 (LMC, #176 – 184) violet

FRI 1 Lenten weekday

Day of abstinence. ▪ The readings present God both as merciful and tolerant (Ezekiel's offer of life after repentance) and as demanding (Matthew). It is a good dual perspective.

▪ FIRST FRIDAY: Because the church wants the Lenten texts to be used virtually every day, votive Masses of the Sacred Heart are allowed on this day only with the explicit permission of the bishop.

#230 (LMC, #176 – 184) violet

SAT 2 Lenten weekday

Deuteronomy recalls the covenant and the commandments that it involves, while Jesus in the gospel calls us to go far beyond those commandments to the law of love.

#25 (LMC, #21) violet

3 Second Sunday of Lent

The Transfiguration of the Lord is celebrated on August 6 in both Roman and Orthodox traditions. Lutherans celebrate this feast on the Sunday preceding Lent because the transfiguration of Christ is an epiphany that foreshadows his cross and resurrection. Our hearing of the transfiguration story today points us toward the paschal mystery, too.

■ MASS: The preface for the Second Sunday of Lent is based on today's gospel. Examining the differences between the liturgical texts for today and for August 6 gives a good appreciation for how to understand transfiguration in Lent. The readings speak of trusting God's promises, as Abram and Jesus did. Remember to ask again how these readings speak to the elect and then share those insights with the whole community.

■ PENITENTIAL RITE FOR THE CANDIDATES: The *Rite of Christian Initiation of Adults*, #459 ff., includes a penitential rite (similar to the scrutinies) for Catholics who are baptized but uncatechized and for those joining the Catholic church from other Christian communions. This rite may be celebrated today. Musicians could consider chanting the intercessions for the candidates during this rite.

The Christian community needs Lent as a time to face honestly the evil that infects and often dominates our lives. We have grown uneasy in recent years in regard to speaking about sin and evil. Reacting against an overemphasis on sin in the preconciliar period, we have perhaps allowed the pendulum to swing too far, so that we are only willing to talk about God's love and our basic goodness. Yet we are still sinners, and our unwillingness to admit this openly and speak about it in community contributes to both our personal and our communal malaise.

Some years ago the great psychologist Karl Menninger wrote a book called *Whatever Happened to Sin?* and noted how our refusal to face our sinfulness often leads to psychological illness. As communities, too, many of our parishes seem unable to deal realistically with problems because we are reluctant to admit that sin is a reality in our midst that needs to

be confronted, opposed, repented and forgiven. In parishes as in families, no true common life can survive without regular forgiveness, and forgiveness presumes the ability to admit and name our sinfulness.

Lent is a time for such honest confronting of ourselves and the demons in our lives. The penitential rite for the candidates and the scrutinies for the catechumens offer an opportunity for parishes to learn again to speak of the sin and evil that exist in our midst. These rites are celebrated around the candidates and catechumens, but they should lead the whole community to pray for release from the power of the evil that infects both our personal lives and our communal activities. A good way for planning teams to begin Lenten planning would be to brainstorm a list of the real evils and sins that need to be confronted locally. Then this penitential rite, the scrutinies, Lenten homilies and other planning can all seek to confront those realities with a bracing honesty that will enable the community to repent and be freed from the power of evil. When that happens, new life then may be experienced and celebrated during Easter.

M O N 4 #231 (LMC, #176–184)   violet
Lenten Weekday

Casimir, optional commemoration. ▪ Parishes with a Polish heritage will probably include Casimir on the Lenten saints' list for this year. If so, the proper collect can be used and intercessions voiced for Poland and its people. This young prince, an exceptional student, was sent to Hungary to be king. But he returned to Poland and resolved never to be involved in war. He made a vow of celibacy, and his deep devotion to Christ in the eucharist and to Mary motivated his charity to the poor. He

died in 1483 while still in his early twenties and was buried in Vilnius, Lithuania, suggesting prayers for that land, too.

Today's first reading offers a clear call to honesty about our sinfulness, while the gospel reminds us both of God's compassion toward us and of our call to show compassion toward others.

T U E 5 #232 (LMC, #176–184)   violet
Lenten Weekday

Both readings call us to humility; Isaiah reminds us of our sinfulness but also of God's forgiveness, and the gospel attacks hypocrisy and pride.

■ PURIM: Today is Purim, a festival of liberation for our Jewish neighbors. It celebrates the events in the book of Esther, a story of trust in God.

W E D 6 #233 (LMC, #176–184)   violet
Lenten Weekday

Today's readings speak of the fate of almost every true prophet—rejection and unjust suffering. Not only do they call us to be open to the prophets in our time, but they also challenge us on our willingness to be prophets!

T H U 7 #234 (LMC, #176–184)   violet
Lenten Weekday

Perpetua and Felicity, martyrs, optional commemoration. ▪ Arrested as catechumens (along with three men), baptized in prison and martyred at Carthage in 202, Perpetua and her slave Felicity are named in the first eucharistic prayer. They offer a powerful witness to catechumens and to faithful alike. Today's first reading calls us to place our trust and hope in the Lord, a call the martyrs followed to the end. The gospel reminds us of the folly of trusting in wealth and ignoring the needs of the poor.

F R I 8 #235 (LMC, #176–184)   violet
Lenten Weekday

Day of abstinence. ▪ *John of God, religious founder, optional commemoration.* ▪ John had been a soldier and then a slave overseer before a conversion experience at age 40 led him to a life devoted to the sick and the poor. He offers an example to us of openness to God's call to change. If he is commemorated locally, include in the intercessions the sick and the poor whom he served.

Another of the great Lenten stories is presented in the lectionary today. The story of Joseph, told in Genesis and recalled in Psalm 105, was seen by our Christian ancestors as portraying the infidelity present in families and the treachery shown in Jesus' passion, the sin for which Lent bids us all repent. The gospel reveals the treachery of the chief priests and the elders, easily related to the Joseph story.

S A T 9 #236 (LMC, #176–184)   violet
Lenten Weekday

Frances of Rome, married woman, religious founder, optional commemoration. ▪ Like Elizabeth Ann Seton at the turn of the nineteenth century, Frances was a wife and mother before founding a religious community in the fifteenth century. Her followers were dedicated to helping the poor and the sick, particularly the most difficult cases.

The beautiful passage from Micah in the first reading today, praising God's merciful forgiveness, provides a perfect prelude to the gospel of the Prodigal Father.

☀ 10 #28 (LMC, #24)   Violet
Third Sunday of Lent

▪ PRAYERS FROM THE SACRAMENTARY: In the opening prayers, the Lenten disciplines of prayer, fasting and almsgiving are echoed once again, a reminder that Friday abstinence is only a minimum of Lenten observance. (In the alternative text, "brothers and sisters" would be more inclusive than "brothers"). When scrutinies are included in the Mass, the presidential prayers and the eucharistic prayer insert for the ritual Mass of scrutinies may be used. The preface is specifically composed for this Sunday's gospel (P14).

▪ LITURGY OF THE WORD: Today's scriptures return us to the theme of thirst, whether in the desert (Exodus) or at the well (gospel). For what are the elect and the candidates thirsting? What thirst in all of us can be quenched only by Christ? Are we as anxious for the water of life as the Israelites were for water from the rock? Paul reminds us of how much God loves us, since Christ died for us while we were still sinners. What consolation for the catechumens and for us!

▪ FIRST SCRUTINY: The paragraph numbers refer to the *Rite of Christian Initiation of Adults:*

• Invitation to prayer (#152): After the homily, the elect and their godparents gather before the presider and the assembly. Try to position them so they face the congregation, perhaps with the presider in the center aisle. Or position pairs of elect and sponsors throughout the assembly. The presider directs the elect to bow their heads (or kneel) and pray; silence is observed "for some time."

• Intercessions for the elect (#153): Godparents place their right hands on the shoulders of the elect for the intercessions. Note that these are prayers for the elect and are not the usual general intercessions. The intercessions as they are given are too general and too weak. Many parishes adapt them to pray for the power of Christ to overcome what is sinful in the elect and in the community. Musical and other suggestions are found on page 99.

• Exorcism (#154): A central part of the rite, the exorcism consists of two prayers and a powerful ritual gesture. Between the prayers, the presider places his hands (both hands) on the head of each of the elect (in many parishes, catechists or godparents also lay on hands) in unhurried *silence.* Overcome the temptation to "cover" this action with a hymn or instrumental music—silence is an integral part of this act.

The rite suggests that the exorcism be concluded with an appropriate psalm or with a song. The community might select one of the psalms suggested there and sing it at each of the scrutinies. Note that one of the suggested psalms is Psalm 51, also a good choice for the responsorial psalm during Lent. Because the scrutinies are meant to uncover, then heal all that is weak and sinful, musicians might opt for a hymn that speaks of healing at this point in the rite. For the first scrutiny, consider Michael Joncas's arrangement of the traditional Baptist hymn "O healing river." (GIA, G-2594) Appropriate hymns for the second scrutiny might include "Amazing Grace" ("was blind but now I see") or Marty Haugen's "Awake, O sleeper" (its text echoes the day's second reading). For the third scrutiny, the refrain from Suzanne Toolan's "I am the Bread of Life," repeated a few times, is fitting. Two other possibilities for the third scrutiny are "God is our fortress and our rock" (the translation by Michael Perry found in GIA's *Worship* Third Edition is a fine setting), or "Now the green blade rises," found in GIA's *Gather* hymnal.

- Dismissal (#155): An optional text is provided in case the elect are not dismissed—but it is an option that should rarely be used.

- After the scrutiny rite (#156): The general intercessions and the profession of faith should not be omitted (see page 97). Remember that the order is reversed after the scrutiny. The introduction to the general intercessions might link them to the prior prayers for the elect (e.g. "We now continue our ministry of intercession, praying for the needs of all").

MON 11 #238 (LMC, #176–184)   violet
Lenten Weekday

Today's cure of Naaman in the first reading takes on new significance when Jesus uses it to challenge his hometown on their rejection of him.

TUE 12 #239 (LMC, #176–184)   violet
Lenten Weekday

In today's readings, the prayer of the three men in the furnace stands as a model of the humility and trust that Jesus invites in the parable of the unforgiving official.

WED 13 #240 (LMC, #176–184)   violet
Lenten Weekday

Today's readings call us to be mindful of God's commands and to fulfill them. Fulfillment, in this case, means more than obeying the letter but living out the spirit of the commandments.

THU 14 #241 (LMC, #176–184)   violet
Lenten Weekday

Today's psalm sets the theme of the readings clearly: "If today you hear God's voice, harden not your hearts." How open are our hearts to God's word today?

FRI 15 #242 (LMC, #176–184)   violet
Lenten Weekday

Day of Abstinence. ▪ Hosea calls the people to abandon idols and trust in the Lord. Jesus quotes Deuteronomy and invites us to the same single-hearted trust in God.

SAT 16 #243 (LMC, #176–184)   violet
Lenten Weekday

Today's readings call us to give God love, not mere religious observance. Neither Temple sacrifices nor the Pharisee's proud religiosity substitute for loving service of God and neighbor.

17 #31 (LMC, #27)
violet or rose
Fourth Sunday of Lent

The antiphon of the introductory rites sets the traditional tone for this day, "Rejoice, Jerusalem! Be glad for her, you who love her; rejoice with her, you who mourned for her." These verses from Isaiah have given this Sunday its title; this is Laetare or "Rejoice" Sunday, with rose vestments and flowers allowed (the custom of bringing spring roses led to the color of the vestments). The hymn "Lift high the cross" (CRUCIFER) would serve well in today's liturgy. Several settings by Carl Schalk (Concordia) and Richard Hillert (GIA) have optional choral and instrumental parts. This hymn is also useful on Holy Thursday and during the Easter season.

In our history, Laetare Sunday signaled more than a few ritual variations. In Rome, the pope celebrated Mass this day at the basilica of Santa Croce in Gerusalemme

(a link to the introit antiphon). In the era of more severe penitence and fasting, people looked to Sundays and to this mid-season Sunday in particular for a break in the fast. Now we know that Sundays are not a "break" from Lent, but this day still reminds us that the season is more than half over.

▪ PRAYERS: The first of the opening prayers reflects this day's position in mid-Lent: "Let us hasten toward Easter." In the alternative prayer, "humanity" or "us" is more inclusive than "mankind." Once again, the presidential prayers associated with scrutinies may be used, as appropriate (for notes on the scrutinies, see last Sunday).

▪ READINGS: Today our focus shifts from thirst to blindness, as Samuel learns to see as God sees and the man born blind receives his sight. Paul also speaks of living in the light. What blindness are the catechumens experiencing? How clearly do we all see as God sees? What happens to those who learn to see from God's perspective? Will we be rejected by the powers-that-be as the man in the gospel was? Be sure that the intercessions for the scrutiny reflect the real evils the catechumens and the community must overcome.

▪ ST. PATRICK: Liturgically, the patron of Ireland does not even get a commemoration this year, but in many parts of the United States, parades, parties and green clothing will mark this day. In one sense, such celebration is not inappropriate for this "Rejoice" Sunday. And we can find ways to relate Patrick to Lent; his *Confessions* are fine Lenten reading (a portion is in the Office of Readings for his memorial). The shamrock was a teaching device for the catechumens preparing to be baptized at Easter in the name of the

Trinity. The legend of Patrick chasing the snakes out of Ireland reminds us of the need to chase evil from our lives. Green became the ritual color associated with penitents returning to the church at Easter, as white is associated with the newly baptized. It is even claimed that Patrick kindled (and "christened") the Celtic May Day bonfire as part of the *lucernarium* ritual of the Easter Vigil.

■ THE WEEK AHEAD: The solemnity of St. Joseph will interrupt the weekday readings on Tuesday. Since the passages assigned to Tuesday are not linked closely to either Monday or Wednesday, they can be omitted. But if you wish to draw on the images of water in Tuesday's passages, they could replace Wednesday's.

MON 18 #245 (LMC, #176–184)   violet
Lenten Weekday

Cyril of Jerusalem, bishop, doctor of the church, optional commemoration. ▪ Cyril, a fourth-century bishop of Jerusalem, is known as the greatest catechist among the early Fathers. His best-known works were written for catechumens during the "golden age" of the catechumenate; an excerpt is in the Office of Readings today. His postbaptismal, or mystagogical, catecheses give wonderful treatments of the sacraments.

Today we begin the semicontinuous proclamation of the Gospel of John on weekdays until Wednesday of Holy Week. The beautiful prophecy from Isaiah finds the beginning of its fulfillment in the healing power of Jesus.

TUE 19 #543 (LMC, #272)   white
Joseph, husband of the Virgin Mary
SOLEMNITY

Pope John XXIII named Joseph patron of the universal church and included his name in the first eucharistic prayer. The preface today sums up Joseph's life: "He is that just man, that wise and loyal servant, whom you placed at the head of your family. With a husband's love he cherished Mary, the virgin Mother of God. With fatherly care he watched over Jesus Christ your Son, conceived by the power of the Holy Spirit."

■ LITURGY: The Lenten set of acclamations can continue today. A hymn or two about St. Joseph would be helpful, along with the singing of the Gloria and perhaps the creed. *Worship* offers two hymns to St. Joseph, and the hymn "By all your saints still striving" (*Worship,* #706) includes a verse for St. Joseph. The *Collegeville Hymnal* also offers two hymns for this solemnity. G. W. Williams's thoughtful text, "Come now, and praise the humble saint," deserves consideration. You will find it in *Worship* coupled with the well-known and singable American melody, LAND OF REST. Flowers are allowed in the church on this weekday (and on the Annunciation). If there is a statue of the saint in the church, this is the most, obvious place for the flowers. Parishes named after Joseph,

as well as religious communities under his patronage, may consider holding a vigil service on the eve, using the texts and outline found in appendix I of the Liturgy of the Hours.

■ ST. JOSEPH'S TABLE: The Italian tradition of the St. Joseph's table began as a meal to which all, particularly the poor, were welcomed without cost. It was often a way to thank and honor St. Joseph for a favor granted. This worthwhile custom, adapted and adopted by many groups, combines the three Lenten disciplines of prayer, fasting and almsgiving in a single event. Prayers and songs, both for Joseph and for Lent, are customary. The table features meatless dishes and a collection is made for the poor. An "Order for the Blessing of a St. Joseph's Table" is found in chapter 53 of the *Book of Blessings*. His litany is found in *Catholic Household Blessings and Prayers* (page 346), which also contains domestic prayer for this day on page 165.

WED 20 #247 (LMC, #176–184)   violet
Lenten Weekday

Isaiah offers a message of hope and of God's unending love. Jesus insists that he and the Father are fully united; thus God's love and power to give life are revealed in him. If you use Tuesday's pericopes, the focus on water offers an obvious link to baptismal themes.

Today is also the spring equinox, reminding us that the term "lent" comes from the Middle English "lente," meaning springtime. Lent should be a time of new life and growth for us.

THU 21 #248 (LMC, #176–184) violet
Lenten Weekday

Today's readings raise the issues of idolatry and testimony to the truth. Both can help us face honestly our own addictions to falsehood and to false gods.

FRI 22 #249 (LMC, #176–184) violet
Lenten Weekday

Day of abstinence. ▪ Both readings today raise the issue of the rejection and mistreatment of the just one. Every age has difficulty dealing with those whose lives bear silent witness against the evils and compromises of society.

SAT 23 #250 (LMC, #176–184) violet
Lenten Weekday

Toribio de Mogrovejo, bishop, optional commemoration. ▪ Toribio was archbishop of Lima, Peru, in the sixteenth century and worked tirelessly to implement the reforms of the Council of Trent there. His commemoration offers an opportunity to pray in solidarity with South American Christians.

Both of today's passages continue yesterday's theme. Nicodemus speaks up for justice, but his wisdom is rejected, too.

✴ 24 #34 (LMC, #30) violet
Fifth Sunday of Lent

▪ PASSION: Both opening prayers reflect the shift of emphasis at this point—our focus now is more on the passion of Christ. The gospel of Lazarus also points the elect and the assembly to the meaning of baptism as incorporation into Christ's death and resurrection. Invite the assembly once again to walk with the catechumens as they hear the promise of new life from Ezekiel, Paul and Jesus.

While maintaining the core of your Lenten repertoire, consider this an appropriate day to add one or two passion-oriented hymns, such as "O sacred head" or "What wondrous love." Don't miss the opportunity to repeat these hymns next Sunday and at Masses during this week.

On this day in 1980, Oscar Romero, then archbishop of San Salvador, was assassinated as he presided at the eucharistic liturgy. He stands as a modern example of trust in the promise of resurrection. Pray for justice and peace in that nation and throughout the earth.

▪ SUMMON THE ASSEMBLY: In today's homily, in a parish-wide mailing, in local newspaper announcements and in various other ways, the entire parish should know the details of the coming celebrations. Even more importantly, they need to be inspired, to be invited into the celebrations, to know that they are expected. Several sermons in the Office of Readings provide models for today's homilists or newsletter writers: Athanasius, this past Friday and today (second half); Gregory Nazianzen, this coming Saturday (second half); Andrew of Crete, on Passion (Palm) Sunday.

On a more practical level, the announcements this week must focus on Palm Sunday details. Where will the assembly convene for the procession? How will procedures be worked out so that those who participate in the blessing and procession can easily be seated when they arrive at church?

▪ THE WEEK AHEAD: Monday's feast displaces the weekday readings, which are powerful passages; they could be used on Tuesday, but Tuesday's pericopes contain the images of the saraph serpent and Christ being lifted up for salvation; so perhaps Susanna should be skipped this year.

MON 25 #545 (LMC, #274) white
The Annunciation of the Lord
SOLEMNITY

▪ HISTORY: Many theories have been put forward to explain the dating of this feast. Today's gospel notes that Elizabeth was six months pregnant; since the angel's appearance to Zechariah was probably on Yom Kippur, September 25, this puts the conception of Jesus on this date and his birth on December 25. Another ancient belief was that Jesus died on this date and that he had been conceived on the same date that he died. Other historians put more emphasis on the spring equinox, long observed as a festival in pre-Christian times.

In ancient liturgical calendars, the annunciation was celebrated near Christmas—for example, on December 26 or on the Sunday before Christmas, and echoes of that tradition remain in the Advent liturgy on the Sunday and weekdays just before Christmas.

This is also Greek Independence Day (marking independence from Turkey in 1821), a fact important to the Greek Orthodox and to Greek Catholics.

▪ FEAST OF THE LORD: Today many Catholics still think of the

Annunciation as a Marian feast, but the calendar reforms of 1969 returned the feast to its origins as a feast of the Lord. A similar shift was made on February 2. The title of the feast reminds us to keep the liturgy focused on Christ, though Marian hymns and references also find their place this day. All of this, of course, falls within Lent, which suggests a perspective on the Annunciation as the beginning of our redemption.

■ LITURGY: This is one of the two days each year when all are invited to genuflect during the profession of faith. However this was carried out at Christmas should be repeated on this weekday—kneeling for the whole line that ends with the incarnation phrase or genuflecting only for the phrase itself. Introduce the creed with appropriate instructions. This is one of the three days in Lent this year when flowers are allowed in the church. They might be placed by the Marian shrine or by an icon depicting the Annunciation.

T U E #253 (LMC, #176–184)   violet
26 **Lenten Weekday**

Today's readings parallel the bronze serpent raised on a pole for healing with Jesus raised up on the cross for salvation. The readings are clearly moving toward the Triduum!

W E D #254 (LMC, #176–184) violet
27 **Lenten Weekday**

The gospel today speaks of the truth that sets us free, a freedom that Shadrach, Meshach and Abednego knew.

T H U #255 (LMC, #176–184) violet
28 **Lenten Weekday**

Today's readings recall Abraham and God's covenant with him; Jesus' insistence that Abraham saw his day can remind us of God's continuing faithfulness to the covenant with us—a reassuring truth when life is difficult.

F R I #256 (LMC, #176–184) violet
29 **Lenten Weekday**

Today's readings show us both Jeremiah and Jesus facing threats and relying on the Lord. We are invited to trust God's promises, too, when we face opposition or persecution.

S A T #257 (LMC, #176–184)   violet
30 **Lenten Weekday**

Today's readings focus on Christ's mission of reconciliation, "gathering into one all the dispersed children of God." It is a good reminder of what our mission is, too.

✸ 31 #37–38 (LMC, #33)   red
Passion (Palm) Sunday

HOLY WEEK

This week is called holy because it includes the Triduum, the great days of our redemption, preceded by the final days of Lent. It is followed by the Easter octave, and no other feast can be celebrated during these two weeks.

This week is easily misunderstood as a historical drama, so care must be taken to celebrate the Paschal Mystery as a present reality into which we must enter.

Songs like "The palms," "The holy city" and "The old rugged cross" are inappropriate because they foster the historical drama approach. Celebrating Palm Sunday does not require a live donkey. Holy Thursday's evening Mass of the Lord's Supper is not celebrated in the context of a Seder meal, nor is the washing of the feet restricted to 12 males. Good Friday's solemn liturgy is not a passion play. We celebrate liturgy so that we can be plunged into the mystery.

The liturgies of this week are celebrated only once a year; hence they do not need novel adaptations every year. The reforms of Holy Week in the 1950s, confirmed and enhanced after Vatican II, restored the authentic tradition of worship. The challenge is to celebrate the traditional rituals as given fully and prayerfully.

THE COMMEMORATION OF THE LORD'S ENTRANCE INTO JERUSALEM

■ THE PALMS: Palms are an important, concrete symbol of this day and this week. Order enough so that you can give each person a reasonable symbol. Invite a group of parishioners for a palm-stripping gathering the day before Palm Sunday. Decorate with full palm fronds so people can make some connection between the piece in their hand and the actual plant.

The procession for Passion Sunday should include a large number of people moving, with music and singing and palms waving, from the place where the palms were blessed to the main worship space. Everyone who is not incapacitated by age or illness should participate; advance planning, signs and well-prepared ushers can enable the assembly to gather in the proper place. The rubrics restrict the procession to the principal Mass, not to restrict the parishioners' experience of this rite but to call for one grand liturgy for all parish members—just as it is done during the Triduum. If this is not possible, the solemn entrance should be used at the other Masses.

■ RITUAL OUTLINE: Quotes given here without reference are taken from the sacramentary. Others are from the Ceremonial of Bishops (CB).

- Gathering: All assemble in a place "distinct from the church to which the procession will move."

- Branches are distributed: Palm branches are already in the hands of the assembly before the presider and other ministers arrive.

- Red vesture: The deacon and presider wear red Mass vestments, although the presider may wear a red cope.

- Song: As the presider and assisting ministers arrive, or after all are gathered, everyone sings the antiphon (Matthew 21:9) "or any other appropriate song." The "Hosanna to the Son of David" text recommended for this time is found in the Passion Sunday section of *Worship* set to chant mode VII, adapted by Richard Proulx. Taizé (GIA) offers several "Hosanna" and "Benedictus" antiphons that would serve well as gathering and processional music. Also consider "O Christe Domine Jesu" from the same source. Richard Proulx also has arranged a choral setting of "Hosanna to the Son of David," titled "Fanfare for Palm Sunday" (GIA, G-2829), which is based on the traditional chant; it is short but very effective. Another effective option is Christopher Walker's Paschal/Palm Procession ("We are your people," St. Thomas More Collection—OCP, 8680). The refrain should be altered, since, for some reason, the final word of the

text is "alleluia." The words "sing, hosanna" could easily replace the final "alleluia." Walker's tune is characteristically rhythmic and could serve as part of the processional music.

- Sign of the cross: The presider leads all in the sign of the cross (CB, #266).

- Greeting: The presider gives the liturgical greeting (the one used on the other Lenten Sundays).

- Introduction: If not using the introduction that is in the sacramentary, parish coordinators should prepare one with equal content and style. This introduction also can be given by the deacon or by a concelebrant (CB, #266).

- Blessing: The presider voices the prayer of blessing (with hands joined); the first of the optional prayers is preferable.

- Sprinkling: The presider silently sprinkles the branches that are held by the people. Encouraging everyone to hold their branches high may help people appreciate that the water is being sprinkled on the palms. In a large congregation, this action should take some time, with the presider walking among the people.

- Preparation for the gospel: The presider and the other ministers who have not carried branches from the beginning now take them (from a table or pedestal). Incense is placed in the censer, and the deacon who is to proclaim the gospel is blessed. During these preparatory actions, a "suitable song" is sung (CB, #268). This is one of the few examples of a pre-gospel hymn in our tradition.

- Gospel: The deacon, a concelebrant or the presider (in that order of preference) proclaims Luke's gospel of the entry into Jerusalem.

- Homily: "A brief homily may be given." The preacher may want to link this brief homily with the main homily after the passion, i.e. a two-part homily.

- Invitation to the procession: The deacon (or presider) invites the

assembly to join in the procession, using words such as those in the sacramentary (perhaps preceded by practical instructions given as briefly as possible).

- Procession participants: All carry palms unless they already are bearing a liturgical object such as a thurible, cross or candle. The procession follows this order:
  • thurifer, with plenty of smoke billowing out of the censer
  • cross bearer, "with the cross suitably decorated with palm branches" (CB, #270), flanked by two candle bearers
  • deacon carrying the book of the gospels
  • lectors
  • concelebrants
  • presider and assistants
  • choir
  • assembly

- Processional route: The procession can move in a straight line toward the church, or it might take a longer route around the parish property. Be sure that the thurifer and the cross bearer walk slowly enough to keep the procession together.

The route may necessitate the collaboration of the police, or a permit may be required. Some cities require permission for the use of audio systems outdoors (even on private property). These permits are not difficult to obtain; they just require a bit of time and forethought.

Walk through the processional route beforehand, looking for possible trouble spots as you go. Will the banners and the cross fit through any tight places? Will the head of the procession—with the cross prominent—be clearly visible? Are there places where part of the procession can bog down, where people can trip easily or become confused or take shortcuts?

- Processional music: "All glory, laud and honor" is a once-a-year text that everyone will come to associate with Passion Sunday if it is used consistently. Set to the tune ST. THEODULPH, it is solid and easily sung in procession with leadership by the choir and portable instruments (drums, flutes, bells). Search for a descant (see GIA's small descant books) that the sopranos could sing for the "refrain" of the hymn, even in procession. If you wish to sing different music for the outdoor procession and begin the hymn as the procession enters the church building, consider one of the alternatives mentioned in the "song" section of the ritual outline on page 112, or use the "Hosanna" antiphon from Howard Hughes's "Mass of the Divine Word" (GIA, G-2415 or *Worship*) with choir or cantor interjecting the "Blessed is he. . . ." The tonality of this piece is compatible with the rhythmic chant setting, but the "Hosanna" will have to be transposed to begin on B-flat if the ST. THEODULPH tune will follow.

- Entrance into the church: As the procession enters the church, the music continues. Additional responsory texts with the imagery of entrance are suggested in the sacramentary. The presider venerates the altar with a kiss and with incense, then changes from cope to chasuble if necessary.

- Invitation to prayer: After the ushers have helped all find places, the presider, standing at the chair, invites everyone to pray. (The formulas given for this invitation are helpful.) An extra measure of silence—to help participants quiet their hearts after the rousing procession—should follow.

- Opening prayer: The alternative opening prayer is difficult to comprehend. Use the first one.

■ AT THE OTHER MASSES: At the other liturgies of the day, the "Solemn Entrance"—with the following adaptations—is a practical alternative. The assembly is handed palms as they enter the church, perhaps with the singing of one of the Taizé ostinatos beginning at least ten minutes before Mass is scheduled to start. At that time, the presider and other ministers "go to a suitable place in the church outside the sanctuary so that most of the people will be able to see the rite." The choir loft in an old building or a raised area near the doors might work well. As in the principal Mass with the procession, the palm branches are blessed and the gospel of the triumphal entry is proclaimed; then the ministers process through the assembly toward the altar while everyone sings a rousing entrance hymn.

LITURGY OF THE WORD

■ READINGS: The lectionary notes that "for pastoral reasons" the first two readings might be omitted, but it is "strongly recommended that all three readings" be used. These readings are powerful and important; people who come this day know that Mass will be a bit longer than usual.

■ PSALM: Settings of Psalm 22 suggested for this day include:

- "My God, my God" in *Songs of Israel* by Alexander Peloquin (GIA, G-1666)

- "My God, my God" in *Psalms for Feasts and Seasons* by Christopher Willcock (Liturgical Press)

- "My God, my God" by Marty Haugen in *Gather*

- "My God, my God" by David Isele in *Psalms for the Church Year* (GIA, G-2262)

- "My God, my God" by Christopher Walker (OCP–from his collection *Out of Darkness*)

■ THE PASSION ACCORDING TO MATTHEW is narrated without candles, incense, preliminary greeting or signing of the book. Note that the passion may be read in parts, but need not be. The practice of the assembly reading "crowd" parts rarely works well because it forces the community to read along. The scriptures are to be listened to, never read along with the lector.

A hymn interpolated throughout the reading can engage the assembly in active reflection on the Passion text. Either "O sacred head surrounded" or "My song is love unknown" would serve well. Choose carefully the places where the gospel will be interrupted, and mark the text clearly.

After the verse about the death of the Lord, all kneel for a time of complete silence (*Ceremonial of Bishops,* #273).

■ HOMILY: The homily may be brief in light of the length of the passion, but it is important. It might even be done in two short parts, the first after the procession gospel and the second after the Passion. It should serve as an invitation to keep Lent through Holy Thursday and then to enter fully into the observance of the Triduum. It is a call to keep the great Paschal fast and to engage in prayerful reflection from Thursday night until Sunday—three days like no other in the year. See appendix three in Gabe Huck's *The Three Days* (LTP) for some homily ideas.

The homily might also address the potential for anti-Semitism flowing from the passion account. See the fine document on this question by the Bishops' Committee on the Liturgy, God's *Mercy Endures Forever,* #21–25.

■ DISMISSAL OF THE CATECHUMENS AND THE ELECT: One of the Lenten dismissals continues to be used.

■ PROFESSION OF FAITH AND GENERAL INTERCESSIONS follow in their regular Lenten pattern. Good ideas for intercessions can be found in Morning Prayer for this day.

LITURGY OF THE EUCHARIST

For the eucharistic prayer (with or without variable prefaces), the communion rite and the concluding rite, continue to use the Lenten format for texts and music established for the season.

TAKING IT HOME

Catholic Household Blessings and Prayers (page 140) contains a short rite for the "Placing of Branches in the Home." Prayers for the Triduum begin on page 143. This might be a good time to make this important book available for purchase. It is a good reminder of the importance of domestic prayer, family customs and observing special days outside the church building, too.

■ THE WEEK AHEAD: When you encourage all to attend the Triduum liturgies, also remind the assembly that Daylight Savings Time begins next Sunday morning, lest they arrive an hour late for Easter Sunday Masses.

April

M
O #258 (LMC, #176–184) violet
N **Monday of Holy Week**

The first readings for these three days of Holy Week are the first three "Suffering Servant" songs from Isaiah; the fourth is used on Good Friday. The gospels recount the events immediately preceding the Passion in John, which is used on Friday. Appendix I of the sacramentary provides a sample set of intercessions for these days (#7), but the general Lenten ones also can be used. The preface

titled "Passion of the Lord II" (P-18), is so specific to these days that it might be used, even if another preface has been used consistently for Lent.

T
U #259 (LMC, #176–184) violet
E **2** **Tuesday of Holy Week**

The mission of the servant in today's first reading is clearly described as a universal one, reminding us of the scope of Christ's redemptive mission. The gospel begins the account of the Last Supper, highlighting Judas's betrayal.

W
E **3** #260 (LMC, #176–184) violet
D **Wednesday of Holy Week**

This day already was known to Christians as the "day of the betrayal" in 250. Its denotation as "Spy Wednesday" has been forgotten in our own era, but today's gospel continues the tradition.

T
H **4** #39–40 white
U **Holy Thursday**

■ THE CHRISM MASS should draw representatives from every area of the diocese. The renewal of priestly commitment in that liturgy is secondary to the blessing of oils and the consecration of the chrism. Many dioceses move the Mass to an earlier day during Lent. Whenever it is celebrated, consider using a van or bus to bring parish members to the cathedral. Their experience of the oils, of ministries and of the gathered local church will add greatly to the richness of this week. See page 130 regarding the rites for receiving the oils in the parishes.

■ MORNING AND AFTERNOON: Even though the Triduum does not begin until this evening, eucharistic celebrations, even for funerals, are not permitted. The reason is simple: The entire parish—even mourners, those who commute to work, schoolchildren, senior citizens and col-

lege students—is expected to gather tonight to begin the Christian Passover. This expectation, written into our rubrics, suggests that we take great pains to invite all the groups, communities and ages of the parish to attend all the liturgies of the Triduum. The permission to hold a Mass earlier in the day, granted by many bishops, should be employed only in unusual circumstances, for people who truly *cannot* attend the evening celebration.

■ SCHOOL ASSEMBLIES: Because Catholic schools often are in session this day, various practices have developed for their gathering this morning. The observance cannot be a Mass, but it can be a prayer service that is an extended prelude or "call to worship" for the Triduum. Students should be expected to attend the Triduum liturgies; encouraging attendance is a profound favor to young people because these liturgies will help form the students in the Catholic way of life. See the outline of ideas for this morning in the *Leader's Manual of the Hymnal for Catholic Students* (page 90).

INTRODUCTORY RITES

Greeting

The grace and love of Jesus Christ, who calls us to conversion, be with you all.

Invitation to the Penitential Rite

WEEKS 1 TO 4:
As we begin this eucharist, let us heed the Lenten call to conversion of heart and, by acknowledging our sins, seek reconciliation and communion with God and our neighbor.

WEEK 5 AND WEEKDAYS OF HOLY WEEK:
Acknowledging that we are all sinners cleansed by the blood of Christ, let us pardon one another from the depths of our hearts and ask pardon from God who is merciful and just.

Penitential Rite

The Confiteor (I confess) followed by a sung Kyrie is appropriate during the first four weeks of Lent.

Or:

FOCUSING ON INITIATION:
By water and the Holy Spirit, you have given us a new birth in your image: Lord, have mercy.

You have sent your Spirit to create a new heart within us: Christ, have mercy.

You called us to your supper to partake of your body and blood: Lord, have mercy.

FOCUSING ON RECONCILIATION:
You command us to forgive each other before we come to your altar: Lord, have mercy.

You asked your Father to forgive sinners as you hung upon the cross: Christ, have mercy.

You have entrusted your church with the ministry of reconciliation: Lord, have mercy.

LITURGY OF THE WORD

Dismissal of the Catechumens and the Elect

The Rite of Christian Initiation of Adults provides proper texts of dismissal for the Rite of Sending, the Rite of Election and the Scrutinies.

AT OTHER EUCHARISTS:
My dear friends: With the assurance of our loving support this community sends you forth to reflect more deeply upon the word of God we have shared. May Christ who is the power and wisdom of God challenge you to be one with us in the disciplines of prayer, fasting and almsgiving, that you may be one with us at last in the paschal feast of the Lord's table.

General Intercessions

Invitation to prayer

In this, the acceptable time, the Lenten spring, the Lord invites us to be renewed in mind, purified in spirit, and more responsive to the needs of others. Let us ask God to accompany us on our journey to conversion, and to draw all the human family to the waters of life and the paschal feast.

For the church

For the unity of the church
and the holiness of all who have
	been baptized:
let us pray to the Lord.

For the church,
that with Christ we may turn from evil
and be obedient to God's word:
let us pray to the Lord.

For the world

For prisoners and those unjustly detained,
for exiles and all who are without homes,
and for those who are oppressed:
let us pray to the Lord.

For the safety and peace
of the Russian people
and for harmony among their neighboring
	lands:
let us pray to the Lord.

For various needs

For those who are sick,
and for those who remember them and
        care for them:
let us pray to the Lord.

For those who love us and those
who hate us,
for those we have forgiven
        and those whom we cannot yet forgive:
let us pray to the Lord.

For the local community

That God will lead this community from
death to life:
let us pray to the Lord.
For this community of faith,
that we be freed from the darkness of sin
and made holy by Christ:
let us pray to the Lord.

For the catechumens and the elect

For the elect and the candidates
        of the church,
that Christ lead them to the table
        of his love:
let us pray to the Lord.

For those called to the sacraments
of the Lord,
that Christ may now be their strength:
let us pray to the Lord.

For the dead

For those who have died in Christ,
who are remembered forever by God:
let us pray to the Lord.

Concluding Prayers for the General Intercessions

FIRST SUNDAY OF LENT
Lord our God,
in every age you call a people
to hear your word
and to do your will.

Renew us in these Lenten days:
washed clean of sin,
sealed with the Spirit,
and sustained by your living bread,
may we remain true to our calling
and, with the elect, serve you alone.

Grant this through Christ, our liberator
        from sin,
who lives and reigns with you in the unity
        of the Holy Spirit,
holy and mighty God for ever and ever.
—© ICEL

SECOND SUNDAY OF LENT
Holy God,
from the dazzling cloud
you revealed Jesus in glory
as your beloved Son.

During these forty days
enlighten your Church with the bright glory
        of your presence.
Inspire us by your word,
and so transform us into the image
        of the risen Lord,
who lives and reigns with you in the unity
        of the Holy Spirit,
holy and mighty God for ever and ever.
—© ICEL

THIRD SUNDAY OF LENT
O God, living and true,
look upon your people,
whose dry and stony hearts are parched
        with thirst.

Unseal the living water of your Spirit;
let it become within us an ever-flowing
        spring,
leaping up to eternal life.
Thus may we worship you in spirit
        and in truth
through Christ, our deliverance and hope,
who lives and reigns with you in the unity
        of the Holy Spirit,
holy and mighty God for ever and ever.
—© ICEL

FOURTH SUNDAY OF LENT
God our Creator,
show forth your mighty works
in the midst of your people.
Enlighten your Church,
that we may know your Son
as the true light of the world
and through our worship confess him
as Christ and Lord,
who lives and reigns with you in the unity
        of the Holy Spirit,
holy and mighty God for ever and ever.

FIFTH SUNDAY OF LENT
Merciful God,
you showed your glory to our fallen race
by sending your Son
to confound the powers of death.
Call us forth from sin's dark tomb.
Break the bonds which hold us,
that we may believe and proclaim Christ,
the cause of our freedom
and the source of life.
who lives and reigns with you in the unity
of the Holy Spirit, one God forever and ever.
—© ICEL

PASSION (PALM) SUNDAY
O God of eternal glory,
you anointed Jesus your servant
to bear our sins,
to encourage the weary,
to raise up and restore the fallen.

Keep before our eyes
the splendor of the paschal mystery
    of Christ,
and, by our sharing in the passion
    and resurrection,
seal our lives with the victorious sign
of his obedience and exaltation.

We ask this through Christ, our liberator
    from sin,
who lives with you in the unity
    of the Holy Spirit,
holy and mighty God for ever and ever.
—© ICEL

LITURGY OF THE EUCHARIST

Eucharistic Prayer Inserts

SUNDAYS IN EUCHARISTIC PRAYERS II AND III:
    See page 85.

ANNUNCIATION IN EUCHARISTIC PRAYER II:
    Lord, you are holy indeed,
    the fountain of all holiness.
    We gather here before you,
    and in communion with the whole
        church
    we celebrate the day the Virgin Mary,
    through the Holy Spirit,
    conceived your eternal Son.
    Through him, who became our Savior,
    we pray:
    Let your Spirit come upon . . .

ANNUNCIATION IN EUCHARISTIC PRAYER III:
    . . . a perfect offering may be made
    to the glory of your name.
    This is why we gather before you,
    and in communion with the whole
        church
    we celebrate the day the Virgin Mary,
    through the Holy Spirit
    conceived your eternal Son.
    Through him, who became our Savior,
    we bring you these gifts.
    We ask you to make them holy . . .

Introduction to the Lord's Prayer

Let us come before the compassionate God
with hearts full of forgiveness toward others,
so that we may offer our prayer in the words
Jesus taught us to pray:

Prayer for Peace

Lord Jesus Christ, through the mystery of
your death and resurrection you sealed the
covenant of peace between heaven and earth:
Look not on our sins . . .

Invitation to Communion

This is the Lamb of God, who takes away the
sins of the world: our Passover sacrificed for
us, our peace and reconciliation. Happy are
those who are called to his supper.

CONCLUDING RITE

Dismissal of Eucharistic Ministers

Go forth in peace to the sick and homebound
members of our community, bearing the word
of life and the Body of Christ, together with
the assurance of our love and concern. May
these gifts strengthen our absent brothers and
sisters in their communion with us through
the pilgrimage of Lent to the paschal feast of
the kingdom.

Dismissal

As a people called to conversion on a journey to
new life, go in peace to love and serve the Lord.

The *Circular Letter Concerning the Preparation and Celebration of the Easter Feasts* suggests that an appropriate way to mark the First Sunday of Lent with penitential solemnity would be to begin the liturgy with a procession during which the litany of the saints is chanted. Reference is made to #261 of the *Ceremonial of Bishops,* which describes how the procession is held.

- The community assembles in a place apart from the place where Mass will be celebrated.

- While a gathering song is sung, the presider and ministers go to that place.

- The presider (who may be vested in a cope) greets the assembly with the sign of the cross and then the seasonal liturgical greeting.

- The presider or a deacon or other minister offers a brief introduction, for example:

  We have come to the beginning of our Lenten spring, the season to prepare the holy Passover that will bring our catechumens to the saving waters of rebirth, the Passover that will be, for those of us already initiated, a pilgrimage of conversion.

  Lent is a journey with the Lord who longs to draw us more closely to himself that he might speak to our hearts. Along the way we will be challenged to recognize Christ in the scriptures we read, in those we love and serve, and in those whom we so often neglect to love and serve — for surely Christ is most specially present in them.

  Therefore, let us begin the journey!

  Our procession is in the spirit of the pilgrimage of the Israelites, our forebears in faith. We call upon the saints, our holy ancestors, who remind us that we do not journey alone.

  Let us move forward in joy, keeping our eyes fixed on the goal of our Lenten journey, which is Jerusalem, the holy city of God.

- The presider offers a collect: either that of the Holy Cross, September 14; or "For Forgiveness of Sins" in the back of the sacramentary (#40); or for the local church (under Masses and Prayers for Various Needs and Occasions); or from the prayers over the people in the sacramentary (especially #6).

- Incense is placed in the thurible, and the deacon announces: "Let us go forth in peace."

- The litany of the saints is sung as the procession moves to the church. Saints from the local parish's heritage should be added in their proper places, along with patrons of the diocese, place or parish.

- When the ministers reach the altar, the presider reverences it, kisses it and may incense it. The presider then goes to the chair (changing from cope to chasuble), and when the litany ends, chants the opening prayer of the Mass, omitting the penitential rite.

TEXTS FOR THE ANOINTING OF THE SICK WITHIN MASS

Introduction/Reception of the Sick

Though he was in the form of God, Christ emptied himself, becoming one of us, indeed the servant of all. It was our infirmities he bore, our sufferings he endured, becoming obedient for us even unto death, death on a cross. As we gather in this holy season of Lent to celebrate the sacraments of anointing and eucharist, let us recall that by baptism into Christ's death, we have become heirs with him to the glory of resurrection. Through this celebration may ours be a share in his redemptive suffering and risen glory.

Prayer after Anointing

God of the covenant,
in this, the acceptable time of your favor,
on this, the day of salvation,
you offer in Christ the healing power
    of your love
through the laying on of hands
and anointing with holy oil.
Immersed in Christ's life through baptism,
and now joined more closely to his passion,
may our brothers and sisters
    come to share fully
in the triumphant power of his resurrection,
who lives and reigns for ever and ever.

TRIDUUM

Introduction to the Season

THE three days that compose the Triduum are the central days of the whole liturgical year. They are the Christian "High Holy Days," as it were, the days when we celebrate most fully our identity as followers of Christ and the meaning of our lives. These are the days we need to celebrate most richly and most completely. They ought to be the days that draw the largest crowds and have the greatest impact on parish life. It could be said that our celebration of these three days provides a good barometer of the level of liturgical development of the parish. To the extent that the whole parish has come to understand and appreciate the liturgy and the liturgical year, to that extent they will enter eagerly into the celebration of the Triduum.

This could, of course, be cause for discouragement in parishes where the Triduum liturgies still draw only a small percentage of the parish. A realistic yardstick is important here. The ideal is that every member of the parish will recognize the importance of these days and strive to celebrate them with the community. But the ideal will never be fully realized. And perhaps it never was in the past, either. While it is probable that Christians in the early centuries had a better understanding of their role

in worship than many do today, it is almost certain that the church has always included some members who are unwilling to do more than the minimum required. Moreover, in earlier centuries, participation in church-centered celebrations was often a major means of both socialization and recreation. Without the communication media and the means of travel common to the modern world, earlier generations had far fewer distractions to fill the days. Our contemporary culture also works against full participation in the Triduum. Many people must work on Good Friday and sometimes even on Saturday and Sunday. Society does not organize its calendar around church feast days as it did in medieval Europe.

So our goal must always be to encourage full participation in well-prepared and well-attended liturgies, but we should take heart from whatever progress is evident and not let the progress not yet realized discourage us or deter us from offering the best liturgies that we can arrange. Our focus really should be on preparing to celebrate well with whoever comes; a tradition of consistently well-prepared worship will gradually draw more and more parishioners to participate. Recognizing the importance of these days should lead us to careful preparation and prayerful celebration of the liturgical moments that mark them.

The Triduum is best understood as a unified observance that extends over three days. It stands between Lent and Easter as the hinge not only of this major festal cycle, but of the whole year. The Three Days are marked by a variety of liturgical services, but the Triduum is more than its liturgies. While much effort is needed to prepare for these major celebrations, it is important to see that keeping these days holy means observing the entire three days well, both in church and at home.

The Triduum begins with the Evening Mass of the Lord's Supper and concludes with Evening Prayer on Easter Sunday. Throughout this period, the church is called to pray, to fast and to keep vigil. The principal liturgies even suggest the unity of the Triduum by the way they end and begin. On Thursday, there is no dismissal or conclusion; on Friday we gather and leave with no introductory or concluding rites, and at the Vigil we gather around the fire and begin without the usual introductory rites. We begin on Thursday, and we don't conclude until after the Vigil, with Easter Sunday as a kind of extension of the celebration of the Vigil.

Understanding the Triduum as one three-day-long liturgy can help us find the right approach to each of the ritual moments within it. The Evening Mass on Holy Thursday is a liturgy of entrance into the Triduum, not primarily a celebration of the institution of the eucharist or of the ordained priesthood. Good Friday's main liturgy commemorates the death of the Lord, but as a part of the whole paschal mystery (we call it "Good" Friday), which is celebrated in its fullness at the Easter Vigil, when our newest members enter into the death and resurrection of the Lord through the waters of baptism. Easter Sunday is a day of reveling in the mystery we celebrate at the Vigil, a day for the glow of the feast to be enjoyed and savored.

As the Lent–Easter cycle is the core of the year, so the Triduum is the core of Lent–Easter. The Triduum gives meaning to Lent, which precedes it, and to the Fifty Days of Easter, which follow it. These days are central because they draw us into the heart of our identity as church. The mystery of Jesus' death and resurrection is the core of our faith, and our participation in that mystery through the celebration of baptism defines what it means to be Christian and what it means for the community to be church.

As always, we must overcome the tendency to approach liturgy as historical drama. When we celebrate these liturgies, we are not pretending that we are standing at the foot of the cross in first-century Palestine or waiting to see if Christ will rise on Easter Sunday. We know that these events have already occurred, once and for all; Christ does not die again, for death has no more power over him. The death and resurrection we celebrate is not just the historical event in the past, but our dying and rising in Christ today. We focus our celebration especially around the catechumens who enter the watery tomb and rise from it to resurrected life for the first time. Along with them, we are all called to reenter the mystery each year, to die more fully to self and to rise in the Lord. Leo the Great makes the point succinctly:

> The body that lies lifeless in the tomb is ours. The body that rose again on the third day is ours. The body that ascended above all the heights of heaven to the right hand of the Father's glory is ours. If then we walk in the way of his commandments . . . we too are to rise to share his glory. (Office of Readings, Thursday of the Fourth Week of Lent)

Thus we renew each year the promises of our baptism. We gather around the font and remember who we are as we welcome new members into the order of the faithful.

The Triduum finds its climax and ultimate meaning in the celebration of the Vigil. The centrality of the Vigil should be obvious by the way we approach the various celebrations of the Triduum. The Evening Mass on Holy Thursday is the beginning of the Triduum and should not compete with the Vigil in splendor or importance. Good Friday is both solemn and austere, and it waits for the Vigil to complete its meaning. The Vigil itself is the highest moment of celebration, which is then extended throughout Easter Sunday.

Even more than in the 40 days of Lent, this time must not allow for business as usual. And it is possible for the most part with some foresight. We should all abstain from normal activity on these days. The usual routines of life are interrupted so that we can spend these days as a time of "retreat," a time of intense engagement with the paschal mystery. During the three days, we gather frequently for prayer and celebration, but every moment of these three days should be marked by prayer and reflection.

The rituals of the Triduum provide a framework of common worship to support and focus our personal prayer. As once-a-year rituals, they need very little in the way of adaptation or creative innovation. What is important is that they be prepared well and celebrated with care and reverence. This is a time to follow the ritual books closely and to establish an annual tradition of music and ritual that will be comfortable, yet powerful. The temptation to do something different each year should be firmly resisted.

Semitic scholar and liturgist Anton Baumstark's insight that the most important days in a community's calendar change the least over centuries also points to a very important pastoral principle: Unique rituals, such as those of the Triduum, can be fully effective only if they are substantially the same from year to year so that people can enter into them confidently. Rather than spending time thinking up innovations, those responsible for the liturgy should focus on steadily improving the care and fullness with which the official rituals are carried out. Making ever fuller use of the basic symbols and actions of our worship can lead us to an ever deeper appreciation of the fundamental mystery we celebrate.

THE PASCHAL FAST

One of the best ways for all of us to enter into the spirit of these days is by keeping the paschal fast. The Second Vatican Council issued this appeal in its *Constitution on the Sacred Liturgy:*

> Let the paschal fast be kept sacred. Let it be observed everywhere on Good Friday and, where possible, prolonged through Holy Saturday, as a way of coming to the joys of the Sunday of the resurrection with uplifted and welcoming heart. (#110)

Though Catholics are accustomed to fasting on Good Friday, the paschal fast is not generally understood. It is not part of the Lenten fast, and it is not penitential as much as it is preparatory. It is fasting in anticipation of the coming feast. It is preparation for the Vigil, for the work of initiating new members into the paschal mystery of Christ. It is the fasting of those who are too excited to eat. We have all known times when the anticipation of a coming event has made us so excited that we didn't even think about eating (perhaps on our wedding or ordination day). And we've known times when we've gotten so engrossed in something (perhaps a novel or a project) that we simply forgot to stop for a meal. Ritual fasting attempts to re-create such experiences in reverse, as it were, letting the fasting from food lead us back to such an excitement of anticipation or such a preoccupation with Christ. It is a larger expression of the same impulse that leads us to fast before communion (even if that is only an hour now). And

it is a powerful way of marking these days as unique; nothing about our lives is as usual, not even our eating and drinking.

The paschal fast is not just from food and drink. If the purpose of the fast is to focus our lives on the mystery, it may be more important to fast from television, radio and whatever other distractions usually fill our lives. The goal is to keep these days special, to keep them holy, to keep ourselves focused on the Lord and on the meaning of these days.

The fast is only strictly required on Good Friday, but the Council urged its extension through Saturday, and subsequent documents have reinforced that idea. The *Rite of Christian Initiation of Adults* provides a strong focus for the fast; for the catechumens, it is immediate preparation for approaching the waters of the font, and the whole community joins them, fasting on their behalf and also preparing for their own baptismal renewal. From that perspective, Saturday seems even more appropriate for the fast than Friday, since it is closer to the Vigil. The church community needs to find ways of keeping this fast honestly and communally. Each individual will want to create his or her own routine of prayer, reflection and fasting for these days, but it is done in the context and with the awareness of the fact that we keep these days and this fast together, supporting one another and uniting in prayer especially for those to be baptized and received into the church at the Vigil.

■ STRUCTURE OF THE SEASON: The season contains three main liturgies—the Evening Mass of the Lord's Supper, the Celebration of the Lord's Passion and the Easter Vigil. Then the liturgies on Easter day are a bit simpler. As Anscar Chupungco summarizes in *Liturgies of the Future:*

> The Mass and vespers of Easter day are like a passage formally concluding a musical composition.... This implies that the Easter day liturgy must not be so elaborate as to become the center of the Triduum. Yet it must not be so plain and ritually impoverished that it appears like any ordinary Sunday liturgy. For the faithful, Easter Sunday as the conclusion of the Triduum is the fitting occasion to reminisce about the Easter vigil and recall the Easter sacraments. (pp. 173, 184)

Those who prepare the liturgies of these days should be realistic about parish resources, especially in terms of prayer leaders and liturgical ministers. This *Sourcebook* offers a multitude of possible events for these three days. Better to do a few very well than to attempt too many and do them poorly. After scheduling the three main liturgies and as few Sunday morning Masses as possible (everyone should be at the Vigil!), other events may be scheduled. The liturgical books indicate that the next liturgies developed should be the preparation rites for the elect on Holy Saturday and Evening Prayer on Easter Sunday.

After these liturgies, Morning Prayer on each of the three days (perhaps combined with the Office of Readings on Good Friday and Holy Saturday to form Tenebrae—see page 134) can be added to the parish schedule over a period of years. Other hours and rites are described in the Triduum calendar section of this book. The hours not mentioned here are never celebrated publicly due to the major liturgies.

Other devotions are on a still lower level. Stations of the cross, for example, may find a proper place in the Triduum, but they should never compete with the full liturgy of the church on these holiest days.

An African American Perspective

IN celebrating the Triduum we are at the heart of who we are: a people made whole in the death–resurrection of the Lord. It is at the very heart of the spirituals. The number of spirituals that would be appropriate for the Triduum is vast. Two deserve special attention: "Ride on, King Jesus" and "Were you there?"

RIDE ON KING JESUS

Ride on, King Jesus,
No man can a-hinder me.
Ride on, King Jesus,
No man can a-hinder me.

I was but young when I begun,
No man can a-hinder me.
But now my race is almost done,
No man can a-hinder me.

King Jesus rides on a milk white horse . . .
The river of Jordan he did cross . . .

If you want to find your way to God . . .
The gospel highway must be trod . . .

Our entry into our yearly celebration of the paschal mystery begins on Passion (Palm) Sunday. More than recapturing some past event, this is an entrance into a current mystery: our salvation won through the death–resurrection of the Lord. It is a mystery, a reality that we celebrate here and now. Here is a song that compels us to do what Jesus did, to die for the life of the world. African American insurrectionists of old used this song to remind them that the death–resurrection of the Lord did more than bring about inner healing. This song spurred then on to continuing liberating as Jesus did. In this song they were made confident that

> [Jesus'] role as a current, loyal companion and leader in [the] battle [for freedom] was equally, if not more significant. . . . In this song, we can feel the resolve of generations of African Americans who have used it to bolster their persistent ride on the road to freedom. With its lively and spirited rhythms, we sense that the ancestral composer of this song intended its power to be experienced in the personally and socially transformative circle of the ring shout, strengthening even further the mounting resistance to decades [centuries] of slavery. In singing and dancing this song, we can be sure that each participant felt, with complete determination, "no man can a-hinder me!" (Arthur C. Jones, *Wade in the Water*, Maryknoll: Orbis 1993, p. 54)

And no one can hinder those of us today who struggle for justice, mercy and peace. Our entering into this holy week is entering into that certainty.

WERE YOU THERE?

Were you there when they crucified my Lord?
Were you there when they crucified my Lord?
Were you there when they crucified my Lord?
Oh! Sometimes it causes me to tremble, tremble, tremble.
Were you there when they crucified my Lord?

Were you there when they nailed him
to the tree? . . .
Were you there when they pierced him
in the side? . . .
Were you there when the sun refused
to shine? . . .
Were you there when they laid him
in the tomb? . . .

Perhaps the most well-known and widely-used spiritual during Pasch is this one. Its use should be encouraged, particularly if one understands its anamnetic quality. This is not some maudlin song about a "dead Jesus" but a song about the crucified Lord of life. This song is more than an objective "Christ has died. Christ is risen. Christ will come again."

But rather "We were there when they crucified the Lord"—in the pain of the Middle Passage and in sight of a trembling crack baby. "We were there when they nailed him to the tree"—in the anguish of slavery and the embrace of a son or daughter withered with AIDS. "We were there when they pierced his side"—in the daily discrimination of a racist society and in the streets running red with blood spilled in violence. "We were there when the sun refused to shine"—in the battered spouse and forgotten parent and in the unemployment that makes tonight's dinner more of a dream than a reality. Indeed, it causes one to "tremble, tremble, tremble." And we tremble with the reality of a God who brings life from suffering and death, hope from a stinking tomb and love in the midst of abandonment. (Richard E. McCarron, "Our Yearly Feast," *Plenty Good Room,* November/ December 1993, 2–3)

The Hispanic Mística and the Liturgy

ALTHOUGH it has been reformed and simplified twice in this century, the most liturgically complex week of the church year in any Catholic parish is still Holy Week. It can seem even more complicated in a Hispanic parish because of the many extras that seem to crop up on unsuspecting non-Hispanic liturgical ministers. For some who are not Hispanic, accommodating traditional Hispanic devotional practices during this week poses not only logistical but theological problems, since the popular stress of these days seems to be almost entirely on the suffering and death of Jesus with very little attention paid to the resurrection. If one were to judge on the basis of attendance, Holy Thursday and especially Good Friday enjoy much more popularity than the Easter Vigil or even Mass during the day on Easter.

It would be a mistake, however, to assume that this emphasis is caused by a morbid preoccupation with Christ's suffering and death. Rather, the stress on the suffering of Christ and

Mary during the days of Holy Week and Triduum evokes the important relationship that many Hispanics see between these rituals and their own lives. Hispanic spirituality and popular piety is strongly rooted in a cultural value called *personalismo,* or the dignity of the person and personal relationships as central to living a truly human life. This value is well expressed during this holiest week of the year. The dramatic and paradoxical suffering of Jesus as the innocent Son of God atoning for the sins of humanity resonates deeply in the hearts of most Hispanics, principally because of their long experience of oppression and marginalization, even in their own land. The depiction of the agony of Christ venerated by the *confradías* (the pious fraternities) throughout the Hispanic world, such as Jesus as *El Nazareno* (Jesus just after the scourging at the pillar) of New Mexico and Colorado, illustrates the dignity in suffering of those unjustly persecuted.

Our response as followers of the suffering Christ is not to try vainly to alleviate suffering—which we know to be impossible—but to accompany the suffering savior through the agonies of the passion, as we would a friend and brother. The belief in the redemptive power of suffering is central to the Hispanic understanding of Holy Week and of the entire paschal mystery. For this reason, *not* to emphasize the suffering of Christ and move directly to the resurrection is to falsify and trivialize the reality of the redemption. It is clear, of course, that this focus on suffering can be exaggerated, but it can also be a good tonic for the rest of the U.S. church, which tends to rush to the risen Christ after what is often portrayed as the brief inconvenience of the cross.

Hispanics accompany the suffering savior throughout these days. The traditional vigil at the reserved sacrament after the Mass of the Lord's Supper on Holy Thursday is called *El Santo Dolor del Huerto*—"The Holy Agony of the Garden." The popularity in Hispanic parishes around the country of the "living way of the cross," a reenactment of Jesus' walk after being condemned by Pilate, is another way in which the whole parish and neighborhood accompanies the suffering savior on Good Friday. Finally, Hispanics extend to Mary the same respect given to any mother who has lost her son. Late afternoon and evening on Friday is the usual time to go to church and offer the *Pésame a la Virgen* (condolences to the grieving Virgin Mary).

One cannot help but think of the expression used at the time of death to show support of the one in grief, *"Yo te acompaño en tus sentimientos,"* literally, "I accompany you in your sorrow." Much as at a traditional wake, the rosary is prayed and hymns are sung in the presence of a *La Dolorosa,* a statue of the sorrowful Mary placed before an empty cross. Through these celebrations, Hispanics enter fully into the tragedy of Christ's pain and death, and also "rehearse" accompanying others in their moment of suffering and loss—aware, however, of the resurrection that is to come.

Preparing the Parish

IN one sense, preparing the parish to celebrate the Triduum well is what the liturgical renewal is all about. The more the parish assembly accepts its central role in creating good worship and the more they understand the inner meaning of the liturgical year, the more fully the parish will enter into the spirit and meaning of these days. All the effort we make to develop a liturgically based spirituality in the parish comes to its ultimate fruition in the Triduum.

Viewed from the opposite perspective, leading the assembly to celebrate these days well will also foster more involved and powerful worship all year long. So there is good reason to focus specifically on the meaning and importance of these days. Awareness of that importance will grow gradually through the example and catechesis offered by parish leaders year by year.

The example offered by all members of the parish staff is crucial. Parish leaders might find much benefit in common study of a text like Gabe Huck's *The Three Days* (LTP; revised edition, 1992), so that all can share a common vision of the goal to be sought in making the Triduum central in the life of the parish.

Then practical steps are needed to communicate the importance of these days to the whole parish. If we consider how the parish goes about promoting other events, we may see parallels that could be helpful. If your parish has a festival, for example, what are the various means by which participation in the event and excitement about it are communicated? Should we do more to communicate the importance of and excitement about the Triduum, the days when we welcome new members to the sacraments and redefine our very identity?

The key word may be *excitement.* Despite the fact that these are the greatest feasts of the year, they are not listed as holy days of obligation, perhaps because participation in the Triduum should not be a matter of obligation. It should flow from a sense that something important and wonderful is happening which we want all to share. Generating such excitement is easier when the Triduum has been celebrated well in previous years, but it ultimately flows from a conviction that there is nothing we do as a community that is more important to our life together as church than celebrating these days.

Every committee and group in the parish might be visited by a member of the staff or worship committee during Lent (or earlier) with encouragement to participate in the Triduum. Confirmation candidates should see such participation as part of their commitment to being full members of the church. All those who schedule events in the parish should place the Vigil and other Triduum events at the center of their annual calendars. Asking for this is simply a matter of calling the church to its roots and its foundation.

Schedules for the Triduum services might be printed on a bulletin that makes clear the importance of the Triduum and how it might be well observed. *Three Days to Save,* published by LTP, is a good example.

Planners should also consider practical steps that will facilitate participation by all members of the parish. A simple parish supper may enable workers to come directly to church on Holy Thursday. Provisions for transportation and assistance to the disabled will signal the importance of including everyone in these celebrations. Arrangements for child care during services, perhaps with parents rotating coverage every half hour, would encourage those with small children to consider greater participation.

Taking It Home

THOUGH it is natural that our attention focuses on the parish liturgies, keeping these three days holy must include both personal and family prayer outside the church building. This provides the basis for deep participation in the liturgies. One of the fundamental ways that we should prepare is by observing the paschal fast. Since fasting is only minimally observed among most Catholics today, it will take time to make this special fast an integral part of Catholic practice. Steady catechesis and the example of parish staff and leaders will gradually enable the whole community to recover the values of this ancient tradition.

LTP's *Take Me Home* resource book has activities for the Paschal Triduum and for Easter Sunday. *Catholic Household Blessings and Prayers* contains many texts for observing the Triduum (pp. 143–52). These materials include meditations, an antiphon to echo through the days, texts of the baptismal renewal and a blessing of Easter foods. Homebound parisioners have a special place in domestic prayer. They might all be given a copy of *Catholic Household Blessings and Prayers* as a gift from the parish community inviting them to pray with and for the whole church.

Families might also be encouraged to make and/or decorate their own Easter candles. Such candles could be used during the Vigil in place of the individual tapers and then used through the Fifty Days of Easter at home.

Triduum. Communal penance services certainly should not be scheduled during the Triduum, and many parishes and dioceses avoid scheduling individual confessions after Wednesday of this week, though an individual request for this sacrament will always be met when possible.

- Anointing of the sick may be celebrated in cases of emergency, but normally this sacrament would not be scheduled during the Triduum.

- On Holy Thursday and Good Friday, communion cannot be distributed outside the liturgy except to the sick. On Holy Saturday, communion can be given only as viaticum.

- Funeral Masses are not celebrated during the same period; if a funeral cannot be delayed until Monday, the funeral is conducted without Mass and without music or flowers. Paragraph 179 of the *Order of Christian Funerals* allows for the funeral rites to take place at sites other than the church. During the Triduum, the rite that begins at #183 must be used, and readings consonant with the day should be selected, using a few of the readings from the day's liturgies. These texts of the day help mourners experience the consolation of the death and rising of Christ. A eucharist should be scheduled for the bereaved during the Easter octave. Pastoral workers should help mourners appreciate the importance of the Easter Vigil. No wake should compete with it. Perhaps those who grieve may choose to pray in vigil for the deceased by coming to at least part of the Easter Vigil.

Other Ritual Prayer and Sacraments

THE sacramentary on Good Friday notes: "According to the church's ancient tradition, the sacraments are not celebrated today or tomorrow." Besides the obvious inappropriateness of celebrating baptism or confirmation during the Triduum (or even during Lent itself) and the fact that no Masses are celebrated on these two days prior to the Vigil, this brief reminder points to several regulations:

- Weddings are not celebrated from Holy Thursday (all day) through Easter. While weddings are allowed on Easter Sunday (with the readings and prayers of the day), they should be considered pastorally inappropriate.

- Though the sacrament of Penance may be celebrated, it properly belongs in Lent, not during the

The Worship Environment

IT is important to do most of the work for the Triduum before the Three Days arrive. Long before Holy Thursday, the church should be thoroughly cleaned. Only last-minute tasks should be left for the days of Triduum, and these should be thought through and assignments made earlier in Holy Week, freeing coordinators and pastors to enter fully into the Triduum.

■ VESSELS AND OTHER OBJECTS: A careful review of liturgical ceremonies will help sacristans prepare a thorough list of items needed for each liturgy, from towels for the foot washing to congregational candles at the Vigil to flowers or Easter eggs for all. Helpful "requisites" lists are provided for each day in the *Ceremonial of*

Bishops (#299, #315, #336). Sample lists can be found in the Triduum calendar section, pages 130–150 of this book. Thomas Ryan's *The Sacristy Manual* (LTP, 1993) provides similar lists and a great deal more of interest to those who tend to the material requirements of the liturgy.

■ VESTURE FOR THE TRIDUUM: Thursday calls for white vestments. These should be a simple white, not the festive Easter vestments.

Red is the color for Good Friday, without ornament (certainly without Pentecost symbols). The sacramentary calls for red Mass vestments—chasuble for the presider, dalmatic for the deacon.

Violet is the color for Holy Saturday's liturgy of the hours or for the preparatory rites. Copes should not be used on this simplest of days.

The vesture to be worn throughout the Fifty Days of Easter should be worn for the first time at the Vigil. To add solemnity, consider vesting the cantors and lectors, especially the person who will sing the Exsultet, in albs. Albs are simply baptismal garments. They should be ready for all the neophytes this night.

■ LITURGICAL BOOKS should be worthy of the holy mysteries they serve, beautiful reminders of the presence of the word of God. The sacramentary, perhaps suitably covered by local artisans, is to be held by the assisting ministers—no flimsy missalette should be juggled by those attempting to draw the assembly into the sacred mysteries. The lectionary and any book of the gospels should tell even the youngest participant that this is important.

For the Triduum, three other books should be considered. First, the book or scroll from which the Exsultet is sung should be beautiful. Second, most parishes will need to create a book for use by leaders of the liturgy of the hours. The variety of adaptations and the importance of locally selected music demand a tailor-made presider's book. An artistically designed binder or a beautifully bound book (perhaps with blank pages) should be obtained. Removable tape and photocopiers allow for all the texts to be placed without damaging the book. A third book may be a locally arranged leaders' book for the Vigil—for presider, music director and anyone who needs the complete outline of this complicated liturgy. This book would include the appropriate texts from the sacramentary and the initiation rites, music and marginal notes to

remind pastors and music directors of previously agreed on actions and signals.

■ DECORATIONS: The sacramentary and other official liturgical documentation should guide sacristans through these days.

• *Thursday evening (before Mass):* "The tabernacle should be entirely empty." That implies that the veil is removed, the vigil light is removed and the doors are left open. That rubric, as well as the norms of the sacramentary for Lent, implies that the entire church is stripped and cleaned—without candles or cloths or any unnecessary furniture (see page 101 in the introduction to Lent). This bareness conveys the austere solemnity of these days and should contrast with the splendor of Easter to come.

• *Thursday evening (for the end of Mass):* The place for the transfer of the eucharist is described as "a chapel suitably decorated" and "conducive to prayer and meditation" (*Circular Letter,* #49). Remember that it is Good Friday eve, so the watchword is simplicity. Candles should not exceed the number usually used at Mass. Save the flowers for Saturday night. The *Newsletter* of the U.S. Bishops' Committee on the Liturgy (March 1993) emphasized that the place of reposition should be "either the chapel of reservation, if the church has one, or a chapel set up apart from the church." A side altar in the main nave does not suffice!

• *Thursday evening (after Mass):* Crosses are to be removed from the church or veiled. It also is customary to remove holy water from the fonts to await the Easter water. The removal of crosses, however, is a logical part of the church cleaning earlier in Lent or even before Ash Wednesday. There should be little to strip from the church tonight except the altar cloth and the furniture used in the washing of the feet. Anything not part of the building itself (credence tables, kneelers, etc.) should be removed. The few items needed for the celebration tomorrow can be brought in for the service and then taken away. Although there is no ceremony for removing the altar cloth, strip the altar with great reverence and dignity. This action was for years a sign of our entering into the paschal fast. It took place during the singing of Psalm 22. The psalm still may be prayed by those performing this ministry.

• *Thursday midnight:* All candles, except for the candle near the tabernacle in the chapel of reservation, are extinguished at the conclusion of eucharistic adoration or night prayer (whichever comes later). All other decorations are taken from the eucharistic chapel before the first hour of prayer on Friday.

- *Friday (before the Celebration of the Lord's Passion):* Only those items of furniture needed for the rite are set out. Candles are to be ready near the cross for its solemn entrance, and an altar cloth is kept to the side for later use. All else is bare.

- *Friday (after the communion rite):* At the conclusion of the rite, any remaining eucharist is brought to a separate, private place to be kept for viaticum. This must not be the eucharistic chapel, for the reservation is not provided for visitation or private prayer.

- *Friday (after the Celebration):* The altar and sanctuary again are completely stripped except perhaps for the cross. The cross (which was carried in during the celebration) is placed (perhaps with lighted candles) in a place conducive both to quiet prayer and to reverencing the cross with a touch or kiss. The *Circular Letter* (#71) suggests the now-empty eucharistic chapel. If the cross is a stationary one—for example, the one suspended over the sanctuary—then candles (and perhaps a spotlight) might grace it.

- *Saturday in general:* The church should be decorated as late as possible so that it is bare for the liturgy of the hours, the preparatory rites or other assembly. The enshrined cross remains in place.

- *Saturday morning:* The *Circular Letter* (#74) suggests that an image or two may be introduced into the space for the whole day.

  The image of Christ crucified or lying in the tomb, or of the descent into hell, the mystery which Holy Saturday recalls, and also an image of the sorrowful Virgin Mary, can be placed in the church for the veneration of the faithful.

- *Saturday night (Vigil):* The *Ceremonial of Bishops* (#48) contains an interesting note: The rubrics ban the use of flowers from "Ash Wednesday until the Gloria at the Easter Vigil." For centuries, a reverent procession of flower bearers and veil removers (recall the rubrics regarding the removal of veils from the statues) took place at the Gloria.

■ RITES SHAPE ARCHITECTURE: Good ritual celebrations demand appropriate spaces, and the liturgies of the Triduum raise several important issues. This is not the time for pastors and liturgical planners to worry about renovation plans, but it is the perfect time to jot down notes about what would have enhanced and facilitated the prayer of the assembly.

- *Thursday:* The place of reposition is the eucharistic chapel, if this is separate from the main worship space. A parish that ordinarily uses a side altar for the tabernacle should set up another room for reservation this night. And then it should add this to the list of renovation topics. The liturgy of the church calls for a chapel of reservation for the tabernacle that is separate from the space for celebration of the eucharist.

- *Thursday (and later days):* When the elect and catechumens are dismissed before the general intercessions, they go to the *catechumeneon* (see page 101)—a space apart.

- *Friday:* The size and location of the cross that will grace the worship space are directly related to the veneration on this day. A suspended cross must be attached in such a way that the assembly can touch or kiss it—no substitute cross should be brought in for this moment, especially if the regular cross is hanging overhead. The Roman Rite's preference for the church's regular cross to be a processional cross—not a permanently fixed cross—rises in part from this rite and its centrality in linking the parish to its cross.

- *Saturday night (and other days):* Because every household should come to the Vigil, a child-care facility will be needed. This is not peripheral to good liturgy. For 20 years, the *Rite of Baptism for Children* (#14) has called for an auxiliary room where children and infants should be taken until the time of baptism. The possible presence of infants to be baptized at the Vigil lends further strength to this Triduum requirement.

- *Saturday night (Fire):* The service of light makes particular architectural and landscaping demands. Renovation plans must consider the full observance of this liturgy, with all gathered in a place separate from the main worship space.

- *Saturday night (Water):* An immersion font is called for. The National Statutes for the Catechumenate, approved by the United States Conference of Bishops in 1986, tells us that immersion is the preferred mode of baptism (#17). If a permanent immersion font is not yet part of your worship space, a temporary font large enough for an adult to kneel in the pool while water is poured over the head (a graceful position for baptism) is easily devised. See "Testing the Waters" in the April 1992 issue of *Environment & Art Letter* (LTP).

  Liturgical design committees continue to argue over the best place for the font, but it certainly is not right next to the other sacred furnishings. If you are constructing a font for this occasion, be aware that front and center is not always best. Allow this sacred action to unfold in its own area of the church, one that would allow for processions both to and from the site.

April

4 #39 white
Holy Thursday

ENTERING THE TRIDUUM

Preparing the Triduum liturgies is a unique undertaking in several respects: The liturgies include numerous once-a-year rituals; the days themselves are the most solemn and significant of the year; the sacraments of initiation at the Vigil make the Triduum the sacramental and emotional high point of the year for the initiates and for the community as a whole; the ceremonies are ancient and rich with symbol; and the whole Triduum is essentially one long liturgy with multiple assemblies and ritual moments.

While planners must always prepare liturgies with an eye to the season and what precedes and follows a particular Sunday or feast, the Triduum demands an even more holistic approach. Each of the ritual moments carries such weight that it is easy to see them as self-contained. The temptation is to focus on each day of the Triduum separately rather than to see them as parts of an integrated celebration.

Thus, Holy Thursday is not primarily a day to celebrate the institution of the eucharist or the ordained priesthood. It is, first and foremost, the beginning of the Triduum. The entrance antiphon in the sacramentary makes clear the proper focus of the celebration: "We should glory in the cross of our Lord Jesus Christ, for he is our salvation, our life and our resurrection; through him we are saved and made free." All other "themes" in this celebration are subordinate to the fundamental theme of the Triduum, the death and resurrection of the Lord. It is inevitable that the institution of the eucharist will be noted, this being the day of the Last Supper, but the eucharist always celebrates the whole paschal mystery. And we will wash feet this night, but that should remind us of what it means to be Christians and follow the one who gave his life for us. Those who prepare this liturgy should begin by understanding Holy Thursday as a threshold liturgy that leads us into the Triduum and points us toward the Vigil.

HOLY THURSDAY CHECKLIST

Sacristans and planners may find a list similar to the following helpful from year to year:

- Get holy oils from cathedral or dean
- Prepare pitcher(s) and bowl(s) and towels
- Clean censer, fill boat with incense
- Clean cups for both species
- Measure wine needed
- Prepare bread or count hosts for Thursday and Friday
- Prepare baskets or other receptacles for gifts at Mass for the poor
- Use white altar paraments and vestments
- Prepare humeral veil(s)
- Prepare altar of reservation
- Empty the tabernacle; leave open

- Tell server about bells during Gloria
- Train servers for procession
- Prepare inserts for eucharistic prayer
- Arrange for stripping of altar and church after Mass
- Announce adoration until midnight

MASS OF THE LORD'S SUPPER

Introductory Rites

■ THE OPENING HYMN: Like the antiphon in the sacramentary, this song should reflect the whole paschal mystery. An ancient text by Venantius Fortunatus that is highly appropriate for the beginning of this celebration is "Sing, my tongue, the song of triumph." It is most effectively sung to the Mode III chant ("Pange lingua") but can be found in *Worship* coupled with PICARDY; it also fits LAUDA ANIMA. Using the same melody for this text to begin and the "Pange lingua" text at the transfer of the eucharist helps knit the many rituals of this evening into one unified celebration. "Lift high the cross" is another excellent choice for the opening hymn because it appropriately directs the assembly's attention to the heart of the entire feast. Other possible music for gathering includes "Praise to you, O Christ our Savior" (Farrell, OCP #7126) and Marty Haugen's "We remember."

■ RECEPTION OF THE HOLY OILS: Three ministers might carry the vessels of oil blessed at the Chrism Mass in this evening's entrance procession, placing them on pedestals or on a small table near the altar. After the greeting, the presider speaks briefly about the significance of the oils in the life of the church (for sample texts, see page 152). The oils then are taken to the repository (often by the font), where they are to be reserved. A good musical accompaniment to this rite is the "Rite for Receiving the Holy Oils" by John Schiavone (OCP, 9120). This rite reminds us again that we are entering into the Triduum—the premier time for initiation, in which the chrism is used.

■ GLORIA: Consider one of "Two Plainsong Gloria Settings with Handbells" by Richard Proulx (GIA, G-3638). The first is a setting of John Lee's Gloria found in *Worship* and the second is arranged from chant Mass VIII, "Missa de Angelis." If the parish's Gloria to be sung this night has a refrain, consider a random handbell ring during the refrain.

Tradition calls for church bells to be rung during tonight's Gloria. Though this assumes the use of tower bells, some parishes, especially those who do not have functioning tower bells, have invited parishioners to bring bells from home to ring during the singing of the Gloria this night and at the Vigil. The music ministers should be consulted first to see if such a custom accords with the music chosen.

■ OPENING PRAYER: The opening prayer for this night was written with little attention to the fullness of the paschal mystery. Opening prayers A and B for the Votive Mass of the Holy Eucharist are more in spirit with this threshold moment.

Liturgy of the Word

■ CHILDREN'S LITURGY OF THE WORD: On this night the whole community gathers together; no other eucharist is permitted. Since this liturgy celebrates our unity in Christ, children ought not be sent to a separate liturgy of the word this night. The readings are straightforward, and the washing of the feet is a powerful ritual in which the children should be included. It is incumbent upon the homilist to preach in a manner that is accessible to all ages on this special night.

■ THE READINGS: All three readings call our attention to the paschal mystery and remind us that this night is about life and death. In the first reading, the blood on the doorposts guarantees protection from the angel of death. Paul reminds the Corinthians that the eucharist proclaims the Lord's death until he comes. And the gospel speaks of betrayal as it calls us to imitate the one betrayed.

■ THE PSALM: Psalm 116 is the appointed psalm for this evening. Michael Joncas's setting (NALR, JO 07-JON-SM) is a wonderful choice, but it should be noted that some material from the verses is taken from sources outside the given psalm. Marty Haugen's setting, found in *Gather*, is also a fine choice. A highly skilled cantor is needed for Charles Conley's setting with the refrain "What return can I make to the Lord?" (GIA, G-2528) and for the lovely refrain and challenging verses of Stephen Dean's "How can I repay the Lord" (OCP, 7119).

■ THE WASHING OF THE FEET: This ritual is technically optional, but it should be included in every parish. It is a powerful symbol of our identity as a servant people and a kind of visual homily. There are no words of introduction to the ritual, so the spoken homily should lead naturally into the washing of feet. Ample towels, adequate washbasins and pitchers of warm water can be brought from the sacristy as the singing begins and the participants move to their places. This singing continues throughout the washing and during any followup washing of the hands of the ministers, ending just before the intercessions.

Some parishes have experimented with washing hands instead of feet so that all can participate; such experiments have generally been less than successful. The ritual action is grounded in the historical event recounted in tonight's gospel; it should not be altered so drastically. Washing feet is quite different from washing hands; it is more intimate, more unusual, and thus more awkward. Yet all of that is integral to what Jesus did and what we are called to do. The humility required to wash feet (and to have one's feet washed) is lost when only hands are involved.

The sacramentary does not speak of washing the feet of "twelve" people, which reminds us that the ritual is not historical drama. Parishes might consider ways in which larger numbers might have their feet washed, perhaps with more than one person washing or even with a procession to several stations for foot-washing. Parishes might also ask whether there are others (the poor, the homeless, people with AIDS) who might be invited to have their feet washed as a sign of the community's commitment to serve.

The music of the mandatum must be selected carefully and performed to complement the ritual. The entire assembly should be able to watch or participate in the foot-washing. A hymn, by its complexity of text, forces the assembly to choose between participating in the singing or participating in the ritual action. Some pieces that are responsorial and worth learning for this annual moment are Chrysogonus Waddell's "Jesus took a towel" (*Worship,* GIA), a remarkable and powerful piece; "Jesu, Jesu," #431 in *Worship,* a song from

Ghana that speaks in concrete terms of our "mandatum" to serve as Jesus did; and the recitative setting of the "Mandatum Novum" of Taizé (GIA, G-2433). "Faith, hope and love" by Christopher Walker is based on the mandatum text with alternate verses derived from "Ubi caritas" (OCP, 7149). The choral arrangement of the verses is masterful and when done *a cappella* is striking. It is well worth the work. Consider looking at Alexander Peloquin's "A simple command" (GIA, G-2483). This piece is composed for use at the communion rite, yet its text, even though eucharistic in nature, could be appropriate here. The choral parts are challenging at first, until one notices that the composer has each verse modulating up a half step to the next refrain. "Hosanna" could be substituted in the final verse, which has "Alleluia" as its text.

■ DISMISSAL OF THE CATECHUMENS AND THE ELECT: The elect and the catechumens are sent forth following the washing of feet. It might not be necessary for a catechist to leave the eucharist to accompany them on this night; at this stage, the elect and catechumens should be able to continue their reflection and discussion on their own, perhaps with some prepared questions to guide them.

■ GENERAL INTERCESSIONS: For an example of appropriate prayer themes at the start of the Triduum, see the intercessions for today's Evening Prayer (a liturgy celebrated only by the homebound). In accord with the usual style of the general intercessions, however, these texts need to be recast as invitations to the assembly to pray to the Father rather than petitions addressed directly to Christ. Remember to pray for our Jewish brothers and sisters, who begin their celebration of Passover tonight.

Liturgy of the Eucharist

■ PREPARATION RITES: The sacramentary notes that "at the beginning of the liturgy of the eucharist, there may be a procession of the faithful with gifts for the poor." The *Circular Letter* (#52) notes that these gifts might be "especially those collected as the fruit of Lenten penance." Canned goods for a food bank, filled "rice bowls" for Catholic Relief Services or similar gifts could be collected in this procession. The procession would be completed by those bringing up the bread and wine for the eucharist.

"Ubi caritas," the appointed song, is straight from the Reichenau Abbey of the year 800. No other preparation rite has a song assigned to it. Few hymns have such a venerable history. Richard Proulx's setting for unison choir/ cantor and congregation, "God is love" (GIA, G-3010) is worth examining. The Taizé mantra "Ubi caritas" (*Worship,* GIA) establishes a calm, prayerful environment and lends itself to embellishment so that it can be sustained throughout the ritual. "Where charity and love prevail," is another fine choice; you will find it with inclusive language in the *People's Mass Book* (World Library Publications) and in *Gather.* Due to its brevity, musicians may call upon an instrument (flute or oboe work well) to play interludes between the verses, which can be easily composed from similar thematic material. A finely crafted choral piece that can be sung after the chant "Ubi caritas" is Randolph Currie's "The love God has for us" (GIA, G-2963).

■ EUCHARISTIC PRAYER: There are three inserts for Eucharistic Prayer I tonight. Sample inserts for Eucharistic Prayers II and III are on page 151. Richard Proulx's

fine setting of the *Corpus Christi Mass* utilizes the familiar tune "Adoro te" throughout the sanctus, memorial acclamation and Amen. It is for unaccompanied choir, cantor and congregation. This tune is so familiar that it gets an immediate response from the congregation.

■ BREAKING OF THE BREAD: Even if the parish has not yet learned to use loaves or hosts large enough to break for the community at every Mass, this night cries out for such bread. The breaking of the one bread is an important symbol of the meaning of eucharist. The bread for tomorrow should be broken tonight as well.

■ THE COMMUNION PROCESSION: Psalm 34 is a happy choice for communion this night. Engaging settings include James Moore's "Taste and see" (GIA, G-2802), which begs for a cantor who can take some liberty with the wonderful gospel-style verses, and Stephen Dean's "Taste and see" (OCP, 7114). "Love is his word" (*Worship,* GIA) gathers many of the images of this evening in a graceful musical setting by Robert Hutmacher, which is effective with cantor or choir singing the verses while the assembly responds. Michael Joncas's "Take and eat" (GIA, G-3435) is a wonderful choice for communion this night. Musicians might consider repeating it for the communion procession for the Vigil. Choral settings of "O taste and see," one by Ralph Vaughan Williams (Oxford) and another by Richard DeLong (E. C. Schirmer) will make excellent offerings. Mozart's "Ave verum" is another choral possibility. Whatever is chosen for the assembly's song, this night's communion refrain must resound.

■ DISMISSAL OF EUCHARISTIC MINISTERS: The *Circular Letter* (#53) reminds us that the homebound should be included in this Triduum celebration:

It is appropriate that the eucharist be borne directly from the altar by the deacons or acolytes or extraordinary ministers at the moment of communion, for the sick and infirm who must communicate at home, so that in this way they may be more closely united to the celebrating church.

■ AFTER COMMUNION: The vessel with the eucharistic bread for Good Friday's communion is left on the altar. After a period of silence, the prayer after communion is sung or said. The procession follows immediately.

Transfer of the Holy Eucharist

■ PURPOSE: This rite of transfer of the holy eucharist is just that, a transfer for reservation until Good Friday—omitted if the Celebration of the Lord's Passion will not be held in the same church.

■ PREPARING FOR THE PROCESSION: The presider stands before the altar and places incense in the thurible. Kneeling, he incenses the eucharist three times. Meanwhile, the assisting ministers and all others kneel. The presider puts on the humeral veil, takes the vessel with the eucharist in it and covers the vessel with the ends of the veil. At the same time, the ministers who will lead the procession gather in the correct order. If the largest vessel available is not large enough to contain the bread for Good Friday, a second vessel should be carried by a deacon or concelebrant also wearing a humeral veil.

■ PROCESSION: The cross bearer and two acolytes lead the procession, followed by deacons, concelebrants, two censer bearers, and the presider with the eucharist. Other ministers and members of

the assembly follow the presider into the reservation chapel, if there is room.

"Pange lingua/Sing my tongue" is a touchstone in Catholic ritual music. Verses can be sung in Latin or in English, or the two can be alternated. Musicians should coordinate with those who arrange the procession so that the procession will last until the last two verses ("Tantum ergo").

■ CONCLUSION OF PROCESSION: The presider sets the vessel down in the tabernacle (leaving the door open) or just in front of it. He then removes the humeral veil, kneels and incenses the vessel with one of the thuribles. Then all sing the last two verses of the "Pange lingua" ("Tantum ergo sacramentum"). The deacon places the eucharist in the tabernacle (if the presider did not) and closes the door. A period of silent adoration follows. Then the altar is stripped (see page 128) in silence; people are free to stay for prayer and leave when they choose. Note that there is no dismissal, no real ending of this liturgy; people simply disperse and continue their prayer and fasting at home.

EUCHARISTIC ADORATION

During the hours from the transfer of the eucharist to midnight, all should be encouraged to continue in prayer. The *Circular Letter* (#56) calls for chapters 13–17 of John to be read as part of this time of prayer. Many parishes encourage participation in this prayer by involving different groups in the vocal praying and in the singing—religious communities, prayer groups, Bible-study groups or others. With a little coordination and division of time,

the chapel can be filled for hours with public prayer (it should be parish prayer and not the devotions of any one particular group or individual). See page 128 for notes on the environment of this adoration and on the stripping of the altar.

NIGHT PRAYER

Many parishes conclude the period of adoration by singing Night Prayer together just before midnight.

PASSOVER SEDERS AND AGAPE MEALS

Some parishes have developed the custom of celebrating a Passover seder or a parish agape meal on this night. Holding such a meal after the Mass of the Lord's Supper is inappropriate, because it conflicts with the spirit of silence and prayerful adoration following the transfer of the eucharist and because it is contrary to the spirit of the paschal fast. The counting of the Three Days is based on the ancient view that the day begins and ends at sunset. Hence, the first day of the Triduum runs from sunset Thursday until sunset Friday, and the second day until sunset on Saturday, after which the Vigil is celebrated. Thus the two days of the paschal fast begin on Thursday night. If any parish supper is held on Thursday, it would precede the evening Mass and might take the character of other Lenten parish meals. Such a supper could be advantageous for people who would be coming to church directly from work this night, though proper attention should be paid to the question of the fast before communion.

The custom of celebrating a Jewish seder meal might best be done on some other night so that this night the Mass of the Lord's Supper stands as our true liturgy. This year Passover begins on this very night, so a seder cannot be held the same night as the Jews. If the parish wishes to experience a Passover seder, the advice of the U.S. Bishops' Committee on the Liturgy should be heeded:

> It is becoming familiar in many parishes and Catholic homes to participate in a Passover seder during Holy Week. This practice can have educational and spiritual value. It is wrong, however, to "baptize" the seder by ending it with New Testament readings about the Last Supper or, worse, turn it into a prologue to the eucharist. Such mergings distort both traditions.
>
> When Christians celebrate this sacred feast among themselves, the rites of the *haggadah* for the seder should be respected in all their integrity. The seder . . . should be celebrated in a dignified manner and with sensitivity to those to whom the seder truly belongs. The primary reason why Christians may celebrate the festival of Passover should be to acknowledge common roots in the history of salvation. Any sense of "restaging" the Last Supper of the Lord Jesus should be avoided. . . . The rites of the Triduum are the [church's] annual memorial of the events of Jesus' dying and rising. (#28, *God's Mercy Endures Forever*)

LTP's *The Passover Celebration,* a *haggadah* prepared by Rabbi Leon Klenicki, is faithful to the Jewish Passover tradition.

5 #41   red
Good Friday

TENEBRAE

Before Vatican II, "Tenebrae" was the title for the Office of Readings combined with Morning Prayer, during which candles were extinguished as morning came. In recent centuries, despite the early-morning images, this was sometimes moved to Wednesday night, a sort of prelude to the Triduum, which led to the creation of various meanings for the diminishing candles. The *Ceremonial of Bishops* (#296), the *Liturgy of the Hours* (#210) and the *Circular Letter* (#40, #62) call for a return of the original Tenebrae. While more permanent rites for combining these hours are prepared, parishes should make a choice: use either the Office of Readings or Morning Prayer, or combine these two liturgies using the *General Instruction of the Liturgy of the Hours* (#99) for structural guidance. The combined office follows this outline:

- invitatory antiphon (Office of Readings [OR]) and invitatory psalm
- hymn (samples listed under "Holy Week," just before Passion [Palm] Sunday texts)
- antiphons and psalms (OR)
- verse (OR)
- scriptural reading, with responsory (OR)

- patristic reading with responsory (OR)
- antiphons, psalms and canticle (Morning Prayer [MP])
- scriptural reading (MP)
- antiphon (MP; same as Thursday's Night Prayer)
- antiphon (MP) and canticle of Zechariah
- intercessions (MP), Lord's Prayer, and prayer (MP)
- blessing and dismissal

CHILDREN AND TRIDUUM

Those who prepare the liturgy must consider the inclusion of children in the prayer of the church. Child care for the youngest ones should be provided, at least for the main celebrations on these Triduum days. Ways to involve preschool and older children should be planned carefully. Possibilities include:

- Midday Prayer (or stations of the cross), with some of the musical repertoire taught to the children during religious education classes
- references to the faith life of children as part of the homily
- participation of the children in preparing the church building for the Triduum
- a catechetical assembly for all children of the parish on the morning of Good Friday and the morning of Holy Saturday

■ CATECHETICAL ASSEMBLIES: One way to encourage young people to participate in the liturgies may be to hold catechetical assemblies of all parish youth on Good Friday and Holy Saturday mornings. Parents will appreciate the attempt to draw their children into the great mystery of faith, and children will enjoy the gatherings if the assemblies are planned well. Such events could involve all youth from preschool through grade six or so. They would gather each day for an hour-long event organized more or less as a celebration of the word. What distinguishes this from being a children's liturgy that competes with the principal liturgy is that it must clearly point to the parish assembly—a kind of rehearsal and preparation to enable children to participate fully in the principal liturgies.

On Good Friday morning, such an assembly might include:

- music that speaks of the passion and the cross and that will be used at the Celebration of the Lord's Passion

- a reading or two from the day's liturgy of the hours, using images with which children can identify

- instructions, given by one or more of the catechists, that introduce the liturgy that the children will enter later in the day. Instructions may be given in smaller groups by age level.

- rehearsal of and explanations for the solemn actions that they will perform with the adults later on

- some preparation of the physical requirements of the principal liturgy: For example, the children can see the stripped-down church and reflect on it, help to prepare a resting place for the cross or get the cross out of storage and bring it to the place from which it will be carried in solemn entrance.

- praying some of the general intercessions chosen from the Celebration of the Lord's Passion.

MIDDAY PRAYER

Many people come to church at noon today. If the Celebration of the Lord's Passion is at 3:00 PM or later, this is a good opportunity to celebrate Midday Prayer. A passion-oriented hymn follows the regular words of introduction. A psalm antiphon referring to noontime follows. After the

psalms, a powerful passage from Isaiah is followed by the proper antiphon that the community of Taizé has made popular in its music: "Jesus, remember me." A simple prayer concludes the service. If a longer service is desired, this format can be expanded with readings from the Office of Readings in Holy Week, with a homily or with long periods of silence between the psalms.

GOOD FRIDAY CHECKLIST

A list similar to what follows may be helpful for sacristans and planners:

- Practice singing intercessions

- Arrange microphones for Passion if extra readers are used

- Cross, candles and matches in back

- Altar cloth and corporal on credence table

- Arrange for collection for the Holy Land

- Empty holy water fonts

- Prepare red vestments

- Key in tabernacle (reservation chapel)

- Place prepared to keep any remaining hosts after service

CELEBRATION OF THE LORD'S PASSION

Introductory Rites

■ SILENCE: This liturgy begins in complete silence, without the usual procession. The priest and deacons enter simply, with no cross or candles. Avoid the temptation to replace the silence with a solo instrument, choral motet or drum beat.

■ FALLING PROSTRATE: The presider and assisting ministers reverence the bare altar and then fully prostrate themselves. The

Circular Letter (#65) stresses the importance of this ritual gesture: "This act of prostration, which is proper to the rite of the day, should be strictly observed, for it signifies both the abasement of 'earthly man' [sic] and also the grief and sorrow of the church." If the physical arrangement of the room allows (a rare thing), the whole assembly can join in the prostration; otherwise the assembly kneels. Prostrate or kneeling, all pray silently—as the sacramentary suggests, "for a while," that is, long enough for this silence to become prayer.

■ OPENING PRAYER: Going to the chair, the presider neither greets the people nor uses the traditional "Let us pray." With hands outstretched, the presider simply offers the prayer and sits down for the liturgy of the word. Thus this liturgy begins almost as a continuation of last night's liturgy, reminding us that the whole Triduum is one integrated period of worship.

Liturgy of the Word

■ LITURGY OF THE WORD FOR CHILDREN: Again, it may be best to let the children be part of the main assembly rather than having a separate liturgy of the word. Children learn the meaning of these days gradually through yearly participation with older parishioners. Though the Passion is long, it is a story that even children can follow. If a separate assembly is held, the children might return before the intercessions or before the veneration of the cross. In the latter case, their own intercessions should be as broad as those of the sacramentary, and then they might enter in procession with the cross.

■ THE PSALM: The psalm will be the first music of this gathering.

The absence of musical instruments can be remarkably powerful during this celebration. Choose music that is sung easily and is well understood without accompaniment; chant would serve well. Consider using the setting of Psalm 22 that was used for Passion Sunday. Psalm 31, "Father, I put my life in your hands" (*Worship,* #814) is also an effective and simple setting. Francis Strahan's simple refrain, "Father, Father," found in the *People's Mass Book* is a fine alternative, especially if it is done *a cappella* with the verses chanted freely.

■ THE PASSION: The proclamation of the passion offers several possibilities. The singing of the passion by three strong singers (GIA, G-1795) can be effective. Deacons, presbyters, cantors or capable lectors can chant the parts of Christ, narrator and speaker. This is performed with simple austerity, without incense and candles and without the greeting and the signing of the book. After the verse about the death of the Lord, all kneel and a brief silence is observed.

Also effective is a strong proclamation of the passion by a single, well-trained lector. Or it might be proclaimed by several lectors, each taking a section of the story, with a musical refrain repeated by the assembly between each section. An appropriate refrain would be the parish's normal setting of the memorial acclamation "Lord, by your cross." This text is fitting given John's focus on the triumph of the cross.

Several missalettes involve the congregation in the reading of the passion with a "crowd" part, but this requires the assembly to read along rather than listen. Communities that have such missalettes might remove them from the pews today or at least encourage people to put them down and listen attentively to the word proclaimed.

Musicians should check the various publishers' catalogues to review sung settings of the passion. Some require months of rehearsal, yet if learned over a period of a few years could be a mainstay for the parish for years to come.

■ HOMILY: The homily today should avoid any language that gives the impression that the Jewish people as a whole are responsible for Christ's death. In fact, the homily may need to correct any such impression left by John's Passion. The revised lectionary, when it comes into use, will help by distinguishing between the Jewish leaders and the whole people; but we have centuries of misunderstanding to overcome. The homilist should take to heart these comments from the U.S. bishops:

> The message of the liturgy in proclaiming the passion narratives in full is to enable the assembly to see vividly the love of Christ for each person, despite their sins, a love that even death could not vanquish. . . . To the extent that Christians over the centuries made Jews the scapegoat for Christ's death, they drew themselves away from the paschal mystery. For it is only in dying to one's sins that one can hope to rise to new life. (*God's Mercy Endures Forever,* #22)

■ DISMISSAL OF THE ELECT AND THE CATECHUMENS: The elect and the catechumens should not be present for the general intercessions, which are prayers of the baptized faithful. They may leave with a catechist or on their own to continue their reflection on the passion and perhaps return to the assembly space after the liturgy to venerate the cross.

■ GENERAL INTERCESSIONS: The intercessions are an important part of the ministry of the baptized this day. Most Catholics today seem to lack a proper sense of the importance of the general intercessions in every Mass as a time of service to the world through prayer. The intercessions this day can help us all learn to see these prayers as part of the way we carry on the mission of Christ, who gave his life for all. In preparing the intercessions, consider carefully how they can best involve the assembly in prayer. The key to good prayer here is taking time to do the intercessions well. They are proclaimed as follows:

1. The introduction to each petition should be said or sung by the deacon (or another minister). If a deacon is not present, then a female voice would provide contrast with a male presider singing the orations.

2. The assembly can respond to the invitation to prayer by kneeling for silent prayer, by a sung response, or both. If kneeling is used, the deacon should direct the assembly to kneel and stand. Be sure to allow time for real silent prayer, lest it become a "bobbing exercise." If a sung response is used, someone may need to lead the assembly for a strong response.

Some parishes have successfully used an ostinato refrain sung in response to the intercessions. The choir and assembly could continue to hum the melody of the ostinato quietly as the next intention is announced. Bob Hurd's "O God, hear us" (OCP) is a marvelous refrain which fits the tone of the day very well. Hurd's "Oyenos, mi Dios" (OCP) offers another possibility in this style, especially if the intercessions are to be done in Spanish and English.

3. The presider then sings the oration, and the assembly responds with the Amen.

Veneration of the Cross

■ THE CROSS: No single answer can be given to the question of which cross to use. Venerating the cross that is used all year long in the worship space (there should be only one!) is most appropriate. Other values to consider are using a cross rather than a crucifix, using a wooden cross (we proclaim "This is the wood of the cross. . ."), and using a cross or crucifix that has special significance to the parish.

The sacramentary makes it clear (#19 on Good Friday) that only one cross is to be used. If worshipers are numerous, a large cross will allow two lines of people to process simultaneously, as ushers graciously direct the flow. The alternative is for the presider to invite the people to venerate the one cross by holding it up for them to worship from their places in silence, but this loses much of the power of the ritual. There is no need to rush today; let the veneration take whatever time is necessary.

■ SHOWING THE CROSS: The two options given in the sacramentary are an "uncovering" and a "bringing in." The "uncovering" form is necessary if the cross for this liturgical space is suspended or otherwise stationary. Even here, architects or interior designers should have planned for lowering it for this rite. Note carefully what the rubrics say: The veiled cross is not carried in and unveiled in stages along the way. Rather, the gradual unveiling occurs entirely in one place.

Just as the processional cross is preferred for the parish's one cross, so, too, the "bringing-in" option is the preferred format. The presider or deacon moves through the assembly with the cross, making three stops: at the entrance to the worship space, in the middle of the assembly and in front of the assembly. At each stop, the cross is acclaimed and the assembly responds in song and then kneels for silent veneration. This movement is patterned after the

bringing in of the paschal candle, a nonverbal link between Good Friday and the Easter Vigil. Other ministers can surround the cross bearer with incense and candles, as in a gospel procession. The cross is not carried over the shoulder; it is carried the way one holds a processional cross. At the three stations, the cross should be hoisted high and held steady, a feat that is possible if rehearsed well. After the final station, assistants might come to help hold the cross, and the candles and incense (in bowls?) can be placed nearby.

■ VENERATING THE CROSS: Some parishes make sure that the cross always is held by people during the veneration, and some parishes simply lay it flat or on the steps before the altar. The cross should not be propped up on furniture, much less on the altar.

For the veneration, the assembly comes forward to reverence the cross. There is a simple genuflection "or another sign of reverence . . . for example, kissing the cross." Local custom in many places is a genuflection (or prostration) and a kiss. It is not necessary to explain to the assembly how to venerate the cross; let the first people who venerate the cross do so with broad, authentic gestures, enabling those who come after to feel free to honor the cross as they choose.

A powerful gesture on this day is for all ministers—indeed, all the people—to come to the cross barefoot or in stocking feet. While it is not mentioned in the sacramentary, the *Ceremonial of Bishops* (#322) calls for the presider to leave his chasuble and shoes at the chair. They should be taken off before the entrance of the cross so that the procession flows into the veneration. This tradition, observed by many monastic orders

and mentioned by ancient writers, catches on quickly—if the presider and other assisting ministers handle it with grace. Announce it in the participation booklet or in a brief verbal invitation. If the presider is seen taking his shoes off while others in the sanctuary do the same, the assembly will feel comfortable removing their shoes.

■ MUSIC FOR THE VENERATION: When selecting music for the veneration of the cross, keep in mind that during each of the Triduum gatherings we celebrate the full paschal mystery; on this day, we believers display the cross not in grief and despair but as a trophy and triumphant symbol of life and hope. Our primary means of expressing this attitude is music. One way to establish this mood is by an invitation to come and adore, sung by the cantor near the cross and followed by a strong proclamation of praise such as "Agios, o Theos/Holy is God," composed by Howard Hughes (in *Praise God in Song,* GIA, G-2270).

This procession will take time and cannot be rushed. Prepare plenty of music and vary the styles and musical forces (mix congregational singing with pieces sung by the choir; using cantor or soloist in either case will add further interest). Begin and end with music that involves the assembly. "Sing, my tongue, the song of triumph" is appropriate, with its final two verses addressed to "faithful cross" and "tree of glory"; the PICARDY melody found in *Worship* is well suited, particularly if used last evening. Consider Marty Haugen's "Tree of life" (GIA, G-2944), appropriate throughout the Triduum. Taizé (GIA, G-3719) offers several wonderful ostinati for this purpose: "Crucem tuam," "Adoramus te, Domine I" (*Gather,* #221) and "Jesus, remember me" (*Gather,* #167) are all strong choices. A setting of "Wood of the cross," composed by Owen Alstott (OCP, 8826) for choir and congregation, combines the refrain "Behold the wood of the cross" with verses of Psalm 22, providing very strong and moving music for this ritual. The "Lamentations of Jeremiah," found in the appendix of Gabe Huck's "The Three Days" (LTP), is a wonderful, haunting chant. The refrain "Jerusalem, Jerusalem" could easily be sung by the assembly without any rehearsal.

Choral music would also effectively serve this rite: Consider settings of "Populus meus" by Palestrina, Victoria or Colin Mawby. Robert Scholtz's arrangement of the American hymn "Wondrous love" (MSM 50-9017) and John Ferguson's setting of the German Chorale "Ah, Holy Jesus" (MSM 50-3012) are beautiful alternative settings. Lotti's "Surely he has borne our griefs" offers another possibility.

Taizé-style ostinati are simple and evocative and can be used with great success "as is" or with various instruments, choral (or congregational) harmonies and cantor verses. This music's beauty is in its flexibility and adaptability to different situations and musical forces.

Two extraordinary pieces of music for the veneration of the cross bear investigating: "By the blood with which we marked the wooden lintels," composed by Joseph Gelineau, is found in the hymnal *Cantate Domino* (Oxford University Press). The translation by Fred Pratt Green of a Didier Rimaud text employs our finest Catholic tradition of piling one image or type on another. For wonderful images of our tradition put in a fresh light, see "The tree of life," an Eric Routley paraphrase of a text by Imre Pecsely Kiraly (copyrighted by Hinshaw Music).

The meter is compatible with the familiar passion tune HERZLIEBSTER JESU, and a fine original tune is provided by K. Lee Scott (Morning Star Music, MSM-50-3000). This setting for choir and congregation provides a congregation page that may be reproduced if quantity copies are purchased for the choir.

Holy Communion

■ COMMUNION: See the rubrics in the sacramentary regarding the simple transfer of the eucharist to the altar, where the altar cloth, corporal and book have been placed. The candles carried with the cross are arranged by the altar. The communion music from last night might be repeated tonight; "Now we remain" (*Gather*, GIA) is especially appropriate.

■ AFTER COMMUNION: Before the prayer after communion, the eucharist remaining (for Holy Saturday viaticum) is carried without ceremony by an assisting minister to a suitable place outside the church.

■ PRAYER OVER THE PEOPLE: Without offering the traditional greeting, the presider extends hands toward the assembly and offers this prayer. Like last night, there is no dismissal.

NIGHT PRAYER

This liturgy, perhaps after a parish supper in the spirit of the paschal fast, includes the same proper antiphon as last night and this morning: Christ was obedient unto death.

violet
6 Holy Saturday

PREPARATION FOR INITIATION

■ PREPARATION RITES FOR THE ELECT: The *Rite of Christian Initiation of Adults* (starting at #185) calls for preparation rites on Holy Saturday: song and greeting, reading the word of God and homily, and celebrating certain rites (presentation of the Lord's Prayer if deferred, the "return" of the creed and/or the *ephphetha* rite).

These rites can be scheduled on their own, with the full participation of parish members encouraged. They also could be part of one of the liturgies from the *Liturgy of the Hours*. In this case, the preparation actions would follow the proper psalmody and scripture reading.

Notice that the anointing with the oil of catechumens is no longer a part of these preparation rites. The current edition of the rite prescribes this anointing as a repeatable rite for the period of the catechumenate.

■ RITE OF RECEPTION OF CHILDREN: If infants will be baptized at the Vigil, #28 of the *Rite of Baptism of Children* calls for a preparatory rite with the infants, their parents, the sponsors and parish members. Except in danger of death, baptism of infants ought to be deferred during Lent. Easter is the traditional time for baptizing. Some are hesitant to baptize infants at the Vigil because of its length and the danger of disruption from crying. But the Vigil is the time for initiation, and we want the babies' families at the Vigil just as we want everyone there. Unless they go to two Easter Masses, the babies' families will skip the Vigil if we celebrate the infant baptisms on Easter Sunday morning. Infant baptisms also can be celebrated on the Sundays of Eastertime.

Given all of this, a preparatory rite for all those involved with the infants to be baptized on Holy Saturday may be necessary. It would involve at least the rite of receiving the children (at the door), the prayer of exorcism and the anointing with the oil of catechumens. This may be celebrated before a "fasting lunch" or in conjunction with one of the hours of the liturgy.

■ COMBINED PREPARATION RITE: A service combining this reception of infants with the preparation of the elect is possible, uniting in one assembly the prayers and expectation of the elect, the parents, the sponsors and the catechists.

- gathering hymn with the entire assembly at the entranceway

- rite of receiving the infants (*Rite of Baptism for Children* [RBC], #35–41)

- procession of all, with refrain or hymn sung by all, to seating near the ambo

- liturgy of the hours option: psalms and scripture of the appropriate hour of day

  or

  liturgy of the word option: reading(s) related to the preparatory rites, followed by a psalm (the possible rites are listed in the RCIA, #185.2; the readings are at #179–180, #194, #198)

- homily

- preparation rites for the infants: prayer of exorcism (RBC, #49) and, possibly, the anointing with the oil of catechumens (RBC, #50)

- one or more of the preparation rites for adults and children of catechetical age: the presentation of the Lord's Prayer (RCIA, #180 ff.), the recitation of the Creed (RCIA, #195 ff.), or the *ephphetha* (RCIA, #199)

- singing of a hymn or of the gospel canticle (if this is part of Morning or Evening Prayer)

- intercessions: from Morning or Evening Prayer of Holy Saturday, supplemented with prayers for baptized candidates for full communion

- prayer of blessing (RCIA, #204)

- dismissal (RCIA, #205)

OFFICE OF READINGS AND MORNING PRAYER

A suggested outline for this service (sometimes called Tenebrae) is given in this book under the entry for Good Friday (page 134).

Many parishes combine some or all of Morning Prayer with the preparation rites for the elect or with the rite of reception of children (before infant baptism) on this day. Notes regarding such a service are given under the previous section on Preparation for Initiation.

MIDDAY PRAYER

The preparation rites for initiation could be celebrated at Midday Prayer. This also may be a good time to gather the children for a special assembly preparing them for the Vigil. This liturgy also may mark the end of the cleaning time or precede a fasting meal. Until the 1950s, the Easter Vigil was held on Saturday morning, and many came afterward

for the blessing of foods. When the Vigil was moved to its proper time, the Vatican reformers noted that the blessing should be moved to Easter as well. See chapter 54 of the *Book of Blessings,* and notes here on page 149.

CATECHETICAL ASSEMBLY FOR CHILDREN

See the introduction to this idea under Good Friday on page 134. Today's catechetical session may include any of these items:

- the participation of the children in the preparation of the elect, especially if children of catechetical age will be prepared

- the participation of the children in any of the liturgies of the *Liturgy of the Hours* that follow; if the children will be present in large numbers, those who plan the session could select psalms and prayers that facilitate the children's entrance into this

- the painting of Easter eggs to be distributed to all after the Vigil

- hearing (and dramatizing) scriptures from the Vigil

- preparing the worship space for the Vigil

These activities are meant to prepare the children for the Vigil and should presume their participation in it.

EVENING PRAYER

Depending on the time of the Vigil, this hour may be best for the preparatory rites for the elect. It also may be the best prayer hour to link to a fasting meal. If the Vigil is very late or just before dawn, those in the habit of coming to church at an early evening hour for Mass may appreciate the scheduling of Evening Prayer at that time.

@**6-7** #42 white
Easter Vigil

THIS MOST HOLY NIGHT

On this most holy night, when our Lord Jesus Christ passed from death to life, the church invites her children throughout the world to come together in vigil and prayer. This is the passover of the Lord: If we honor the memory of his death and resurrection by hearing his word and celebrating his mysteries, then we may be confident that we shall share his victory over death and live with him for ever in God. (Sacramentary, Easter Vigil)

All Christians are invited to come together this night in vigil and prayer. If your parish has begun to appreciate this to the point that space is a problem (a happy problem!), consider the options:

- Celebrate the Vigil in a larger space, such as a school auditorium or a civic center.

- Celebrate the Vigil in a tent. If the tent is near the church building, the procession before initiation could bring the elect into the church's baptistry.

- Begin the Vigil after nightfall and then hold another Easter Mass at midnight or before dawn. This second Mass utilizes elements from the vigil: candlelight for all (candles in everyone's hands can be lit from the paschal candle, which is already lit when the worshipers arrive), the liturgy of the word of the Vigil, other texts of

that Mass and the renewal of baptismal promises.

EASTER VIGIL CHECKLIST

The following sample list of items and groups to be prepared should be adapted to your local situation.

Items to be in place

- Fire, matches, wood
- Paschal candle, scribe, nails, incense
- Censer, charcoal (one or two at base of fire), incense, tongs
- Wooden tapers to light candle from fire
- Sacramentary
- Flashlight
- People's candles (bobeches, windguards)
- Water container, full
- Aspergillum and bucket (or branches and bowls)
- Holy-water-font fillers
- Chrism
- Baptismal candles
- Towels for baptized and for floor around font
- Baptismal garments
- Exsultet music
- Hymnals where needed
- Bells for the Gloria
- Gospel candles on credence table
- Wine, chalice, cups for assembly's communion, purificators
- Bread and additional plates for distribution
- Music for eucharistic prayer; sheet for concelebrant

Instructions for Various Groups

Candidates / Sponsors

Procession during litany

Candles for candidates at fire (but not for catechumens)

Lighting candles of all after baptism

Petitions for Prayer of the Faithful

Procession with gifts

Dressing the altar

Instructions for receiving communion – "Amen"

Sacristan

Lights on *after* Exsultet

No hosts from tabernacle; tabernacle empty

Neophytes bring gifts

Ushers collect candles after money?

Ushers

Give candles to all who come

Facilitating procession in

Collecting candles and money

Let neophytes receive communion first

Servers

No cross tonight

Things needed at fire

Lighting candles of all during procession

Holding candles for singing the Exsultet

Bells at the Gloria

Light altar candles at Gloria

Water bearer during sprinkling

Fill holy water fonts during sprinkling

Deacon

Third proclamation of "Christ our Light" after all are in place

Singing Exsultet; if deacon is not singing, assist presider or cantor

Who will incense Exsultet and candle?

Deacon incenses gospel

Calling up catechumens and candidates

Leading baptismal procession with paschal candle

THE SERVICE OF LIGHT

■ THE DARK: "The entire celebration of the Easter Vigil takes place at night. It should not begin before nightfall; it should end before daybreak on Sunday." (Sacramentary, #3 under Easter Vigil)

The Vigil begins after nightfall, not after sunset. Lighting an Easter fire and the paschal candle in the brightness of dusk destroys much of the power of this ritual. We need to experience the power of darkness before the light of the Risen One can be fully experienced in contrast. Since Daylight Savings Time will not begin until tomorrow morning, it will be dark early and there is no need to begin before full darkness.

■ THE FIRE: The Latin word for this fire is *rogus*, "bonfire." This means a real fire, outdoors, one that gives off heat and light. A fire can be built on a lawn with no harm if a thick tarp is put down and then about ten inches of sand laid over it—a good job for the youth group or scouts! A large trough made for watering livestock also can be used to contain the wood, if sand or cinder blocks are placed underneath as insulation. Some parishes that have renovated their churches or built new ones have constructed appropriate places for this fire, with plenty of room for people to gather around.

Everyone should meet around the fire, which can be lighted even before most arrive. Bad weather, short of a blizzard or downpour, should not deter us. If some parishioners insist on going inside, be sure that all who want to be at the fire are encouraged to do so. Those who do not gather outside should be asked to move to the sides of the church so that those who enter in procession can enter the pews from the center aisle.

For safety's sake, remember that a bonfire can become dangerous on a windy night. Good dried hardwood is safer than pine or other quickly consumed woods. The fire

department or fire marshal's office may have to be consulted. Many communities have regulations about fires, even if set up on private property. Public safety and pollution controls need not be seen as anti-liturgical, but if the civic administrators are unwilling to cooperate, options are possible. Mount a campaign to get an exemption—thus giving members of the parish who are lawyers and politicians a good way to prepare for the Triduum. Or do what the liturgy calls for in a reasonable, safe way and cite the freedom of religious expression and the rubrics if you are questioned. Or construct the fire in a way that meets local codes.

No responsible pastor would allow civic (or even religious) officials to strip away one of the central instruments of this service of light: the lighted candle in every person's hand. Of course, ushers should be alert, with full knowledge about how to snuff out a fire using a thick blanket. One should be kept on hand along with fire extinguishers.

■ THE BLESSING OF THE FIRE AND THE LIGHTING OF THE CANDLE: The rubrics specify that the paschal candle must be made of wax, must never be artificial (this also outlaws liquid wax in a plastic cylinder), must be renewed each year and must be sufficiently large in size. No matter what certain manufacturers and suppliers of church goods claim, only real wax candles fulfill the liturgy's requirements.

An acolyte carries the unlit candle to the fire. The censer bearer carries the empty censer. No cross or other candles are carried. The presider leads all in the sign of the cross (*Ceremonial of Bishops,*

#339) and gives one of the greetings. Then he, a deacon or a concelebrant gives the "instruction" using what is in the sacramentary or similar words.

After the blessing of the fire, which may include a sung acclamation (see "Acclamations for the Easter Vigil" in David Haas's *Who Calls You By Name,* volume I–GIA), the paschal candle is prepared and lit. Though optional, the symbolic decoration of the candle should not be lightly abandoned; it includes beautiful expressions of Christ's importance to all ages. The wax nails included with most paschal candles are just a colorful way to attach the grains of incense, which are the real symbols. A tight bundle of thin wooden sticks will transfer the flame from the fire to the candle better than a wax taper, which will melt near a bonfire.

■ PROCESSION: The censer is supposed to be prepared by the lighting of coals from the fire and the addition of incense at this point. It takes time, however, for the coals to burn before they are ready to receive incense. The charcoal can be placed in the fire before the liturgy begins and then removed at the appropriate time with long-handled tongs.

The deacon carries the candle (held high, the sacramentary says), preceded only by the censer bearer and followed immediately by the presider. They lead the procession into church. Everyone's candles should be lit early in this procession. Careful planning with several acolytes passing the flame will avoid a lengthy delay in the procession. The one who will chant the Exsultet—perhaps wearing a cope—carries a fine book or scroll with the text and music. If the deacon will sing this proclamation, an assisting minister carries the scroll.

If the fire is built some distance from the church, consider constructing a beautiful glass windguard for the candle. The people's candles can be lit before the procession if you also provide windguards for these. Paper cones are available; Orthodox church-goods stores offer red plastic windguards designed to be placed on the substantial candles they use in their processions.

The "Light of Christ, thanks be to God" acclamation becomes the processional song, but it can be augmented by fuller acclamations in honor of Christ. Because it is from this ritual that we derive any other evening service of light or *lucernarium,* one recommendation is to intersperse the verses of the classic evening hymn "O radiant light" *(Phos hilaron)* set to the chant melody JESU DULCIS MEMORIA between these brief acclamations. The coordination of movement, music and ministers cannot be left to chance. Be sure, for example, that the pitch for the acclamation is clear and matches the key of the hymn; if each acclamation or hymn verse will be sung at a higher pitch, carefully prepare and rehearse the transitions.

■ PREPARATION FOR THE PROCLAMATION: The candle is honored with incense when it is placed in its stand, which is normally near the ambo where the Exsultet is sung. The censer bearer stands nearby. If a deacon sings the Exsultet, he asks for and receives a blessing in a low voice.

■ THE EASTER PROCLAMATION: Despite the suggestion in the sacramentary, do not turn the electric lights on until after the Exsultet is sung. (Some lights might remain dimmed until the Gloria.) This proclamation is one of the most beautiful examples of solo repertoire that has survived the nearly 2,000-year history of Christian music. Like the presidential prayers, it is solo music, sung by the deacon, presider, or cantor (male or female). The person selected to chant the Exsultet should be a confident singer, able to bring this marvelous text to life with strong music and clear diction. "Exsultet" by Robert Batastini (GIA, G-2351) is a smooth working of the English text to the traditional chant melody for a single cantor. Christopher Walker offers a setting for cantor and SATB choir in which the assembly enters for the concluding Amens (St. Thomas More, OCP, #7175). The beautiful setting by Everett Frese (Pastoral Press) also respects the integrity of the text for cantor and successfully incorporates the assembly in brief opening and closing sections.

LITURGY OF THE WORD

■ CHILDREN AND THE LITURGY OF THE WORD: The whole church—including the children and the parents of babies—should be here tonight. Child care should be available throughout, but the toddlers who are able to appreciate the service of light should be at the fire. They can be taken to the nursery before the liturgy of the word.

■ NUMBER OF READINGS: LTP's *A Triduum Sourcebook* contains tables of all the traditional readings for the Easter Vigil, if your parish is ready to add to the nine readings in the lectionary. If you have omitted several of the assigned readings in the past, think about gradually restoring them, perhaps adding one more each year, until the parish learns to value the riches of the full vigil.

■ PSALMODY: Musicians should work with planners of this evening's liturgy to explore creative ways to incorporate music into the liturgy of the word. For instance, if the long form of the creation story is chosen, consider simply chanting "Evening came and morning followed, and God saw that all this was good" following the proclamation of each day of creation. Also note that the response after the mandatory Exodus reading, which is at the core of the meaning of the entire Triduum, could follow immediately upon the proclamation of the text. Rather than the lector reciting the closing line of the text, "Let us sing to the Lord . . . ," this text could be sung immediately following the line of the lector, "Then Moses and the Israelites sang this song to the Lord." Having the lector turn in the direction of the cantor at this point is most effective. This great song of the Israelites must be rhythmic and alive, accompanied by percussion instruments. Tambourine lends an Eastern flare to this great song.

Robert Batastini's "You Will Draw Water" (GIA, G-2443) is a noble setting for the response to the Isaiah 55 text. The handbell accompaniment is lovely, and the water imagery suggested by the use of handbells is quite effective.

■ GLORIA: The position of the Gloria in this liturgy is a remnant from the time when the readings from the Hebrew Scriptures comprised "the Vigil," which was followed by baptism (or at least the blessing of water) and then by "the Mass of Easter," which began with the Gloria. Though arguments can be made for relocating the Gloria, it may be best to live within the present order, to ensure continuity from year to year. If earlier experiments have led to a parish tradition placing the

Gloria elsewhere, be sure the ritual outline is comprehensible enough for new worship coordinators, musicians and pastors to understand.

A Gloria with a repeated refrain is an appropriate choice for this night, when some members are new and many visitors may be present. Some options include "Glory to God" by Peter Jones (OCP), Richard Proulx's "Gloria for Eastertime" based on "O filii et filiae" (GIA, G-3086 or the choral version G-3087) or Peloquin's "Gloria of the Bells" (*Worship*, #258). According to the sacramentary, the candles on or near the altar are lit during the hymn (and if all the lights in the church were not put on after the Exsultet, the rest may be turned on now). Church bells are rung now, announcing the good news to the neighborhood. Parishioners might bring bells from home, too.

See page 129 about the possibility of decorating the worship place at this point. This can be accomplished with the following simple steps: When volunteers and ministers are arranged for the Triduum, ask certain groups (the confirmation class or altar guild, perhaps) to help with a procession of flowers and decorations. If the flowers are delivered Saturday morning, have the volunteers come to a brief late-morning rehearsal. They can help place the flowers (and other material) where they should end up at the Gloria, assign zones to different clusters of volunteers, and then bring the material to a side room (or rear pew). During the last reading and psalm before the Gloria, the bearers join in their clusters (quietly and unobtrusively, of course) by their materials and form one or more double lines. As the Gloria begins, the groups each go in procession to the correct places for their flowers or material.

■ GOSPEL ACCLAMATION: The gospel acclamation must be carefully selected in light of the fullness of the procession. Processions are meant to be seen by all—with movement, incensations, banners, candles and the gospel book held high. We do not serve this ritual well if we ask people to bury their heads in a hymnal or pamphlet. Choose something well crafted and easily sung, and repeat it with the addition of choir, bells, brass, organ; welcome the alleluia back into our worship with everything you can muster.

The presider or cantor intones the alleluia three times, each time at a slightly higher pitch (Chant Mode VIII; see *Worship*, #826). All repeat the alleluia each time. The cantor then sings the verses of Psalm 118. All sing the same alleluia after each verse. Other very effective settings of this psalm, by Haugen and Haas, are in *Gather* (#50–51).

Alternatively, the cantor or choir can intone the Easter alleluia while the procession comes together and incense is placed on the coals; this might be followed immediately with a vibrant singing of the "Celtic Alleluia" (*Gather*, GIA, or OCP, 7106) with handbells, if possible. The "Easter Alleluia" (*Gather*) based on the traditional "O filii et filiae" tune with verse by Marty Haugen is another festive possibility. Richard Proulx's setting of "Alleluia and Psalm for Easter" (GIA, G-1965), specifically written for this night, uses the familiar mode VI alleluia often used at Easter. It involves congregation, choir, cantor, organ and handbells. The alleluia sung at the Vigil may be the one heard throughout the Fifty Days, or it may be reserved for this procession and perhaps the end of this Mass and for Sunday Evening Prayer on Pentecost.

■ THE GOSPEL PROCESSION: Tonight's gospel demands a long procession. The deacon, carrying the book, and censer bearers (but no candle bearers) can process around the assembly while all the verses of Psalm 118 are sung.

■ HOMILY: Preachers sometimes feel at a loss for words, so powerful are the actions and mysteries of this night. They might look at the paschal homilies found in the Office of Readings over the coming days and at the prefaces of Easter, or consider a homily in the style of the Exsultet ("This is the night when . . ." with examples from the local community). Another effective approach is to build on the whole schema of readings, which have recounted the history of salvation, and proclaim God's continuing work of establishing a new creation in the present time among the people, especially evident in those to be baptized, confirmed and brought to the table this night.

INITIATION AT THE VIGIL

What the sacramentary refers to as the "Liturgy of Baptism" will take one of several forms, depending on the parish situation.

- *Parishes with elect to be baptized and candidates to be received into the full communion of the Catholic church:* This outline is followed in the commentary that follows and in the *Rite of Christian Initiation of Adults* (RCIA), appendix I, 4. Some of these parishes also may decide to baptize infants at the same assembly.

- *Parishes with elect to be baptized but without candidates for reception into full communion:* Follow Part I of the RCIA and use the elements commented on in the following section. These elements are arranged, however, in a different order. See the note on page 132. Some of these parishes also may decide to baptize infants at the Vigil.

- *Parishes with only infants to be baptized and with candidates for full communion:* Use the same outline as listed previously for parishes with both elect and candidates. Follow the rubrics given for infant baptism at the vigil in #28 of the *Rite of Baptism for Children.*

- *Parishes with only infants to be baptized and with no candidates to be received into full communion:* Follow the RBC, noting the rubric at #28. Although that rubric notes that the presentation of the lighted candle is omitted, it may be appropriate to keep it.

- *Parishes without baptisms but with candidates to be received into full communion:* Use RCIA, appendix I, 4, beginning with #580.

- *If no one is to be baptized or received,* follow the order given in the sacramentary. The renewal of baptismal promises may be enhanced with some of the following elements of the rite of baptism.

INITIATION: CELEBRATION OF BAPTISM

■ PRESENTATION: The RCIA outlines three methods for the presentation of those to be baptized (#219 or #568). This presentation is connected to the procession to the baptistry. Almost every parish can use Form B well, regardless of the placement of the font. The summoning of the elect and their godparents (and infants and their parents) should be carried out solemnly, with the names called loudly and slowly.

■ PROCESSION TO THE BAPTISTRY: Those who are to be baptized process to the baptistry, following the paschal candle carried by an acolyte. The elect, the godparents and the parents of any infants are followed by the deacon, the presider and the assisting ministers. If the baptistry is outside

the main assembly area, others can process as well. This procession should take a long route through the church to the baptismal font.

■ LITANY OF THE SAINTS: The litany of the saints is the song that accompanies this procession. As noted in RCIA, #221 (and #570) and in the sacramentary at #41, the following names should be added to the litany: the titular of the church (if it is a saint), patron saints of the area (diocese, city), the patrons of those to be baptized and the patrons of those to be received into the church.

The list of those to be added should be checked against the martyrology or a thorough collection like *Butler's Lives of the Saints.* Of course, the names of the saints have a seemingly endless number of language variations. They are organized according to their type and inserted into the litany with the others of that type. The "types" are: titles of Mary; angels; prophets and ancestors of the faith; apostles and disciples of Christ; martyrs; bishops and doctors; priests and religious; and holy women and men.

If the litany of the saints is used as the processional music to the font, a musical setting with some internal drive is appropriate. John Becker's wonderful "Litany of the Saints" (OCP) is easily learned and can be adapted to include the saints' names to be added this night. David Haas's Litany of the Saints (volume I of *Who Calls You By Name*) offers another possibility. Consider learning a new litany especially if the parish's singing of the traditional chanted litany has tended to drag. The litany is the great call to all who have gone before us in faith to surround us this night at the font and at the table.

■ INVITATION TO PRAYER: If Form B (RCIA, #219 or #568) was used, this invitatory (RCIA, #220 or #569) comes after all are at the font and the litany has ended.

■ BLESSING OF WATER: This prayer of blessing can include repeated sung acclamations, even alleluias. David Haas's "Blessing of Water" (*Who Calls You By Name,* volume II, GIA) offers a fine musical setting of the blessing, which includes the "Springs of Water" refrain that concludes it. Because the chant line to this setting (O filii et filiae) is familiar to most presiders, it is easily learned. Rehearsal time should be arranged with the choir and cantor. If the presider is unable to sing the text, consider using this arrangement with the presider boldly speaking the text. Continue to punctuate this long prayer with the alleluia refrains followed by the "Springs of Water." If blandly spoken, this text falls flat. Its imagery of the history of water in our salvation is too wonderful to be missed by a quickly read rendition.

The rubric that calls for plunging the candle into the font (once or three times) should not be overlooked. This is a great example of archetypal symbol language that needs no explanation. If the font is visible from the assembly area, sight lines should be kept clear.

At the end of the blessing, the sacramentary calls for an acclamation by the people and suggests "Springs of Water." Suitable music at this point includes:

- "Springs of water" by Thomas Savory (GIA, G-2549); cantor verses use Psalm 118.

- "Springs of water" by Donald Fellows (GIA, G-3639); cantor verses use text from the sprinkling rite "I saw water flowing . . ."

- "Rite of Sprinkling" by Richard Proulx (GIA, G-3097); uses the general verse "Cleanse us Lord from all our sins . . ." and could also be used at other times.

■ THE PROFESSION OF FAITH: Scholars remind us that the profession of faith is at the heart of baptism, the immediate prelude to the water bath. Follow the rite closely—and, unless there are dozens of elect, ignore the options given "if there are a great many to be baptized." The elect are asked to renounce sin as a group or individually. The questions of the profession of faith are asked of each individual, who then is baptized immediately. Parents and godparents of any infants to be baptized are then addressed and questioned as in the RBC, #58, #60–61.

■ BAPTISM: The preferred method of baptism in the Roman Catholic church is immersion. If your permanent font does not allow for that, consider making temporary arrangements until a full renovation of the font is possible. As each person rises from the waters of baptism, an acclamation is sung by the assembly. You can leave the assembly free to watch the ritual *and* sing an acclamation by using the call and response form; the cantor sings a line and the assembly repeats it. Suggestions include: "You have put on Christ" by Howard Hughes (GIA, G-2283) and "Rejoice, you newly baptized" by Arthur Hutchings (*ICEL Resource Collection,* GIA, G-2514). "Song Over the Waters" *(Gather)* by Haugen is a mellifluous baptism song that could work well here or at the sprinkling rite. The refrain "Happy are those who are washed clean, washed in the blood of the Lamb! Alleluia!" is set with cantor verses by Lynn Trapp in "Rite of Christian Initiation of Adults" (Morning Star MSM-80-907A). John Olivier's "You have put on Christ," found in the *People's Mass Book,* is worth looking

at. Whatever choice is made, consider having one "standard" acclamation each time the community celebrates baptism, at the vigil and throughout the year.

■ EXPLANATORY RITES: If there are infants, they are anointed with chrism after the prayer (RCIA, #228 or #577 or RBC, #62).

The newly baptized are now dressed in their baptismal garments. A room for parents to diaper and dress the infants should be prepared with enough dressing tables for the number of babies to be dressed (diapers, powders and lotions could be brought there by the parents before the liturgy). Godparents should assist adult neophytes in drying off as they emerge from the font and in robing (in a side room) while other professions of faith and baptisms continue. The words at the robing (RCIA, #229 or #578) can be omitted or said in private by the parents and godparents as the newly baptized are dressed.

The presentation of the baptismal candle is described in RCIA, #230 or #579. The presider and godparents pass the light to the neophytes. Plain, small paschal candles, with candle followers, make good baptismal candles if the parish paschal candle is sufficiently larger. Some candle makers offer smaller versions of their paschal-candle designs for this purpose (e.g. Marklin Candles Design, PO Box 1001, Nashua NH 03061; 603-595-2981).

Those parishes with baptisms but without receptions into full communion should read the section titled "Initiation: Rites after baptism when there are no receptions" (page 146) before reading the next three sections of commentary.

INITIATION: RENEWAL OF BAPTISMAL PROMISES

The RCIA presumes that the baptismal promises are spoken from the font and that the water comes from the font. If the font is in a separate place, the renewal will follow a procession back to the assembly area. The candidates for reception join in the renewal—which is placed here (RCIA, #580 ff.) so that their reception flows from it.

All stand, and the candles of the assembly are relit. The neophytes might be the ones to share the flame from their baptismal candles. Consider singing the renewal of baptism promises. How sad it is when the community at large has been catechized throughout Lent to look forward to their own renewal of baptism promises only to reach the vigil and blandly respond "I do" to the set of questions. David Haas's setting of the renewal (*Who Calls You By Name,* volume I, GIA) is a gem and worth investigating. Instead of having the entire assembly sing the entire refrain Haas has composed for their assent to the credal questions, consider having the cantor simply intone "We do believe," with the assembly responding with its own "We do believe" each time. After the final credal question, the choir could continue with Haas's entire refrain. Musicians should investigate other creative ways to enliven the renewal musically.

When the renewal of vows is completed, water is drawn from the font (if it has not already been brought from the font). During the sprinkling or signing, parents and godparents of any newly baptized infants bring them back to their places in the assembly.

■ SPRINKLING: The act of sprinkling should be as full as possible. People should feel the water. This may mean that assisting minis-

ters sprinkle the side aisles while the presider takes time with one section of the assembly. Branches from evergreen bushes or trees make excellent sprinkling implements. Tie several together to form a full, generous surface. Tape the stems at the bottom to form a handle and also to keep sap off people's hands. Colorful ribbons may be added. Each person who sprinkles might be accompanied by an assistant who carries the bowl of water.

During the sprinkling, acolytes can take water to all the holy water fonts in the church.

■ SIGNING: In place of a sprinkling, everyone in the assembly might be invited to come to the font (if it is in the worship space) or to bowls filled with water drawn from the font. The people may approach the font or the bowls from all sides and sign themselves or others with the water.

■ MUSIC FOR THE SPRINKLING OR SIGNING: The music used at the end of the blessing of water (see page 144) might be repeated here, providing a sense of unity to the use of water tonight. "Lord Jesus from your wounded side" by Richard Hillert in *Worship* is an Easter piece that would also serve well for the sprinkling. Michael Joncas's adaptation of the Baptist hymn "O healing river" (GIA) offers another possibility.

INITIATION: CELEBRATION OF RECEPTION

■ PROCESSION: If the font is in a separate building, the procession occurs before the renewal. If the neophytes and the ministers are in the main church building, they now return in procession from the font to the front of the main worship space. Following the paschal candle, neophytes carry their lit baptismal candles.

RCIA, #584, suggests a hymn at this time. The *Ceremonial of Bishops* (#366) suggests "You have put on Christ." Another appropriate text is "Baptized in water" by Michael Saward, coupled in *Worship* with the familiar Gaelic melody BUNESSAN. The Taizé ostinato "Beati in domo domini" is another good choice, particularly for its flexibility if the procession will not be lengthy.

■ RECEPTION: The rite of reception (RCIA, # 584 ff.) is brief, but it demands solemnity and deliberateness. The neophytes and their godparents should be nearby, but not blocking the assembly's relationship to this act. Those being received and their sponsors should stand in such a way that the congregation can see their faces. Consider concluding the receptions with a repeat of an earlier acclamation. An alleluia is appropriate.

INITIATION: CELEBRATION OF CONFIRMATION

If both neophytes and newly received are present to be confirmed, the introduction given at RCIA, #589, is used. Confirmation is the same for both the newly baptized and those received into the church. They are not anointed in any particular order. A Taizé ostinato, such as "Veni, Sancte Spiritus" or "Confitemini Domino," can be sung throughout the laying on of hands, prayer and chrismation; the song may continue to be sung quietly (or hummed) during the prayer. Another effective piece to use in this way is Christopher Walker's "Veni, Sancte Spiritus" (St. Thomas More/OCP, 7116). The refrain repeats the text several times and is graceful and easily singable; omit the overlaid cantor

verses for this occasion, unless the number to be confirmed is large. "Spirit blowing through creation," "Send us your spirit" (both found in *Gather*) and "Lord, send out your Spirit" (*Glory and Praise*, #117) are also appropriate and usable musical selections for the celebration of this sacrament.

Consider using the traditional hymn "Come, Holy Ghost" during the chrismation. An effective way to sing this hymn is to begin with piano or guitar simply playing it through, a solo instrument singing the melody line. The assembly could then be invited to begin the hymn, quietly at first, eventually adding organ and perhaps other instruments to the latter verses. Arranging a hymn in this way preserves some of our tradition and communicates a sense that the Spirit has indeed visited this place.

After all are signed with chrism, they take their places in the assembly. If neophytes will lead the general intercessions, they might go directly to the ambo. The neophytes continue to wear their robes throughout the Vigil.

INITIATION: RITES AFTER BAPTISM WHEN THERE ARE NO RECEPTIONS

When there are baptisms but no receptions, the procession from the font to the front of the assembly area takes place after the explanatory rites (RCIA, #231). Confirmation (#233 ff.) follows, using the musical suggestions highlighted previously. Then the renewal of baptismal promises (#237 ff.) leads to the signing or sprinkling of all, as described above. During the signing or sprinkling, the neophytes return to their places in the assembly.

INITIATION: GENERAL INTERCESSIONS

Their initiation into the order of the faithful brings neophytes "for the first time" to one of the central tasks of the church: to lift up the needs of the world and church to God. These intercessions could be sung, or just the people's response might be sung. The form and musical response for the general intercessions might be established here and remain consistent throughout Eastertime. Look to the Kyries of Taizé, which are intended to be sung with movement and energy, or to Ronald Krisman's "Gracious Lord, hear us, we pray," found in *Worship*. For multilingual communities, the intercessions offer an opportunity to allow all the languages to be spoken, perhaps with a common refrain. Bob Hurd's "Oyenos, mi Dios" (OCP) is an appropriate choice for English/Spanish celebrations.

If there are newly received Catholics, one or two petitions can be drawn from the RCIA, #496. Worthy of special mention tonight are all those who are to be initiated in the parish in the weeks and months ahead—confirmation candidates, catechumens, babies who will be baptized and children preparing for first eucharist.

LITURGY OF THE EUCHARIST

■ PREPARATION RITES: This is the perfect time for the choir to show its artistry. The neophytes bring up the bread and wine for the eucharistic meal in which they will share for the first time.

■ EUCHARISTIC PRAYER: Singing the whole eucharistic prayer lends appropriate solemnity to this liturgy. Advance preparation and

practice will be necessary, however, to include the proper preface and inserts. The preface of Easter I is used with the words, "on this Easter night." Eucharistic Prayer I contains two or three inserts:

- "Remember . . ." from the ritual Mass of baptism if there were baptisms (post the godparents' names in the sacramentary).

- "In union . . ." for the Vigil and octave (printed under the prayer in the sacramentary).

- "Father, accept . . ." from the ritual Mass of baptism if there were baptisms *or* for the Vigil and octave (printed under the prayer in the sacramentary) if there were no baptisms. The two versions of this insert start the same, but the initiation text is richer.

Special inserts are available for Eucharistic Prayers II and III:

- For the beginning of the prayer ("Lord, you are holy indeed . . ." in II; "And so, Father, we bring . . ." in III), see the "Easter Vigil and Octave of Easter" inserts translated from the French sacramentary (pages 151–152).

- For the paragraph remembering the church, see the inserts in the U.S. sacramentary at the ritual Mass of baptism. Other nations use a close equivalent of these inserts for the Vigil and the days of the octave, whether or not there were baptisms in the local community (see pages 151–152). Copy these inserts and post them in the proper place in the sacramentary.

■ COMMUNION RITE: The RCIA notes: "Before saying 'This is the Lamb of God,' the presider may briefly remind the neophytes of the preeminence of the eucharist, which is the climax of their initiation and the center of the whole Christian life" (#243). A similar note appears at #594 for the newly received.

For the communion procession, Tom Parker's "Praise the Lord, my soul" (GIA, *Gather* or G-2395) is full of baptismal imagery and

appealing musical material for choir, cantors and assembly. In light of the presence of the newly initiated at the Lord's table, settings of Psalm 34 with the refrain "Taste and see the goodness of the Lord" are fitting; so is "I received the living God" in *Worship,* also found in a striking choral setting (one step higher than the hymnal version) by Richard Proulx (GIA, G-3071). The moving Taizé antiphon "Eat this bread" (GIA, G-2840) has become a favorite in many communities. "You will show us the path of life" (*Gather,* #277) is also an affirmation of our Easter relationship with the Risen Christ. Michael Joncas's "Take and eat" (GIA) is a wonderful piece for communion this night, especially if it was sung on Thursday evening.

CONCLUDING RITE

Ideas for the solemn blessing can be found on page 162. The dismissal, with its double alleluia, might be sung to the Gregorian melody. Note that it is sung at least every day of the octave, which includes next Sunday, and then again on Pentecost. In the Episcopal church, this dismissal is sung throughout the Fifty Days. Some Roman Catholic parishes have begun doing the same.

THE BLESSING OF FOOD AND FOOD FOR ALL

While discouraging the blessing of foods earlier on Holy Saturday, chapter 54 of the *Book of Blessings* provides texts and outlines for tonight's blessing of food for the first meal of Easter.

If you distribute Easter eggs or hold a parish Easter breakfast this night, include these foods in the blessing. Such a breakfast is not just a "reception" for the neo-phytes, although they will certainly be recognized there; the gathering is a time for the whole parish to share Easter joy.

Be sure Easter water is available for people to take home tonight and tomorrow. Easter eggs (and fresh flowers) may be given to all as they leave or during the breakfast. The eggs might have been colored at the catechetical assembly of children earlier or prepared and distributed by the candidates to be confirmed during Easter's Fifty Days.

7 #43 (41, 46)   white
Easter Sunday

MORNING PRAYER

The popularity of Easter sunrise services suggests that many might welcome the opportunity to greet the dawn with Morning Prayer. Individual candles can be lit again from the paschal candle, as all sing the glorious psalms and antiphons of Easter. This service is also a good format for Easter dawn ecumenical services, where Catholics can invite others to share our way of greeting the risen Christ, the Sun of righteousness. Such a service could take place in church or outdoors; but wherever the setting, a "sunrise service" should begin while it is still dark, so that dawn is experienced during the prayer.

MORNING MASS

■ THE ASSEMBLY: Many who will come today come only at Christmas and Easter; they will not be won over by chastisements. They need to hear the good news of reconciliation, forgiveness, peace, and the invitation to believe. Model the homily after John Chrysostom's Easter words: "And you who did not fast, come and rejoice as well!"

■ MUSIC: The Easter musical tradition has been fully established at the Vigil, but most of the Sunday morning worshipers were probably not in attendance at the Vigil. So this is the time to reassert and emphasize the Alleluias and acclamations of the Easter celebration. It will be important to hear and sing traditional Easter hymns, just as it is important to hear and sing traditional Christmas carols on December 25. Pull out all the stops, tune up all the instruments, warm up all the music ministers, and continue the Easter joyousness. We are continuing to set the tone for the entire Easter season, and it should be inspiring to all involved!

Choral offerings might include "Alleluia for Christ the Lord Is Risen" by J. S. Bach (Concordia 98-2101), "Christ the Lord is risen again" by John Rutter (Oxford), "Eastertide Carol" arranged by Richard Proulx (GIA, G-3668), Charles Wood's "This joyful Eastertide" found in *Carols for Choirs 3* (Oxford), "Love is come again," a French carol arranged by John Erickson (AMSI 206) and "Sing praise to Christ" by J.S. Bach (Concordia 98-1377). A more contemporary choral piece for Easter, which can be repeated later in the season, particularly when the Emmaus gospel is proclaimed, is Michael Ward's "In the breaking of the bread" (World Library Publications).

■ INTRODUCTORY RITES: The renewal of baptismal promises and the sprinkling take place after the homily, so water is not used at the opening rites; in light of this renewal ritual, the penitential rite might best be omitted. Let the Gloria be full and joyous. In the alternative opening prayer, "those" would be more inclusive than "men."

■ LITURGY OF THE WORD: The fifty days of readings from Acts of the Apostles begins today. The seasonal psalm and seasonal gospel acclamation for Eastertime should be used this morning. Any sung alleluia can be used as a psalm response during Eastertime.

After the reading from one of the Pauline letters, the sequence is sung. Another sequence will grace the final day of Eastertime, Pentecost. Their power and their ability to frame the fifty days should place them high on the list of musical elements to be prepared before the Triduum.

The Mode I chant setting of the "Victimae Paschali" text translated by Peter Scagnelli is available in *Worship* (#837); the same hymnal also offers a hymn based on the sequence, "Christ the Lord is risen today." A lively, rhythmic setting of the chant with congregational refrain is "Easter Sequence" (GIA, G-3088), arranged by Richard Proulx.

The sequence prepares the way for a gospel procession in scale with the day and the crowds—with plenty of incense, a gospel book worthy of public viewing and an acclamation that is strong and festive. At this morning Mass, the gospel proclamation can be from either Matthew (lectionary #42) or John (#43).

■ RENEWAL OF BAPTISMAL PROMISES: The sprinkling action today, as last night, may involve several buckets and sprinklers, or perhaps instead of sprinkling, the entire congregation might be invited to come to the font for a ritual signing with the Easter water (see the notes on the Vigil). Buckets or bowls (if used) should be filled from the font at this time.

■ LITURGY OF THE EUCHARIST: The preface of Easter I is prescribed. Inserts in the eucharistic prayers are at the bottom of prayer I in the sacramentary; also see page 151–52 here for prayers II and III.

■ CONCLUDING RITE: See the Easter season notes (page 162) for the solemn blessing. As on Christmas, the seasonal greetings and statements of appreciation should not perpetuate a sense that "the priests and the parish staff thank you for how you helped them at Mass." Don't forget the double Alleluia at the end of the dismissal, which is best sung.

■ HOSPITALITY: Give every worshiper (not just the children or women) a spring flower as they leave Mass after the Vigil or today. Easter eggs also can be given to all. After-worship gatherings today can include various traditional items: hot-cross buns and eggnog after Mass, an egg hunt for adults and children alike, or a parish breakfast that breaks the paschal fast.

BLESSING OF FOODS

Blessing Easter food is not just an ethnic custom but is a part of Christian tradition that can become part of the parish's liturgical life: Throughout Lent, remind people to bring baskets of food as well as children's Easter baskets to any Mass on Easter Sunday,

including the Vigil. Tables may be set up to hold the baskets. Ushers should be informed so that they can direct people to place their food on these tables, especially at the Easter Vigil, when people arrive in the dark. Alternatively, household members can keep the foods with them in their places, ready to raise them up for the blessing prayer.

The brief prayer of the "Order of the Blessing of Food for the First Meal of Easter" should be used from the *Book of Blessings*. This blessing can take place after the prayer after communion (#1723) or at the start of post-Mass refreshments.

MIDDAY PRAYER AND EASTER DINNER

Midday Prayer might be welcomed by those who were at the Vigil but not at morning Mass. The blessing of food could serve as the conclusion to Midday Prayer.

The blessing also can be a service on its own (*Book of Blessings*, #1707–1719). This works best when the parish holds a festive Easter dinner—for homeless or elderly people, for those who might otherwise eat alone, for those who prefer to eat their meal and sing their songs in a community bigger than the domestic one. Twenty minutes for this blessing prayer and for Easter carol singing would be just the right length of time.

AFTERNOON MASS

Those parishes who regularly have a Sunday afternoon or evening Mass should probably have one today, too. The ministers may be exhausted, but this may be the only paschal experience for many in the congregation.

Those who prepare the liturgy should arrange for musicians and

other ministers for this Mass—perhaps those who would have been at the Vigil but have a lighter schedule in the morning. The lectionary suggests a special gospel for this evening (#47), and its content may direct the choice of hymnody.

PASCHAL VESPERS

The liturgical books and their commentaries (the *Circular Letter*, #98; the *Ceremonial of Bishops*, #371; and the *General Instruction of the Liturgy of the Hours*, #213) advocate the restoration of "Baptismal Vespers" to complete the Triduum. If you have not yet implemented this, perhaps this is the year to do so. This is an appropriate way for the parish community and its neophytes to revel in the afterglow of the Vigil.

This outline is suggested:

• The paschal candle has been kept burning all day or is relit before the assembly gathers. All assemble near the candle with booklets and small candles.

• Service of light (found, for example, in GIA's *Worship*) begins. All candles of the assembly and of the church are lit from the paschal candle. No electric lights are turned on, to emphasize the gathering shadows of evening.

• Opening dialogue

• Hymn praising Easter light, sung by all. The hymn "Rejoice, Angelic Choirs" (*Worship,* #455) is set to the tune MIT FREUDEN ZART. The hymn text is a paraphrase setting based on the opening section of the "Exsultet" and will continue to draw on the images and exuberance of the Easter Vigil.

• Thanksgiving for light, sung by the cantor. Easter texts are available in two books from GIA: *Praise God in Song* and *Worship: Liturgy of the Hours—Leader's Edition.*

- The assembly's candles can be extinguished as whatever lights are needed are turned on for the psalmody. The appointed psalms have wonderful antiphons.

- During the canticle from Revelation, a congregational alleluia should be repeated often as cantors sing the verses. This is the music to accompany a procession of all to the font. The shortest route does not have to be taken. All follow the incense bearer, a minister bearing the paschal candle and the presider.

- Depending on the size and location of the baptistry, all remain there until after the baptismal commemoration or until the end of the service.

- Hebrews 10:12–14, or the gospel about the Emmaus experience (Lectionary #47, at the end of the Easter pericopes), or a patristic selection from the Easter octave may be read.

- A brief homily might focus on the symbols of Easter.

- Silence

- Responsorial song or the proper responsory listed at Easter Sunday Evening Prayer

- Prayer over the blessed Easter water (adapted from RCIA, #222 D or E; or from option C of the sacramentary's sprinkling rite).

- All approach the font and sign themselves or each other. Meanwhile, all sing an antiphon such as the one from the blessing of water at the Vigil.

- The Magnificat is sung with its proper antiphon as all are honored with incense. All might process to the altar before or during this canticle.

- Intercessions can be drawn from the *Liturgy of the Hours*.

- Lord's Prayer

- Prayer of Easter

- Solemn blessing of the day

- Dismissal with the traditional sung double alleluia

- Recessional hymn sung by all, e.g., "Come ye faithful, raise the strain" (GAUDEAMUS PARITER)

LITURGY OF THE WORD

Concluding Prayers for the General Intercessions

EASTER DAY
God of undying life,
by your mighty hand
you raised up Jesus from the grave
and appointed him judge of the living and
    the dead.

Bestow upon those baptized into his death
the power flowing from his resurrection,
that we may proclaim near and far
the pardon and peace you give us.

Grant this through our Lord Jesus Christ,
    firstborn from the dead,
who lives with you now and always in the
    unity of the Holy Spirit,
God for ever and ever.
—© ICEL

EASTER AFTERNOON/EVENING
O God, worker of wonders,
you made this day for joy and gladness.
Let the risen Lord abide with us
    this evening,
opening the Scriptures to us
and breaking bread in our midst.
Set our hearts aflame and open our eyes,
that we may see in his sufferings
all that the prophets spoke
and recognize him at this table,
the Christ now entered into glory,
    firstborn from the dead,
who lives with you now and always in the
    unity of the Holy Spirit,
God for ever and ever.
—© ICEL

LITURGY OF THE EUCHARIST

Eucharistic Prayer Inserts

HOLY THURSDAY IN EUCHARISTIC PRAYER II:
    Lord, you are holy indeed,
    the fountain of all holiness.
    We gather here before you,
    and in communion with the
        whole church

we celebrate the most holy day
our Lord Jesus Christ was handed over
    for us.
Through him whom you glorified,
our Redeemer and our Savior,
we pray:
Let your Spirit come upon these gifts to
make them holy,
so that they may become for us
the body and blood of our Lord,
Jesus Christ.
Before he was given up to death,
a death he freely accepted—
this very day
He took bread and gave you thanks.
He broke the bread . . .

HOLY THURSDAY IN EUCHARISTIC PRAYER III:
    . . . a perfect offering may be made
    to the glory of your name.
    This is why we gather before you,
    and in communion with the
        whole church
we celebrate the most holy day
our Lord Jesus Christ was handed over
    for us.
Through him, our Redeemer and savior,
whom you glorified,
we bring you these gifts.
We ask you to make them holy by
    the power
of your Spirit,
that they may become the body
    and blood
of your Son, our Lord Jesus Christ,
at whose command we celebrate this
eucharist.
On the night he was betrayed—
this very night—
he took bread and gave you thanks
    and praise.
He broke the bread . . .

EASTER VIGIL AND THE OCTAVE OF EASTER
(INCLUDING THE SECOND SUNDAY OF
EASTER) IN EUCHARISTIC PRAYER II:
    Lord, you are holy indeed,
    the fountain of all holiness.
    We gather here before you,
    and in communion with the
        whole church

we celebrate the most holy night (day)
our Lord Jesus Christ rose according
 to the flesh.
Through him, whom you raised to your
 right hand,
we pray:
Let your Spirit come upon . . .

. . . and all the clergy.
Remember those whom you raised on
 this Easter feast
in water and the Holy Spirit
to a new life in Christ.
Remember our brothers and sisters . . .

EASTER VIGIL AND THE OCTAVE OF EASTER
IN EUCHARISTIC PRAYER III:
 *. . . perfect offering may be made
 to the glory of your name.*

This is why we gather before you,
and in communion with the
 whole church
we celebrate the most holy night (day)
on which our Lord Jesus Christ
rose according to the flesh.
Through him, whom you raised to your
 right hand,
we bring you these gifts.
We ask you to make them holy . . .

*. . . and the entire people your Son
 has gained for you.*
Remember those whom you raised on
 this Easter feast
in water and the Holy Spirit
to a new life in Christ.
Father, hear the prayers of the family . . .

TEXTS FOR THE RECEPTION OF THE HOLY OILS

The "Order for the Reception of the Holy Oils," now recommended for use at the Evening Mass of the Lord's Supper on Holy Thursday, will appear in future editions of the sacramentary. Its ceremonial is described on page 109. These texts are to be adapted as needed:

Oil of the Sick:

This oil of the sick has been blessed by our bishop for the healing of body, mind and soul. May the sick, who are anointed with it, experience the compassion of Christ and his saving love.

Oil of Catechumens:

This oil of catechumens has been blessed by our bishop for the anointing of those preparing for baptism. Through this anointing they are strengthened by Christ to resist the power of Satan and reject evil in all its forms, as they prepare for the saving waters of baptism.

Holy Chrism:

This holy chrism, a mixture of olive oil and perfume, has been consecrated by our bishop and the priests of our diocese. It will be used to anoint infants after baptism, those who are to be confirmed, bishops and priests at their ordinations, and altars and churches at the time of their dedication.

EASTER

Introduction to the Season

THE joy of resurrection life—that's the motif for the Fifty Days of Easter. As with Lent and Triduum, Easter is best understood from the viewpoint of those initiated at the Vigil. What is it like to be fresh from the waters of baptism, newborn from the womb of the church? What do the readings, prayers and songs of the season say to those who have just joined the order of the faithful? What does it mean to live the resurrected life of Christ? What does it mean to be church? How do we live our lives now that we have died and been raised up? During the Fifty Days the church continues to instruct the neophytes (newly baptized) about the new life they have embraced.

In the process, all the members of the community are called to reflect on the meaning of their own baptisms and the shape of baptismal living. Even more than during Lent and Triduum, during Easter the journey of the neophytes and the journey of the community are united. The neophytes now stay for the whole eucharist and their main catechesis takes place through the homily of the Sunday Mass. So we all are cate-chized again, we all are called to reflect on the implications of the resurrection and of baptism, by which we share in Christ's resurrection.

The catechesis proper to this season is called *mystagogical catechesis.* The term *mysta-gogy* comes from the same word as *mysteries,* an ancient term for sacraments. Based on the principle that one learns something best after experiencing it, this time is devoted to catechesis on what the newly baptized experienced at the Easter Vigil and what it all means for their lives now as members of the order of the faithful. It thus offers the whole assembly an opportunity to unpack the experience of the Easter sacraments.

The readings of the Easter Sundays offer opportunities for such reflection, especially in Year A: the focus of the readings is on the life of the church community after the resurrection. In 1996, the first readings of these Sundays are from the Acts of the Apostles, the second readings are from 1 Peter (except on Pentecost), and the gospels are from John except for the Third Sunday, which has the Emmaus story from Luke.

The readings from Acts give us a picture of the life and preaching of the early church as it began to develop. The passages from 1 Peter form a kind of postbaptismal instruction on living out the implications of baptism. And the gospel pericopes present the Lord as the Risen One; the one present in the breaking of bread; the Good

Shepherd; the way, the truth and the life; and the one who promises the Spirit to strengthen and sustain the church.

These readings present us with a model by which we can see what baptismal living involves. Like the early church, we also are a people called to live a new life, to leave sin behind, to proclaim the good news of the resurrection, to endure suffering joyfully, and to be filled with the Holy Spirit. The task of the preacher is to make these themes concrete for this local community in this time and place. What are the ways in which we share the good news with others during Easter and all year long? What obstacles to living out our baptismal commitment do we face? What does faithfulness require in our own time? What signs of the Risen One can we see in our midst today? How is the Spirit active among us? What reasons do we have to give thanks and to rejoice throughout the Fifty Days?

There is a danger that by focusing on the life and mission of the early church and its implications for us, we will experience the burden of the gospel more than the joy. This is a season for rejoicing, for an extended celebration for a week of weeks. The challenge is to experience the gift of new life so powerfully that the mission flows from our joy and our excitement rather than from duty or guilt. And perhaps the best way to find that joy and excitement is to share the experience of the newly initiated members in our midst. The *Rite of Christian Initiation of Adults* (#246) puts it this way:

> The neophytes, with the help of their godparents, should experience a full and joyful welcome into the community and enter into closer ties with the other faithful. The faithful, in turn, should derive from it a renewal of inspiration and of outlook.

■ HISTORY OF THE FEAST: The fifty-day feast of Easter developed from the harvest feast of ancient Israel known as "Shavuot," or the "Feast of Weeks." It was a period of seven weeks (a "week of weeks") plus one day, beginning with Passover and concluding with the fiftieth day, the day of Pentecost. The fiftieth day marked the end of the barley harvest and included an offering of the first fruits. By the time of Jesus, this festival also had become a celebration of the giving of the Law on Mount Sinai.

The themes of harvest, Exodus and the Law also became part of the Christian celebration. Christians celebrated the Passover of Jesus through death to new life and the Covenant that was established in him. Images of Christ as paschal Lamb and as first fruits are the earliest Easter images, used by St. Paul.

Easter was the first of our feasts to develop beyond the weekly Sunday celebration. This fifty-day period of rejoicing seems to have been adopted by all Christian communities by the second century. Within a few centuries, however, the unity of the feast began to weaken, and the resurrection, the ascension, and the descent of the Holy Spirit began to be celebrated separately. Easter and Pentecost became two separate days rather than the two names for the same fifty-day period. Only in our own time has the unity of this celebration been reestablished, at least in the liturgical books. The pastoral challenge is to reestablish it in the minds and hearts of the parish, and the best way to do that is by celebrating the whole feast well.

■ STRUCTURE OF THE SEASON: Within the unity of the Fifty Days, we can discern three phases:

- Octave: The first eight days are celebrated almost as one exuberant festivity, with each day ranked as a solemnity. The tradition of mystagogical catechesis during this time influenced the selection of scriptural passages.

- The 31 middle days: The gospels of the Sundays give focus to Eastertime: The first three Sundays of Easter relate postresurrection appearances, the Fourth Sunday always focuses on the powerful image of the Good Shepherd, and the next three Sundays of the season (and many of the weekdays nearby) draw from what has come to be known as the "farewell discourse" or "high-priestly prayer" in the Gospel of John. These paschal references and the overall unity of the Fifty Days should not be compromised by excess attention to May as "Mary's month." The paschal season can include references and hymns to Mary, but they must never dominate. See the notes at May 1 in the calendar section.

- The final days: The nine days following Ascension (the original novena) and Pentecost Sunday itself are days of intense prayer for the Holy Spirit. Before Vatican II, Pentecost day had an octave and there was some confusion about when Easter ended. Today it is clear: Easter ends with Pentecost Sunday.

■ CELEBRATING FOR FIFTY DAYS: Every year, parishes across the land observe Lent with vigorous penance and a variety of renewal programs, service projects, penance services and other prayer opportunities. They celebrate the solemn liturgies of the Triduum with care and devotion. They muster all their musical and homiletic resources for a joyous Easter Sunday. And then things tend to fall flat! Both as individuals and as parishes, we seem to know better how to do penance during Lent than how to celebrate the Fifty Days of Easter.

Part of the problem is that we do not know how to celebrate well, even for a short time, much less for fifty days! Celebrating conflicts with the serious-minded, productivity-oriented attitude that is assumed to make America great. Despite the license of recent years in certain areas, Puritan and Jansenist influences still inhibit a real sense of festivity. Our culture commonly assumes that people can celebrate only with lots of alcohol, drugs or sex, so that celebrating becomes a way to escape reality. True celebration, however, does not seek to escape reality but to enter more deeply into it. We need to celebrate the profound goodness of reality, a goodness we have come to recognize as deeper and stronger than the evil that is also part of reality. Christian celebration does not deny the reality of evil; the cross is a constant reminder of evil's presence and power in the world. But Christians believe in love that is stronger than hate, grace that is more abundant than sin, light that is not overcome by darkness, and life that conquers even death. We celebrate the victory of Christ over sin and death, and we need to celebrate that truth long and well. This kind of celebration is much more profound and powerful than the mindless superficiality of drugs, alcohol and casual sex. We need to recover the ability to celebrate the deepest meaning of life, and Easter is the perfect time to do so, as we celebrate the ultimate victory of life over death.

Another part of our problem with celebrating the Fifty Days is that we still don't view Easter instinctively as one extended feast. Our recent history led most Catholics to see Easter, Ascension and Pentecost as three separate and independent feast days, each with their own themes. At various times, we have had a period of fast between Ascension and Pentecost and an octave period following Pentecost, both suggesting that Pentecost was not part of Easter. The custom of extinguishing the paschal candle on Ascension contributed to the same impression. Another difficulty is with our recent stress on Lent as *the* religious period for Catholics. Easter Sunday still seems to be the end point of Lent for many people; on Easter Monday, it's back to everyday life as usual. Recovering Easter as a fifty-day feast, therefore, requires preparing the whole Lent-Triduum-Easter cycle as a unit.

Within Easter itself, it is important to make decisions that emphasize the unity of the fifty days. The continued use of the paschal candle at all gatherings for prayer and worship, the retention (and replacement when needed) of Easter flowers, the continuing use of Easter banners and other decor, the regular use of the sprinkling rite, the continuing visibility of the neophytes (in Easter white?) and the constant use of Easter music throughout the fifty days (even on Mother's Day!) can help everyone learn to see the fifty days as one unified feast. Efforts at catechesis and items in the bulletin can help, too, but it is the way we celebrate that indicates most clearly and convincingly the unity of this "great Sunday."

One point that may need some catechesis is the use of the terms "Easter" and "Pentecost." Both are used in two senses, to refer to a day and to refer to the whole fifty days. Easter is Easter Sunday and also the fifty-day feast. Pentecost is the fifty-day period and its final day of celebration. This ambiguity is rooted in our history, and there is no need to abandon these traditional usages, but care in written and spoken communication with the parish can make clear how these various usages intertwine.

Images of the Season

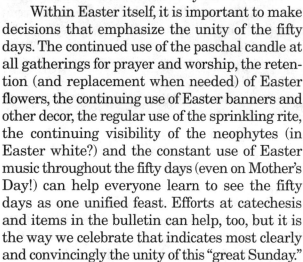

THE most central images of Easter are human images, the neophytes who were baptized at the Vigil. They are the ones in whom the death and resurrection of the Lord is most clearly visible this year, and they remind us that Easter is the primary time for celebrating the initiation sacraments. Other initiates are powerful symbols of the season, too: adults entering into full communion, youths being confirmed and children making their first communion. The initiates reminds us all of our identity and the new life we share.

Many other rich images, linked in various ways to initiation, pervade the Fifty Days. The paschal candle, baptismal water, white garments and Easter flowers remain as central, visual reminders of the Vigil itself. The resurrection inaugurates a new creation, the eighth day, a new Pentecost, a new covenant, a new way of life. The Christ is the Risen One appearing to the disciples, the shepherd of the flock, the true vine with many branches, the stone rejected by the builders that became the cornerstone, the light of the world, the way and the truth and the life, the first fruits of the new creation, the glorified Lord ascending, and the ever-present companion through the gift of the Spirit. In Jesus' holy name, the gospel is preached, the lame walk, the dead are raised to life, the Apostles rejoice in being found worthy of persecution, Stephen accepts the crown of martyrdom, and Paul is converted on the way to Damascus. The baptized form a new people of God, the body of Christ, the flock of the Good Shepherd, fed in the breaking of bread and enlivened with the breath of the Spirit. That Holy Spirit is a gift of God, conveyed in the breath of the Risen One, descending as wind and fire, guiding the early church, prompting an ever-expanding mission, showering the baptized with gifts for the common good, choosing individuals for various tasks and making the whole world new.

■ EASTERTIME SAINTS: The time frame of this season can differ by up to a month from year to year, so the saints included in it change somewhat. Three feasts occur this year: Mark, Philip and James (together), and Matthias. No Marian feast occurs during this season this year. Two obligatory and up to eight optional memorials may be celebrated. All feasts and memorials that are observed should be celebrated in a way that makes it clear they are part of the paschal season.

An African American Perspective

FOR fifty days we rejoice. And the spirituals once again aid us in our celebration. "He arose" and none of us will ever be the same. Not only has each one of us been redeemed, all creation has been restored and renewed in Christ's liberating death–resurrection. We can most assuredly sing, then, that God "has the whole world in his hands." As Gerard Manley Hopkins expressed it so beautifully, all creation sings, even where

. . . generations have trod, have trod, have trod;
and all is seared with trade; bleared, smeared
    with toil;
. . . Because the Holy Ghost over the bent
world broods with warm breast and ah!
    bright wings.

For fifty days we awake as we did on Easter Sunday morning: "I woke up this morning with my mind stayed on Jesus." With our minds and hearts fixed on Jesus we necessarily focus on what he does: the care of his flock. ("You can hear the lambs a-crying").

Our festival is made all the more joyous by our desire to serve. Great joy is derived from sharing news that is almost too good to be true: Jesus Christ is risen as he said. How can we do anything but let the light that has been given to us shine, shine, shine? In truth, "This little light of mine, I'm gonna let it shine . . . "Everywhere I go, I'm gonna let it shine. Let it shine, let it shine, let it shine!"

Perhaps the song which best captures this season is "Wade in the water."

Wade in the water,
Wade in the water, children,
Wade in the water,
God's a-going to trouble the water

With its surface emphasis on baptism, this spiritual reveals a symbolic meaning

whose underlying significance in encouraging deep immersion in the spiritual waters of the soul is readily evident when one takes the time to think about it in that way. . . . On this level the lyrics communicate that if one follows the song's advice about engaging in a deep exploration of the waters of the spirit [which we did for the 40 days of Lent], a transformation will occur [the Triduum]; God's-a gonna trouble these spiritual waters, and the affected person will never be the same. And when one listens to or sings this song, the lively rhythm and infectious melody provide further confirmation; one is indeed a new person! (Jones, 97)

Could there be a more appropriate song to accompany the sprinkling rite as we continue to wade in the turbulent waters of violence, in the undulating waters of hopelessness, or in the flood of poverty and homelessness that threaten to drown us even now? God has troubled the waters, and though we waded through it "chilly and cold," we have come forth renewed for the life of the world.

The Hispanic Mística and the Liturgy

IT may seem strange to many post–Vatican II Catholics who were not raised with an intense Marian piety that devotion to Mary should figure so prominently in the worship life of a Hispanic parish during the Easter season. In some parishes, especially those that have retained the Spanish custom of processions around the town with *pasos* (floats) carrying statues of the suffering Christ and of the sorrowful Mother, the dramatic custom of the *santo encuentro* (holy meeting) is especially important. A statue of the resurrected Christ and another of the Virgin Mary are carried in procession from two different points in the town and meet in front of the church before Mass at dawn on Easter Sunday. Those who have accompanied Jesus and his Mother in their suffering during Holy Week, who have expressed their *pésame* (condolences) to Mary on Friday evening, see this *encuentro* as a particularly appropriate (if not biblically recorded) way of celebrating the joy of the resurrection and the reunion of son with mother. Thus, drama and human relationship, aspects of liturgy and life prized by Hispanics, are used to celebrate this particular and very human facet of the good news of Easter.

This emphasis on Mary during Eastertide is not completely unfamiliar to Catholics raised before the Council. The traditional Easter hymn *Regina Coeli, Laetare,* which called upon Mary to rejoice because Christ has risen as he promised, is part of the tradition of European as well as Hispanic Catholics. But Hispanic Marian piety has its own set of cultural references and should not be immediately conceptualized by non-Hispanics as simply "old fashioned" or even theologically naive. The U.S. Bishops' Pastoral Plan for Hispanic Ministry states quite plainly that "the Hispanic people find God in the arms of the Virgin Mary. That is why Mary, the Mother of God, as goodness, compassion, protection, inspiration, example . . . is at the heart of Hispanic spirituality" (*Origins,* 17, Dec. 10, 1987, 46). Therefore, it should not come as a surprise to find a popular emphasis on Mary during this time of year.

Marian piety during the month of May offers interesting possibilities for bringing together various groups within a multicultural parish.

Catholics from many cultural backgrounds share a devotion to Mary and usually express this love by "May Crownings" at which a statue of Mary is crowned with a wreath of flowers after a procession and Marian hymns. Hispanics also practice a devotion called *Las flores de Mayo* (the flowers of May); little girls daily offer flowers to Mary during a recitation of the rosary. These devotions could be the occasion for a multicultural celebration of prayer at which the various cultural groups of the parish are asked to choose representatives to dress in their native costume and take part in the procession with or to the statue of Mary.

Each culture has Marian hymns in their own language that evoke strong ties with their country of origin. In addition, there is a new tradition of Marian hymnody in Spanish that moves beyond the merely sentimental or doctrinal and speaks of Mary's presence with the people of the Americas in their struggle for justice. Juan Espinosa's *Santa María del Camino* or Cesáreo Gabaráin's "Madre de la Inglesia" can offer a fine justice complement to the more traditional Marian hymns. (Both hymns can be found in *Flor y Canto,* Portland, Oregon: OCP Publications, 1989.) Some parishes have celebrated a May crowning on a Sunday afternoon followed by a dinner at which every group contributes the specialty of their country. In this way, bridges are built between people of different cultures within the parish, many of whom can unite around the image of Mary, the Mother of the Resurrected One.

In preparing these celebrations, the emphasis, of course, is not on Mary alone but on Mary as the Mother of the Resurrected One— our Mother and the Mother of the Church, who points the way to Christ, to resurrection through redemptive suffering. For this reason, symbols of the Easter season need to be incorporated into these celebrations. The Paschal Candle placed near the statue of Mary is an appropriate way of visually uniting Mary and Eastertide.

Preparing the Parish

THE best preparation for Easter is a well-prepared Triduum preceded by an engaging

Lent. Beyond that, some efforts at catechesis through bulletin, newsletter and pulpit can help the parish recognize the duration and exuberance appropriate to Easter. The most effective catechesis, however, is non-verbal — celebrating the Fifty Days year by year.

■ MYSTAGOGY FOR ALL: Eastertime is the season for mystagogy, for unpacking the meaning and import of the Easter sacraments of initiation and thus the meaning and implications of church membership. The mystagogical homilies of the early church, captured in the Office of Readings in the early days of Eastertime, show how to open the sacramental actions just experienced. Reflecting with the neophytes on the meaning of their Vigil experiences provides an opportunity for the whole parish to deepen its living of resurrection life.

■ CATECHESIS BEFORE FIRST EUCHARIST: Many parishes celebrate first communion for children during the Fifty Days. It is important for this event to be seen as part of the Easter celebration of initiation. The final weeks of catechesis should clearly link the coming celebration with the Easter Vigil sacraments. Children preparing for first eucharist should have been present at the Easter Vigil, and they might meet during the Fifty Days with any children of catechetical age who were initiated at the Vigil.

Taking It Home

DOMESTIC PRAYER: Seven sections of *Catholic Household Blessings and Prayers* offer material useful at home in Eastertime: the blessing at table (page 84), the blessings of homes (page 153), the blessing of children before confirmation (page 230) or before first eucharist (page 231), a blessing for Mother's Day (page 197), intercessory prayers for the blessing of fields and gardens (page 166) and a fine prayer for Pentecost day itself (page 157).

A family Easter candle might be the focal point for family prayer and/or for the family dinner each day during Easter. Families should be encouraged to continue a spirit of celebration throughout the fifty days with special foods or family outings, for example. Each day should

include some reminder, however simple, that it is Easter!

LTP's *Take Me Home* has pages for each week of Easter and for Pentecost Sunday.

■ BLESSING OF HOMES: The *Book of Blessings* (chapter 50) speaks of both Christmas and Easter as traditional times for blessing homes. An interesting rubric (#1599) notes that "a home should not be blessed unless those who live in it are present," reminding us that blessings are times for prayer, not magical rites.

■ BLESSING OF GARDENS, FIELDS, ORCHARDS, FLOCKS, SEEDS: In the medieval and post-Tridentine church, rogation days (April 25 and the three days before Ascension Thursday) were times for fervent prayer for growth and fruitfulness. The *Book of Blessings* contains both an order for the blessing of fields and flocks (chapter 26) and a blessing of seeds at planting time (chapter 27). Other prayer materials mindful of the rhythms of the earth are available from the National Catholic Rural Life Conference, 4625 N.W. Beaver Drive, Des Moines IA 50310.

The Mass

INTRODUCTORY RITES

THROUGHOUT Easter, the choices made for music, texts and ritual should make it abundantly evident that the celebration is part of the great feast of Easter. This is perhaps most important at the entrance rites, so that the assembly is aware from the beginning that they are gathering within the Fifty Days.

The penitential rite on Sundays might well be replaced with the blessing and sprinkling (or signing) with water (Prayer C in the sacramentary or the example on page 176), with music drawn from the rich Easter and baptismal collections of our tradition. Select music that the congregation will sing well, and then repeat it each Sunday. The water should come from the baptismal font. If the water has already been blessed, see the RCIA, #222, D and E for thanksgivings to replace the blessing. If a penitential rite is used, forms C*v*, C*vi* and C*vii* in the sacramentary are most appropriate. Also see the example on page 174.

■ THE GLORIA: The Gloria should certainly be sung every Sunday in Easter as well as each day during the Octave. Richard Proulx's fine "Gloria for Eastertime," based on the alleluia from "O filii et filiae" (O sons and daughters), is available for cantor and congregation (GIA, G-3086) or for two-part mixed/equal choir and congregation (GIA, G-3087) with optional trumpet fanfare and descant. Other festive refrain-style settings include Christopher Walker's "St. Augustine's Gloria" (OCP #7107) and Peter Jones's "Glory to God" (OCP #7110). Both setting have optional brass parts. The Gloria from "Mass of Creation" by Marty Haugen (GIA, *Gather*) has proven to be an effective and singable piece familiar to many assemblies. John Rutter's lively and straight-forward setting of the "Gloria" (*Worship*, #276) is well worth adding to the parish repertoire.

■ OPENING PRAYERS: See page 180 for suggested presidential prayer texts for Masses with children during the Easter season.

LITURGY OF THE WORD

■ ACTS OF THE APOSTLES: The Sunday and daily readings from Acts continue an ancient tradition, focusing on the work of the Spirit in the primitive Christian communities and calling our own community to the enthusiasm of those early days.

■ THE PSALM: Psalm 118 is the premier Easter psalm. It is the core of the gospel acclamations for the Easter Vigil and for the octave weekdays, and the proper psalm of Easter Sunday and its octave. Michael Joncas's rhythmic setting found in *Psalms for the Cantor,* Vol. I (World Library Publications) is a delight for both the cantor and the congregation. Richard Proulx's classic setting is joyful in tone and easily embellished by canonic singing of the refrain and descant; the octavo edition offers parts for handbells, triangle and tambourine (GIA, G-1964). A setting by Christopher Willcock (*Psalms for Feasts and Seasons,* Liturgical Press) has a strong refrain in 7/8 rhythm, with lively verses for the cantor. Christopher Walker's "This day was made by the Lord" is a lively, dance-like setting and its assembly's "echo" within the verses is a delight! Scott Soper's "This is the day" (OCP) is a new, easily sung setting of this Easter psalm.

■ GOSPEL ACCLAMATION: Bring out your best settings for this season. The exuberant "Celtic Alleluia" (OCP, #7106) with Easter verses serves well, as does the more gently moving Robert Hutmacher "Gospel Processional" (GIA, G-2450). "Gospel Fanfare for Easter Morning" (GIA, G-2719) is a fine choice if you have brass available. The familiar alleluia refrain from "O sons and daughters" is particularly appropriate for this season; see the arrangements by John Schiavone for Easter Sunday, Ascension and Pentecost (GIA, G-2162) and Marty Haugen's "Easter Alleluia" (*Gather,* GIA), which provides verses for each of the season's Sunday gospels. Jeremy Young's setting of the familiar "Easter Alleluia" in the Cantor/Congregation Series (GIA, G-3175) has appropriate settings of the verses for each of the Sundays of Easter.

■ HOMILY: The RCIA says simply that the homily "should take into account the presence and needs of the neophytes" (#248). The homily is the main component of the mystagogical catechesis for the newly-baptized, so the whole assembly is invited to share in this process. There are two main components of mystagogy: to reflect on and "unpack" the experience of the sacraments and to make ever clearer the implications of initiation for daily living as baptized members of the body of Christ. Preachers who prepare well to help the neophytes will also be helping the whole assembly deepen their baptismal awareness and commitment.

■ DISMISSAL OF CATECHUMENS: While we pray for and work toward the full incorporation of the neophytes into the life of the church, many communities also have other catechumens who are still preparing for the Easter sacraments—perhaps in 1997. They continue to be dismissed for their own reflection on the word after the homily. See the sample dismissal on page 174.

■ GENERAL INTERCESSIONS should take on a seasonal cast. Form 8 in the appendix to the sacramentary is a model, but it needs a petition or two added for the neophytes. Other examples for the season begin on page 174.

LITURGY OF THE EUCHARIST

■ EUCHARISTIC PRAYER: The Eucharistic Prayer for Masses with Children III provides three variable parts for this season. The words and the format—more frequent acclamations—may make it a candidate for continual use in a parish with large numbers of children.

Five prefaces are designated for the Fifty Days, with two more added to the list during the last days (Ascension) and with one more possible for Pentecost. The sacramentary provides varied inserts for Eucharistic Prayer I: for the octave, for the Ascension, for Pentecost (all printed at the bottom of the prayer text). On page 176, see samples of inserts for Eucharistic Prayers II and III. Presiders in parishes with a strong musical tradition might consider singing the whole Eucharistic prayer throughout the Octave and on the Sundays of Easter.

Three festive settings of the eucharistic acclamations that work well are "Festival Eucharist" by Richard Proulx (GIA, *Worship* or G-1960), which adapts well for a cantor when the choir is not present; Paul Inwood's "Coventry Acclamations" (OCP, #7117); and "Festival Mass" by Christopher Walker (OCP, 7154). All three settings have brass and percussion parts.

■ COMMUNION RITE: See page 177 for suggestions for Eastertime for the communion rite. Music for the communion rite might include Suzanne Toolan's "I Am the Bread of Life," Richard Hillert's processional "Worthy is Christ (also called "This is the feast") or Richard Proulx's arrangement of "I received the living God." All these pieces are found in *Worship*. From the Taizé tradition, two ostinato refrain settings, "Surrexit Christus" and "Christus Resurrexit" (GIA, *Music from Taizé,* Volume II, G-2778), employ segments of Psalm 118 for the cantor answered with short acclamations by the assembly. Bob Hurd's setting of "In the breaking of the bread" *(Gather)* recalls the appearances of Jesus to the disciples.

CONCLUDING RITE

■ BLESSING: The sacramentary contains several solemn blessings that may be used this season. Blessing 7 may be memorized by the presider and used throughout the Fifty Days or other texts may be selected on certain days—#6 on Easter Sunday, #8 on the Ascension, #9 on Pentecost.

■ DISMISSAL: The Fifty Days are marked by the addition of a double alleluia after the words of dismissal and after the assembly's response. Musical settings are suggested at the end of the section in this book on the Easter Vigil. This

tradition is prescribed for every day of the Easter octave. An often overlooked rubric calls for its appearance again at the end of the Pentecost eucharist and at the very conclusion to the season—the last lines of Evening Prayer II on Pentecost. Other traditions suggest continuing the chant throughout all the fifty days, better expressing the unity of the season.

MUSIC

The music of the season, perhaps more than any other element, will assist in underscoring the fact that the Easter feast lasts for fifty days. Musicians could ask themselves, "If a stranger came into our church on the Sixth Sunday of Easter, would that person know that the resurrection of Christ is being proclaimed with force and vibrancy?" Easter hymns and music should be sung for the entire season. Texts that point to the historical event, i.e. "Jesus Christ is risen *today*" need not be reserved for the actual feast of Easter Sunday. Using such texts throughout the season helps establish that the entire season is one big Easter.

The strong hymns of this season, such as "Jesus Christ is risen today," "The strife is o'er," and "Hail thee, Festival Day" should be repeated each year. To this staple and familiar repertoire, it might be good to add a few hymns whose tunes are carols. Some are borrowed from Christmas and Advent and may already be familiar to the parish. These include: "This Joyful Eastertide" (VRUECHTEN), "Now the green blade rises" (NOEL NOUVELET), and "That Easter day with joy was bright" (PUER NOBIS). These carol-hymns provide a pleasant contrast to the majestic hymns of the season. A search of the assembly's music resources will surely yield additional music. OCP offers Christopher Walker's "Paschal Procession," which may be used as gathering music for the season. John Foley's "All shall be well," Roc O'Connor's "Behold the Glory of God" and John Dailey's "Rejoice! Rejoice!," all found in OCP's music resources, are wonderful additions to the standard Easter selections.

New choral music to consider adding to the parish repertoire includes: John Ness Beck's "The King of Love my Shepherd Is" (Beckenhorst Press BP1247), Bach's "Sing praise to Christ" (Concordia 98-1377), Michael Ward's "In the Breaking of the Bread" (World Library Publications), Jerry Galipeau's "On the wings of

Change" (World Library Publications) and the wonderful "I will not leave you comfortless" by Everett Titcomb (Carl Fischer CM441), which is particularly appropriate for the final weeks of the season.

Other Ritual Prayers and Sacraments

LITURGY OF THE HOURS

IF the parish has celebrated Morning Prayer or Vespers as part of Lent and/or the Triduum, it should be continued during Easter. Even if the hours are not celebrated through the whole year, gathering for them during Easter indicates that this season is at least as important as Lent. Saturday night resurrection vigils might also become part of the parish's liturgical life. Appendix I of this season's volume (II) of the *Liturgy of the Hours* includes special texts for vigils for each Eastertime Sunday and for the Ascension. See page 178 for notes on the Pentecost vigil.

COMMUNAL ANOINTING OF THE SICK

When the sick are anointed or when a community gathers to share communion with homebound parishioners during Eastertime, the scriptural passages from the Acts of the Apostles listed in the rite are appropriate, as is the Johannine selection on the Good Shepherd. See page 178 for suggested seasonal adaptations for the introduction/reception of the sick and the prayer after anointing.

MARRIAGES

One of the scriptures given in the marriage rite can be used on the Sundays of Eastertime, but all other texts of the day come from the Easter lectionary. On Easter Sunday, on the Ascension and on Pentecost, no such substitution is permitted. The season also invites couples and ministers to look at the passages from First John (lectionary #775.8, #775.9), Revelation (#775.10) and the latter parts of the Gospel of John (#778.8-778.10).

FUNERALS

The first days of the octave may be marked by eucharistic celebrations with the people who buried their loved ones during the Triduum. The scriptures of these days can serve well at these Masses, linking the bereaved to the paschal mystery. The presidential prayers from Funeral Mass C were composed for the Easter season. Because the liturgy will not be concluded by a procession to the cemetery, this is a great opportunity for the parish community to provide food and hospitality.

Funerals later in the season may draw from the readings of the day as well. Within the *Order of Christian Funerals,* the passages from Acts and Revelation and the gospel about Emmaus (Luke 24:13-35) stand out for their Easter echoes. Our tradition does not allow the celebration of funeral Masses on the Sundays of the season or on the Ascension.

OTHER RITES AND BLESSINGS

■ ANNIVERSARY OF BAPTISM: The RCIA (#250) calls for celebrating the anniversary of baptism with the neophytes from the previous year. This presumes that the parish maintains contact with each year's neophytes; if this is not the case in your parish, this is a good time to develop plans for this year's initiates. The celebration need not occur on the exact calendar day but might better be observed as part of Easter. One option is a gathering on some day early in the season—after evening prayer on the octave Sunday may be just right. If the parish is named for an Eastertime saint such as Catherine of Siena or George, the party could be scheduled on the saint's feast, which is observed as a solemnity. Choose the same day each year so that each group of neophytes can anticipate their anniversary celebration. Initiates from several recent years could also be invited to join in the celebration.

The Worship Environment

THE Fifty Days should look and feel like the great festival they are. Those who prepare the environment might consider these traditions:

■ PLACE FOR THE NEOPHYTES: The newly baptized and their godparents should occupy special places in the assembly throughout the Easter season. Perhaps special seats could be reserved for them near the candle and ambo.

■ THE FONT: Use the water blessed at the Vigil throughout the season. Parishes with their font in a separate place sometimes display a large bowl of water somewhere near the front of the church, but it would be better to keep attention fixed on the font no matter where it is located. During the sprinkling rite, maintain some association with the font, even if that means drawing Easter water from it and then carrying this water into the assembly for the prayer of thanksgiving over the water.

■ THE EASTER CANDLE: Is your paschal candle too small for your building or too short for the times it is needed during the year? The problem is sometimes a tiny stand or a narrow fixture for the candle base. Even if it is too late for this year, begin looking for a stand with the right scale and style for your building. It must be right for the Easter Vigil, for the Fifty Days in the main worship area and then for the rest of the year in the baptistry. Some places, faced with a huge worship space and a small baptistry area, use two stands for the same candle.

The candle should be kept lit for every gathering this season. Ideally, it should be shining brightly even before people gather. Once the candle is lit on Easter Eve, it is never extinguished, at least publicly, and other candles can be lit from it.

■ FLOWERS: Consider the entire worship space throughout the period, from the Gloria of the Vigil through Pentecost Sunday. Even if certain flowers will need to be replaced during the Fifty Days, the overall plan should be consistent.

■ OTHER DECORATIONS: If the worship space will be decorated with Easter banners, they should not duplicate the imagery already present in the worship environment, such as water, candle, font, cup, and book. Illustrate the paschal stories: the creation, Jonah, the Exodus, the giving of the Law at Sinai, Daniel in the lions' den, the three youths in the fiery furnace, Esther and Mordechai. Or use non-representational banners; large drapings of yellow-gold and white material can lend a festive air to the whole assembly space. Any of this large-scale decoration should direct attention to—and not draw attention from—the altar, ambo, chair, font, paschal candle and cross. And don't forget the assembly's spaces: portals, walls, interior floors and exterior sidewalks and walkways are too often ignored as potential places for art. Whatever is added for special celebrations (first communion, confirmation, Pentecost, etc.) should be integrated into the Easter decor, which should remain primary.

■ VESTURE: Use the same festive vesture for Easter Sunday and for the rest of the season. Let the clothing itself say that these days are one unified feast. The red days provide exceptions: apostles, martyrs and, of course, Pentecost. This red vesture may be unique to Eastertime, not the more somber vesture of the passion.

Ideally, whatever fabrics and trim patterns were chosen for vesture, altar cloths and book covers for the previous Sundays of Eastertime can be reflected in the Pentecost vesture. Only the colors of these fabrics would change, thereby establishing a strong connection.

April

MON 8
#261 (LMC, #185 – 192)   white
Easter Monday
SOLEMNITY

■ EASTER OCTAVE: In the early centuries of Christianity, the newly baptized gathered each day during the octave for mystagogical catechesis. This may not be possible in many parishes, but here are some alternatives to consider:

- a gathering of the neophytes with those baptized on previous Easters

- evening eucharists with extended mystagogical sharing

- neighborhood suppers with the neophytes of each section of the parish

Parishes without neophytes should also consider ways to gather for rejoicing. Liturgical planners and volunteers, at least, should gather to swap stories, make notes for next year, sing Easter songs and treat each other to Easter foods.

■ LITURGICAL PATTERNS: For Morning Prayer and Evening Prayer, the same psalms, canticles and antiphons from Easter Sunday are used all through the week — a reminder that the octave is like an extended Easter day. The same principle underlies the status of each day this week as a solemnity (though without the Profession of Faith). All Masses this week should be fully festive, with sung Gloria (and Easter sequence?), the sprinkling rite, Easter hymns and the double alleluia at the dismissal. The gospel acclamation verse each day will repeat the refrain, "This is the day the Lord has made; let us rejoice and be glad." Let it look and sound and feel like Easter Sunday all week.

The first reading at Mass throughout the Fifty Days is taken from Acts. The gospels this week recount the appearances of the risen Lord.

■ PARISH SCHOOLS: On one of the first days back to school, students might assemble for a seasonal liturgy. This, too, should follow the parish's Easter patterns. See the ideas for curriculum and liturgy in the *Leader's Manual of the Hymnal for Catholic Students,* pages 92 – 96.

TUE 9
#262 (LMC, #185 – 192)   white
Easter Tuesday
SOLEMNITY

In Acts today, continuing from yesterday's passage, Peter proclaims the good news of the resurrection to those gathered in Jerusalem on Pentecost. The gospel reminds us that it was through women that this good news was first proclaimed.

WED 10
#263 (LMC, #185 – 192)   white
Easter Wednesday
SOLEMNITY

Today's gospel presents the beautiful story of the disciples on the way to Emmaus, which is also told this year on Easter Sunday for an afternoon or evening Mass and on the Third Sunday of Easter. In Acts, Peter and John cure a crippled man in the name of Jesus. It's a good day to ask where we find the Risen One in our midst and how his power is evident in our lives.

THU 11
#264 (LMC, #185 – 192)   white
Easter Thursday
SOLEMNITY

The second reading from the Office of Readings today provides a model for mystagogy and homilies. It speaks directly to the neophytes and to all of us: "You were led into the font . . ." The gospel reminds us that we are called to be witnesses to the death and resurrection of Christ, while Acts shows Peter fulfilling that mandate. While we rejoice in the glow of Easter, we are reminded that our joy must be shared. The reading from Acts might also prompt some explanation of the role of the Jews in Christ's death, noting Peter's assumption that those who put Jesus to death acted out of ignorance.

FRI 12
#265 (LMC, #185 – 192)   white
Easter Friday
SOLEMNITY

Today's gospel again suggests the mission of the church to gather in all people, while Acts reminds us that this mission often brings opposition and persecution.

In some parts of Europe, this is a favorite day for "Easter hikes" or pilgrimages with banners flying and hymns filling the air. Church communities in the United States might collaborate with each other, bringing diverse congregations together into a joyous throng for at least one day of the Fifty. The diocesan assembly with the neophytes may be one such occasion.

SAT 13
#266 (LMC, #185 – 192)   white
Easter Saturday
SOLEMNITY

Today's gospel summarizes three post-resurrection appearances and again links them to the missionary mandate. Acts offers an answer to all who oppose such preaching: "Judge for yourselves whether it is right in God's sight to obey you rather than God."

Because today ranks as a solemnity, the Mass of the day is used for weddings. One of the readings from those given in the rite of marriage may be used. The nuptial blessing and the special final blessing may also be used.

This day's intercessions might also include prayers for our Orthodox neighbors, who tonight begin their celebration of Easter.

✹ 14 #44 (LMC, #37) white
Second Sunday of Easter

In a previous calendar, this Sunday was called *Dominica in albis,* "Sunday in whites." The neophytes wore their baptismal garments for the whole of Easter week, laying them aside after Vespers today. Another old designation for this day, "Low Sunday," often left us with the wrong impression. The words "high" and "low" meant beginning and end (of the octave), not big and little.

What is crucial is that the joy and splendor of Easter Sunday continue today and throughout the season. Many parishes with strong ethnic traditions observe this "second Easter Sunday" as a day for a parish potluck supper where folks bring ethnic specialties for a parish Easter feast.

The gospel on this Octave Sunday is the same every year, which indicates the importance that our tradition assigns to this passage. Since the first part of the passage is repeated on Pentecost, the story of Thomas's doubt and faith draws our attention today. The first two readings this year reflect how the apostolic faith shaped the early life of the church (Acts) even in times of suffering (1 Peter). Preachers might find ideas in the marvelous example of mystagogy from Augustine in today's Office of Readings, too.

In many parts of the world, this Sunday is the traditional day for children to receive their first communion.

■ ORTHODOX PASCHA: Orthodox Christians celebrate Easter today. Include prayer for them and for the eventual reunion of our churches in today's intercessions.

MON 15 #267 (LMC, #185–192) white
Easter Weekday

As we move into the central section of Eastertime, the semicontinuous readings from Acts are joined by a similar unfolding of John's gospel. Jesus tells Nicodemus that he must be born of the Spirit, and the early Christians experience that Spirit giving them complete assurance as they speak God's word in the face of threats.

Parishes named after the various saints eclipsed by Holy Week and the Easter Octave would normally move their "titular solemnities" to this first open day after those weeks.

TUE 16 #268 (LMC, #185–192) white
Easter Weekday

Today's account in Acts of the communal sharing of the early church might prompt reflection on how we today share the gifts God has given us, material as well as spiritual. Such charity arises from the power of the Spirit in those who have been baptized (gospel).

■ HOLOCAUST MEMORIAL DAY: Today is also Yom Hashoah, the Day of the Destruction. On the Jewish calendar, this occurs on Nisan 27 (12 days after Passover). The Israeli Knesset seems to have had a two-fold reason for selecting this date. It is near Israeli Independence Day, and the Warsaw Ghetto uprising in 1943 ended on Nisan 27. The intercessions today should include prayers for the victims and their survivors and for the healing of the whole world. *Catholic Household Blessings and Prayers* (page 190–91) has prayers for this day. Interreligious services could also be planned. Great care should go into the selection of texts and images used today. Helpful resources include *When Catholics Speak about Jews; Thank God: Prayers of Jews and Christians Together* and *From Desolation to Hope: An Interreligious Holocaust Memorial Service,* all from LTP. See the chapter on this day in Michael Strassfeld's *The Jewish Holidays: A Guide and Commentary* (New York: Harper & Row, 1985).

WED 17 #269 (LMC, #185–192) white
Easter Weekday

The continuing opposition to the apostles' preaching in Acts finds its explanation in today's gospel: "The light came into the world, but people loved darkness rather than light because their deeds were wicked."

THU 18 #270 (LMC, #185–192) white
Easter Weekday

Jesus urges Nicodemus to believe in and obey the Son in order to have life eternal. Peter follows this principle when he insists: "Better for us to obey God than human beings!"

FRI 19 #271 (LMC, #185–192) white
Easter Weekday

The first reading reminds us that persecution and martyrdom do not stop the progress of God's work. The gospel story of the loaves and fish might lead to reflection on the eucharist as one of the initiation sacraments in which we meet the Risen One.

SAT 20 #272 (LMC, #185–192) white
Easter Weekday

Today's readings remind us of the challenge of change and growth in the church. The passage from Acts shows the early church developing new ministries to meet community needs, and the gospel story of Jesus walking on the water invites us to trust in the Lord in difficult times.

☀**21** #47 (LMC, #40)   white
**Third Sunday
of Easter**

Today's gospel is the wonderful Emmaus story, which offers an ideal time to reflect on the liturgy of the word and the liturgy of the eucharist. Though it was also used on Easter Sunday afternoon or evening, most parishioners didn't hear it then. The first reading was also used on Monday of the Easter Octave. The passage from 1 Peter gives a succinct summary of the paschal mystery.

M
O **22** #273 (LMC, #185 – 192)
N   white
Easter Weekday

The martyrdom of Stephen is recounted today and tomorrow, reminding us that witnessing to the resurrection often requires accepting the cross. The gospel might prompt reflection on the goals we pursue in life.

Today is the 26th annual Earth Day, which ought to find a place in our prayer. Liturgical planners should be sensitive to environmental questions, both in church decor and in the implications of an incarnate liturgy, for how we treat the created world.

T
U **23** #274 (LMC, #185 – 192)   white
E   **Easter Weekday**

George, martyr, optional memorial / red. ▪ George was probably a martyr who died at Lydda in Palestine in 303. The story of George slaying a dragon and rescuing the king's daughter is a twelfth-century Italian fable, which is perhaps best understood as a symbol of George's triumph over evil. He was a favorite patron of the Crusaders and is the patron saint of England, Portugal, Germany, Aragon, Genoa and Venice.

The death of Stephen is described today as an imitation of the death of Jesus, reminding us that all Christians, not only martyrs, are to walk in the footsteps of the Master. The gospel reminds us that Jesus is the living bread come down from heaven to give us life.

W
E **24** #275 (LMC, #185 – 192)
D   white
Easter Weekday

Fidelis of Sigmaringen, presbyter, religious, martyr, optional memorial / red. ▪ Frustrated by injustices against the poor, Fidelis abandoned a career in law and joined the Capuchins, preaching against heresy in Germany and Switzerland in the early seventeenth century. He was murdered at age 46 when he refused to renounce his faith.

Acts presents the death of Stephen as the beginning of a persecution of the church in Jerusalem (see Acts 11:19), in which Saul takes an active role. God can draw good from evil, however, and the persecution leads to the spreading of the Good News as the disciples disperse. Jesus' promise of eternal life in the gospel no doubt sustained those undergoing persecution, in the early church and in the seventeenth century.

T
H **25** #555   red
U   **Mark, Evangelist**
       FEAST

The gospel assigned to today's feast is an Easter appearance of the Risen Lord, who sends the Eleven on a mission. The passage from 1 Peter is used here because it indicates that Mark accompanied Peter, leading to the belief in the early church that Mark's gospel reflected Peter's preaching.

The hymn "By all your saints still striving (*Worship*, #706) includes a verse for St. Mark.

Mark's feast is one of the traditional rogation days—days of asking for blessings from God for our earth and its peoples. Other rogation days in our tradition are the three days just before Ascension Thursday. See page 162 for blessings appropriate to this time of year.

F
R **26** #277 (LMC, #185 – 192)
I   white
Easter Weekday

The conversion of Saul (Paul) is related in Acts, one of the classic descriptions of a reversal of one's life. Note the question of Christ, "Saul, Saul, why do you persecute *me*?" Christ lives now in his members; we who share his resurrected life form his body in the world. This gives added insight into the gift of the eucharist proclaimed in today's gospel.

▪ ARBOR DAY: Remember to pray for deeper respect for creation as God's gift and greater care for the garden entrusted to us.

S
A **27** #278 (LMC, #185 – 192)
T   white
Easter Weekday

Today's reading from Acts presents Peter as a healer; he brings "the words of eternal life" (gospel) to people in Lydda and Joppa, literally giving new life.

☀**28** #50 (LMC, #43)   white
**Fourth Sunday
of Easter**

▪ THE GOOD SHEPHERD: The beautiful image of the Good Shepherd appears on the Fourth Sunday every year. Today's texts in the sacramentary, the lectionary and the *Liturgy of the Hours* present a picture of the Good Shepherd that is much more than a gentle herdsman. This is the shepherd who is also the gate through which the sheep must pass to have life to its fullest. The first and second reading remind us that the shepherd gave his life for the sheep. Excellent quotations on the image of the shepherd are found in the chapter for this week in LTP's *An Easter Sourcebook.*

■ WORLD DAY OF PRAYER FOR VOCATIONS: This Sunday has been designated Vocation Sunday since 1964. While this is an important issue in the church, it can easily overwhelm the Sunday. Express this special concern in a petition in the intercessions, with bulletin inserts and perhaps with a reference or two in the homily. Use the texts of the Fourth Sunday and continue the ritual patterns set out for the season. This allows the Good Shepherd texts to be the context of prayer for vocations to the priesthood and religious life, as the original planners envisioned. The prayers and readings for vocations found at the back of the liturgical books are not to be used today.

■ MUSIC: Hymns that would emphasize the image of the Good Shepherd include "The king of love my shepherd is" (ST. COLUMBA) and "The living God my shepherd is" (BROTHER JAMES' AIR). *Worship* includes a contemporary hymn, "Jesus, shepherd of our souls" with an interesting text by Fred Kaan and a tune by Alexander Peloquin; it also offers the African American spiritual, "The Lord, the Lord, the Lord is my shepherd." Tobias Colgan's "Gentle shepherd" is included in OCP's *Breaking Bread* and the *Music Issue.* Marty Haugen's "Shepherd me, O God" (GIA) could be used effectively as a communion refrain this day. John Ness Beck's choral setting "The King of love my shepherd is" (Beckenhorst Press, BP1247) offers a beautifully lyrical setting of this hymn.

■ SACRAMENTS IN EASTERTIME: This Fourth Sunday of Easter is chosen by many parishes as first communion day. Both confirmation and first eucharist are best celebrated on Eastertime Sundays. The readings and prayers for this Fourth Sunday of Easter should not be changed, however; first eucharist is an initiation sacrament, a sharing in the Easter mystery.

#279 (LMC, #185–192) white

MON 29 Catherine of Siena, virgin, doctor of the Church
MEMORIAL

This fourteenth-century mystic and doctor of the church attracted many followers and played a role in papal politics, encouraging Gregory VI to move from Avignon to Rome and supporting his successor, Urban VI, against an antipope. When declaring her a doctor in 1970, Pope Paul VI termed her "the mystic of Christ's Mystical Body."

A special first reading is suggested as an option for the memorial (#557), but today's assigned reading from Acts is an important explanation of the Gentile mission. The gospel continues the Good Shepherd imagery from yesterday, stressing that Jesus is the way to salvation for all, Jews and Gentiles alike.

#280 (LMC, #185–192) white

TUE 30 Easter Weekday

Pius V, pope, religious, optional memorial, white. ▪ Pius was elected three years after the end of the Council of Trent and accepted the task of reform mandated by that council. He published a Roman catechism, the Breviary and the Missal used for 400 years until 1970. His work and the reforms of Vatican II remind us that the church is continually in need of renewal, both institutionally and personally.

Today's reading from Acts shows how even persecution led to the spread of the gospel; it also recalls the first use of the term "Christians" to designate the followers of Christ. The gospel continues the Good Shepherd image.

May

#281 or 559 (LMC, #185–192) white

WED 1 Easter Weekday

Joseph the Worker, optional memorial / white. ▪ This memorial was established by Pope Pius XII in 1955 to place May Day, a worker's holiday, in a Christian context. In the United States we celebrate this theme on Labor Day, so it might be best to omit the memorial today and use the St. Joseph texts in September.

■ MARY, QUEEN OF APOSTLES: Many people still think of May as a time of devotion to Mary, but this devotion should never eclipse the paschal nature of the Fifty Days. Even the desire of some faithful to highlight a statue of Mary during this month may compromise the season's visual unity. If the Marian shrine is to be highlighted, it should be done for all 50 days.

Devotional gatherings such as May processions and May crownings should not take place on Ascension. On other days, Marian devotions should have clear Easter flavor: praying the Regina Caeli instead of the Angelus, singing Easter hymns (such as "Be joyful, Mary") and remembering the witness of Mary praying with the apostles before Pentecost. This last image is the most traditional form of devotion to Mary in the Fifty Days: honoring her as one open to the Spirit. While votive Masses generally are restricted to Marian shrines in Eastertime, prayer texts for other devotions can be drawn from the Mass of "Queen of the Apostles" in the *Collection of Masses of the Blessed Virgin Mary* (Liturgical Press).

In the gospel, Jesus speaks the word of God; in Acts, the disciples are guided by the Spirit. We might reflect on whose words we speak and how much the Spirit of God shapes our attitudes and our actions. Are we influenced more by the word of God and the Spirit of God or by societal attitudes and media commentators?

T H U 2 #282 (LMC, #185–192) white
Athanasius, bishop, doctor of the Church
MEMORIAL

Athanasius, the fourth-century bishop of Alexandria in Egypt, played a leading role in the Council of Nicaea and was a great champion of the faith against the Arian heresy, which denied the divinity of Christ. The special first reading suggested for the memorial (#560) reflects that issue. Athanasius was exiled five times for his defense of orthodox teaching, which the optional gospel reading reflects.

In today's weekday readings, Paul recounts the history of salvation from the Exodus through the coming of Jesus as the world's savior, and the gospel reminds us that we are to imitate the Savior, the Master who became a slave for our sake.

F R I 3 #561 (LMC, #452–455) red
Philip and James, apostles
FEAST

Philip brought Nathaniel to Jesus and was the intermediary for the Gentiles who wanted to speak to Jesus. James, the cousin of the Lord, is traditionally considered by the West to have been the bishop of Jerusalem, though the Eastern tradition on this is different. This joint celebration can

be traced in the Roman church to the time when their relics were placed in the Church of the Twelve Apostles in 570. Its date of consecration (May 1) was their feast until 1955, when the institution of "Joseph the Worker" occasioned a shift of date.

"By all your saints still striving" (*Worship,* #706) includes a verse for these two apostles.

S A T 4 #284 (LMC, #185–192) white
Easter Weekday

Acts recounts the conflict between the Christians and the Jews as the gospel spread to the Gentiles. In the gospel, Jesus insists on his unity with the Father.

5 #53 (LMC, #46) white
Fifth Sunday of Easter

■ GOSPEL: Today's gospel selection marks the first of three Sundays when the gospel reading is from the Last Supper discourses found in John. Two of the more important commentaries are found on pages 581–782 in Raymond Brown's *The Gospel According to John* (XIII–XXI), Anchor Bible 29A (Garden City NY: Doubleday, 1970), and on pages 972–79 in Pheme Perkins' "The Gospel According to John" in *The New Jerome Biblical Commentary* (Englewood Cliffs NJ: Prentice Hall, 1990). They note that these discourses follow the standard literary practice of attributing farewell speeches to great heroes. Today's passage includes most of yesterday's verses.

The first reading today recounts the choosing of the seven known as the first deacons, and the second reading speaks of all of us as living stones; both suggest some attention to the ministry and mission we share.

M O N 6 #285 (LMC, #185–192) white
Easter Weekday

In Acts, Paul and Barnabas have to insist they are human, not divine. Jesus promises to send the Paraclete to instruct us in the truth.

T U E 7 #286 (LMC, #185–192) white
Easter Weekday

Jesus promises peace in the gospel today, but the first reading makes it clear that this peace does not mean the absence of conflict. Those who know that the Risen One is with them can undergo trials with an inner peace and assurance.

This is National Teacher Day, a good day to pray for those who have educated us and those who continue to teach both children and adults.

W E D 8 #287 (LMC, #185–192) white
Easter Weekday

Today's passage from Acts reminds us that disagreement is normal in the church, and the gospel reminds us that we must stay united on the vine even when we disagree.

T H U 9 #288 (LMC, #185–192) white
Easter Weekday

The first reading today records the discussion at the first council of the church in Jerusalem; the decision of the council not to burden the Gentile converts is a practical application of the gospel command of Jesus to keep his commandments and live in his love.

F R I 10 #289 (LMC, #185–192) white
Easter Weekday

Today's readings echo yesterday's, describing in more detail the decisions of the council of Jerusalem and Jesus' command to love. Note the role of the Spirit in the council: "It is the decision of the Holy Spirit, and ours too. . . ."

S A T 11 #290 (LMC, #185–192)   white
Easter Weekday

In the passage from Acts today, Paul and Timothy continue to spread the Word of God under the forceful guidance of the Spirit. In the gospel, Jesus reminds his disciples that they will suffer hatred and opposition just as he did.

12 #56 (LMC, #49)   white
Sixth Sunday of Easter

Today's readings point us toward Pentecost and the coming of the Spirit, promised by Jesus in the gospel and bestowed on the Samaritans through Peter and John. First Peter gives good advice about being always ready to explain the basis of our hope but speaking gently and respectfully. These texts might lead to some reflection on the ministry of evangelization today, a ministry inspired by the Spirit.

■ MOTHER'S DAY: While this observance should not in any way eclipse the liturgy of Easter, people's desire to pray for mothers should be acknowledged. Three sample intercessions are found in the *Book of Blessings,* #1727. The prayer over the people for the conclusion of Mass today from the *Book of Blessings,* #1728, seems a good recognition of this day's cultural power. *Catholic Household Blessings and Prayers* (page 197) provides a similar prayer for use at home. A more extensive blessing for home use may be found in Edward Hays, *Prayers for the Domestic Church,* page 80; this prayer would require rewording for use in a communal context. In

all other ways, the Masses this day should follow the seasonal Easter pattern already in place.

M O N 13 #291 (LMC, #185–192)   white
Easter Weekday

These three days before the Ascension were once designated as Rogation Days. See page 162 regarding blessings for fields and gardens appropriate to these days. The gospel today speaks of the coming Spirit, while Acts continues to describe the missionary journeys of Paul.

T U E 14 #564 (LMC, #293)   red
Matthias, apostle
FEAST

Matthias's election was part of the disciples' prayer and action immediately before Pentecost, and the feast was moved to this date recently so that it would be before Pentecost each year. The gospel affirms Christ's closeness to his disciples, whom he calls friends, not just servants.

"By all your saints still striving" (*Worship,* #706) includes a verse for this apostle.

W E D 15 #293 (LMC, #185–192)   white
Easter Weekday

Isidore the Farmer, married man, optional memorial/white. ■ This twelfth-century Spanish farmer's memorial offers an opportunity to pray for those who till the soil, for good crops to feed the world, for those of Spanish ancestry, and for all married persons. (In Spain, Isidore's wife, Maria, is also honored as a saint.)

The account of Paul's failure in Athens reminds us that reason does not always bring people to faith. It is the Spirit's inspiration that enables people to come to the truth.

T H U 16 #59 (LMC, #185–122)   white
The Ascension of the Lord
SOLEMNITY

St. Paul wrote to the church in Ephesus: "The fullness of Christ fills all in all." That is what we celebrate on Ascension Day. This day is not about the absence of Christ. It is about Christ's presence. At the conclusion of Matthew's gospel, Jesus says, "I am with you always." (*Companion to the Calendar,* page 21)

This Eastertime day is so central that Masses for funerals, weddings and anointings cannot be celebrated today. The celebration should follow the same patterns established for all of Eastertime, with the few exceptions noted below. If a school liturgy is scheduled, see the notes on page 96 of the *Leader's Manual of the Hymnal for Catholic Students.*

■ INTRODUCTORY RITES: A strong opening hymn such as "Hail the day that sees him rise" (LLANFAIR) or "A hymn of glory let us sing" (LASST UNS ERFREUEN) sets the tone for this wonderful Easter liturgy.

■ LITURGY OF THE WORD: Today's responsorial psalm is one of great exultation; it might be used as the seasonal psalm for the days from the Ascension to the Saturday before Pentecost. Choose one setting of Psalm 47 that is worthy of the solemnity and that you will want to use each year. Richard Proulx's setting fits these criteria admirably (*Worship,* #851). Other recommended settings include

- Hal Hopson's offering in *Psalms for All Seasons* (NPM), "Sing out your praise to God"

- Christopher Willcock's Psalm 47, "God mounts his throne," in *Psalms for Feasts and Seasons* (Liturgical Press)

- Marty Haugen's "God mounts his throne" in *Gather* (GIA)

■ LITURGY OF THE EUCHARIST: The first Ascension prefaces is the richer one and may provide a bulletin summary (the week before) of what the feast is all about. When preparing the eucharistic prayer, see the inserts on page 178 (prayers II and III) and in the sacramentary (prayer I).

■ THE PASCHAL CANDLE should still be in its Easter location and continues to be lighted until the Fifty Days are completed.

F R I 17 #295 (LMC, #185–192) white
Easter Weekday

Today's gospel speaks of the temporary grief of the disciples until their joy in seeing Christ again. Though this was spoken before Christ's death and it referred to the Triduum, it might also apply to the period from the Ascension to the second coming. The joy of Easter does not disappear with the Ascension, for the Risen One is still among us, assisting the church in proclaiming the good news (gospel).

S A T 18 #296 (LMC, #185–192) white
Easter Weekday

John I, pope, martyr, optional memorial / red. ▪ This sixth-century pope was forced by the Western emperor to head a delegation to the Eastern emperor to urge less harsh treatment of the Arian heretics. The outcome of the mission is unclear, but the Western emperor was suspicious of John and had him imprisoned at Ravenna, where he died.

The first reading shows Paul traveling about to proclaim the gospel and to strengthen the disciples; Apollos begins to share the preaching ministry. The gospel encourages us to trust that God will give us what we need, because the Father loves us.

✴ 19 #60 (LMC, #55) white
Seventh Sunday of Easter

Today's texts situate us between Ascension and Pentecost, as the disciples wait in the upper room (first reading), in the world as Jesus goes to the Father (gospel). This Sunday, the music also can facilitate our looking ahead to Pentecost; the familiar Eastertime patterns should remain largely the same, perhaps with a new gathering song and psalm (repeat Psalm 47 from Ascension). Consider "Alleluia, sing to Jesus," with its reference to the Ascension and Christ's promise to remain with us, or "Come down, O Love divine," to the gracious Ralph Vaughan Williams melody, DOWN AMPNEY.

M O N 20 #297 (LMC, #185–192) white
Easter Weekday

Bernardine of Siena, presbyter, religious, missionary, optional memorial / white. ▪ The greatest preacher of the first half of the fifteenth century, Bernardine was a Franciscan with a special devotion to the name of Jesus. He devised the symbol IHS, the first three letters of "Jesus" in Greek, to replace superstitious and factional symbols of the day.

Though the first readings simply continue the cursus from Acts, it is intriguing that the passages for the first three days this week speak of the Spirit—a reminder

of how much the early church relied on the Spirit's guidance. The gospel speaks of the glory of the One who has overcome the world.

Today is also Armed Forces Day in the United States, which might prompt prayers for peace and for those who work for peace.

T U E 21 #298 (LMC, #185–192) white
Easter Weekday

The first reading reminds us that the gift of the Spirit brings us not only peace and joy, but also courage to face chains and hardships. The gospel speaks of Christ's glory and of his prayer for us, who continue to make him present in the world.

W E D 22 #299 (LMC, #185–192) white
Easter Weekday

Paul's farewell speech in Acts offers good guidance not only for church leaders but for all of us. Jesus' prayer in the gospel also applies to all members of the church, not just the apostles.

Today is National Maritime Day in the U.S., pray for those who earn their living on the seas.

T H U 23 #300 (LMC, #185–192) white
Easter Weekday

Today's gospel offers a wonderful reminder that we are to be evangelizers—Jesus prays for those who will believe in him through our words. The dissension among the Jews in Acts reminds us of the importance of the unity for which Christ prayed.

F R I 24 #301 (LMC, #185–192) white
Easter Weekday

The readings explain how Paul ended up in Rome and indicate that the apostle Peter will suffer martyrdom, the final answer to Jesus' question: "Do you love me?"

S A T **25** #302 (LMC, #185–192) white
Easter Weekday

Bede the Venerable, presbyter, religious, doctor of the church; Gregory VII, pope, religious; Mary Magdalene de Pazzi, virgin, religious; optional memorials / white. ▪ Bede was a Benedictine monk and scholar in eighth-century England, noted for his history of the Anglo-Saxon church and people. Gregory was pope in the eleventh century and fought against simony (buying and selling sacred offices and things), unlawful marriage of the clergy and lay investiture (kings and nobles controlling church appointments). As a result, he suffered much persecution, and died in exile. Mary Magdalene De Pazzi was a sixteenth-century Italian Carmelite mystic and promoter of reform after the Council of Trent.

The readings today set the stage for the death of both Peter and Paul in Rome.

☀ **26** #63–64 red
Pentecost
SOLEMNITY

IMAGES

This day should be a great celebration marking the end of Easter. But it is more than a birthday party for the church—it is a day to celebrate again all that Easter means, including the gift of the Spirit we received in the initiation sacraments. Any focus on the gift of tongues, on the wind and fire, or on the different ministries in the church should be clearly situated in a celebration of the new life and joy of the Resurrection. The importance of this festival is the reason most other rites are forbidden this day: funeral Masses and ritual Masses of anointing and the marriage Mass texts.

▪ DAY OF NEOPHYTES: Pentecost became the day for the initiation of those who were sick or otherwise unable to be initiated at Easter. This history and the general Easter focus on baptism should find expression in the liturgies of Pentecost:

- The neophytes should be honored (perhaps in the homily and in post-liturgy hospitality) and prayed for (in the intercessions). Dressed in their white robes, they sit for the last time in their special places.

- Babies baptized at Easter and throughout the past year can be brought to church in their baptismal gowns, accompanied by their parents, siblings and godparents.

- Those who were received into full communion should be included in the intercessions and might have special seating today.

- Young people who were confirmed and who celebrated their first communion during the Fifty Days should also be in our prayers. They also might have special seating and be dressed in the clothes they wore at confirmation or first communion.

▪ DAY OF MINISTRIES: Some books and ministerial training programs have suggested Pentecost as the day for commissioning new ministers of the church. See page 76 regarding other possible (and better) dates and ritual ways to approach this.

EVENING PRAYER I

The Pentecost festival begins on Saturday evening. The traditional hymn "Veni Creator" can be the "ushering in" of this holy day. Even if your parish observes few celebrations of the liturgy of the hours, this great day may suggest a fuller schedule.

SATURDAY NIGHT MASS

Masses celebrated Saturday afternoon or evening use the Vigil of Pentecost texts (#63 in the lectionary). A fuller vigil celebration of the eucharist is recommended by our ancient tradition and by more recent documents. This will not work as a substitute for the regular Saturday afternoon Mass but should be held at a later hour.

PENTECOST VIGIL

Encouragement should be given to the prolonged celebration of Mass in the form of a Vigil, whose character is not baptismal as in the Easter Vigil, but is one of urgent prayer, after the example of the apostles and disciples, who persevered together in prayer with Mary, the Mother of Jesus, as they awaited the Holy Spirit. (*Circular Letter,* #107)

The full observance of Pentecost involves a parish whose consciousness of the countercultural demands of its liturgical life has been raised mightily. And this is something that can happen over years, where parish leadership has remained faithful to year-by-year tradition and where religious education, the parish school and the various ministries of the parish all regard the liturgy as the source and summit of their life together. An outline and texts for the Pentecost Vigil are found beginning on page 178.

MORNING PRAYER

If people appreciated Morning Prayer on Christmas Day or on Easter morning, then celebrate this hour today, perhaps preceded or followed by a breakfast.

MASS DURING THE DAY

Because this day marks such a high point of the year for Christians and because it is about being many yet one, it is an ideal Sunday to cancel as many Masses as possible so that the entire parish can come together at one Mass—the same principle that leads us to hold a single Celebration of the Lord's Passion or a single Easter Vigil. To do this you may have to move outdoors to a field, to a lot behind the church or to a large tent. Some parishes combine different ethnic and language communities as well as different music groups and other kinds of communities. Choose a neutral time and involve everybody in a well-planned joint effort.

■ INTRODUCTORY RITES: The patterns used throughout the Fifty Days should continue today. The sprinkling rite should be carried out well, as on previous Sundays. The beautiful alternative opening prayer from the Vigil Mass might be used at all Masses.

■ LITURGY OF THE WORD: Psalm 104 is appointed for today. Settings include Alexander Peloquin's "Lord, send out your Spirit" (GIA, G-1662) and Robert Edward Smith's more lyrical setting, "Lord, send out your Spirit," (GIA, G-2122). Paul Lisicky's setting of Psalm 104 *(Gather)* is very melodic, with an attractive refrain.

The sequence should be sung. Reciting it makes no more sense and has no more impact than speaking alleluias. Peter Scagnelli's translation found in *Worship*

(#857) and its tune, a rhythmical setting of the traditional chant, are good. Because each of the lines is sung twice to accommodate the text, it would be most practical to alternate the stanzas between the choir or cantor and the congregation. This will allow the assembly to hear each line before singing. The traditional chant "Veni Sancte Spiritus" could be sung here by cantor, small schola or choir. Alerting the assembly to the meaning and significance of this sequence before it is chanted is appropriate.

■ LITURGY OF THE EUCHARIST: There is a proper preface for today as well as inserts for the eucharistic prayers (page 177 for prayers II and III, the sacramentary for prayer I). The acclamations of the Fifty Days should be repeated, perhaps with more instruments and more harmonies.

■ CONCLUDING RITE: The dismissal includes the double alleluia (even if you haven't done it since the Easter Octave), a final reminder that this is still the Easter feast.

■ HYMNODY: A metrical setting by Richard Wojcik of the "Veni creator spiritus" chant is coupled with a John W. Grant translation in "O Holy Spirit, by whose breath" in *Worship* (#475). This can be effective with the choir interpolating the Latin chant verses. Marty Haugen's "Spirit blowing through creation," found in *Gather,* is filled with marvelous Spirit imagery. Christopher Walker's "Veni Sancte Spiritus" (OCP) would provide a lovely gathering song for this feast. It's final modulation will leave the assembly with no doubt as to whether the Spirit is working through the music. "Veni, creator spiritus" is translated poetically by Ralph Wright in the *Hymnal for the Hours* (GIA); sing it with the traditional chant or to an 88.88 meter tune, such as PUER NOBIS.

Another fine and challenging text is "Spirit of God within me" by Timothy Dudley-Smith. It is paired with a Randolph Currie tune in *Worship* and set in a flowing style by Michael Joncas (GIA, G-2831). Another lovely hymn found in most hymnals is "Draw us in the Spirit's tether." A fine choral arrangement of this hymn is by Harold W. Friedell, published by H. W. Gray (CCP/Belwin, Inc.). "Creator Spirit, by whose aid," set to the LASST UNS ERFREUEN tune in OCP's music resources, is a worthy addition, especially valuable for its "Easter" sound.

EVENING PRAYER II

Evening Prayer II marks the end of Eastertime and deserves attention. It ends with the double-alleluia dismissal and is followed by the transfer of the Easter candle to the font. If the candle has been in the midst of the assembly or by the ambo, and the distance to the baptistry is significant, sing the best and longest Easter hymn as all follow the candle to the font and then sign themselves with the saving waters.

DOMESTIC PRAYER

Prayers for home use are found in *Catholic Household Blessings and Prayers* (page 157). The Eastertime table prayer still is appropriate today (page 84).

INTRODUCTORY RITES

Greeting

The God of life, who broke the bonds of death and raised Jesus from the tomb, be with you.

Rite of Sprinkling Holy Water

Dear brothers and sisters: Let us implore the blessing of God that this rite of sprinkling may revive in us the grace of baptism through which we have been immersed in the redeeming death of the Lord, that we might rise also to the glory of new life.

O God Most High,
from the Lamb sacrificed for us upon
    the cross
you have made spring up for us fountains
    of living water:

R. Alleluia.

O Christ,
you have renewed the youthfulness
    of the church
in the cleansing of water with the word
    of life: R.

O Spirit,
you have brought us up
from the waters of baptism
as the firstfruits of a new humanity: R.

Almighty God,
who in the sacred signs of our faith
renews the wonders of creation and
    redemption,
bless this water
and grant that all who have been born
    again in baptism
may be heralds and witnesses
    of the paschal mystery,
which is forever renewed in your church.
We ask this through Christ our Lord. Amen.
—from the Italian and Spanish sacramentaries

Penitential Rite

For weekday Masses or Sunday Masses when resources would not permit the sprinkling rite to be done well.

Christ, risen from the dead, shines upon us, the people he redeemed with his own blood. Coming together at his call to celebrate the paschal feast, let us die to our sins and rise with him to newness of life.

Lord Jesus, you are the faithful witness, the firstborn from the dead: Lord, have mercy.

You have loved us and have washed away our sins in your blood: Christ have mercy.

You have joined us to your death through baptism to make us one with you in resurrection: Lord, have mercy.

LITURGY OF THE WORD

Dismissal of the Catechumens

My dear friends: With the assurance of our loving support, this community sends you forth to reflect more deeply on the word of God we have shared. May Christ who is risen from the dead, and who shines with special radiance among us in this Easter's newly baptized, fill you with joyful hope and steadfast perseverance, so that in the beauty of an Easter yet to come, you, too, may be one with us in the paschal feast of the Lord's table.

General Intercessions

Invitation to Prayer

By the resurrection of Christ, God has given us a new birth unto a living hope. Let our Easter prayer embrace the needs of all the human family, as we offer it through Christ who intercedes for us at the Father's right hand.

For the church

For the holy church throughout the world,
that Christ may be known in the works
    we do:
let us pray to the Lord.

For the church throughout the world,
born into new life by water and
    the Holy Spirit:
let us pray to the Lord.

For the world

For all who carry the Good News of Christ
    to the world,
and for Christians who witness
    in places hostile to the gospel:
let us pray to the Lord.

For our enemies and those who wish
    us harm,
and for all whom we have injured
    or offended:
let us pray to the Lord.

For various needs

For seasonable weather,
an abundance of the fruits of the earth,
and the well-being of all who work with
    the land:
let us pray to the Lord.

For those in our town
who are without food or shelter,
that they find in us generous friends:
let us pray to the Lord.

For the local community

That the violence and rage
    in our lives and our towns
give way to a desire
    for compassion and respect:
let us pray to the Lord.

For the children and the parents,
the students and the teachers,
the simple and the wise:
let us pray to the Lord.

Attuned to the Sunday readings

That Christ the Good Shepherd
may gather those who have been scattered,
bring back those who have wandered away,
and unite us in faith:
let us pray to the Lord.

For neophytes and catechumens

For the newly baptized
and newly received members of the church,
that Christ pour out his spirit upon them:
let us pray to the Lord.

For the catechumens of the church,
that their doubts give way to faith
and their fears be turned to trust:
let us pray to the Lord.

For the dead

For those who have died in Christ,
that God may call them
to the company of all the saints:
let us pray to the Lord.

Concluding Prayers for the General Intercessions

SECOND SUNDAY OF EASTER
God of life,
source of all faith,
through the waters of baptism
you have raised us up in Jesus
and given us life that endures.

Day by day refine our faith,
that we who have not seen the Christ
may truly confess him as our Lord and God,
and share the blessedness of those
    who believe.

Grant this through Jesus Christ,
    the resurrection and the life,
who lives and reigns with you in the unity
    of the Holy Spirit,
God for ever and ever.
—© ICEL

THIRD SUNDAY OF EASTER
O God of mystery,
out of death you delivered Christ Jesus,
and he walked in hidden glory
    with his disciples.

Stir up our faith,
that our hearts may burn within us
at the sound of his word,
and our eyes be opened to recognize him
in the breaking of the bread.

Grant this through Jesus Christ,
    the firstborn from the dead,
who lives and reigns with you now and
    always in the unity of the Holy Spirit,
God for ever and ever.
—© ICEL

FOURTH SUNDAY OF EASTER
O God,
you never cease to call even those far away,
for it is your will
that all be drawn into one fold.

Attune our ears to the voice
    of the Good Shepherd,
who leads us always to you,
that we may find under your tender protection
life in all its fullness.

We ask this through Jesus Christ,
    the resurrection and the life,
who lives and reigns with you in the unity
    of the Holy Spirit,
God for ever and ever.
—© ICEL

FIFTH SUNDAY OF EASTER
We have beheld your glory, O God,
in the face of Christ Jesus your Son.

Enliven our faith,
that through Christ we may put our trust
    in you.
Deepen our faith,
that in Christ we may serve you.
Complete our faith,
that one day we may live with you
in that place which Christ prepares for us,
where he lives with you now and always in
    the unity of the Holy Spirit,
God for ever and ever.
—© ICEL

SIXTH SUNDAY OF EASTER
Faithful God,
who love us in Christ Jesus,
send your Spirit of truth to dwell within us,
that we may always reject what is false,
live by the commands of Christ,
and be true to the love you have shown us.

Grant this through Jesus Christ,
    the resurrection and the life,
who lives and reigns with you in the unity
    of the Holy Spirit,
God for ever and ever.
—© ICEL

THE ASCENSION OF THE LORD
God of majesty,
yours is the power that raised Christ
    from death,
yours the glory that exalted him to your
    right hand.

By the mystery of the Ascension,
sustain our hope
as we bear witness to our baptism.
By the perpetual outpouring of your Spirit,
confirm your Church
in its mission of salvation.

Grant this through Jesus Christ,
    the firstborn from the dead,
who lives and reigns with you now and
    always in the unity of the Holy Spirit,
God for ever and ever.
—© ICEL

SEVENTH SUNDAY OF EASTER
God our Father,
glorify your Son
in the lives of the people called by his name.
Through no merit of ours, you have made us
    your own,
to be your witnesses on earth.
Keep us true to the name we bear,
that people everywhere may know
that you are the God and lover of us all.

We ask this through Jesus Christ,
    the resurrection and the life,
who lives and reigns with you in the unity
    of the Holy Spirit,
God for ever and ever.
—© ICEL

LITURGY OF THE EUCHARIST

Eucharistic Prayer Inserts

EASTER VIGIL AND THE OCTAVE OF EASTER
(INCLUDING THE SECOND SUNDAY OF
EASTER) IN EUCHARISTIC PRAYERS II AND III:
    See pages 151–152.

EASTER SUNDAYS III–VII IN EUCHARISTIC
PRAYERS II AND III:
    See page 84.

ASCENSION IN EUCHARISTIC PRAYER II:
    Lord, you are holy indeed,
    the fountain of all holiness.
    We gather here before you,
    and in communion with the whole church
    we celebrate the most holy day
    your only Son, our Lord,
    after taking on our weakness,
    brought it to glory in your presence.

Through him, who from now on sits
  at your right hand,
we pray:
Let your Spirit come upon . . .

ASCENSION IN EUCHARISTIC PRAYER III:
  . . . a perfect offering may be made
  to the glory of your name.
  This is why we gather before you,
  and in communion with the whole church
  we celebrate the most holy day
  your only Son our Lord,
  after taking on our weakness,
  brought it to glory in your presence.
  Through him, who from now on sits
    at your right hand,
  we bring you these gifts.
  We ask you to make them holy . . .

PENTECOST IN EUCHARISTIC PRAYER II:
  Lord, you are holy indeed,
  the fountain of all holiness.
  We gather here before you,
  and in communion with the whole church
  we celebrate the most holy day
    of Pentecost
  on which the Holy Spirit appeared
    to the apostles
  in countless fiery tongues,
  and we pray:
  Let your Spirit come upon . . .

PENTECOST IN EUCHARISTIC PRAYER III:
  . . . a perfect offering may be made
  to the glory of your name.
  This is why we gather before you,
  and in communion with the whole church
  we celebrate the most holy day
    of Pentecost
  on which the Holy Spirit appeared
    to the apostles
  in countless fiery tongues.
  And so, Father, we bring you these gifts.
  We ask you to make them holy . . .

Introduction to the Lord's Prayer

We are called children of God, and by baptism that is indeed what we have become; and so we have the courage to pray:

Prayer for Peace

Lord Jesus Christ,
on the day of your glorious resurrection
you greeted your disciples
and offered them your gift of lasting peace:
  Look not on our sins . . .

Invitation to Communion

This is the Lamb of God, who takes away the sins of the world:
Christ our Passover who was sacrificed for us:
Happy are those who are called to his supper.

Dismissal of Eucharistic Ministers

Go forth in peace to the sick and homebound of our community, bearing the word of life and the Body of Christ, together with the assurance of our love and concern. By your presence and the holy gifts you share, remind them of the communion that is ours in the risen Lord whose paschal mystery has made us one Body and one Spirit, in the one baptism by which we have been born to new life.

CONCLUDING RITE

Blessing

The God of peace, who brought Jesus the great Shepherd back from the dead through the blood of the everlasting covenant, make you perfect in every good work and pleasing in his sight.
  And may almighty God bless you . . .

TEXTS FOR THE ANOINTING OF THE SICK WITHIN MASS

Introduction/Reception of the Sick

In the joy of the Easter season, the church celebrates the Lord's passover from death to life, his conquering of sin and death. With the Prophet Hosea and the Apostle Paul, God's people sing: O death, where is your victory? O death, where is your sting? Gathered to celebrate the sacraments of anointing and eucharist, may we, who in baptism died with Christ to share his resurrection, rejoice in the triumph of the Lord and claim for ourselves a share in his victory and new life.

Prayer after Anointing

In the surpassing glory of Christ's
    resurrection,
you have filled your church, Lord God,
    with new hope.
Touch with your healing power
those on whom we have laid our hands
    in Christ's name.
Transform with your saving grace
those we have anointed with holy oil.
Surrounded by the love and concern
of all who have been baptized into Christ,
may our brothers and sisters experience
the victory of the cross
and the triumph of new life.
We ask this through Christ our Lord.

A VIGIL SERVICE FOR PENTECOST EVE

If Mass begins in the usual way, after the Kyrie the priest offers the prayer "God our Father . . . ," which is the alternative opening prayer of the Pentecost Vigil Mass.
The liturgy of the word is expanded this night. The presider instructs the assembly in these or similar words:

Dear brothers and sisters: We gather this holy night, following the example of the apostles and disciples who, with Mary, the Mother of Jesus, persevered in prayer, awaiting the Spirit promised by the Lord. Let us listen now with quiet hearts to the word of God. Let us contemplate how much God has done for us, and let us pray that the Holy Spirit, whom the Father sent upon those first believers, will bring God's work to perfection throughout the world.

All the "first readings" from the Vigil Mass in the lectionary are proclaimed in the following order:

Reading I

Reading

Genesis 11:1–9

It was called Babel for there the speech of the whole world was put to confusion.

Psalm

Psalm 32:10–15

Prayer

Grant, we pray you, almighty God,
that your church may always be
    that holy people
gathered together by the unity
of the Father and of the Son and
    of the Holy Spirit,
so that it may manifest
    to all the world
the mystery of your unity
    and holiness
and itself come to the perfection
    of your love.
We ask this through Christ our Lord.

Reading II

Reading

Exodus 19:3–8, 16–20

The Lord descended on Mount Sinai in the sight of all the people.

Psalm

Canticle of Daniel 3:52–56

Or:

Psalm 18:8–11

Prayer

O God, who in smoke and fire
  upon Mount Sinai
gave the old law to Moses,
and who this day revealed the
  new covenant
in the fire of the Spirit:
grant, we pray, that kindled
  by that same Spirit
which you wondrously poured
  forth upon your apostles,
and gathered from among all
  peoples to be the new Israel,
we may receive with joy
  the eternal commandment
  of your love.
We ask this through Christ our Lord.

Reading III

Reading

Ezekiel 37:1–14

Dry bones, I will send spirit into you and you will live.

Psalm

Psalm 106:2–9

Prayer

Let your people ever exult, O God,
renewed in youthfulness of soul
  by your Holy Spirit:
that we who now rejoice to have
  restored to us
the glory that is ours as your
  adopted children,
may look forward in sure and
  certain hope
to that great day of resurrection
  and reward.
We ask this through Christ our Lord.

Reading IV

Reading

Joel 3:1–5

I will pour out my Spirit upon my servants and hand-maids.

Psalm

Psalm 103:1–2a, 24 and 35c, 27–28, 29bc–30

Prayer

Graciously fulfill, O Lord,
the promise you have made
  in our regard:
that your Holy Spirit,
  when the Spirit comes to us,
may make us witnesses
  before all the world
to the gospel of our Lord
  Jesus Christ,
who lives and reigns with you
  forever and ever.

Gloria

Opening prayer

Taken from either the first or alternative opening prayers for the Pentecost Mass during the Day in the sacramentary. After the opening prayer, the liturgy of the word continues with the reading from Romans and the gospel, and Mass continues in the usual way.

Dismissal

In dismissing the people, the deacon or the presider adds the double alleluia to the invitation as do the people to their response.

IF EVENING PRAYER IMMEDIATELY PRECEDES THE VIGIL

The celebration begins either with the introductory verse, "O God, come to my assistance," and the hymn, "Veni, Creator Spiritus," or with the entrance antiphon from the Pentecost Vigil Mass. The presider greets the people, omitting the penitential rite (cf. General Instruction on the Liturgy of the Hours, #94 and #96).

Evening Prayer may begin with a lucernarium, *the thanksgiving for light, except that the paschal candle would already be lit as everyone gathers.*

The psalmody of Evening Prayer follows up to, but not including the short reading. After the psalmody, the presider offers the prayer "God our Father . . . ," which is the alternative opening prayer of the Pentecost Vigil Mass. The vigil then continues with the introduction and readings above.

A Vigil that has combined Evening Prayer with the Vigil Mass ends in this way: After communion the Magnificat is sung with its antiphon from Evening Prayer, "Come, Holy Spirit." Then the prayer after communion is offered and the concluding rite takes place as usual.

Opening Prayer

Great and powerful God,
in these days of Easter
you have taught us how great
    and how beautiful
is your love for us:
Help us to journey with the risen Jesus
toward that joy which lasts forever.
We ask this through your Son, our Lord
    Jesus Christ,
who lives and reigns [with you in the unity
of the Holy Spirit, one God] forever
    and ever.

Prayer over the Gifts

Holy God,
receive your church's gifts in this
    happy season.
You are the source of all our joy:
Help us always to be joyful in your Spirit.
We ask this through Christ our Lord.

Prayer after Communion

O good and loving God,
you have given us Jesus, the bread of life,
to be our food.
May we all work together
as we journey together with you
    to your house,
our heavenly home.
We ask this through Christ our Lord.

SUMMER AND FALL
ORDINARY TIME

Introduction to Ordinary Time

AFTER the intensity of Lent, Triduum and Easter, we return to Ordinary Time with a sense of relief and relaxation. Summer itself encourages such an attitude, and it is important to have time to catch our breath a bit and relax with a more routine pattern of celebration.

Summer and Fall Ordinary Time compose the longest continuous portion of the liturgical year, this year covering more than six full months of the calendar. It would be a mistake, though, to see this long stretch of Ordinary Time as a merely routine time when nothing important is happening. This is a time of opportunity, not a time of boring blandness.

Ordinary Time provides space for the whole assembly to reflect upon and internalize the teachings of the Lord. The readings for these counted weeks offer us a rich treasury of stories, parables and sayings of Christ along with selections from the Jewish Scriptures and from the letters of St. Paul and other New Testament figures. We are given time to dwell upon the word of the Lord and see how well we are living out the implications of the great mysteries we celebrate in the festal cycles.

Recall, too, that in the earliest centuries of our history, there were no feast days and festal cycles other than the weekly cycle and the weekly celebration of the resurrection on Sunday. Sunday is the original feast day, and the early church saw every day as a holy day, a day that belongs to Christ, a day of salvation. Ordinary Time gives us an opportunity to focus on the celebration of Sunday as the most basic feast of our liturgical cycle. This is the "ordinary" way the early church celebrated God's love and salvation all year long.

The problem with Sunday is that it occurs every week, and so it is easy to take it for granted and to become apathetic or even sloppy about our preparation and celebration of our weekly worship. Ordinary Time is an excellent time to review the basics of good worship, to see how we can improve our "ordinary" mode of celebration.

This is a good time to review the basic musical repertoire of the parish and to introduce new pieces on a periodic basis. Consider especially the acclamations for the eucharistic prayer, the responsorial psalms and gospel acclamations, and other parts of the Mass that are frequently repeated. Would a new setting or two enhance the parish worship?

Ordinary Time is also a good time to look at basic environmental issues that affect our worship: improving sound systems and lighting, raising issues of needed renovations of the space to make it more adequate for our renewed worship, repairing and repainting, and asking whether the arrangement of furniture and decor could be improved. There is little time to address these questions during the festal seasons; now we have more leisure to look at such fundamental questions.

This is also an opportunity to improve the basic symbols we use in worship. The bread for eucharist should look and taste like bread. It should be able to be broken and distributed among the faithful, as the sacramentary requires. The cup should be offered to the assembly at all Masses. Baptism should be celebrated by immersion, the preferred method in the Roman Catholic church. All ministers need to know how to use gestures well. Fake candles and fake flowers are never appropriate for worship, and a good artistic sense is needed by those charged with preparing the space for worship.

Ordinary Time is also best for training new liturgical ministers and retraining experienced ones. Lectors, communion ministers, acolytes, ushers, choirs, sacristans, musicians, cantors and even presiders all can benefit from regular sessions aimed at improving skills and deepening their appropriation of the wonder and beauty of our worship and the spirituality that underlies it and flows from it.

This also is a good time to focus on the role of the assembly in worship. The assembly must come to know and accept the important role they have in making good worship happen. They are responsible for creating a hospitable atmosphere among themselves, as well as for visitors and strangers, as they gather. They need to sing robustly and pray fervently. They must learn to sit together when the church is not full and to seek the seats closest to the altar and ambo first. What kind of instruction and formation will help the assembly "get more out of Mass" by putting more of themselves into it? Advance planning during the summer may lead to good adult education and formation in the fall.

THE PACE OF SUMMER AND FALL

With all the opportunities discussed so far, it is clear that Ordinary Time is not "time off" for parish liturgists. Yet there is a different pace to summer and autumn. Summer may be more relaxed and informal, and many of our members will be away at some point while many visitors may be joining us for worship.

Autumn brings increased activity as schools resume and vacation times generally come to an end. This may be the best time for ministry training sessions and renewal days. It is also a season of multiple special collections and "theme Sundays," which should never be allowed to overwhelm parish worship. Autumn harvests and festivals provide opportunities to thank God for the gifts that sustain our life. As autumn moves toward winter, both nature and the liturgy incline our attention to death and the "last things," the eschatological issues that mark the end of the liturgical year.

■ THE SAINTS IN SUMMER AND FALL: Because recent calendar reforms have limited saints' days during the Christmas and Easter cycles, Ordinary Time brings a plethora of saints' days. Other than the usual Solemnities of the Trinity and the Body and Blood of Christ on the first two Sundays, and Christ the King on the last, no other feast will displace a Sunday in Ordinary Time this year. In the course of the 208 days of this period, there are eight solemnities (plus All Souls Day, which is treated much like a solemnity), 12 feasts, 42 obligatory memorials, and 43 optional memorials (on 34 dates). Thus a given parish may observe as many as 85 or as few as 42 memorials.

This is a pastoral dimension of the current calendar. Parishes all over the world observe the universal calendar, while nations add several days that relate to their histories. Then, each local community adds those optional days it selects and those local days that define them (the patronal feast and anniversary of dedication). The need for advance planning and discretion in choosing which optional memorials to celebrate should be obvious.

Taking It Home

DURING this long Ordinary Time, parishes can help families celebrate special days and feasts at home by calling attention to prayers and rituals that are available in various resources. *Catholic Household Blessings and Prayers* has prayers (pages 198–200) for Father's Day, Independence Day, Labor Day and Thanksgiving Day. It also has blessings for

Rogation Days (page 166), for Assumption (page 170) and for St. Francis (page 174), as well as prayers for visiting a grave (page 178) and for November (page 181). Other blessings in part IV of this book can be suggested for use at appropriate times, such as the blessing before leaving on a journey (and one for returning); the blessing before leaving home for school, employment or ministry; and the blessing for moving.

Families might also be encouraged to keep Sunday as the primary feast day, keeping it as a day not only for worship but also for family prayer and time spent together in healthy recreation and celebration.

LTP's *Take Me Home* resource has pages for Trinity Sunday, Corpus Christi, Father's Day, the Birth of John the Baptist, SS. Peter and Paul, July 4, Blessed Kateri Tekakwitha, SS. Mary Magdalene, James and Martha, Transfiguration, Assumption, St. Bartholomew, Labor Day, Moses (September 4 in the Eastern Catholic calendar), Nativity of Mary, Triumph of the Cross, St. Matthew, St. Vincent de Paul, St. Michael (the Archangels, September 29), St. Francis of Assisi, Sukkot (September 28 – October 5), St. Luke, Halloween, All Saints, All Souls, St. Martin, Thanksgiving and Christ the King.

The Mass

SEE pages 68 – 70 for a fuller description of the gospel of Matthew and the Mass in Ordinary Time.

Because this part of Ordinary Time is such a long period, it may be helpful both for planning and for celebration to divide the period into sections. Such divisions could then mark times to change to a different set of acclamations, new decor, etc. The basis for dividing the period could be one of several:

- Change at the beginning of each new month.
- Change at mid-summer (July 4), at summer's end (Labor Day) and in mid-autumn (All Saints).
- Change when a new section of the gospel begins. Based on the outline of the Gospel of Matthew (see page 69), new sections of Jesus' teaching begin on June 16, July 14, September 8 and November 3 this year.

- Change when the second readings change. There are basically three letters this year: Romans, Philippians and 1 Thessalonians, beginning on June 23, September 22 and October 20. This would produce a very long first block and perhaps only makes sense if the second readings are the main focus of preaching this year.

INTRODUCTORY RITES

■ PENITENTIAL RITE: Form C*i* or C*viii* can be used each week, with the scriptures of that Sunday providing a phrase for one or all of the invocations. Ordinary Time is also a good time to use form B; if the assembly is unfamiliar with this option, it might be used frequently during these months until it becomes a part of their ritual vocabulary.

LITURGY OF THE WORD

As described in the introduction to the lectionary (1981):

There is a semicontinuous reading of the synoptic gospels [Matthew in Year A]. This reading is arranged in such a way that, as the Lord's life and preaching unfold, the teaching proper to each of these gospels is presented.

This distribution also provides a certain coordination between the meaning of each gospel and the progress of the liturgical year. . . . The liturgical year leads quite naturally to a termination in the eschatological theme proper to the last Sundays, since the chapters in the synoptics that precede the account of the passion treat this eschatological theme rather extensively.

[The Hebrew Scripture] readings have been chosen to correspond to the gospel passages in order to avoid an excessive diversity between the readings of different Masses and above all to bring out the unity between the Old and New Testament. . . .

There is a semi-continuous reading of the Letters of Paul and James. . . .

The [weekday] gospels are so arranged that Mark is read first (First to Ninth Week), then Matthew (Tenth to Twenty-first Week), then Luke (Twenty-second to Thirty-fourth Week). Mark 1 – 12 are read in their entirety, with the exception only of the two passages of Mark 6 that are read on weekdays in other seasons. From Matthew and Luke the readings comprise all the matters not contained in Mark. From all three synoptics or from two of them, as the case may be, all those passages are read that either are distinctly presented in each gospel or are needed for a proper understanding of its progression. Jesus' eschatological discourse as contained in its entirety in Luke is read at the end of the liturgical year.

The first reading is taken in periods of weeks first from the Old, then from the New Testament; the number of weeks depends on the length of the biblical books read.

Rather large sections are read from the New Testament books in order to give the substance, as it were, of each of the letters of the apostles.

From the Old Testament there is room only for select passages that, as far as possible, bring out the character of the individual books. . . .

At the end of the liturgical year the readings are from Daniel and Revelation, the books that correspond to the eschatological character of this period (#105–107, 109–110).

■ RESPONSORIAL PSALM: The common psalms for Ordinary Time are listed in the lectionary at the end of #175. Eight are listed for these weeks, plus one for the final weeks of the year. Praise and petition refrains are also suggested at #174. This is a good time to evaluate all of the seasonal and sacramental uses of psalmody, noting strengths and weaknesses. If the parish is not ready to sing the appointed psalms for each Sunday, consider some of the common psalms that are already appointed to these Sundays:

- Psalm 145, one of the common psalms for Ordinary Time, appears on the Fourteenth, Eighteenth and Twenty-fifth Sundays, with varying refrains. It is also used as one of the praise psalms in Morning Prayer, for confirmation, marriage and the votive Mass of the eucharist. Some good settings of Psalm 145 are by
  - David Haas in *Psalms for the Church Year* (GIA, G-2664)
  - Leon Roberts in *Lead Me, Guide Me* (#539, GIA)
  - Thomas Sullivan in "Psalm 145" (GIA, G-2299)
  - Christopher Willcock in *Psalms for Feasts and Seasons* (Liturgical Press)
  - J. Robert Carroll in *Worship Lectionary Accompaniment* (GIA)
  - Jeanne Cotter in *Gather, Second Edition* (GIA)

- Psalm 63, another of the common psalms, appears on the Twenty-second and Thirty-second Sundays. It is also frequently used as the first psalm of Morning Prayer. It is recommended for the rite of acceptance of catechumens and is one of the best choices for funerals. The Gelineau Psalm 63 with the Proulx antiphon "My soul is thirsting for you, O Lord . . ." (GIA, *Gelineau Gradual*, G-2124) is a worthy setting favored by many assemblies. The simple and direct translation of this psalm from the *ICEL Liturgical Psalter Project* ("God, my God, you I crave . . .") enjoys a sturdy, singable

antiphon and psalm. Look for other settings in collections for Morning Prayer. Other settings of Psalm 63 are by
  - Christopher Willcock in *Psalms for Feasts and Seasons* (Liturgical Press)
  - Richard Proulx in *Worship Lectionary Accompaniment* (GIA)
  - Delores Hruby in *Psalms for Cantor, Volume 1* (WLP)
  - Marty Haugen in *Gather* (GIA)
  - Leon Roberts in *Lead Me, Guide Me* (GIA)
  - Michael Joncas in *Gather, Second Edition* (GIA)
  - Balhoff, Daigle and Ducote in *Gather, Second Edition* (GIA)
  - Tom Conry in "I will lift up my eyes" (OCP)

- Psalm 23 is assigned to the Twenty-eighth Sunday and Christ the King. Though not one of the common psalms, Psalm 23 is one of the most versatile psalms in the rites of the church; it is used for votive Masses of the eucharist, funerals, the second scrutiny and the presentation of the Lord's Prayer, the baptism of children, confirmation, and Evening Prayer. Settings of this psalm abound in hymnals and collections; two that may not be easily found but are worth knowing about are:
  - Steven Warner "Psalm 23; I shall live in the house of the Lord" (*Psaltery*, GIA, G-3445)
  - Dale Wood "Psalm 23" (*ICEL Lectionary Music*, GIA G-2626)

- Psalm 95, assigned to the Twenty-third Sunday, is also a common psalm and is used for the first scrutiny. Good settings include those by
  - David Isele in *Psalms for the Church Year* (GIA, G-2262)
  - Christopher Willcock in *Psalms for Feasts and Seasons* (Liturgical Press)
  - David Haas in *Gather* (GIA)
  - Rawn Harbor in *Lead Me, Guide Me* (GIA)

- Psalm 103, which appears on the Twenty-fourth Sunday, is a common psalm for Ordinary Time and is also used for marriages, funerals and the presentation of the Lord's Prayer. Two settings appear in *Gather–Second Edition* (GIA), one by Jeanne Cotter and the other, the more familiar, by Marty Haugen.

- Psalm 96, also a common psalm, is assigned to the Twenty-ninth Sunday and is also used in the ritual mass for confirmation. Settings of this Psalm include
  - David Haas's "Proclaim to all the nations" (*Gather, Second Edition*)
  - Owen Alstott's "Proclaim his marvelous deeds to all the nations" (OCP, *Respond and Acclaim*)

■ GOSPEL ACCLAMATION: Verses for the gospel acclamation are not usually assigned to specific Sundays in Ordinary Time. Rather than using a different one each week, planners might select one from the lectionary #164 for each section of the season.

▪ GENERAL INTERCESSIONS: Appendix I of the sacramentary has four sample sets for this time of year (#1–2, 9–10). Ordinary Time might also be a good time to learn to sing the petitions, or at least the response, since both the musicians and the assembly have fewer musical demands than during the festal cycles.

LITURGY OF THE EUCHARIST

▪ EUCHARISTIC PRAYER: Besides the variable prefaces for Ordinary Time, be sure to make use of Eucharistic Prayer IV and the Eucharistic Prayers for Reconciliation. Because these have their own prefaces, they are seldom used in festal seasons but should be a part of every parish's repertoire of prayer. See page 228 for special inserts on Sundays and selected feast days.

▪ COMMUNION PROCESSIONAL: Consider using James Chepponis's "Life-giving Bread, Saving Cup" (Gather); Jerry Brubaker's "O Blessed Savior" (WLP); Robert Kreutz' "Gift of finest wheat," found in many hymnals; Richard Proulx's "I received the living God" (Worship and Lead Me, Guide Me); and Bernadette Farrell's "Bread for the world" and "Unless a grain of wheat" (Breaking Bread, OCP). Other choices might include Michael Joncas's "Take and eat" (GIA) and Martin Willet's "Behold the Lamb of God" (OCP). Marty Haugen's "O taste and see" (Gather, Second Edition) is an uplifting, more than merely "catchy," communion refrain. Musicians unfamiliar with this piece should listen to a recording before attempting to bring it to the assembly. David Haas's "Song of the Body of Christ/Canción del Cuerpo de Cristo" is also worth bringing to the assembly's repertoire.

CONCLUDING RITE

▪ BLESSING: The appendix of the Book of Blessings contains four additional solemn blessings for Ordinary Time. Many of the chapters of the same book conclude with blessings that are also appropriate for Sunday. For example, see #88 for a short Trinitarian blessing, #360 for a blessing for God's protection, #658 or #676 or #937 for Labor Day, #741 or #766 for the opening of school and #1020 for Thanksgiving. Planners

should also peruse this book to find fuller blessings that might be appropriate during Sunday Masses in Ordinary Time, such as the blessing for travelers in Chapter 9, #1171.

HYMNODY

The topics of faith, discipleship and the call to serve are strong themes in the readings of Ordinary Time. Some hymns whose texts and images focus on these topics include: "Christ is the King" to the tune GELOBT SEI GOTT (Worship and Collegeville Hymnal); "Jesus lead the way" (Worship); "The church in every age" (Worship); "Jubilate Deo" from Taizé (Worship and Gather); "The kingdom of God" to the tune LAUDATE DOMINUM (Worship and Collegeville Hymnal); "Bring forth the kingdom" (Gather); "Send me Jesus" (Thuma Mina) in Worship and Lead Me, Guide Me; "Sent forth by God's blessing" (People's Mass Book); "O God, beyond all praising" (Worship); "Two Fishermen" (Worship); "For the life of the world" (Gather, Second Edition); "You are all we have" (Gather, Second Edition); "We are called" (Gather, Second Edition); "I want to walk as a child of the light" (Worship, Gather and other sources); "Center of my life" (OCP); and "We walk by faith" (Gather and Worship).

The Worship Environment

BECAUSE Ordinary Time does not have specific, seasonal requirements, it offers the opportunity to focus on basic issues. Two long-term issues are described here.

▪ FLOWERS AND PLANTS: The Ceremonial of Bishops bans altar flowers during Lent and at funerals and calls for "moderation" in Advent (#48, #236, #252, #824). Flowers (like instrumental music) are seen as expressions of festivity. The Order of Christian Funerals used in the United States softens the application of these norms at funerals: "Fresh flowers, used in moderation, can enhance the setting of the funeral rites" (#38).

Environment and Art in Catholic Worship insists that nothing "fake, cheap or shoddy" is appropriate for worship (#22), and this includes flowers and plants.

> Flowers, plants and trees—genuine, of course—are particularly apt for the decoration of liturgical space, since they are of nature, always discreet in their message, never cheap or tawdry or ill-made. Decoration should never impede the approach to or the encircling of the altar or any of the ritual movement and action, but there are places in most liturgical spaces where it is appropriate and where it can be enhancing. The whole space is to be considered the arena of decoration, not merely the sanctuary. (#102)

These principles reject the use of plastic or silk flowers or plants; we are to use the real thing or nothing. Dried flowers are real, however, and can be used when fresh flowers are not available or are not affordable. They would be especially appropriate during autumn, when such drying occurs in nature.

Sacristans and those who prepare the liturgy can ask parishioners to sign up to provide flowers according to seasonal guidelines regarding scale and location. When establishing the flower budget, consider all the locations where flowers will be used—the altar area, the baptistry, tombs, columns, doors and vestibule.

■ CANDLES AND OIL LAMPS: Despite the claims of some manufacturers and retailers, the Roman liturgy does not allow for the use of artificial candles or lamps. An oil lamp may be used instead of a candle as the light indicating the presence of the blessed sacrament in the reservation chapel, but it should then be designed as a beautiful oil lamp, not as a fake candle. Candles at the altar must be real candles, not plastic shells around oil canisters. Hollow metal tubes with tapers inside also violate the principle of authenticity in design.

Candles, by their very nature, burn down. Their length changes as they burn, offering a quiet symbol of giving one's life for God. Some parishes have opted for fake candles because of problems with air conditioning drafts that cause candles to burn unevenly, but other solutions are available, including glass "followers" designed to shield the flame. Check with your local church supply store for workable solutions that use authentic materials.

May

#347 (LMC, #193–231)
green
M O N 27 Weekday

Augustine of Canterbury, bishop, religious, missionary, optional memorial/white. ▪ Sent by Gregory the Great with about 30 monks to evangelize Britain in 596, Augustine died in 604. By that time, the faith was well established in Britain, in large part because the missionaries adapted local customs and temples to Christianity rather than destroying them.

▪ MEMORIAL DAY: This observance began after the Civil War in a spirit that connected remembering those who died in the war to the desperate need to forgive and to rebuild. The "Gettysburg Address," stressing the task that remains for the living, is still apt reading. Special Mass texts for use in the United States may be taken from appendix X, 6, in the sacramentary; the first suggested preface (P82) seems to fit the day, though the exclusive language needs updating.

The readings of the day may be used or pericopes may be chosen from those For Peace and Justice (#831–835). If the readings of the day are used, 1 Peter speaks of the hope of glory that sustains those who die in Christ, and the gospel invites us to devote ourselves to Christ even more than soldiers give themselves for their country.

▪ CEMETERIES: Eucharist might be celebrated in a cemetery today (not on Sunday, when all should celebrate at the parish), or a parish might organize liturgical visits to one or several cemeteries. Chapter 57 of the *Book of Blessings* shows how this can be done as a congregation after the prayer after communion (#1739). A family service can be found in *Catholic*

Household Blessings and Prayers (pages 178, 280).

▪ ORDINARY TIME: The church interior and exterior should look different on this day from the way it looked in the Easter season. Presiders who wish to use the "preceding Sunday" prayers on the "open" weekdays this week should use the Eighth Sunday texts, not the Pentecost texts.

▪ THE READINGS: We rejoin the progression of gospels for Ordinary Time with the tenth chapter of Mark, as Jesus instructs his disciples before heading to Jerusalem. The first readings this week come from 1 Peter (and Jude on Saturday); next week we turn to 2 Peter and then to 2 Timothy. Preachers would do well to spend a few moments with commentaries on these books, or at least the introductions to them found in most Bibles.

#348 (LMC, #193–231)
green
T U E 28 Weekday

Both readings today call us to take seriously God's call to holiness and to rejoice in the gifts God promises to us.

#349 (LMC, #193–231)
green
W E D 29 Weekday

Today's readings invite us to reflect on the sacrifice of Christ as the price of our salvation and as the model for us to follow.

#350 (LMC, #193–231)
white
T H U 30 Weekday

The first reading is a marvelous passage that suggests to many that 1 Peter was composed from a postbaptismal instruction for the neophytes. The gospel cure of the blind man is intended to remind us all of our need for faith to see the truth.

#572 (LMC, #302) white
F R I 31 The Visit of the Virgin Mary to Elizabeth
FEAST

This feast points us to the Christmas season and thus reminds us that the whole life, death and resurrection of Christ forms one great mystery. The first option for the first reading matches the gospel canticle in expressing the joy and expectancy of this feast. The second option calls us to imitate Mary's concern for others.

June

#352 (LMC, #193–231) red
S A T 1 Justin, martyr
MEMORIAL

Justin is known for his writings defending the faith and describing the liturgies of the second century. He was the first Christian writer to link Christianity and pagan philosophy.

The letter of Jude urges us to rely on the power of Jesus to preserve us from sin; in the gospel the Jewish leaders question the authority of Jesus.

#165 (LMC, #158) white
✡ 2 The Holy Trinity
SOLEMNITY

▪ THE SOLEMNITY: The feasts celebrated this Sunday and next are best marked by familiar Trinitarian and eucharistic hymns. "The feast is only a feast if we follow the lead of the assigned scriptures and acclaim a God of love, not dissect an arcane theological treatise" (*Study Text 9,* page 60). Today's scripture passages clearly proclaim God's love manifested in Jesus and sustained by the Holy Spirit.

The music and the decorations should not convey that Eastertime has been extended by two more weeks. Decorations and vestments should be different from and simpler than those of the Easter season. Marty Haugen's "Alleluia, sing!" found in *Gather, Second Edition* can be added to the standard selection of hymns for this feast.

■ INTRODUCTORY RITES: Today's Mass probably should not include the sprinkling rite if it has been used throughout the Easter season. The prayers for this day are found after all the Ordinary Time Sundays. Use a Gloria different from that of Eastertime.

■ BLESSING MARRIED COUPLES: This order, in chapter 1 of the *Book of Blessings,* seems far more appropriate than an annual "renewal of vows" on Valentine's Day or on the feast of the Holy Family. The parish community can make wedding anniversaries part of the Sunday assembly if the integration is handled with sensitivity. The texts of the day would be used, or some of the lectionary and sacramentary texts for "Marriage (anniversary)" may be interpolated with them. One creative approach is to schedule this rite during one or more of the Masses on Trinity Sunday — as one manifestation of triune love enfleshed in our midst.

■ BLESSING OF STUDENTS AND OF TEACHERS: Ordinary time provides two extraordinary times for the young members of the parish: Schools open and schools close. For the closing of school and for graduations, see page 97 of LTP's *Leader's Manual of the Hymnal*

for Catholic Students. One Sunday in June, the Masses could incorporate petitions for teachers and for all students, especially graduates. Suggestions are found in the *Book of Blessings,* #527.

■ THE WEEK AHEAD: Presiders who wish to use the "preceding Sunday" prayers on the "open" weekdays this week should use the Ninth Sunday texts, not Trinity Sunday.

MON 3
#353 (LMC, #193–231)   red
Charles Lwanga, catechist, martyr, and his companions, martyrs
MEMORIAL

These 22 saints, martyred in Uganda a century ago, were led by Charles, the master of pages at the royal court of King Mwanga. They were martyred because they opposed the immorality of the royal court and were canonized by Pope Paul VI in 1964.

Both readings fit this memorial well; 2 Peter speaks of fleeing a world corrupted by lust and living a life of genuine piety; the gospel speaks of the rejection of the prophets and of Jesus himself.

TUE 4
#354 (LMC, #193–231)   green
Weekday

As we approach the end of the millennium and a concern about the end time, 2 Peter gives good advice: "While waiting for this, make every effort to be found without stain or defilement and at peace in his sight." Jesus' dictum in the gospel to "give to God what is God's" might prompt us to ask how much of our lives belongs to God.

WED 5
#355 (LMC, #193–231)   red
Boniface, bishop, religious, missionary, martyr
MEMORIAL

An Anglo-Saxon monk, Boniface preached the gospel in what is now the Netherlands, the Rhineland and Bavaria and part of

France. He is honored today as the apostle and patron of Germany. The opening prayer suggests that the common of martyrs be used for the other orations.

Boniface expresses well the spirit "that makes us strong, loving and wise" (first reading) as well as the belief in the resurrection that the gospel affirms.

THU 6
#356 (LMC, #193–231)   green
Weekday

Norbert, bishop, religious founder, optional memorial / white. ■ This twelfth-century archbishop of Magdeburg founded the Premonstratensians (Norbertines) to combat heresies about the eucharist. He was also a zealous preacher of spiritual renewal. He suffered rejection and persecution, but won over many of his opponents.

Norbert's ministry reflects 2 Timothy's insistence that "there is no chaining the word of God." His preaching called all to fulfill the gospel commands of love of God and neighbor.

FRI 7
#357 (LMC, #193–231)   green
Weekday

Paul writes to Timothy of the persecutions he endured and urges Timothy to be faithful. Jesus confounds the scribes with his clever questions, ultimately hinting at his identity.

SAT 8
#358 (LMC, #193–231)   green
Weekday

Blessed Virgin Mary, optional memorial / white. ■ For the closing of the school year, see Mass #24 ("Seat of Wisdom") in the *Collection of Masses of the Blessed Virgin Mary.*

Paul writes to Timothy about constancy in preaching the word, while the widow in the gospel preaches though action.

9 #168 (LMC, #161)   white
The Body and Blood of Christ
SOLEMNITY

■ HISTORY: This feast developed during the late Middle Ages, at a time of extreme emphasis on the physical presence of Christ in the eucharist. A procession with the eucharist is the most distinctive feature of the feast. Recent reforms have combined the feast of the Precious Blood and this festival, changing the day's name to "The Body and Blood of Christ."

■ MUSIC: "Pange lingua" and "Adoro te" have pride of place in today's feast. Within the church's rich treasury of eucharistic hymns, we should also consider the Eucharistic Congress hymn "Gift of finest wheat." Newer settings appropriate for this day are Jerry Brubaker's "O Blessed Savior" (World Library), Robert Hutmacher's "Love is his word" (*Worship,* #599), Michael Joncas's "Song of the Lord's Supper" *(Gather),* Bernadette Farrell's "Bread for the World" (OCP) and Christopher Walker's beautiful "There is something holy here" (OCP).

An appropriate Mass setting for this day is Richard Proulx's "Corpus Christi Mass" (GIA, G-3693). This setting of the "ordinary" uses the familiar "Adoro te" hymn as the basis for its melodic lines. It is scored for SATB choir, cantor and congregation. The familiar tune enables very successful participation.

Choral music for this feast might include various settings of "Ave verum corpus." The traditional chant is incorporated into Alexander Peloquin's setting "In memory of you" (GIA). There are the rich settings by William Byrd and Mozart. Also consider Gerald Near's setting from his "Three Eucharistic Motets," published by Areole/Paraclete Press. Other appropriate choral music choices are "Very bread" by Randolph Currie (GIA, G-2422) and Healy Willan's "O sacred feast" (H. W. Gray).

■ LITURGY OF THE WORD: The sequence should be sung by all. We have few of these left, and this is a rich text. Search for a setting that the assembly can sing together or in alternation with a cantor.

■ SHARING COMMUNION: There should be no question regarding communion being shared today under both species. It has been many years since the formal approval by Rome of the American Bishops' 1978 resolution permitting reception of communion under both kinds on Sundays and holy days as well as weekdays (which was approved in 1970). People have the option to accept the cup or not, but it is their option. To refuse to share the cup with the assembly makes a mockery of Christ's words, "Take this, *all of you,* and drink from it. This is the cup of my blood. . . ." To proclaim these words and then restrict the cup to the priest or the communion ministers is inconsistent, at the very least. The people of God have a right to the sacraments in their fullness. If the cup is not offered at all Masses in your parish, this is a good Sunday to begin to remedy the situation. The readings today offer an excellent opportunity to reflect on the meaning of sharing both bread and cup.

■ EUCHARISTIC PROCESSION: If a eucharistic procession takes place, the blessing and dismissal are omitted and the order found in *Holy Communion and Worship of the Eucharist outside Mass,* #101–108, is followed. Helpful notes can be found in the *Ceremonial of Bishops,* #387–394.

- As the distribution of communion ends, a monstrance is brought to the altar, and a host consecrated at this Mass is placed in it.

- The prayer after communion is said from the chair.

- Participating priests (of whatever number) may wear white copes.

- The thurible is prepared, and the host is honored with incense as all kneel and begin singing.

- The presider puts on a humeral veil and takes up the monstrance for the entire procession.

- The procession, accompanied by music, proceeds in this order: crossbearer and acolytes with candles, ministers of the Mass (lectors, ministers of the eucharist), deacons or concelebrants, two thurifers with burning incense, the presider carrying the monstrance, and the members of the assembly. The rubrics specify that all the liturgical ministers are to carry lighted candles; certainly everyone else can, too.

- The procession should move from one building to another: to a neighboring parish, from church to parish hall via neighboring streets, or from the church to a cemetery chapel.

- Upon entering the destination, the presider places the monstrance on the altar, lays aside the humeral veil and performs an additional incensation. Meanwhile "Tantum ergo" (or something similar) is sung.

- A prayer from *Holy Communion and Worship of the Eucharist outside Mass* (#98) is said.

- A blessing is given with the monstrance.

- An acclamation or a hymn of praise is sung. The "Divine Praises" can be used if sung.

- The deacon or other minister alone takes the host to the chapel of reservation.

■ THE WEEK AHEAD: If prayers of the preceding Sunday are to be used, they should be from the Tenth Sunday. The feast of Barnabas, on Tuesday, and the solemnity of the Sacred Heart, on Friday, will interrupt the daily readings. Tuesday's first reading might be appended to Monday's, while the gospel could be prefixed to Wednesday's. Friday's first reading could replace Thursday's reading and the gospel could be appended to Thursday's.

MON 10 #359 (LMC, #193–231)   green
Weekday

Today we switch to first Kings and to Matthew, beginning with the Sermon on the Mount. God feeding Elijah (and the widow if Tuesday's passage is appended) links easily with the beatitudes; both readings invite trust in God's providence as the psalm says: "Our help is from the Lord, who made heaven and earth."

TUE 11 #580 (LMC, #193–231)   red
Barnabas, apostle
MEMORIAL

A companion of Paul and an early preacher of the gospel in Cyprus, Jerusalem and Antioch, Barnabas appears frequently in chapters 11 to 15 of Acts. Today's readings speak of the missionary work of Barnabas and of all the disciples of Jesus; the first reading also notes the first time they were called Christians.

WED 12 #361 (LMC, #193–231)   green
Weekday

Today's readings are largely unrelated; the emphasis will fall on the passage from 1 Kings because of its length and drama. It is a story of God's power and the prophet's trust that God would hear his prayer. A link could be made to the gospel in that both passages call upon us to obey the Lord God.

THU 13 #362 (LMC, #193–231)   white
Anthony of Padua, presbyter, religious, doctor of the church
MEMORIAL

Anthony already had joined the Augustinians when he saw the bodies of the first Franciscan martyrs and was inspired to join the Franciscans, hoping to preach to the Moors. Instead, his learning and eloquence led to a life of teaching theology and preaching. This popular saint has been known as the patron of lovers and of marriage, as a help at the time of birth or as a help against infertility, as patron of sailors, travelers, fishermen and mountain dwellers, as defense against fevers, diabolic powers, and plagues among cattle, as a guardian of the mails, and of course, as a finder of lost or stolen items. But in his life, it was his total living of gospel poverty that made his preaching so effective.

Using Friday's first reading might prompt us to reflect on where we look for God. The gospel commands us to forgive, which is often as hard for us as it would have been for Elijah to forgive Jezebel for seeking his death.

FRI 14 #171 (LMC, #164)   white
Sacred Heart
SOLEMNITY

"The day is not meant to be a detached viewing of a sentimentally colored portrayal of Jesus pointing at his large heart. The Mass texts point us beyond the relatively modern image to perennial love of God seen in Jesus" (*Study Text 9,* page 60).

The *Book of Blessings* expresses the goal of images of the Sacred Heart:

We search the deepest reaches
    of his heart,
and our own hearts burn with
    that fire of the Spirit
which he spread in order to renew
    the face of the earth. (#1272)

■ LITURGY: The sacramentary texts are found after the Sundays in Ordinary Time. Parishes and religious communities that have this as their titular solemnity should see the vigil in appendix I of the *Liturgy of the Hours*.

If Flag Day is commemorated, include petitions for peace and justice. Given the feast of the day, however, it would seem inappropriate to focus on the flag by having it displayed in church. Let it wave proudly outside today.

SAT 15 #364 (or 573 for IHM)
(LMC, #193–231)   green
Weekday

The Immaculate Heart of Mary, optional memorial/white; Blessed Virgin Mary on Saturday, op-

tional memorial / white. ▪ The first reading expresses the radical response that God seeks from those called to serve the Lord. The gospel insistence on not swearing is really a call to radical truthfulness so that no swearing is necessary. If the Marian memorial is celebrated, the gospel story of the child Jesus in the Temple links easily with the first reading from the weekday.

❂16 Eleventh Sunday in Ordinary Time
#92 (LMC, #86)   green

▪ BLOCKS OF SUNDAYS: Depending on the approach taken locally, this might be the first of several Sundays with a given set of penitential invocations, common responsorial psalm, gospel acclamation verse, eucharistic prayer, acclamations, communion processional and certain hymns (see page 185).

The readings today focus our attention on God's call and our identity as the people of God, redeemed by Christ's death for us "while we were still sinners." This might be a good choice for one of the two or three days during the year when the parish celebrates the enrollment of catechumens. (See RCIA, #18.3)

▪ FATHER'S DAY: This day should be observed by the church in much the same way as Mother's Day. The *Book of Blessings* (chapter 56) contains three suggested intercessions and a simple blessing. Also call people's attention to the blessing in *Catholic Household Blessings and Prayers* (page 198). A more extensive blessing for home use may be found in Edward Hays, *Prayers for the Domestic Church,* page 81; this prayer would require

rewording for use in a communal context.

MON 17 Weekday
#365 (LMC, #193–231)   green

Today's first reading is a graphic example of the injustice inflicted on the poor by the powerful, but Jesus' insistence on turning the other cheek forbids vengeance as the answer to such injustice.

TUE 18 Weekday
#366 (LMC, #193–231)   green

God's forgiveness of Ahab in the first reading sets the stage for Jesus' teaching about loving our enemies.

WED 19 Weekday
#367 (LMC, #193–231)   green

Romuald, abbot, religious founder, optional memorial / white. ▪ Founder of the Camaldolese Order, Romuald died around 1027. He spent his life as a monk and as a hermit, persevering in prayer even through times of spiritual dryness.

The first readings shift from 1 Kings to 2 Kings, as the ministry of Elijah is taken up by Elisha. The gospel challenges not our religious observances (we are certainly to pray in community as well as in secret) but our motivation.

THU 20 Weekday
#368 (LMC, #193–231)   green

Today we turn to Sirach's praise of the godly summing up the life of Elijah. The gospel account of the Lord's Prayer puts special emphasis on the petition for forgiveness; use the appropriate introduction to the Our Father at Mass today.

FRI 21 Aloysius Gonzaga, religious
#369 (LMC, #193–231)   white
MEMORIAL

This Jesuit seminarian ministered to victims of the plague and con-

tracted the disease himself in 1591, dying at 23. His early death and life-long innocence led to his title as patron of Catholic youth. Many Jesuits and health-care workers would like to see him declared the patron of those with AIDS. Use his memorial as an opportunity to pray for young people and for those living with AIDS.

Today's account of palace intrigue and butchery in 2 Kings is a sordid tale, but it is also a story of God's will being done despite the sinful efforts of Athaliah and a story of covenant renewal. It provides an interesting backdrop to the gospel's call to seek heavenly treasure.

SAT 22 Weekday
#370 (LMC, #193–231)   green

Paulinus of Nola, bishop, optional memorial / white. ▪ *John Fisher, bishop, martyr, and Thomas More, married man, martyr, optional memorial / red; Blessed Virgin Mary on Saturday, optional memorial / white.* ▪ Contemporary and correspondent with Augustine, Ambrose and Jerome, Paulinus was ordained priest with the consent of his wife and later became a bishop "renowned for his love of poverty and concern for his people" (opening prayer). Thomas More and John Fisher both were martyred in 1535 for resisting Henry VIII's takeover of church authority. Choose the memorial that best fits your community, or celebrate each in alternate years.

▪ SOLSTICE: Today marks the official beginning of summer, the longest day of the year. It's a good day to pray that we might always live in the light and avoid deeds of darkness.

☀23 #95 (LMC, #189) green
Twelfth Sunday in Ordinary Time

Today's readings invite trust in God's providence even in the midst of trials and persecution. The last sentence of the second reading might be a solid basis for reflection and for preaching; many Catholics were raised with a sense that sin was stronger and more widespread than grace.

■ THE SUNDAY BEFORE PETER AND PAUL: Coastal communities often celebrate the blessing of the fleet on this Sunday (see chapter 22 of the *Book of Blessings*). Even in communities far removed from the ocean and fishing fleets, those who enjoy fishing could participate in such a prayer service today or next Saturday.

■ DEPARTING PARISHIONERS: The order for blessing parishioners who are about to move (*Book of Blessings*, chapter 67) should be used on a regular basis by every parish. Large communities might schedule such a blessing on a monthly basis. Whatever the schedule, those who are leaving might be prayed for in the intercessions and then called forward after the prayer after communion for the blessing.

■ THE WEEK AHEAD: Monday's and Saturday's solemnities will displace the weekday readings. Monday's first reading might replace Tuesday's, in order to tell of the fall of the Northern Kingdom; the gospel could be prefixed to Tuesday's passage. Saturday's readings could be omitted this year, though the gospel might be appended to Friday's passage.

24 #586–587 (LMC, #316) white
M O N
The Birth of John the Baptist
SOLEMNITY

■ HISTORY OF THE DAY: This feast was placed here because the annunciation to Zechariah took place at Yom Kippur, nine months ago. This may have determined the date for Christmas, because Elizabeth was six months pregnant when the angel appeared to Mary. A simple way to remind people of the connection is to announce today that they only have six months left to shop for Christmas!

■ LITURGY: If the vigil Mass is not celebrated, the gospel for the vigil might be prefixed to the gospel for the day Mass, so that the whole story is heard. Inserts for eucharistic prayers are found on page 228. Several settings of the Canticle of Zachary can be found in resources for the Liturgy of the Hours, particularly *Praise God in Song* (GIA, G-2270). The three-verse setting coupled with ELLACOMBE in the *Hymnal for Catholic Students* is particularly lively and singable. The text, "The great forerunner of the morn," often coupled with the tune WINCHESTER NEW, may also be used with PUER NOBIS.

If John is the parish patron, pastoral planners might schedule an assembly on the evening of the 23rd or the 24th. If the eve is chosen, the texts suggested in appendix I of the *Liturgy of the Hours*

could help to shape an extended vigil. On the 24th itself, use Evening Prayer II, perhaps adding the passage from Augustine in the Office of Readings. Either liturgy or the eucharist itself could be followed by summertime festivities.

25 #372 (LMC, #193–231) green
T U E
Weekday

In the first reading for the day, Hezekiah trusts in the Lord and Jerusalem is saved for now; if Monday's passage is substituted, we hear about the fall of Samaria, which precedes the fall of Judah in Friday's passage. Matthew gives us a series of aphorisms or proverbs from Jesus.

26 #373 (LMC, #193–231) green
W E D
Weekday

The first reading recounts the renewal of the covenant after the book of the law was discovered in the Temple; the king recognizes the need to make our actions correspond with God's word. Jesus calls for good fruit in action, too.

27 #374 (LMC, #193–231) green
T H U
Weekday

Cyril of Alexandria, bishop, doctor of the church, optional memorial/white. ■ This fifth-century saint was a champion of orthodoxy against the Nestorian heresy. He presided as the pope's representative at the Council of Ephesus, which proclaimed that Mary is the Mother of God.

Second Kings recounts the beginning of the end for Jerusalem, with a puppet king installed by Nebuchadnezzar. Jerusalem's fall points out the importance of the gospel teaching on putting God's word into practice.

A student of Polycarp, Irenaeus was bishop of Lyons in the second century. He composed several works against heresy, especially against the Gnostics. He taught that Christ is truly present in the eucharist and that the eucharist was the sacrifice of Christ. He is also an important witness to apostolic succession, having compiled a list of the bishops of the churches founded by the apostles.

The first reading recounts the fall of Judah and the beginning of the Babylonian exile. The gospel passage, perhaps augmented with Saturday's verses, presents Jesus as a healer of great power.

SAT
29
#590–591 (LMC, #319)   red
Peter and Paul, apostles
SOLEMNITY

The opening prayer of the Vigil Mass lauds this pair as "the apostles who strengthened the faith of the infant church."

■ HISTORY: All churches in communion with Rome celebrate their apostolic foundation today.

The two apostles have always been linked in celebration, art and preaching. Because his successors are the popes, Peter stands for the institutional dimension of the church, while Paul represents the more charismatic, Spirit-led dimension. Peter and Paul clashed at times, though they served the same Lord. This day celebrates that at the very moment of its foundation, the church of Rome was marked more by its ability to love in the midst of tension than by its tranquillity.

■ LITURGY: The solemn blessing printed at the Day Mass is also appropriate for the vigil. Appendix I of the *Liturgy of the Hours* has texts for extended vigil; these might be used by the many churches carrying the title of either or both of these apostles. An appropriate hymn for the feast is "By all your saints still striving," with its special verse for Sts. Peter and Paul. "Two noble saints," found in *Worship,* is a hymn particular to this feast.

30
#98 (LMC, #92)   Green
Thirteenth Sunday in Ordinary Time

Today's first reading and gospel speak of welcoming the holy man and the prophet and of the rewards that result from that welcome. We might reflect on how open we are to those who speak the word of God to us.

The general intercessions during the summer might include petitions for those who are traveling during this vacation season (samples in the *Book of Blessings,* #629) and for parishioners who may be moving over the summer (*Book of Blessings,* #1937).

■ BLESSING OF TRAVELERS: Those who are traveling might gather for a special order of blessing led by the pastor or a lay minister (*Book of Blessings,* chapter 9). This would be particularly appropriate for parish tour groups or for any identifiable group (e.g., a local band or sports team) that can be gathered without extraordinary effort. At peak travel times such as this week, parishes might invite all who will be traveling in a given week to stay after Mass. As they gather near the ambo or the doors, the shorter rite (#635–638) would be appropriate in this setting.

■ THE WEEK AHEAD: Wednesday's feast and (probably) Thursday's holiday will eclipse the weekday readings. The passages affected can be omitted.

July

MON
#377 (LMC, #193–231)   green
Weekday

Blessed Junipero Serra, presbyter, religious, missionary, optional memorial / white. ▪ There is little doubt that Fr. Serra played an important role in spreading the gospel in California, even if some of his methods have been questioned lately. Prayers for parishioners of his missions and for Native Americans might be included in the intercessions. If proper presidential prayers are not available, use the Common of Pastors (Missionaries).

The reading from Amos sets out God's anger and disappointment with the chosen people who have not responded to God's goodness by showing love to others. Jesus invites his disciples to follow him completely.

■ CANADA DAY: Prayers for the people of Canada are fitting for the general intercessions today. Canadian parishes have a special set of Mass texts and orders of blessing.

T U E 2 #378 (LMC, #193–231) green
Weekday

The reading from Amos stresses the prophet's obligation to prophesy when God speaks, while Jesus speaks to the wind and the sea; if only people would obey God's voice and acknowledge God's authority as well as the elements do.

W E D 3 #593 (LMC, #193–231) red
Thomas, apostle

Early traditions tell of Thomas's ministry and martyrdom in India; Pope Paul VI declared him patron of India in 1972. Prayers for the peoples of that land are appropriate today. Stories circulated in the fifth century describing the transporting of Thomas's relics to Edessa (in northern Mesopotamia) on July 3, 384. The readings for the feast call us to share Thomas's faith as part of the temple built on the foundation of the apostles and prophets.

T H U 4 #380 or 831–835 (LMC, #193–231) green
Weekday

Elizabeth of Portugal, married woman, queen, optional memorial / white. • *Proper Mass for Independence Day / white.* • Parishes in the U.S. will no doubt celebrate with the special prayers and prefaces available; readings may be chosen from the texts for peace and justice. The prayer used by Archbishop John Carroll at the inauguration of George Washington (*Book of Blessings*, #1965) can provide inspiration for those composing petitions for today. The concluding prayer for the intercessions can be drawn from the various prayers listed in the sacramentary in appendix X, 6.

■ OTHER ELEMENTS FOR INDEPENDENCE DAY: The solemn blessing might be from appendix X, 6, of the sacramentary. A prayer that could be reproduced in the bulletin and used at home is on page 199 of *Catholic Household Blessings and Prayers.*

■ MUSIC: The music for today might include American hymns, but this is not an occasion to fill the liturgy with patriotic songs. Even if they mention God or praise the "divine power," their melodies and associations seem unfit for the celebration of the eucharist. "America the Beautiful" might be appropriate at the closing; it is the only national song that places this country in humility before God, praying for grace and "brotherhood," acknowledging flaws and declaring openness to the refiner's fire "til all success be nobleness and every grace, divine."

F R I 5 #381 (LMC, #193–231) green
Weekday

Anthony Zaccaria, presbyter, religious founder, optional memorial / white. • Anthony was a strong promoter of reform within the church and of the moral renewal of the clergy and the laity after the Protestant Reformation.

Amos's condemnation of injustice and Jesus' insistence that he came to call sinners reminds us of the need to reform our lives and fight injustice today.

S A T 6 #382 (LMC, #193–231) green
Weekday

Maria Goretti, virgin, martyr, optional memorial / red. • *Blessed Virgin Mary, optional memorial / white.* • After her canonization in 1950, Maria became an icon of sexual purity. A more accurate reading of her story is that she was a victim of rape. Pray for all victims of rape today and for an end to violence against all people.

Today's first reading contrasts with most of Amos, prophesying the restoration of Israel and future prosperity. The gospel suggests that the day of rejoicing has come with Jesus, but it also challenges us about the need for true renewal.

7 #101 (LMC, #95) green
Fourteenth Sunday in Ordinary Time

Today's first reading sounds like Palm Sunday or Christ the King. The gospel reminds us that our king is a gentle and humble ruler. Paul calls us to live by the Spirit within us.

■ THE WEEK AHEAD: This week we read from the prophet Hosea, and on Saturday we switch to Isaiah, whom we will read for a week. Some time with commentaries on these prophets will help preachers preach well.

M O N 8 #383 (LMC, #193–231) green
Weekday

Today we begin reading Hosea, who voices God's call to be renewed in love. In the gospel, it is evident that the divine is present in Jesus.

T U E 9 #384 (LMC, #193–231) green
Weekday

Hosea castigates Israel for its idolatry, speaking for God and calling the people to salvation. So, too, Jesus proclaims God's salvation in word and action.

W E D 10 #385 (LMC, #193–231) green
Weekday

Hosea again cries out for reform, and Jesus sends the Twelve out to proclaim the kingdom to the lost sheep of Israel.

THU 11 #386 (LMC, #193–231) white
Benedict, abbot, religious founder
MEMORIAL

Benedict is known as the Father of Western Monasticism; his moderate and balanced rule, combining prayer, study, manual labor and community living, became the basis for numerous other monasteries throughout the centuries. The Benedictine legacy of concern for good worship is worth celebrating.

Today's tender image of God in Hosea is a marvelous expression of God's love seeking to overcome even our sinfulness and ingratitude; it explains the sending of all the prophets and of Jesus himself. Jesus sends the disciples out to give blessings to all, but predicts disaster for those who refuse to listen.

FRI 12 #387 (LMC, #193–231) green
Weekday

Every Friday reminds us of the cross and of our need to repent. Today's readings reflect both of those emphases.

SAT 13 #388 (LMC, #193–231) green
Weekday

Henry, married man, ruler, optional memorial / white. ▪ *Blessed Virgin Mary, optional memorial / white.* ▪ As Duke of Bavaria and later as Holy Roman Emperor, Henry was a competent ruler and a pious promoter of missionary activity and church reform, especially in the liturgy.

God's call of Isaiah to preach God's word is matched by Jesus' instructions to the apostles to proclaim the message from the housetops. Some reflection on our mission of evangelization seems in order and would link easily to St. Henry.

14 #104 (LMC, #98) green
Fifteenth Sunday in Ordinary Time

The first and third readings today speak eloquently of the power of the word of God; this offers a great opportunity to reflect on the liturgy of the word and the experience of Christ's presence it is meant to foster. Paul speaks eloquently, too, linking human salvation with the fate of all creation; this might offer a good time to reflect on the Christian obligation to care for the environment.

Today is Bastille Day in France, a day similar to July 4 in the United States. In the intercessions, remember the French people and all who yearn to be free.

MON 15 #389 (LMC, #193–231) white
Bonaventure, bishop, religious, doctor of the church
MEMORIAL

Bonaventure was a thirteenth-century theologian, superior general of the Franciscans and later Cardinal of Albano. He was a prolific writer whose works include biblical commentaries, ascetical and mystical writings, sermons and a biography of St. Francis. His memorial should be celebrated with the common of doctors and with intercessions for Franciscans, theologians and philosophers.

Isaiah today challenges the sincerity of our religious celebrations, and the gospel (most of which we heard on June 30) reminds us that following Jesus may bring rejection.

TUE 16 #390 (LMC, #193–231) green
Weekday

Our Lady of Mt. Carmel, optional memorial / white. ▪ This memorial is central to Carmelite communities and a festive day for several ethnic groups. In the twelfth century, hermits withdrew to Mt. Carmel and founded an order devoted to the contemplative life under the patronage of the Mother of God.

Isaiah speaks God's word to the king and calls him to faith rather than fear. Jesus rues the refusal of Chorazin, Bethsaida and Capernaum to heed his message. Both readings lead us to ask how well we listen to the word of the Lord.

WED 17 #391 (LMC, #193–231) green
Weekday

Isaiah reminds us of the folly of thinking that we accomplish anything on our own power alone; Jesus suggests the same about our ability to know the Father. Jesus thanks God for giving such revelation to the merest children. How have we come to know God in our lives?

THU 18 #392 (LMC, #193–231) green
Weekday

Today Isaiah speaks of the good things God will make happen for the just. Jesus promises a yoke that is easy and a burden that is light.

FRI 19 #393 (LMC, #193–231) green
Weekday

The healing of Hezekiah in the first reading (and the reversal of the sun) manifests God's power, a power Jesus claims as Lord of the sabbath.

SAT 20 #394 (LMC, #193–231) green
Weekday

Blessed Virgin Mary, optional memorial / white. ▪ In the first reading Micah prophesies that those who perpetrate injustice will be punished. Matthew sees Jesus as fulfilling the role of the servant in Isaiah, an identification Jesus seems to have made himself and one that was very important to the early church as it sought to understand his life, death and resurrection.

⊙21 #107 (LMC, #101)   green
Sixteenth Sunday in Ordinary Time

All three readings today suggest God's patience with our weakness and sinfulness. This might be a good Sunday to reflect on the sacrament of Penance as an important part of Christian life.

■ THE WEEK AHEAD: On Wednesday we begin reading from Jeremiah, with whom we will spend more than two weeks; take time to read some commentary on this great prophet. The daily readings will be interrupted on Monday and Thursday for Mary Magdalene and James. The assigned readings for both days can be omitted.

MON 22 #603 (LMC, #193–231)
white
Mary Magdalene, disciple of the Lord
MEMORIAL

Our tradition refers to Mary Magdalene as *apostola apostolorum,* "apostle to the apostles." She witnessed the crucifixion, saw the body put in the tomb, was the first to see the risen Jesus and was the first to carry the good news of the resurrection back to the apostles.

■ THREE WOMEN: Written and artistic traditions have identified this witness of the risen Lord with two other women: the "sinful woman" (who is described in Luke 7 and has been traditionally pictured as a prostitute) and Mary of Bethany (the sister of Martha and Lazarus). Neither identification was ever given universal affirmation. Ambrose of Milan and many local churches in the East kept the memory of these women separately.

■ LITURGY: Mary's apostolic role is reflected in the gospel passage proper to this memorial and in the day's prayers. The presence of so many proper texts indicates the importance of her memory in earlier generations. The first option for the first reading stresses Mary's love for Jesus, while the second one speaks clearly of the new creation Christ has accomplished (in Mary and in us). A verse for Mary Magdalene appears in the hymn "By all your saints still striving" *(Worship).* She is also mentioned in the hymn "Jerusalem, my happy home" *(Worship* and OCP's *Breaking Bread).*

TUE 23 #396 (LMC, #193–231)   green
Weekday

Bridget of Sweden, married woman, religious founder, optional memorial/white. ■ Bridget was a queen, mother of eight, founder of the Order of the Most Holy Trinity (Brigittine nuns) and a mystic. She was also known for her concern for the poor. Her life reminds us that every vocation is a call to holiness.

The passage from Micah today is really a prayer for God's *hesed,* faithful love and mercy. The gospel reminds us that the gift of God's love and our adoption require that we do the will of the heavenly Father, as Bridget did.

WED 24 #397 (LMC, #193–231)
green
Weekday

Today we hear the call of the prophet Jeremiah to speak God's word. The gospel parable reinforces the importance of listening to those who speak that word.

THU 25 #605 (LMC, #335, 452–455)
red
James, apostle
FEAST

James was the brother of John and one of the three men closest to Jesus. It is strange to hear a gospel proclaimed on this feast that casts James the Great and his mother in such a negative light, jostling for honor. But it also hints at his pending martyrdom; the proper prayers note that he was considered the first of the apostolic martyrs. In the Middle Ages huge numbers of people went on pilgrimages to his tomb at Compostela in northwest Spain. Pilgrims to the shrine of St. James wear a scallop shell—a symbol that traditionally guarantees them the hospitality of any village through which they pass. (The seashell, with its baptismal allusions, thus is a symbol for both John the Baptist and James.) This is good day to review parish hospitality and to consider hospitality to a new breed of "pilgrims"—folks on vacation. Pray today for vacationers and pilgrims.

FRI 26 #399 (LMC, #193–231)
white
Joachim and Ann, parents of the Virgin Mary
MEMORIAL

These saints have been observed separately and moved from date to date over the centuries. Their linking, on the anniversary date of the dedication of the basilica of St. Ann at Constantinople, allows us to pray for parents and grandparents.

Though pericopes are provided in the lectionary at #606, the liturgical calendar from the U.S. Bishops' Committee on the Liturgy lists the weekday readings, perhaps relying on the second paragraph of #8e in the Introduction to the Lectionary:

Sometimes *appropriate* readings are provided to focus on a certain aspect of the spiritual life or the saint's accomplishments. It is not necessary to use these readings every time they are provided, unless pastoral reasons so demand. Generally it would be preferable to use the semi-continuous readings from the book assigned in the weekday lectionary to that liturgical season.

Jeremiah foresees the Lord providing good shepherds for Israel, and Jesus explains the parable of the sower and the seed. God's word calls for our acceptance if it is to bear fruit in our lives.

S A T
27
#400 (LMC, #193–231) green
Weekday

Blessed Virgin Mary, optional memorial / white. ▪ Jeremiah today challenges the honesty of our worship, and Jesus tells a parable (which we heard last Sunday) about the combination of sin and goodness in the church (and in our lives).

☼ 28
#110 (LMC, #104) green
Seventeenth Sunday in Ordinary Time

Solomon asks for and receives wisdom from God rather than wealth or long life or victory, and Jesus urges us to put the kingdom before all else. The passage to the Romans might need some careful explanation of "predestination" in the homily.

M O N
29
#401 and 607 (LMC, #193–231) white
Martha, disciple of the Lord
MEMORIAL

Sister of Mary and Lazarus, Martha enjoyed the friendship of Jesus during his ministry and stands as a model of hospitality.

The first reading is taken from the weekday; the parable of the loincloth speaks of Israel's refusal to listen to God's word. The gospel is from the Proper of Saints, with a choice of passages chosen for their references to Martha. Either passage can be linked to faith in God and acceptance of God's word. Intercessions could include the homeless and immigrants, children and families, and the hope for an increase in hospitality everywhere.

T U E
30
#402 (LMC, #193–231) green
Weekday

Peter Chrysologus, bishop, doctor of the church / optional memorial / white. ▪ Peter, a fifth-century bishop of Ravenna, is called *chrysologus,* "of golden words," because of his excellent preaching. The opening prayer calls him an "outstanding preacher of the incarnate word."

The readings today speak of Israel's guilt and of God's judgment. They also speak of God's mercy and patience with the weeds in the kingdom.

W E D
31
#403 (LMC, #193–231) white
Ignatius of Loyola, presbyter, religious founder
MEMORIAL

Converted by reading the lives of the saints, Ignatius abandoned military life and devoted himself to Christ. The founder of the Jesuits has been a valued guide for countless Christians through his spiritual writings. Pray for Jesuits and for all who use Ignatius' exercises in their search for God.

Jeremiah laments his fate as a preacher of God's word; the Lord promises to sustain him like "a solid wall of brass." As Jeremiah had to give up everything to be a prophet, so Jesus says the reign of God requires such single-minded commitment.

August

T H U
1
#404 (LMC, #193–231) white
Alphonsus Liguori, bishop, religious founder, doctor of the church
MEMORIAL

An eighteenth-century theologian and bishop in Italy, Alphonsus founded the Redemptorists. His theology is noted for its pastoral moderation, and his preaching frequently focused on the eucharist (see the prayer after communion). He is the patron of moral theologians.

Jeremiah offers us a powerful image of Israel as clay in the hands of the divine potter. Jesus compares the kingdom to a fish-net, a kingdom parable that stresses God's judgment.

F R I
2
#405 (LMC, #193–231) green
Weekday

Eusebius of Vercelli, bishop, optional memorial / white. ▪ This fourth-century Italian bishop defended the faith against Arianism, for which he was exiled by the emperor; he is a model of those who are called to stand up to the powerful.

Jeremiah warns the people to heed God's words, but they reject the messenger. In the gospel, Jesus is rejected in his native place, as often happens today.

S A T
3
#406 green
Weekday

Blessed Virgin Mary, optional memorial / white. ▪ Today's readings indicate the risk for every preacher: Jeremiah escapes death for his preaching, but the Baptist loses his head.

☀4 #113 (LMC, #107) green
Eighteenth Sunday in Ordinary Time

We are blessed with rich fare in today's readings. Isaiah invites us to eat and drink freely. Jesus feeds thousands with almost nothing. Paul's poetic words assure us of God's faithful love.

■ THE WEEK AHEAD: The flow of the readings is interrupted by the feast of the Transfiguration on Tuesday and by the feast of St. Lawrence on Saturday. The lectionary already prescribes the use of Tuesday's gospel on Monday. Tuesday's first reading can simply be dropped, as can both passages assigned to Saturday.

MON 5 #407 green
Weekday

Dedication of the Basilica of St. Mary in Rome, optional memorial/white. ▪ Every parish should keep its anniversary of dedication as a solemnity and the anniversary of the dedication of the local cathedral as a parish feast. In addition, all of the churches in the Roman rite remember the dedication anniversaries of the four major church buildings in Rome: St. Mary Major, St. John Lateran (the cathedral of Rome, a feast on November 9), St. Peter (November 18) and St. Paul (celebrated with St. Peter). These days link us to Rome, to the diocese and to our own local church, reminding us of the importance of spaces set aside for worship.

In the readings today, Jeremiah confronts a false prophet who says what people want to hear, and Jesus walks on the water (the pericope is found under Tuesday). Or if the second option for Tuesday is chosen, it would link easily to the false prophet story; this might also be the better choice because the first option repeats next Sunday.

TUE 6 #614 (LMC, #344) white
The Transfiguration of the Lord
FEAST

■ HISTORY: An ancient tradition held that the transfiguration took place 40 days before the crucifixion. Because the cross is celebrated on September 14, this feast was placed 40 days earlier. Other stories explain the date by references to dedication anniversaries on Mount Tabor.

August 6 seems inextricably linked to war. In 1457, the pope put this already ancient festival into the Roman calendar in gratitude for a victory over the Turks near Belgrade on August 6. The anniversary of the bombing of Hiroshima in our own century is changing the observance again and should find a place in our intercessions today.

■ EMBER DAYS: Two days that ought to be ember days in our calendar are August 6 and August 9. *Catholic Household Blessings and Prayers* (page 186) describes the concept of ember days and gives a prayer appropriate for domestic use and for the assembly's intercessions.

■ LITURGY: This is a feast of Christ's glory, similar in tone to Easter and to Christ the King. The account from Matthew, repeating the gospel from the Second Sunday of Lent, is heard in a different way today. The feast's focus, the time of year and the accompanying readings and chants let us see this gospel and the whole feast day as celebrating that "heavenly vision that will give us a share in his radiance, renew our spiritual nature and transform us into his own likeness" (Office of Readings). The proper prayers also highlight our share in that brightness. Two hymns, "'Tis good, Lord, to be here" and "Christ upon the mountain peak" (both in *Worship*) offer good possibilities for this feast.

WED 7 #409 (LMC, #193–231) green
Weekday

Sixtus II, pope, martyr, and his companions, martyrs, optional memorial/red; Cajetan, presbyter, religious founder, optional memorial/white. ▪ Both of today's saints are linked to Rome. Sixtus was pope for only a year before he was martyred in the third-century persecution of Valerian. Cajetan, a sixteenth-century lawyer and priest, founded the Congregation of Clerks Regular at Rome to work for the renewal of preaching and the clergy.

Jeremiah foretells God's restoration of Israel. Jesus' encounter with the Canaanite woman hints at the movement of the good news beyond Israel.

THU 8 #410 (LMC, #193–231) white
Dominic, presbyter, religious founder
MEMORIAL

Founder of the Order of Preachers, Dominic's ideal was to base his preaching on contemplation, to speak with God and of God. He also manifested great concern for the poor, even selling his books to feed the hungry.

Jeremiah's promise of a new covenant is an important passage for the church's understanding of Jesus. Christ's words to Peter indicate the firmness of the new covenant, but he also reminds us that it involves the cross.

FRI 9 #411 (LMC, #193–231)   green
Weekday

Today we hear from the prophet Nahum (the only time he appears in the lectionary), who proclaims the restoration of Israel and the destruction of the evil city of Nineveh, the capital of Assyria, which had conquered Samaria in 721 BC. Jesus calls for commitment to following his way, the way of the cross, to glory.

A prayerful remembrance of the atomic bombing of Nagasaki on this date in 1945 should form part of today's intercessions.

SAT 10 #618 (LMC, #348, 456–460)   red
Lawrence, deacon, martyr
FEAST

Lawrence, archdeacon for Pope Sixtus II, was martyred a few days after him. Legend says he was roasted on a gridiron and joked with his executioners that they could turn him over because he was done on one side. Devotion to St. Lawrence was widespread within a few decades, and his day at Rome was (and is) one of the most festive. The readings reflect Lawrence's reputation for cheerfulness, his concern for the poor and his faith in Christ's promise of new life after death.

#116 (LMC, #110)   green
Nineteenth Sunday in Ordinary Time

Today's readings offer an opportunity to reflect on where and how we look for God. Jesus walking on the water was a mighty manifestation of God's power. So the wind, earthquake and fire in the first reading were considered common manifestations of God's presence. But it is in the tiny, whispering sound that Elijah recognizes the Lord. In the second reading, Paul begins his discussion of the fate of the Jews who did not accept Christ. This passage could inspire some thoughtful preaching about Christian-Jewish relations today.

■ THE WEEK AHEAD: For the next two weeks, we read from Ezekiel; take some time with a commentary. Thursday's solemnity will interrupt the sequence of readings. Thursday's gospel could be appended to Wednesday's for a fuller treatment of forgiveness. The first reading can be omitted.

MON 12 #413 (LMC, #193–231)   green
Weekday

Like Isaiah, Ezekiel was called to speak for God in a mystical vision of God's glory. Jesus claims divine sonship, but pays the Temple tax anyway.

TUE 13 #414 (LMC, #193–231)   green
Weekday

Pontian, pope, martyr, and Hippolytus, presbyter, martyr, optional memorial / red. ■ The Roman presbyter Hippolytus was an important author in liturgy and doctrine, but he quarrelled with Pope Callistus for not being tough enough on heretics and was even elected as an anti-pope. Exiled to Sardinia along with the subsequent pope, Pontian, he was reconciled to the church before they both were martyred. The story suggests prayers for ecclesial unity.

Ezekiel eats the word of God and finds it sweet; after it is part of him, he is able to preach it. Jesus speaks at length on love and care for children, a teaching our society needs to heed.

WED 14 #415 (LMC, #193–231)   red
Maximilian Mary Kolbe, presbyter, religious, martyr
MEMORIAL

A Conventual Franciscan who died at Auschwitz on this date in 1941, Maximilian was canonized in 1982. He volunteered to take the place of a husband and father condemned to death because of the escape of another prisoner; the man he replaced survived the war. Proper prayers are in the current (1985) sacramentary, and proper parts of the Office (including one of his letters) are in *New Memorials for the Dioceses of the United States of America.* Scripture readings, as usual, come from the weekday lectionary (those cited in the sacramentary are only for places that observe his memory as a feast or solemnity).

Ezekiel's vision suggests that only those who lament the evils of the world will be saved. The gospel calls us to resolve our problems within the community and assures us that Christ is in our midst when we gather.

#621–622 (LMC, #193–231, 352)
white

THU 15 **The Assumption of the Virgin Mary into Heaven**
SOLEMNITY

■ HISTORY OF THE SOLEMNITY: Soon after the Council of Ephesus (431) proclaimed Mary to be *Theotokos,* the Bearer of God, a feast of her "dormition," or death, began to spread. Within a few centuries, the church in Rome began observing this feast, which came to be known as the Assumption. At the first National Synod of the American church (1791), the nation was placed under the patronage of Mary with the title of the Assumption. The cathedral of the diocese of Baltimore, at that time the see for the whole country, was given the same name.

In 1950, Pope Pius XII defined the Assumption as dogma. At that time, he listed the benefits which should flow from this proclamation: a stronger piety toward Mary; a more universal conviction of the value of human life devoted to God's will; a repudiation of the materialism that diverts body and soul from their lofty goal; and "Finally, it is our hope that belief in Mary's bodily Assumption into heaven will make our belief in our own resurrection stronger and render it more effective" (*Munificentissimus Deus*, #42).

■ LITURGY TODAY: Recent history has focused strongly on the bodily assumption of Mary. The readings for the vigil and the day, however, suggest a stronger focus on Mary's share in the paschal mystery and on our own share in that same mystery. Planners might review the goals of Pius XII. Have our parish observances of this feast fostered a stronger belief in our own resurrection?

Finding good Marian hymns remains a challenge. Liturgical assemblies should not be asked to sing hymns better suited to devotions or hymns that contain poorly crafted, sentimental texts and/or melodies. A good setting of the Magnificat will reinforce today's gospel and find a place in many other parish celebrations;

Owen Alstott's refrain-style setting "My soul rejoices" (OCP) is a majestic and singable setting. James Chepponis's "Magnificat" (GIA; in *Gather, Second Edition* and in octavo form) is highly recommended for its singable refrain and lilting verses.

The importance of this festival precludes the celebrations of funeral Masses. Any Masses that include marriages must use the texts of the day.

■ LITURGY OF THE WORD: Both the Vigil and the Day Masses offer rich fare. The Vigil Mass sees Mary as the Ark of God and sees the reason for her assumption as her sharing in Christ's victory over death. She is also the premier disciple, hearing and keeping the word of God. The Day Mass begins with a highly poetic description of the woman giving birth and being threatened by the dragon. Evil is foiled, however, and the reign of our God is established, a kingdom in which Mary rejoices. The second reading reminds us clearly that Mary's privilege will be shared by all of us who follow Christ, and the gospel story of the Visitation reminds us of Mary's love for others and God's power at work through her.

An interesting and well-crafted setting of today's Psalm 45 is "Assumption Psalm" by Howard Hughes (GIA, G-2028). A newer setting of this psalm appears in the Second Edition of GIA's *Gather*. This setting, "The queen stands at your right hand," is composed by Diana Kodner. The preface of today's Mass provides more good material for the homilist's interaction with the readings.

■ LITURGY OF THE EUCHARIST: See page 228 for inserts to eucharistic prayers II and III.

■ BLESSING OF PRODUCE: In many countries, this feast is inextricably linked to the blessing of the earth's

bounty. *Catholic Household Blessings and Prayers* (pages 170–71) has a simple order for the blessing, including the litany of Mary. A larger-scale liturgy of blessing the harvest is found in chapter 28 of the *Book of Blessings*.

F R I **16** #417 (LMC, #193–231) green
Weekday

Stephen of Hungary, married man, ruler, optional memorial / white. ▪ Crowned in 1000 or 1001, King Stephen is still revered in Hungary as the one largely responsible for its Christianization as well as for establishing its independence and integrating it into Europe.

There are two choices for the first reading today; the first is longer but easier to understand, and it would be a shame to omit its beautiful story of Israel as a infant growing into a woman. The faithfulness of God to the covenant, despite the people's unfaithfulness, provides a suitable background to Jesus' teaching on marriage.

S A T **17** #418 (LMC, #193–231) green
Weekday

Blessed Virgin Mary on Saturday, optional memorial / white. ▪ The passage from Ezekiel today is famous for expressing each human's personal responsibility for his or her actions. This was a bit of a shift from the common view that children are punished for the sins of their parents, a belief still reflected in Jesus' time (see John 9). In the gospel, Jesus reminds us that children are called to share in the new covenant.

#119 (LMC, #113)   green

☀18 Twentieth Sunday in Ordinary Time

The first reading today sets the stage for Jesus' encounter with the Canaanite woman; God's salvation extends to all the earth. Paul sees himself as apostle to the Gentiles, but he still hopes for the salvation of the Jews, since God's gifts and call are irrevocable. This provides another opportunity to reflect on the relations between Christians and Jews. It would also make a good Mission Sunday, if such designations were based on the readings.

■ THE WEEK AHEAD: Saturday's feast will eclipse the weekday readings. Since the episodes related in the assigned readings are self-contained, there is no need to move them.

#419 (LMC, #193–231)   green

M O N 19 Weekday

John Eudes, presbyter, religious founder, educator, optional memorial/white. ▪ John was an enthusiastic promoter of the reforms of the Council of Trent and founded the Eudists to staff seminaries. He is also remembered for his work to provide decent housing for prostitutes, founding the Sisters of Charity of the Refuge for that work.

Ezekiel is commanded by God not to mourn the death of his wife, as a sign that the Israelites are not to mourn the loss of Jerusalem because they deserved the punishment. This passage and the psalm call for a return to the Lord. Jesus invites the young man (and us) to a deeper commitment to the Lord, too.

#420 (LMC, #193–231)   white

T U E 20 Bernard, abbot, presbyter, doctor of the church
MEMORIAL

Bernard of Clairvaux seems to have been everywhere in the first half of the twelfth century — preaching crusades, revitalizing the Cistercian order, founding monasteries, advising popes and fighting heresy. He was the greatest preacher of his time and a brilliant writer as well.

The first reading speaks to a ruler who does not acknowledge God's rule; Jesus invites his hearers to acknowledge that rule by giving up everything to follow him.

#421 (LMC, #193–231)   white

W E D 21 Pius X, pope
MEMORIAL

Giuseppe Sarto served as pastor, bishop and then patriarch of Venice before being elected pope in 1903. He is remembered as a pastoral pope who promoted the renewal of the church — he fostered more frequent communion, lowered the age for first communion, promoted congregational singing at liturgy, fostered the foundation of biblical institutes, reorganized the Curia and began codifying canon law. His stand against "modernism" was controversial, but his holiness is acknowledged even by his critics.

The famous passage from Ezekiel about the bad shepherds ends with a promise that God will tend the sheep directly. The parable of Jesus makes clear how generous God's love is.

#422 (LMC, #193–231)   white

T H U 22 The Queenship of the Virgin Mary
MEMORIAL

This memorial is like an octave of Assumption, celebrating Mary's share in her son's glory. The preface in Mass #29 of the *Collection of Masses of the Blessed Virgin Mary* serves this day well.

Today's passage from Ezekiel, also used in a longer form at the Easter Vigil, has obvious hints of baptism and the gift of the Holy Spirit. That meshes easily with the gospel parable speaking of those invited into the kingdom to share at the Master's table, which also fits the memorial well.

#423 (LMC, #193–231)   green

F R I 23 Weekday

Rose of Lima, virgin, optional memorial/white. ▪ This first canonized saint of the New World is the patroness of South America. Born in Lima, Peru, she devoted herself to prayer and penance and to service to the elderly, the sick and homeless children, despite much opposition from her parents.

Today's famous "dry bones" passage from Ezekiel is a promise of restoration and new life; the gospel teaching on the great commandments points the way to new life.

#629 (LMC, #360)   red

S A T 24 Bartholomew, apostle
FEAST

Some scholars believe that Bartholomew is the Nathaniel of today's gospel; the first reading celebrates all the Twelve with eschatological imagery. Tradition says he preached the gospel in India and Armenia, where he was skinned alive and beheaded. In Michelangelo's "Last Judgment," he is pictured holding his skin.

#122 (LMC, #116)   green

☀25 Twenty-first Sunday in Ordinary Time

Today's first and third readings are linked by the image of keys as signs of authority. This would be a good day to reflect on the way authority is used in the church. Remember to pray for the current holder of the keys of Peter and for all church leaders. In Romans, Paul concludes his treatment of the Jewish question with praise for God's wisdom.

The blessing of new parishioners, outlined in chapter 66 of the *Book of Blessings,* could be done once a month in large parishes or at the beginning of the school year in others. This blessing could take place at a party or at Sunday Mass. The setting at Mass seems to call for the presentation of the new members (#1932) and a petition in the intercessions (#1933). The service may also take the form of Sunday Evening Prayer.

■ THE WEEK AHEAD: The first readings will be taken from the New Testament for the next four weeks, beginning with 2 Thessalonians and then switching to 1 Corinthians this Thursday. Planners and preachers would benefit from commentaries on these letters. This is the last week spent with Matthew, with passages of woes and warnings about the day of judgment.

The memorials on Tuesday, Wednesday and Thursday all have special readings. If they are used, Tuesday's weekday gospel could be appended to Monday's and the other pericopes may simply be omitted.

MON 26
#425 (LMC, #193–231)
green
Weekday

The two readings provide a marked contrast between the faithfulness of the Thessalonians praised by Paul and the faithlessness of the hypocrites chastised by Jesus.

TUE 27
#426 and 632
(LMC, #193–231)   white
Monica
MEMORIAL

Monica is remembered for her prayers and charity, which led to the conversion of her husband, her mother-in-law, and finally, in the year of her death, her son, Augustine. Her feast is placed here to precede her son in celebration as she did in faith.

The first reading from Paul speaks of the constancy and faith exemplified by Monica, and the gospel for the memorial highlights the relationship of mother and son.

WED 28
#633 or 427
(LMC, #193–231)   white
Augustine, bishop, doctor of the church
MEMORIAL

Augustine looms large in any recounting of church history, as a theologian but also as an adult convert who had a rather wild youth. His famous *Confessions* recount his conversion journey. This is a good day to pray for our own continuing conversion and for the catechumens and candidates in our midst. Born in Numidia, Augustine probably was black; his memorial reminds us of the great contributions of African Christians to our history.

The readings for the memorial reflect Augustine's work as a teacher and his emphasis on love as the foundation of the Christian life.

THU 29
#634 (LMC, #193–231)   red
The Martyrdom of John the Baptist
MEMORIAL

The gospel today tells the story, while the first reading stresses God's strengthening of his prophets. Both readings call us to imitate John's courage in speaking the truth — a ministry much-needed ministry today!

FRI 30
#429 (LMC, #193–231)   green
Weekday

The famous text of Paul insisting that God's wisdom is the opposite of worldly wisdom provides a good context for Jesus' parable of the wise bridesmaids; their wisdom was in being prepared for a long wait until the bridegroom came.

SAT 31
#430 (LMC, #193–231)   green
Weekday

Blessed Virgin Mary on Saturday, optional memorial / white. ▪ In the first reading (also heard on January 28), Paul insists that God chooses the weak and those with nothing in order to shame the wise and the powerful. This provides a healthy caution about trusting too much in our own ability, even as the gospel calls us to use whatever we do have to serve God.

September

SUN 1
#125 (LMC, #119)   green
Twenty-second Sunday in Ordinary Time

In most places, school has resumed by this time. This transition should not pass unnoticed in church. Today's readings might suggest a focus on the cost of discipleship and of being "transformed by the renewal of your mind." Students of all ages might be invited to the front of the assembly (or into the center aisle) prior to the general intercessions. The intercessions given in the *Book of Blessings,* #527, can be added to the ongoing set from the current block of Sundays. Then the presider extends hands over the students and says prayer #528 or #529. The first one has explicit reference to the opening of schools. If it is used, the wonderful phrase in the second prayer can be part of the intercessions, "Let them take delight in new discoveries." The final blessing at the end of this Mass might draw from two other parts of the *Book of Blessings*: #543 for a prayer over the people, or #741 for a solemn blessing.

This is another Sunday also fitting for the blessing of liturgical ministers (page 76). If new members of the pastoral staff are being introduced to the parish, this should be more than a greeting after the communion rite (*Book of Blessings*, chapter 60).

■ THE CATECHUMENATE: The *Rite of Christian Initiation of Adults*, in #18 and #44, calls for each parish to schedule the rite of accepting catechumens on two or three days of the year. Unfortunately, many parishes still organize the catechumenate on an abbreviated, school-year model, with early Advent as a customary time for this rite of acceptance. Pastoral workers should review the National Statutes for the Catechumenate in the United States, printed at the back of every current (1988) U.S. edition of the *Rite of Christian Initiation of Adults*. Statute #6 calls for the periods of catechumenate and enlightenment to last at least 12 months, in addition to precatechumenate and mystagogy. One of the regular dates for the rite of acceptance might be at this time of year. While it might still perpetuate some notions of a "school-year" program, it is better than waiting for Advent.

In the rite itself, whether for catechumens alone or combined with the welcome of previously baptized adults preparing for reception, take special note of the architectural setting (#48, 507).

The rite envisions everyone meeting the candidates outside the main worship space. The dialogues and the rite of signing (of all the senses, with sung acclamations) are followed by a rite of equal importance — the congregation leading the new catechumens in for the celebration of the liturgy of the word.

■ THE WEEK AHEAD: From the beginning of Jesus' public ministry at the synagogue of Nazareth to the confrontations in Jerusalem, we now hear a third evangelist. If special readings are chosen for Monday, the significant readings assigned to that day might replace Tuesday's.

#431 or 907–911 (LMC, #193–231) green/white

**M
O
N 2 Weekday**

■ LABOR DAY: This is a day to remember "that our work forms a bond and a channel of mutual service and charity between the members of the human family; that by our labor we can share in the work of perfecting God's creation" (*Book of Blessings*, #919).

■ TEXTS FOR MASS: A broad range of liturgical texts is available. Certain elements can be used no matter which option is selected — greeting from *Book of Blessings*, #925; intercessions, #932; prayer to end the intercessions, #935; prayer over the people, #937. The readings and presidential prayers may be selected from:

- Prayers from "Masses and Prayers for Various Needs and Occasions, 25, For the Blessing of Human Labor." They can be combined with the weekday readings or with passages selected from lectionary #907–911 ("Blessing of Human Labor").

- Prayers from "Masses and Prayers for Various Needs and Occasions, 21, For the Progress of Peoples," which can be combined with the weekday readings.

- Prayers (May 1) and readings (#559) of "Joseph the Worker," especially in places named after him. Preface P62 should be used.

- Prayers from July 4 or from appendix X, 6 ("Other Civic Observances") can be used with readings from the lectionary "For Peace and Justice."

■ TEXTS FOR OTHER LITURGIES: The Liturgy of the Hours for this day is of the regular weekday. The *Book of Blessings*, chapter 24, has an "Order for the Blessing of Tools or Other Equipment for Work."

#432 (LMC, #193–231)   white

**T
U
E 3 Gregory the Great, pope, religious, doctor of the church**
MEMORIAL

If Monday's readings are used today, Paul reminds us that conversion and faith come from God's grace. Jesus proclaims his mission today in his hometown, but conversion and faith are not the result.

If Tuesday's passages are used, the first reading emphasizes the role of the Spirit in Christian life, while the gospel reveals the authority of Jesus both as teacher and as healer.

#433 (LMC, #193–231)   green

**W
E
D 4 Weekday**

We are sent to continue the mission of Jesus, "to announce the good news of the reign of God." Paul reminds us that it is God who determines the results.

#434 (LMC, #193–231)   green

**T
H
U 5 Weekday**

The last sentence of the first reading is a beautiful expression of the richness of life in Christ. Believing this should enable us to leave all and follow Jesus as Peter, James and John did.

FRI 6 #435 (LMC, #193–231) green
Weekday

Paul's advice to stop passing judgment stands in contrast to the judgment of the scribes and Pharisees in the gospel, but the stronger thrust from Luke is about the newness of the kingdom of God.

SAT 7 #436 (LMC, #193–231) green
Weekday

Blessed Virgin Mary, optional memorial/white. • Both Paul and Jesus were misunderstood and faced opposition; Paul tried to follow Christ's own example of returning blessings for insults.

8 #128 (LMC, #122) green
Twenty-third Sunday in Ordinary Time

Today's readings suggest reflection on the first of the spiritual works of mercy, "to admonish the sinner." God warns the prophet that he will be held responsible if he does not speak out to dissuade the wicked, and Matthew gives us an approach to correction within the church. Paul's words about love of neighbor remind us of the proper motivation for correction.

■ GRANDPARENTS' DAY: The Sunday after Labor Day has been designated as such since 1978. Marian McQuade of West Virginia pressed Congress and the president to make this proclamation. She wanted to honor grandparents, but also wished to help children become aware of the strength, information and guidance older people can offer. In keeping with that broader goal, this might be a fine day for a communal gathering in church or in a nursing home for one of the

"Orders for the Blessing of Elderly People Confined to Their Homes" (*Book of Blessings,* chapter 1, XII). At Mass, intercessions for grandparents, living and deceased, may be welcome.

■ BLESSINGS AS A NEW YEAR BEGINS: See September 1 for notes on the blessing of students and teachers.

■ THE WEEK AHEAD: The feast on Saturday will interrupt the weekday readings. The readings displaced may be omitted, though Saturday's gospel might be appended to Friday's.

MON 9 #437 (LMC, #193–231) white
Peter Claver, presbyter, religious, missionary
MEMORIAL

Peter Claver, a Spanish Jesuit, spent most of his adult life serving black slaves in Colombia in the first half of the seventeenth century. The proper prayer for this American memorial notes how his witness can help all of us overcome racial hatreds. Many parishes with large numbers of black Catholics have special festivities today or on November 3 (Martin de Porres).

Paul calls for a deeper conversion to eliminate sin from our lives. Jesus himself struggled against the power of evil, as today's gospel reminds us.

TUE 10 #438 (LMC, #193–231) green
Weekday

The choice of the Twelve points to the establishment of the church as the new People of God; Paul insists that the church should be able to solve its own disputes without recourse to civil courts — an interesting point for our litigious society.

WED 11 #439 (LMC, #193–231) green
Weekday

Paul's advice about marriage and celibacy flows from his expecta-

tion of the imminent return of Christ: "The world as we know it is passing away." This upending of the world's values is also the point of the beatitudes.

THU 12 #440 (LMC, #193–231) green
Weekday

Paul insists on the priority of love over knowledge, urging the Corinthians to avoid giving any scandal to weaker members. Jesus insists that love must go beyond the usual bonds to include even enemies.

FRI 13 #441 (LMC, #193–231) white
John Chrysostom, bishop, doctor of the church
MEMORIAL

This bishop of Constantinople was renowned as a great preacher, which is indicated by the name *Chrysostom,* "golden-mouthed." Exiled for sermons that made the empress uncomfortable, John died in Lesser Armenia on September 14, 407, the feast of the Triumph of the Cross.

Paul's words about being compelled to preach fit this memorial well, as does Jesus' call to remove the plank from our eye.

SAT 14 #638 (LMC, #370) red
The Holy Cross
FEAST

This feast commemorates the dedication of the church (September 13, 335) erected by Emperor Constantine over the sites of

Christ's crucifixion and resurrection. Contemporaneous documents tell us that this date was selected because it was the anniversary of the finding of the cross by Constantine's mother, a few years earlier. Other sources suggest additional motives: It was the anniversary of the dedication of the temple of Jupiter at Rome; it was a Christian response to Yom Kippur and the motifs of atonement; or it was a continuation of Jewish Sukkoth.

Whatever the reasons for selecting the date, the annual celebration on the 13th was followed by a day to venerate the relic of the true cross kept there. Many churches in the East still keep the 13th as the anniversary of the dedication of the Basilica of the Resurrection. This day, the 14th, celebrating the cross and the redemptive events on the site of that basilica, is one of the few feasts kept on the same day in all Christian communities, both East and West.

Excellent resources for use at a school liturgy today (formally opening the year after the first few days of orientation, perhaps) are found in LTP/GIA's *Leader's Manual of the Hymnal for Catholic Students.*

The Byzantine celebration of Evening Prayer on this night concludes with the assembly coming forward to kiss the cross. Our heritage, the liturgical texts and the enduring need for sacramentals suggest the possibility of Roman rite churches returning to this practice.

■ MUSIC: A venerable hymn for this day, by Venantius Fortunatus, is "Vexilla regis." Two settings of this hymn are found in the Episcopal *Hymnal 1982* (#161 and 162). Both settings are adaptations of the traditional chant tune. Other appropriate hymns are Sydney Nicholson's "Lift high

the cross," found in many hymnals; Isaac Watts's wonderful text "When I survey the wondrous cross," most often sung to the tune ROCKINGHAM; and "Sing, my tongue, the song of triumph," found in *Worship* set to the noble hymn tune PICARDY. From the Taizé tradition, consider "Crucem tuam" (GIA, G-2433).

■ ROSH HASHANAH: Pray for our Jewish brothers and sisters as they enter the year 5756. Although this is commonly called "Jewish New Year," it is also the beginning of the "ten days of awe," a period of intense reflection and repentance, and an anticipation of the day of judgment. The sending of greetings at this time of year includes the wish *L'Shanah tovah tikatevu:* "May you be inscribed (in the Book of Life) for a good year."

#131 (LMC, #125)   green

15 Twenty-fourth Sunday in Ordinary Time

The first and third readings today focus on God's forgiveness, offering an opportunity to preach about that topic at a time other than Lent. Much of the malaise that affects so many of our churches flows from a lack of appreciation of repentance and forgiveness, in our relationships with God and with one another. This topic can be integrated with an emphasis on catechists if that is involved today, since reconciliation is so basic to the whole Christian message. Use the appropriate introduction to the Lord's Prayer, too.

■ BLESSING OF CATECHISTS: Many parishes bless their catechists on this Sunday or another Sunday

in September. The term "blessing" is truer to liturgical form than the term "commissioning." National and diocesan offices often send out suggestions for "Catechetical Sunday." Planners should always evaluate the quality of such suggestions before deciding to use them. The *Book of Blessings,* chapter 4, has a fine "Order for the Blessing of Those Appointed as Catechists." The suggestions given there for inclusion in the Sunday eucharistic celebration include fine intercessions and two possible prayers of blessing over the catechists (who may stand in front of the assembly or in some other visible place during the blessing).

■ THE WEEK AHEAD: The weekday readings will be interrupted on Saturday. There is no strong need to attach the "lost" verses to adjoining days, though Saturday's gospel could replace Friday's brief passage.

#443 (LMC, #193–231)   white

16 Cornelius, pope, martyr and Cyprian, bishop, martyr
MON
MEMORIAL

The inclusion of these saints in Eucharistic Prayer I gives a clue to their importance in the early church. Bishops of Rome and Carthage in the mid-third century, they were both involved in the controversy of the time about the proper leniency to repentant apostates, with Cyprian seeking a middle ground between Rome and the Novation heretics, allowing forgiveness but also requiring rigorous penance. This led to a fuller understanding of the role of the sacrament of penance in the life of the church.

Today's passage from 1 Corinthians ought to give most of our assemblies pause, if we are honest about the divisions among us. The gospel calls us all to the faith of the centurion.

TUE
17
#444 (LMC, #193–231)   green
Weekday

Robert Bellarmine, bishop, religious, doctor of the church, optional memorial / white ▪ This late-sixteenth and early-seventeenth century Jesuit was known as an excellent scholar and teacher and an important apologist during the Counter-Reformation. Cardinal and Bishop of Capua, he lived a simple and austere life.

Paul's discourse on the gifts of the Spirit (today and tomorrow) reminds us that love is the most important gift of all—a caution to those who revel too much in charismatic manifestations of the Spirit. The gospel shows this love in Jesus as he has compassion on the widowed mother.

WED
18
#445 (LMC, #193–231)   green
Weekday

Paul's great hymn of love is familiar from weddings but warrants deeper reflection. The gospel reminds us once again that there always has been opposition to the message of Jesus has always been experienced.

THU
19
#446 (LMC, #193–231)   green
Weekday

Januarius, bishop, martyr, optional memorial / red. ▪ A martyr in fourth-century Naples, San Gennaro is mostly known for the periodic liquefaction of his blood in the Naples cathedral. Whatever the mystical or scientific explanation for this, the worshiping throngs in Naples' cathedral today can remind us of the centrality of blood in our ecclesial life. Appreciation of this core symbol can perhaps deepen and broaden people's participation from the eucharistic cup.

Paul summarizes the good news and then speaks of his apostleship: By God's favor, I am what I am. The woman in the gospel was also blessed by God's favor. Both she and Paul rejoice in God's gift of forgiveness.

FRI
20
#447 (LMC, #193–231)   red
Andrew Kim Taegon, presbyter, martyr, Paul Chong Hasang, catechist, martyr, and their companions, martyrs.
MEMORIAL

One way in which our tradition honors martyrs and recognizes the universality of the gospel is through the merging of groups of martyrs from a particular place into a single memorial. The beginnings of a local church are often consecrated by the blood of martyrs. Thus we remember missionaries martyred at Nagasaki from 1633 to 1637 (September 28), eight Jesuit missionaries to the Huron and Iroquois nations martyred from 1642 to 1649 (October 19), 117 Vietnamese martyrs of 1745 to 1862 (November 24) and the Ugandan martyrs of 1885 to 1887 (June 3). The 103 saints remembered today were martyred in Korea from 1839 to 1867. They included the first Korean priest and pastor, Andrew Kim Taegon, and the lay leader Paul Chong Hasang.

The readings listed with the proper prayers in the sacramentary are only for those liturgical communities that keep this memorial as a feast or solemnity (for example, in Korean communities). Prayers for the nation of Korea are in order as its people struggle for the personal and political freedoms so long denied them.

Paul recalls for us how central the resurrection is for our faith, an appropriate text for this memorial of martyrs. If tomorrow's gospel is used, it would fit well the missionary character of this memorial. Today's gospel passage could remind us of the important role of women in the mission of Jesus and the church.

SAT
21
#643 (LMC, #376, 193–231)   red
Matthew, apostle, evangelist
FEAST

The name Matthew means "gift of God." He was Jewish, a Galilean by birth and a tax collector for the occupying Romans. After Pentecost, he seems to have ministered in Judea and then in some eastern land, perhaps Persia (Iran). Papias of Hierapolis (second century) suggests that he compiled sayings of Jesus in Aramaic and that later writers translated and expanded these. This is one way of describing his role in relationship to the written gospel. Scholars have learned to differentiate between the apostle Matthew and the final author of the Greek-language gospel bearing his name. Matthew has always been venerated as a martyr, but there is little agreement about the place and other details.

Petitions for all peoples in Persia would be appropriate this day, perhaps especially for the small and beleaguered communities of Catholics living in fundamentalist Islamic nations. We might also remember tax collectors and all civil servants. An appropriate hymn, for this or any of the apostles' feasts, is "Let all on earth their voices raise," a setting of which is found in GIA's *Worship*.

#134 (LMC, #128)   green

☀22 Twenty-fifth Sunday in Ordinary Time

The readings today all remind us of the difference between God's wisdom and the ways of the world. Isaiah and Jesus speak of God's generosity, and Paul struggles with the desire to be at home with Christ after death and the need to continue preaching the gospel in this life.

■ FALL EQUINOX: At this turning point of the year, the petitions might include one for a good harvest as autumn begins.

■ THE WEEK AHEAD: This week we switch back to the Old Testament, to the wisdom literature, Proverbs and Ecclesiastes. Once again, a few moments with some good commentaries will yield better preaching.

#449 (LMC, #193–231)   green

MON 23 Weekday

Proverbs gives advice on dealing with our neighbors, while the gospel calls us to share the light with them.

■ YOM KIPPUR: This Jewish Day of Atonement is the holiest day in the Jewish calendar, a day of complete fast and of prayer. The liturgy is rich and complex, and includes the reading of the book of Jonah. At Mass today, announce Yom Kippur and include prayer for the Jewish people in the general intercessions.

#450 (LMC, #193–231)   green

TUE 24 Weekday

Today's collection of proverbs invites us to turn to the Lord and do what is right and just, and the gospel reminds us that our faith must show itself in action.

#451 (LMC, #193–231)   green

WED 25 Weekday

Proverbs prays for neither poverty nor riches but only what one needs. So, too, the disciples are to travel simply and trust God to provide what they need.

#452 (LMC, #193–231)   green

THU 26 Weekday

Cosmas and Damian, martyrs, optional memorial / red. ▪ Legend says they were twin brothers from Arabia and doctors who practiced medicine out of charity, accepting no fees. All we know for sure is that they were martyred in Syria with their three brothers during the persecution of Diocletian (c. 303). Their names are in the Roman Canon (Eucharistic Prayer I), which might be used today.

Ecclesiastes sees only the repetitious cycle of the seasons and of human history; the psalm reminds us that God is present in every one of those cycles and ages; Herod wonders if Jesus is a "recycled" prophet—but there is something new going on in Jesus!

#453 (LMC, #193–231)   white

FRI 27 Vincent de Paul, presbyter, religious founder
MEMORIAL

Founder of the Congregation of the Missions (Vincentians) and (with Louise de Marillac) of the Congregation of the Daughters of Charity, Vincent has long been considered the patron of charitable organizations. This seventeenth-century priest was also concerned with the spiritual formation of priests and seminarians.

Today's famous passage from Ecclesiastes often omits the point made at the end—that God has put the timeless into our hearts. In the gospel Peter names Jesus as the Messiah, and Jesus predicts his own death and resurrection.

#454 (LMC, #193–231)   green

SAT 28 Weekday

Wenceslaus, ruler, martyr, optional memorial / red. ▪ *Lawrence Ruiz, married man, martyr, and his companions, martyrs, optional memorial / red.* ▪ *Blessed Virgin Mary optional memorial / white.* ▪ Wenceslaus, the "good king" of the carol, was king of Bohemia and a model Christian ruler who promoted peace. The other memorial remembers 16 lay and ordained missionaries who were martyred in Nagasaki. Lawrence Ruiz was a husband and father and the first Filipino to be canonized (1987). Pray for those lands. If the proper texts are unavailable, use the Common of Several Martyrs.

Qoheleth insists again that "all things are vanity," but the point of the passage is that young people should remember their Creator in the midst of the world's pleasures and troubles. The gospel reminds us how slow the disciples were to understand that Jesus would suffer and die.

■ SUKKOT: The eight-day Jewish festival of harvest booths, or shelters, begins today. Catholics, especially in organized small groups, should consider visiting a synagogue or Jewish center to experience the joy of standing within a *sukkah* (plural, *sukkot*). (*Sukkot* are the huts that harvesters build in the fields so they can work uninterruptedly.) The moon is full at this festival, just as at Passover.

#137 (LMC, #131) green

☼ 29 Twenty-sixth Sunday in Ordinary Time

The first reading and the gospel insist that a person's ultimate decision for good outweighs the initial rejection of God's will. Philippians offers us a wonderful passage, probably based on an early Christian hymn, describing Christ's self-emptying *(kenosis)* and exaltation.

Announce that Daylight Savings Time ends next Sunday.

■ BLESSINGS: With their materials on the blessing of the parish pastoral council and other parish societies, chapters 64 and 65 of the *Book of Blessings* should be used at least once a year, preferably in Ordinary Time. These blessings would often be used at organizational meetings, but the importance of the parish pastoral council suggests that its blessing take place at the Sunday eucharist. The simple outline given in #1900–1902 can be given some local embellishments — a formal calling of the individual council members forward, a hymn such as "The church of Christ in ev'ry age" *(Worship)* before the intercessions, a reception honoring the council after Mass, and photographs and brief biographies in the bulletin or on a special program sheet.

■ THE WEEK AHEAD: This week we read from the book of Job; reading the whole book through will be helpful for the context of the selected passages. The memorial of the Guardian Angels on Wednesday impedes the normal progression of the readings. The passages that will be omitted do not seem crucial for continuity.

Optional readings are also available for Tuesday and Friday, but it might be best to use the weekday passages, lest we miss too much of Job.

#455 (LMC, #193–231) white

MON 30 Jerome, presbyter, doctor of the church MEMORIAL

Jerome had a strong temper and was often argumentative. But he was also a brilliant scholar and is renowned for translating the Bible from the Greek and Hebrew into Latin, producing the Vulgate translation used for centuries in the church. "To be ignorant of the scriptures" he said, "is not to know Christ."

Today we begin the story of Job, a model of acceptance of God's will; the gospel reminds us that what makes us important in the kingdom is it not wealth or power like Job had, but humble service.

October

#456 or 649 (LMC, #193–231) white

TUE 1 Theresa of the Child Jesus MEMORIAL

Therese Martin, long known as the Little Flower, is now honored with her name in religious life. Entering the Carmelite convent at age 15, she lived a humble and hidden life, dying at age 24. Yet she was declared Patroness of the Missions by Pius XI because she offered her life for the salvation of souls. Her "little way" of holiness has inspired many.

Job's lament today seems less accepting than yesterday's passage, but it can remind us of the painful burdens carried by so many in our world. Jesus' response to James and John indicates clearly that vengeance is unacceptable, even when we have been mistreated.

#650 (LMC, #193–231) white

WED 2 The Guardian Angels MEMORIAL

The proper prayers and scriptures tell us what we celebrate this day: God's protective guidance.

#458 (LMC, #193–231) green

THU 3 Weekday

Despite his misery, Job trusts in God to be his vindicator in the end. As Jesus sends out the seventy-two, he makes it clear that the response to their preaching may not always be positive. (Note the similarity to the sending of the Twelve on September 25.)

#459 (LMC, #193–231) white

FRI 4 Francis of Assisi, religious founder MEMORIAL

Francis is one of the most popular of the saints, even among non-Catholics. He is a powerful example of taking the gospel seriously and living it almost literally. His close identification with his Master is symbolized in the stigmata, the wounds of Christ that appeared in his flesh.

Job's recognition of his insignificance before God leads him to close his mouth; this passage's view of God as creator might remind us also of Francis's love for all of creation. Jesus' sadness over Chorazin, Bethsaida and Capernaum can remind us to open our ears to God's word as Francis did.

The *Leader's Manual of the Hymnal for Catholic Students* (pages 62–64) contains excellent resources for celebrating this day in a school setting. If this is your titular solemnity or if there is a Franciscan community in your parish, shape the entire schedule of this day to allow everyone to hold high the festival.

■ BLESSING ANIMALS: The blessing of animals is traditional in many places on this day. See the *Book of Blessings* (chapter 25) and *Catholic Household Blessings and*

Prayers (page 174) for resources. This might also remind us of Francis's recently accorded role as the patron of the ecological movement.

S A T 5 #460 (LMC, #193–231)   green
Weekday

Blessed Virgin Mary on Saturday, optional memorial/white. • Job accepts God's sovereignty and is greatly blessed. Jesus tells the disciples to rejoice that they, too, are blessed, and he praises the Father for revealing to the merest children what is hidden from the learned and the clever.

6 #140 (LMC, #134)   green
Twenty-seventh Sunday in Ordinary Time

Today's song of the vineyard changes its focus somewhat between the first reading and psalm and the gospel. In Isaiah and the psalm, the vineyard is the house of Israel and God is angry at the lack of fruit. In the gospel, the owner's anger is directed to the wicked tenant farmers, presumably the leaders of Israel. To whom would the point be directed in our own time?

The general intercessions might also include the U.S. Supreme Court, which opens its annual session this week.

■ THE WEEK AHEAD: This week we return to the New Testament with Paul's letter to the Galatians. As always, time with the commentaries will be valuable.

M O N 7 #461 (LMC, #193–231)   white
Our Lady of the Rosary MEMORIAL

This feast was established to commemorate the naval victory over the Turks at Lepanto, which was attributed to Mary's intercession. It is the reason that October has become known as the month of the Rosary. When parishioners gather to pray the rosary communally, often they do so immediately before or after Mass. Pastoral ministers can help them (and everyone) appreciate the difference between liturgy and devotions. Devotions ought to be scheduled separate from Mass.

Resist efforts to add the "Hail Mary" to the general intercessions or to recite a decade of the rosary somewhere in the Mass. Vatican congregations, liturgists and sensible observers of every ideological bent have always condemned the insertion of devotions into the liturgy. The texts of the Mass and the other sacraments are prayed to God; the Hail Mary is addressed to one of our companions in prayer. We should offer the Mass in union with the company of saints, not to them.

Paul's insistence that there is no other gospel and that no one should dare to alter it might make us more attentive to today's gospel and all proclamations of the word of God. Often we "alter" the gospel by selective hearing, ignoring what we don't like to hear.

T U E 8 #462 (LMC, #193–231)   green
Weekday

Today's story of Mary and Martha, and Paul's description of his conversion might make us examine our own response to the presence of God in our lives.

W E D 9 #463 (LMC, #193–231)   green
Weekday

Denis, bishop, martyr, and his companions, martyrs, optional memorial/red; John Leonardi, presbyter, religious founder, optional memorial/white. • St. Denis is the apostle and patron of France. A bishop of Paris, he was martyred about 258 with Rusticus, a priest, and Eleutherius, a deacon. John Leonardi founded the Clerks Regular of the Mother of God in 1574 to carry out the reforms of the Council of Trent and assisted the reform of several other religious communities. Parishes with French heritage would probably celebrate Denis. Celebrating John as a reformer is also a good choice in this age of renewal. Parishes may want to celebrate each in alternate years.

Paul's challenge to Peter in today's first reading stands as a reminder to all church leaders that they must be open to the prophetic voices that challenge them. The gospel account of the Lord's Prayer with its petition to "forgive us our sins, for we too forgive all who do us wrong," reminds us that forgiveness is necessary for our life as church.

T H U 10 #464 (LMC, #193–231)   green
Weekday

Paul is blunt today about the tendency of the Galatians to revert to living by the law rather than by the Spirit. Jesus promises that the Father will give the Spirit to those who ask.

F R I 11 #465 (LMC, #193–231)   green
Weekday

Paul continues today to discuss the futility of seeking salvation through the law; we are saved by the power of the Spirit through faith. Jesus insists that it is the power of God that enables him (and us) to overcome evil.

S A T 12 #466 (LMC, #193–231)   green
Weekday

Blessed Virgin Mary, optional memorial/white. • Today's passage from Galatians offers us a helpful image of the law as monitor (or tutor) until the coming of

Christ. Paul also gives us a beautiful statement of unity, all divisions having been overcome by Christ's reconciliation. The gospel reminds us to keep our view of Mary based on her keeping of God's word.

#143 (LMC, #137)   green
☀13 Twenty-eighth Sunday in Ordinary Time

The first reading, the psalm and the gospel present us with the image of the banquet today. While the central point of the readings focuses on God's gift of salvation, it is not a distortion to note the connections with the eucharistic banquet, which anticipates the heavenly banquet. The first reading also invites reflection on the rich symbolism of communion under both species of bread and wine, a topic that needs periodic attention in most assemblies as we still seek to recover the fullness of our sacramental practice.

■ HOLIDAY WEEKEND: In many areas of North America blessed by beautiful autumn scenery, this is a big weekend for travel. All travelers can be provided a warm welcome and whatever materials and orientation necessary to help them take an active role in the liturgy.

■ THE WEEK AHEAD: This week we continue with Galatians until Thursday, when we begin more than two full weeks of readings drawn from Ephesians. The readings will be interrupted this week by the feast of St. Luke on Friday and perhaps by the memorials on Tuesday and Thursday. Both of Friday's passages (and even the

beginning of Ephesians from Thursday) can precede Saturday's passages. If the memorial reading is used Tuesday, append Tuesday's passage from Galatians to Monday's. If both memorial readings are used Thursday, the weekday gospel can be appended to Wednesday.

#467 (LMC, #193–231)   green
M O N 14 Weekday

Callistus I, pope, martyr, optional memorial/red. ▪ Upon Callistus's election as bishop of Rome, the presbyter Hippolytus refused to recognize the election and became the first anti-pope. (Hippolytus was reconciled by Callistus's successor, Pontian, eighteen years later. They died as prisoners of the Roman empire; their joint feast is August 13.) It seems that today's saint was too lenient for the tastes of Hippolytus.

■ COLUMBUS DAY: The prayers at Mass could also be taken from a number of places in the sacramentary — see especially the ones under "civic observances" for July 4 and in appendix X, 6, of the sacramentary.

■ CANADIAN THANKSGIVING DAY: Canadian parishes can join their prayers to that nation's observance of Thanksgiving today, using Masses "In Thanksgiving" or "After the Harvest."

Paul speaks of liberty in Christ and urges us to stay free (tomorrow's passage may be appended, too), and Jesus condemns the current generation for not listening to his words.

#468 (LMC, #193–231)   white
T U E 15 Teresa of Jesus, virgin, religious, doctor of the church
MEMORIAL

Formerly known as Teresa of Avila, this sixteenth-century Carmelite mystic was a reformer of her order and co-worker with St. John of the

Cross. Her writings include her autobiography, *The Way of Perfection,* and *The Interior Castle.* She was declared a doctor of the church in 1970.

Paul's talk of circumcision and Jesus' attack on mere external observance might lead us to examine ourselves on what enslaves us or what empty rituals we practice.

#469 (LMC, #193–231)   green
W E D 16 Weekday

Hedwig, married woman, religious, optional memorial/white; Margaret Mary Alacoque, virgin, religious, optional memorial/white. ▪ Today's options for celebration include a Polish mother of seven who lived in a monastery after the death of her husband and used her wealth for the care of poor, and a seventeenth-century French mystic who spread devotion to the Sacred Heart based on her private revelations.

Our last passage from Galatians contrasts the fruits of the law and the spirit, and Jesus attacks those who observe the law without a true spirit of faith and love.

This day is designated by the United Nations as World Food Day, a concern that might be included in the intercessions.

#470 or #660 (LMC, #193–231)   red
T H U 17 Ignatius of Antioch, bishop, martyr
MEMORIAL

One of the greatest and earliest of the martyrs, Ignatius was thrown to wild animals on this date in about the year 107. He is well known for the seven letters he wrote on his journey from Antioch to Rome. One of the most famous passages links martyrdom and eucharist:

> I will gladly die for God if only you do not stand in my way. I plead with you: show me no untimely kindness. Let me be food for the

wild beasts, for they are my way to God. I am God's wheat and shall be ground by their teeth so that I might become Christ's pure bread.

In the weekday readings, Ephesians begins with a hymn of praise for what God has done in Christ, but the gospel reminds us that Christ's ministry of reconciliation was neither easy nor universally accepted. Both readings fit well with the memory of this early martyr. The optional readings for the memorial also focus on martyrdom.

The United Nations designates today as World Day for Overcoming Extreme Poverty; remember the poor in the intercessions.

FRI 18 #661 (LMC, #396) red
Luke, evangelist
FEAST

The New Jerome Biblical Commentary summarizes the earliest testimonies on Luke's identity: From the New Testament itself, we can deduce that he was a physician and a companion of Paul; from later traditions we understand that he was a Syrian from Antioch who wrote what is now called the third gospel (and Acts of the Apostles); from more recent scholarship, we think that he wrote the gospel at Antioch a little after AD 80.

The liturgical texts for today include one of the rare references to Luke in the scriptures. They also remind us of the attention he gives to God's love for the poor and invite us to live in the faith of the gospel he preached.

#472 (LMC, #193–231) red
Isaac Jogues and John de Brebeuf, presbyters, religious, missionaries, martyrs, and their companions, martyrs
SAT 19
MEMORIAL

The "North American Martyrs" met death in New York and Canada. Isaac is mentioned first in the title of the day in the United States because he is the better known here. John receives first billing in other countries (and in the opening prayer). All eight martyrs worked with the Huron and Iroquois nations in the early seventeenth century.

Celebrating these missionaries invites us to pray also for the people among whom they preached the gospel. The shrine to these saints at Auriesville, New York, is at the site of Mohawk village, where Kateri Tekakwitha was born a decade after their martyrdom. The intercessions this day could include Native Americans, missionaries, a resurgence of enthusiasm for the gospel and courage in adversity.

Combining Friday's weekday passages with today's, Ephesians speaks of God's choice of both Jews and Gentiles, and prays for continued growth in faith. Jesus warns the disciples to be on guard but also to trust God's providence and depend on the Spirit's guidance when they are brought to trial.

#146 (LMC, #140) green
20 Twenty-ninth Sunday in Ordinary Time

The readings today speak of the relationship between the civil and the spiritual realms. Cyrus was not a Jew, but God used him to restore Israel. Jesus' answer to the Pharisees still leaves the question open: What is there that does not belong to God?

■ MISSION SUNDAY: If the diocese is using this title for today, great care needs to be taken to keep the focus on Sunday. Proper intercessions, a special collection and perhaps a fitting hymn should be the regular ways of incorporating the missions into an Ordinary Time Sunday. This year, the readings also offer an opportunity to speak of the church's mission: especially Isaiah's words, "so that toward the rising and the setting of the sun all may know that there is none besides me," and Paul's comments about preaching the gospel in the Holy Spirit and out of complete conviction.

Some coordinators of this observance unfortunately press pastors to use the prayer texts from Masses and Prayers for Various Needs and Occasions, 14, For the Spread of the Gospel. The rubrics printed with those two sets of formularies also give encouragement for this. Whatever is decided about the prayer texts, no parish should drop the Sunday readings for thematic ones.

The words of Isaiah might also suggest using Eucharistic Prayer III ("from east to west").

MON 21 #473 (LMC, #193–231) green
Weekday

Recognizing that salvation is God's free gift, not our own doing (Ephesians), would keep us from attempting to secure our future by our wealth (gospel).

TUE 22 #474 (LMC, #193–231) green
Weekday

Today's beautiful passage from Ephesians presents the basis for our unity in the church. Together with all who believe, we anticipate the Lord's return (gospel).

WED 23 #475 (LMC, #193–231) green
Weekday

John of Capistrano, presbyter, religious, missionary, optional memorial / white. ▪ John was a fifteenth-century lawyer who was married but received a dispensation to become a Franciscan priest. He was known especially as a great preacher, and he was instrumental in the renewal of the Franciscans and the Poor Clares. Pray today for lawyers, preachers, Franciscans and Poor Clares.

Today's passage from Ephesians speaks of the salvation of Gentiles—most of us—and of Paul's ministry. The gospel again sounds an eschatological note, but we have no need to fear that day if we live as faithful servants.

T H U 24 #476 (LMC, #193–231)
green
Weekday

Anthony Mary Claret, bishop, religious founder, optional memorial/white. ▪ Anthony founded the Claretians in Spain to continue his ministry of preaching retreats and writing. Then he served as bishop of Santiago, Cuba, from 1850 to 1857, trying to reform the church there despite much opposition. Prayers for Cuba would be appropriate. Today is also United Nations Day, so pray for peace among all nations.

Today's section of Ephesians is a beautiful prayer, which could even be used again as the final blessing of Mass today. The gospel reminds us that opposition is often the lot of the Christian.

F R I 25 #477 (LMC, #193–231)   green
Weekday

Paul's beautiful exhortation is based on the unity expressed at the end of the passage. The gospel reminds us to be attentive to the signs of God in our lives lest, like many in Jesus' time, we miss the presence of God in our midst.

This is one of two days designated for the celebration of the anniversary of the dedication of a church when the actual date is unknown; the other is the Sunday before All Saints Day (see entry at October 27).

S A T 26 #478 (LMC, #193–231)
green
Weekday

Blessed Virgin Mary on Saturday, optional memorial/white. ▪ Paul speaks of the various gifts needed for the good of the whole body. Jesus calls us to reform and warns that the time may be short. Both readings invite us to deeper faith.

☀ 27 #149 (LMC, #143)   green
Thirtieth Sunday in Ordinary Time

The first reading and the gospel call those who love God to show it by love of neighbor. The second reading invites joy and praise of God for the grace of conversion.

▪ REFORMATION DAY: Intercessions for our Protestant neighbors are in order. There is much to regret when remembering the Reformation, but most churches have let this day evolve into a prayer for ongoing reformation— a hope for all Catholic, Orthodox and Protestant Christians.

▪ DEDICATION ANNIVERSARY: Today can be a local solemnity observing the anniversary of dedication in many parishes. If a parish's dedication date is unknown, there are two choices for its observance: October 25, if the community will always be free on this day to make a true solemnity, or the Sunday before All Saints. Even if the date is known, this Sunday may be chosen. (See the footnote to paragraph 52c of *General Norms for the Liturgical Year and Calendar* that is found only, apparently, at #3818 in *Documents of the*

Liturgy [Collegeville: The Liturgical Press, 1983]) Such an observance brings great liturgical options to the fore and links this Sunday celebration closely to the solemnity of All Saints.

THE WEEK AHEAD

The weekday readings will not be heard on Monday, Friday or Saturday. Monday's readings could be combined with Tuesday's. Friday's and Saturday's passages can be omitted this year.

The presence of so many possibilities for scriptures on All Souls and the frequent advantage of combining verses in the weekday lectionary show the problem with using anything other than the full lectionary for proclamation. Missalettes and loose-leaf lectionaries regularly narrow the legitimate choices and keep the eclipsed weekday readings out of reach— even though the *General Instruction of the Roman Missal* (#319) calls for such combining and substitutions.

M O N 28 #666 (LMC, #401, 452–455)
red
Simon and Jude, apostles
FEAST

Tradition says that Simon preached in Egypt and Jude in Mesopotamia, and that they worked together in Persia, where they were martyred. We know little for certain, but this feast invites us to celebrate and continue the mission of the apostles.

Pope John Paul II was installed on this day in 1978. Remember him and his office in the intercessions today.

29 TUE
#480 (LMC, #193–231)
green
Weekday

The first reading (including yesterday's verses) is typical of Paul's approach to morality—it flows from what God has done for us. It is important to understand Paul's point about husbands and wives—that every part of our lives should now be transformed because it is lived "in Christ." In the gospel (again including yesterday's), Jesus reveals the presence of God's kingdom despite the opposition he meets and suggests that the kingdom is a hidden reality that acts on its own power.

30 WED
#481 (LMC, #193–231)   green
Weekday

Ephesians continues the discussion of household virtues that began yesterday; Jesus warns that the door to salvation is narrow and many who expect to enter will be surprised.

31 THU
#482 (LMC, #193–231)   green
Weekday

Our concluding section from Ephesians reminds us that proclaiming the gospel brings resistance, as Jesus himself experienced.

■ HALLOWEEN CUSTOMS: We can be happy that so much attention is given to this night, one of the few vigils to survive. Yet many of the trappings of the day flow from Druid festivals and other pagan customs. The Jewish and Christian tradition links harvest time with God's harvest of the faithful. Churches too often fail to make clear that ghosts and skeletons and cemeteries point to the heavenly Jerusalem.

November

THE MONTH OF NOVEMBER

Catholics have long seen this month as a time to remember the communion of saints and to pray for all the souls who have gone before us. The reformed calendar and rites have strengthened this attention to All Saints and All Souls and to the Second Coming; these two great days mark the entrance to the month. As the month progresses, the texts in the sacramentary, lectionary and *Liturgy of the Hours* move us deeper into the intense hope and expectation of the "last days."

■ THE WEEKDAYS: The last two weeks of this month move more and more into themes of the end time. This year we read from the book of Revelation, and the gospel selections for the same period are increasingly eschatological.

THE MASS IN NOVEMBER

■ INTRODUCTORY RITES: The same opening hymn, such as "For all the saints" (SINE NOMINE), might be used for the whole month. The litany of the saints (with local patrons included) also might serve as processional.

The penitential invocations at C*ii* in the sacramentary are fitting, or, to set a more explicitly paschal tone, the rite of blessing and sprinkling may be used instead of the penitential rite for each of these Sundays.

■ LITURGY OF THE WORD: The common psalm is Psalm 122 (Lectionary 175). It is available in several fine settings, including

- Christopher Willcock, "Let us go rejoicing" in *Psalms for Feasts and Seasons* (Liturgical Press)

- Robert Kreutz, "I rejoiced when I heard them say" in *Psalms* (OCP)

- the A. Gregory Murray antiphon with a Gelineau tone (*Worship*, #67)

- Joseph Smith, "I rejoiced when I heard them say" (GIA, G-2775).

- Michael Joncas, "Let us go rejoicing" *(Gather)*

- David Haas, "I was glad" (GIA, *Gather, Second Edition*)

All of these Sundays (and weekdays) can draw from the gospel acclamation verses listed at the ends of lists in the lectionary at #164 and #509. They evoke well the spirit of these days.

The intercessions could be common for the month. They could include extra petitions for the dead (see samples in the *Order of Christian Funerals* and in the sacramentary, appendix I, #11). Some places have even used the litany of the saints (suitably adapted with local patrons) as the intercessions this month. It works only if sung, and only if sung fast enough. It is one of the traditional ways in which the church has prayed its intercessions. For example, at the celebration of infant baptism and at ordinations, the invocation of the saints and sung petitions form the general intercessions.

■ LITURGY OF THE EUCHARIST: The preface for Sundays in Ordinary Time VI (P34) is appropriate for November 2 and the Sundays before Christ the King. Acclamations could be the same for all November assemblies.

■ CONCLUDING RITE: Solemn blessings are suggested for November 1 and for November 2 (sacramentary, #20). The latter might be used for all the Sundays. Its translation in the *Book of Blessings* (#25 in appendix II) changes "man" to "us." An alternative for month-long use that can be taped into the sacramentary is the hidden treasure at #1438 of the *Book of Blessings*.

■ HYMNODY FOR NOVEMBER: A review of the parish's familiar Advent hymns would be a good beginning for this month's planning. Certainly any setting of the Beatitudes could be used all month; you may want to acquaint yourself with Suzanne Toolan's setting (GIA, G-2132) and David Haas's "Blest are they" *(Gather);* both lend themselves well to the communion procession.

"Christ is the king" to the bright Vulpius tune GELOBT SEI GOTT in *Worship* recalls the faith of "Christ's brave saints of ancient days" and urges us to seek again their way of hope and faith; this hymn could be introduced on All Saints' Day and sung throughout November, especially on the final Sunday for the solemnity of Christ the King. Another appropriate hymn, found in *Worship* and a number of other hymnals, is "How firm a foundation" to the tune FOUNDATION. Bernadette Farrell offers two pieces that speak to the mysteries of life and death that we celebrate this month: "All that is hidden" (OCP, 7161) and "Unless a grain of wheat" (OCP, 7115). Both are appropriate for the communion procession.

Some hymns that speak of harvest time—fitting for these final weeks—are "For the fruits of this creation," sung either to EAST ACKLAM or to the more familiar Welsh tune AR HYD Y NOS, "Praise and thanksgiving" (BUNESSAN) in *Worship,* and "Sing to the lord of the harvest" to the tune by John Steurlein in the *Collegeville Hymnal.* Marty Haugen's "Bring forth the kingdom *(Gather)* is also appropriate for these times, as is "The king shall come when morning dawns," found in the second edition of *Gather* (with its more haunting hymn tune CONSOLATION) as well as the OCP resources. Jeremy Young's "We shall rise again" (GIA, G-2983 and *Gather*), fitting for this time in the liturgical year as well as the Easter season, speaks well of the mysteries of death and resurrection and would be suitable for the parish All Souls celebration. A good choral piece to sing during this time, that could perhaps be repeated on Thanksgiving Day, is John Rutter's "For the beauty of the earth," well worth the time and effort.

THE WORSHIP ENVIRONMENT FOR NOVEMBER

■ REMEMBERING THE DECEASED: A blank book in which members of the assembly can inscribe the names of the deceased might grace the assembly space (near the baptismal font, perhaps) throughout November. LTP has published a beautifully bound book for this purpose, *The Book of the Names of the Dead.* The book can be honored with incense, at least on All Saints and All Souls.

■ CEMETERIES: How cemeteries are cared for is a sign of respect not only to the dead but also to the bereaved and to the descendants who visit. Parishes with such a responsibility should think about decorating the entranceway, about posting signs telling the significance of November and its feasts, and about leaving special prayers in weatherproof containers along walkways.

DOMESTIC PRAYER IN NOVEMBER

Catholic Household Blessings and Prayers (pages 178–83) includes prayers for this month plus an order for a family's visit to a cemetery. This is found in an expanded format in the *Book of Blessings* and is discussed in the November 2 entry of this *Sourcebook.* See LTP's *A Sourcebook about Death* (1989), divided into 30 sections for day-by-day reading this month.

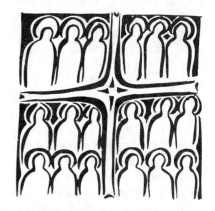

F R I #667 (LMC, #402) white
All Saints
SOLEMNITY

HISTORY OF ALL SAINTS

By the fourth century, most churches in the East observed a festival in honor of all martyrs. The date varied from region to region, but generally it was kept in relation to the great Fifty Days of Easter—Friday of the Easter Octave, May 13 or the Sunday after Pentecost (the date it has retained on the Byzantine calendar). The observance gradually became a commemoration for all saints and was moved to November 1. This new date seems to have originated in Ireland as a replacement for a Celtic pagan feast: Druids celebrated New Year's Day on November 1. However, once the transfer was incorporated into Western churches, some of the paschal content was lost. People seemed to focus on the dead and the saints with little reference to Easter.

LITURGY FOR ALL SAINTS

This feast begins at sunset on Thursday. Due to its importance, funeral Masses are forbidden, and any wedding Masses must use the festival's texts. Inserts for

Eucharistic prayers II and III are on page 228.

■ MASSES THURSDAY EVENING: Many parishes schedule a Mass with children on this eve, early enough to allow youngsters to go on their rounds. Participation in costume can be fun and a kind of eschatological sign, although pushing for "saints only" costumes is not necessary. The sung litany of the saints is a good opening to Mass or a fine form of the intercessions. Be sure to include the local saints. "When the saints go marching in" is justly popular. Parishes with a cemetery by the church building should consider a procession (with music) through it as an opening, or else a visit to it after Mass (see the notes under November 2). A cemetery visit should not be avoided as too scary for children. With adult participation and liturgical forms that do not play up the "spooky," this can be a grand experience to begin November. For other ideas, see pages 64–67 of the *Leader's Manual of the Hymnal for Catholic Students.*

■ VIGIL FOR HALLOWEEN: Three services can be noted for those who have begun weekly or periodic vigils.

- "Vigil for the Eve of All Saints' Day" is in *The Book of Occasional Services* (Episcopalian). A baptismal vigil, it calls for a service of light, three or more readings and psalms before the gospel, then the sacraments of initiation or a renewal of baptismal vows. While Catholic tradition reserves the initiation of adults to the Easter Vigil, the readings given there provide valuable material for any prayer service this day.

- The same book has an exciting "Service for All Hallows' Eve," meant to be combined with "suitable festivities and entertainment" or a communal visit to a cemetery. The rite begins with a service of

light and continues with two or more readings and psalms (the witch of Endor, the vision of Eliphaz the Temanite, the valley of dry bones and the war in heaven). It concludes with a homily and the Te Deum.

- Appendix I of the *Liturgy of the Hours* contains texts proper to this night. The wonderful canticle of Tobit and the gospel citations commend those pages to everyone preparing the liturgy for this day.

■ MASSES ON FRIDAY: A procession through the cemetery before Mass or following the prayer after communion would be appropriate. For a fitting gathering song, consider a setting of the litany of the saints. John Becker's setting (OCP, 8877) could be used effectively here and then could be used at other times, e.g. at the Easter Vigil. Its rhythmic quality is definitely processional in character.

#668 (LMC, #193–231)
white, violet or black
SAT 2 All Souls

MASS ON NOVEMBER 2

■ MUSIC: The gentle Taizé ostinato "Beati in domo domine" ("Happy they who dwell in God's house") would be an effective beginning for today's liturgy; consider also a hymn from the parish's funeral repertoire. The Sanctus and Agnus Dei from the old funeral chants (Mass XVIII) can be used, particularly if they have also been used in Lent. Consider Jeremy Young's

"We shall rise again" (GIA, G-2983; also in all editions of *Gather*) for the All Souls Mass. Its text is moving and pastorally suited to those who have been in grief.

■ TEXTS: Any readings from the section "Masses for the Dead" may be used: Daniel 12:1–3, Psalm 122, Revelation 21:1–5, 6–7 and Luke 12:35–40 are particularly appropriate this day.

The various Mass prayers do not have to be used in tandem with each other, staying under one or another numerical heading. They can be drawn from the six pages of texts in the sacramentary.

■ CONCLUDING RITE AND VISIT TO THE CEMETERY: The *Book of Blessings* (chapter 57) contains the "Order for Visiting a Cemetery on All Souls' Day." It may be used on other days or apart from Mass. The order includes a procession after Mass from the church to the cemetery.

OTHER LITURGIES

For school assemblies and prayer, see page 67 of the *Leader's Manual of the Hymnal for Catholic Students.*

Since this evening begins the celebration of Sunday, Masses for All Souls this year should be in the morning. Evening Masses should be of the Sunday.

VESTURE

White, black or violet vestments may be worn. Because we still seem to be moving away from the negative and morbid, violet or white should probably be used at funerals. Many liturgists, however, wonder if black was too quickly removed from the range of vesture options. This might be the right day to bring out any black sets from storage, if they are in good condition.

THE HISPANIC MÍSTICA AND THE LITURGY

Perhaps no other Catholic cultural group celebrates All Souls Day with as much enthusiasm and color as the Hispanic community. Especially for those of Mexican background, *El Día de los Muertos,* or "The Day of the Dead," is one of the most important holidays in the calendar. In Mexican neighborhoods during late October, it is not unusual to see posters and papier maché or wooden figurines shaped as skeletons going about all kinds of daily activities such as cooking, repairing a car, sweeping the floor and dancing. Children take delight in *calaveras* (sugar or chocolate candy shaped in the form of a skull) and *entierritos*—toys made from shoe boxes that display a funeral procession made of paper entering one end of the shoe box and going out the other.

The customs surrounding this celebration may appear to non-Hispanics to be almost macabre, but they reflect a deeply held conviction about the interconnectedness of the living and the dead. In mocking death, Hispanics challenge with faith the fate that awaits us all. These practices also echo the famous phrase of St. Augustine that at the death of a Christian "life is changed, not taken away."

The most important custom of this time of year is visiting the graves of loved ones in order to clean the place of burial and set out flowers (the traditional flower of this day is the marigold). Members of the family bring food and light candles in order to keep vigil for those who have died, because death has not separated them from the family. In several regions of Mexico families spend the whole night in the cemetery in vigil.

In some areas of this country, the custom called *pan de muertos* (the bread of the dead) is observed. This bread, baked in the shape of human beings, is blessed during the Mass on All Souls Day and then distributed after Mass to the faithful, who take it home and share it at a meal during which the beloved dead of the family are remembered.

Finally, the tradition of the *altarcito,* or home altar, present in many Hispanic homes, also features prominently during this day. An *altarcito* is usually a small table, set in a niche in the family room or master bedroom of the house, on which statues of Christ, Mary or another favorite saint are placed. A candle is kept lighted on this home altar as a sign of presence and prayer. In addition to the statues, it is also common to see pictures of the dead of the family. For the Day of the Dead the *pan de muertos* and special flowers are placed on the altar.

Some parishes in the U.S. have adapted this custom by inviting people of the parish, especially families who have lost loved ones during the year, to set up *altarcitos* in an assembly hall, much as they would in their own homes—with statues, candles, pictures of the dead and flowers. In the room with the *altarcitos,* arrangements are made to serve a potluck supper after the All Souls Day Mass. For those who cannot physically visit the cemetery, this adaptation of tradition provides an important means of observing this day. The dead are memorialized in the context of the entire community and once again the pattern of *misa, musa* and *mesa* (Mass, artistic expression and food) assures a genuine Hispanic celebration.

⊛3. Thirty-first Sunday in Ordinary Time

#152 (LMC, #146)   green

The prophet Malachi chastises first the priests of Israel and then the people for their unfaithfulness. Jesus tells the people not to imitate the example of the scribes and the Pharisees but to follow their teachings. Paul gives us an example of a good church leader in the second reading.

Remember to encourage and pray for conscientious voting on Election Day this Tuesday.

■ THE WEEK AHEAD: This week we hear from Paul's letter to the Philippians. The feast on Saturday will interrupt the daily readings. The displaced gospel verses can be appended to Friday's; the passage from Philippians can simply be omitted.

MON 4 Charles Borromeo, bishop
MEMORIAL

#485 (LMC, #193–231)   white

Another saint from the period after the Council of Trent, Borromeo worked tirelessly for the reform and renewal of the church. Appointed archbishop of Milan in 1560, he also served as papal Secretary of State to his uncle, Pius IV, during the later sessions of the council. Finally able to return to his diocese in 1566, he set out to be a model bishop, implementing the council. His example became an inspiration for the church in his time and might serve our own time of renewal, too.

Today's brief readings speak clearly of the attitudes that should mark the Christian community, especially concern for the needs of others.

5 T U E #486 (LMC, #193–231) green
Weekday

Though every year we hear it on Palm Sunday and the feast of the Triumph of the Cross, and on September 29 this year, the beautiful hymn from Philippians bears repeating often. The gospel connects with it easily as it reminds us that we should include those whom the world would despise as unworthy and unimportant.

Today is Election Day for president and congress as well as for local offices and issues; pray for conscientious voting and for true service from all who win.

6 W E D #487 (LMC, #193–231) green
Weekday

Paul's encouragement to persevere in Christ links well with Jesus' parables about being prepared to carry out the commitment to be disciples.

7 T H U #488 (LMC, #193–231) green
Weekday

Jesus tells parables that insist that God seeks out the lost. Once he was found, Paul considers all else as "loss" in light of Christ.

8 F R I #489 (LMC, #193–231) green
Weekday

Paul exhorts us to stand firm as we await the Lord's coming, and Jesus encourages the use of initiative in serving God, not money (as do Saturday's verses).

#671 (LMC, #406, 442–446) white

9 S A T **The Dedication of the Lateran Basilica in Rome**
FEAST

■ THE BUILDING: In the early fourth century, Constantine gave land on a hilltop near central Rome to the bishop of that city. The property included a large basilica, or meeting hall. A number of buildings have come and gone in that complex of buildings that was called "the Lateran." Some reports say that on this day in 324, the central basilica was dedicated to the Most Holy Savior. Since then, it and its successively rebuilt walls have housed the *cathedra* of the bishop of Rome. A baptistry soon was added to the side of the worship space. The same 1500-year-old building is still used for baptizing the faithful of that parish.

As the worship buildings and palaces evolved, the name "the Lateran" came to carry the same weight as the name "the Vatican" does now. Growth was accompanied by a name change, from Most Holy Savior to St. John (the Baptist). Thus the name St. John Lateran (which sounds like a saint's name) signifies a complex of buildings that were and are (at least in terms of the pope's role as the bishop of Rome) the "Mother and Head of All Churches in the City and throughout the World," which is the inscription at the east entrance.

■ LITURGICAL CELEBRATION: The texts for this day require some advance planning. The day's entry in most editions of the lectionary sends readers to the common of the dedication of a church, where choices abound. Pick readings that fit November. Isaiah and Ezekiel seem properly eschatological, and Psalm 122 is the common psalm for November.

The sacramentary's section on this day is even shorter than the lectionary's. There are texts for an "Anniversary outside the Dedicated Church" and a proper preface. The hymn "What is this place?" (GIA) is appropriate for the feast.

#155 (LMC, #149) green

10 **Thirty-second Sunday in Ordinary Time**

The first reading today speaks of keeping vigil for wisdom as the bridesmaids keep vigil for the groom. Paul speaks about those who have died and about the Second Coming. The themes of November are evident today. Note that the five sensible bridesmaids were prepared for a long wait until the groom arrived; some reflection today on the folly of predicting the end of the world may be appropriate.

If the relatives of those who were buried over the past year were not made a special part of the liturgy on November 2, parishes might make one of the Sunday Masses a memorial for parishioners and mourners (perhaps to be followed by lunch for all).

■ THE WEEK AHEAD: This week we read from the books of Titus, Philemon, and 2 and 3 John.

There is a special gospel for Monday's memorial, so Monday's assigned passage could be prefixed to Tuesday's.

#491 and #673 (LMC, #193–231) green

MON 11 **Martin of Tours, bishop**
MEMORIAL

Martin left military service because of his commitment to Christ. He founded a monastery near Poitiers (France) and allowed himself to be schooled in the faith by that city's bishop, Hilary (see January 13). He is praised for his nonviolent witness (together with Saints Justin and Cyprian) in the U.S. bishops' pastoral letter on peace. The letter quotes Martin's decision to leave the military for Christianity: "Hitherto I have served you as a soldier. Allow me now to become a soldier of God. . . . I am a soldier of Christ. It is not lawful for me to fight."

■ VETERAN'S DAY: The memory of Martin seems appropriate on this civil holiday, which commemorates the end of hostilities at the eleventh hour of the eleventh day of the eleventh month in 1918. Intercessions for peace and for the dead, especially for those who died in war, would be appropriate.

The letter to Titus today gives the characteristics of good presbyters and bishops, ideals that Martin fulfilled. The gospel for the memorial highlights Martin's concern for those in need. Pray for both civil and church leaders.

#492 (LMC, #193–231) white

TUE 12 **Josaphat, bishop, religious, martyr**
MEMORIAL

An Orthodox Lithuanian bishop, Josaphat sought reunion with Rome and was killed by those who opposed it. Pray today for the many Christians (in communion with Rome or not) who still carry the hurts from their persecution at each other's hands, and for the courageous leaders on all sides who are trying to forge new collaborations.

The letter to Titus gives advice for a rightly ordered life, a proper response to God's gift of salvation. The gospel reminds us that we do not earn God's favor, for God's grace is always a free gift.

#493 (LMC, #193–231) white

WED 13 **Frances Xavier Cabrini, virgin, religious founder, missionary**
MEMORIAL

Born in Italy and founder of a religious congregation there, Frances spent the second half of her life founding schools and hospitals in both North and South America. She died in Chicago in 1917 and was the first citizen of the United States to be canonized (in 1946). The proper opening prayer evokes well the spirit of her life.

The letter to Titus reminds us that God saved us, not because of anything we did, but because of God's mercy. The gospel calls us to gratitude for God's gifts.

#494 (LMC, #193–231) green

THU 14 **Weekday**

Today's passage from Philemon is used in part on the Twenty-third Sunday of Ordinary Time in Year C. It is a masterful appeal by Paul for the freeing of a slave, expressing the fact that everything changes when the gospel is accepted as a basis for life. The gospel today moves into Luke's eschatological material.

#495 (LMC, #193–231) green

FRI 15 **Weekday**

Albert the Great, bishop, religious, doctor of the church, optional memorial/white. ■ The Common of Doctors provides another opportunity to praise God for intellectual gifts on the feast of this great thirteenth-century Dominican scholar who linked Aristotle's philosophy and Christian faith. His best student was St. Thomas Aquinas.

The reading from 2 John reminds us of the fundamental command of love that motivated Albert and should motivate all of us, even toward our "enemies." The gospel warnings of the end time remind us of the urgency of true conversion in our lives.

#496 (LMC, #193–231) green

SAT 16 **Weekday**

Margaret of Scotland, married woman, queen, optional memorial/white. ▪ *Gertrude the Great, virgin, religious, optional memorial/white; Blessed Virgin Mary on Saturday, optional memorial/white.* ▪ Both Queen Margaret and the mystic Gertrude are strong women who deserve to be placed on the parish calendar; perhaps in alternating years. Margaret was raised at the court of St. Stephen of Hungary and later became the wife of King Malcolm of Scotland. Her holiness came in her life as wife and mother of eight and was manifested by a special concern for the poor. Gertrude, a thirteenth-century Cistercian nun, teaches the importance of a spirituality based on the liturgy.

The gospel parable urges us to pray always and not lose heart, and 3 John encourages care for our "brothers" even if they are strangers. Both readings give good advice for those who seek to imitate the holiness of today's saints.

17 **Thirty-third Sunday in Ordinary Time**

#158 (LMC, #152)   green

Today's first reading and gospel call us to use well the talents God has given us. Paul strikes a clearer eschatological note, calling us to live as children of the light.

■ THE WEEK AHEAD: Special readings are available for tomorrow's memorial of the Dedication of the Basilicas of Peter and Paul. If they are used, the weekday readings can be omitted this year.

MON 18 **Weekday** MEMORIAL

#497 or 679 (LMC, #193–231)   green

The Dedication of the Basilicas of the Apostles Peter and Paul in Rome, optional memorial/white; Rose Philippine Duchesne, virgin, religious, missionary, educator, optional memorial/white. ■ Most parishes will elect to remember one of the newest saints on the American calendar (canonized in 1988). She died in Missouri in 1852 after spending a long life teaching in France and in cities in the United States. Her desire to teach Native Americans was frustrated by her inability to speak their language, but she lived among the Indians, who named her Woman Who Prays Much. Her proper prayers (and the Common of Virgins) are to be joined to the weekday readings. Or, keep the anniversary of the dedication of the churches, uniting the weekday community to the basilicas of Peter (at the Vatican) and Paul (on the road to Ostia). In this option, the readings and prayers are proper to the memorial.

If the weekday readings are used, the reading from Revelation calls for repentance of those who "have turned aside from your early love." The healing of the blind man might lead us to pray for clear sight to see our own need to renew our love.

TUE 19 **Weekday**

#498 (LMC, #193–231)   green

Revelation today challenges lukewarm Christianity, and Zacchaeus offers an example of a wholehearted response.

WED 20 **Weekday**

#499 (LMC, #193–231)   green

John has a mystic vision in Revelation of the throne of God, the four living creatures (see below) and twenty-four elders. The gospel, like Sunday's passage from Matthew, reminds us to use well what God gives us.

■ SYMBOLS OF THE EVANGELISTS: From at least the second century, the four living creatures (ox, lion, eagle, angel or human) described in Revelation 4:7 were taken as symbols of the four evangelists. The creatures, often called the "tetramorph" or four forms, appear in Ezekiel 1:5. They were seen as the epitome of creation. Hundreds of years prior to this, they were (as they still are) the four "fixed signs" of the zodiac—Taurus at the zenith of Spring; Leo at midsummer; Scorpio, which was in antiquity an eagle, at autumn's peak; and Aquarius (man or angel) with the fullest form of winter.

A few early Christian commentators used the lion to represent Matthew. But soon the universal tradition came to be Matthew represented by a winged human (or angel). The classical explanation, best articulated by Jerome and Augustine, is that his gospel starts with the human genealogy

of Jesus. Mark is represented by a lion, the king of the desert, where his gospel opens. Luke is represented by the ox, perhaps for his scene at Bethlehem, and John by the eagle, for his high theology.

Throughout the history of liturgical art, the four creatures have appeared around Christ: at the four ends of a cross, at the four sides of a mosaic, at the corners of a gospel-book cover. Even agnostic astrologers, when visiting ancient Christian churches or looking at liturgical book covers, can exclaim: There is the Eternal One surrounded by the four symbols of fullness!

THU 21 **The Presentation of the Virgin Mary** MEMORIAL

#500 (LMC, #193–231)   white

Two foundations exist for what is in Western churches a minor memorial for Mary. One is the anniversary of the dedication of the Church of Santa Maria Nova in Jerusalem (November 21, 543). That's why the German calendar calls this day "Our Lady of Jerusalem." The second source of great festivity in the East is apocryphal—the story of Mary being presented in the Temple at the age of three in order to be raised there by "temple virgins." While the books that contained such stories were not made part of the canon of scripture, communities in the East often saw such stories as orthodox and as befitting a festival. A recognition of Mary as the new Temple could be seen as underlying both foundations for this memorial.

Today's passage from Revelation gives praise to the Lamb who was slain and is victorious. Jesus weeps over Jerusalem because it did not recognize its visitation by God. We must each decide where we will stand.

FRI 22 #501 (LMC, #193–231) red
Cecilia, virgin and martyr
MEMORIAL

Devotion to St. Cecilia dates to the fifth century, and her name is mentioned in Eucharistic Prayer I, which might be used today. She was a Roman of a patrician family who, legend says, converted her husband and his brother; the three devoted themselves to charitable works and to burying martyrs until they joined their ranks. Over the centuries, Cecilia became associated with church musicians, due to the erroneous application of a passage in her proper office at that time *("cantantibus organis")*.

Like Ezekiel (see August 13), John eats the scroll, but it turns sour in his stomach, perhaps a reminder that prophecy does not always meet with acceptance. Jesus' prophetic challenge in the Temple did not gain him acceptance, either.

SAT 23 #502 (LMC, #193–231) green
Weekday

Clement I, pope, martyr, optional memorial / red. • *Columban, abbot, missionary, optional memorial / white.* • *Blessed Miguel-Agustín Pro, presbyter, religious, martyr, optional memorial / red.* • *Blessed Virgin Mary on Saturday, optional memorial / white.* • Clement was the third successor of St. Peter. Columban was the greatest of the Irish missionaries to Europe in the sixth and early seventh centuries. The new commemoration of the Mexican priest Miguel-Agustín might be the best choice, especially in Mexican-American parishes. Accused and executed as a conspirator against the government in 1927, he was immediately considered a martyr by Mexican Catholics. He stands as a witness to the troubled history we have inherited and, because of

the widely circulated photograph of him kneeling before executioners, as a twentieth-century icon of courage. His last words, fittingly recalled this week, were *"Viva Cristo Rey."* Either the prayers found in *Sacramentary Supplement* (Catholic Book Publishing Company) or the Common of One Martyr can be used.

See the *Collection of Masses of the Blessed Virgin Mary,* #25 ("Image and Mother of the Church") and #37 ("Mother of Divine Hope") for prayers that express the sense of church and of the last things common to these weeks.

The two witnesses in Revelation may be Moses and Elijah, but their predicted witness, death and raising imitates Christ and holds out promise for all of us. The gospel dispute gives Jesus an occasion to affirm the resurrection of the dead, which is our hope.

24 #161 (LMC, #155) white
Christ the King
SOLEMNITY

Today's solemnity echoes Ascension, Epiphany and Palm Sunday—all ancient celebrations of Christ's rule. It was instituted by Pope Pius XI in 1925 as an antidote to the destructive forces in the world of his day: the Bolshevik revolution of 1917, the rise of fascism in Italy, the loss of political power for the church in most countries, and the rampant

materialism of the "roaring twenties." Times and politics change, and the day is seen less as a medicine and more as a fitting way to remember the Second Coming. The readings this year focus on the judgment of the sheep and goats, a healthy reminder of what it means to serve our king.

Music for this feast might include "To Jesus Christ our sovereign king," and "Jesus the Lord" (New Dawn), found in *Gather, Second Edition,* "The king shall come when morning dawns," "Rejoice the lord is king," All hail the power of Jesus' name" and "Crown him with many crowns." A choral piece for this feast worth investigating is H. Hamilton Smith's "Choral Fanfare for Christ the King" (GIA, G-2393).

■ THE LAST WEEK OF THE YEAR: The three days before Thanksgiving in the United States are proposed as ember days in *Catholic Household Blessings and Prayers* (page 188). Proper readings for Thanksgiving Day may replace the assigned passages. If so, Thursday's gospel can be appended to Wednesday's, and the passage from Revelation can be dropped. Saturday's feast will displace the weekday readings; both of Saturday's passages could be appended to Friday's or the verses from Revelation could be omitted. From Tuesday through Saturday, the verses from Luke are clearly appropriate for these last days. They provide us with the entire eschatological discourse, positioned by Luke just before the Last Supper and the passion narrative.

If prayers from the "preceding Sunday" are to be used on any of these days, they are from the "Thirty-fourth Week," not from Christ the King.

MON 25 Weekday
#503 (LMC, #193–231)   green

Revelation gives us the vision of the 144,000 before the throne. Those who imitate the generosity of the poor widow with her two copper coins will be among their number.

TUE 26 Weekday
#504 (LMC, #193–231) green

The image of harvest in the first reading suggests we should be mindful of the end time. Jesus also indicates that the status quo will not endure forever, but cautions against following those who proclaim that the time has arrived.

WED 27 Weekday
#505 (LMC, #193–231) green

If special readings will be used tomorrow, combine Thursday's gospel with today's; these verses urge patience through all the trials of the end time. Revelation offers us the hymn of those who are victorious over evil.

THU 28 Weekday
#506 or #881–885 (LMC, #193–231)   green or white

■ THANKSGIVING DAY: See the special votive Mass printed after November 30 in the sacramentary. These texts can be supplemented by material in chapter 58 of the *Book of Blessings,* a blessing of food for Thanksgiving, either that to be eaten by the assembly or foods to be given to the poor; #1764 is a good greeting for any assembly today; #1760 suggests intercessions. Consider the preface for weekdays in Ordinary Time IV instead of the preface designated "Thanksgiving Day." Musical choices for a parish Thanksgiving Mass might include "The works of the Lord are created in wisdom" *(Worship)* as well as "Father, we thank thee

who has planted." If the choir is singing for the celebration, consider using John Rutter's "For the beauty of the earth" (Hinshaw, HMC-550).

If the readings of the weekday are used, Revelation gives us reason to give thanks for the victory of the Lamb, and Jesus foretells terrifying events but also notes that our ransom is near at hand.

FRI 29 Weekday
#507 (LMC, #193–231) green

Along with possible misinterpretations of "a thousand years," the first reading gives us the beautiful image of hope of a "new heavens and a new earth." If Saturday's passage is appended, we end with Christ's promise to come soon. The gospel (combined with tomorrow's verses) reminds us that God's word will remain through all that is coming but that we must pray constantly for the strength to endure, too.

SAT 30 Andrew, apostle
#684 (LMC, #423, 193–231) red
FEAST

Andrew was a disciple of the Baptist before he met Christ and brought his brother Peter to the Lord. A very old tradition says he was crucified on an X-shaped cross. John Chrysostom's words in today's Office of Readings offer a picture of Andrew and ourselves as we move toward another Advent: "a soul waiting with the utmost longing for the Messiah, looking forward to his appearing from heaven, rejoicing when he does appear, and hastening to announce so great an event to others." We are continually sent forth from Mass (missa, "dismissal") to spread the gospel.

LITURGY OF THE WORD

Concluding Prayer for the General Intercessions

TRINITY SUNDAY
Lord, merciful and gracious God,
you showed the fullness of your love
when you gave your only Son for
    our salvation.

Complete within us the work of your love
by renewing our trust in him,
that we may come to share
the undying life he lives with you,
in the communion of the Holy Spirit,
God for ever and ever.
—© ICEL

THE BODY AND BLOOD OF CHRIST
The bread we break, O God,
you have made the body of your Son;
the cup we bless,
our communion in his blood.

Grant that we who bow before the mystery
of this most holy sacrament
may know him also in the needy of this
    world
and share with them
the life you share with us.

We ask this through our Lord Jesus
    Christ,
    your Son,
who lives and reigns with you in the unity
    of the Holy Spirit,
God for ever and ever.
—© ICEL

ELEVENTH SUNDAY IN ORDINARY TIME
Compassionate God,
your word calls laborers to the harvest.

Send us who are blest with the gift
    of your kingdom
to announce its coming with gladness
and to manifest its healing power.

We make our prayer through our Lord
    Jesus Christ, your Son,
who lives and reigns with you in the unity
    of the Holy Spirit,
God for ever and ever.
—© ICEL

TWELFTH SUNDAY IN ORDINARY TIME
True and faithful God,
you give courage to the fearful
and endurance to martyrs.

Sustain us as followers of your Son Jesus,
that with boldness and conviction
we may acknowledge him before the world.

We ask this through our Lord Jesus
    Christ, your Son,
who lives and reigns with you in the unity
    of the Holy Spirit,
God for ever and ever.
—© ICEL

THIRTEENTH SUNDAY IN ORDINARY TIME
All-powerful God,
your incarnate Word commands
    our obedience
and offers us true life.

Make our ears attentive to the voice
    of your Son
and our hearts generous in answering
    his call,
that we may take up the cross with trust
    in his promises.

We ask this through our Lord Jesus
    Christ, your Son,
who lives and reigns with you in the unity
    of the Holy Spirit,
God for ever and ever.
—© ICEL

FOURTEENTH SUNDAY IN ORDINARY TIME
Father, Lord of heaven and earth,
by whose gracious will
the mysteries of the kingdom are revealed
    to the childlike,
make us learn from your Son humility
    of heart,
that in shouldering his yoke we may find
    refreshment and rest.

We ask this through our Lord Jesus
    Christ,
    your Son,
who lives and reigns with you in the unity
    of the Holy Spirit,
God for ever and ever.
—© ICEL

Fifteenth Sunday in Ordinary Time
God of the heavens,
God of the earth,
all creation awaits your gift of new life.

Prepare our hearts
to receive the word of your Son,
that his gospel may grow within us
and yield a harvest that is a hundredfold.
We ask this through our Lord Jesus
    Christ, your Son,
who lives and reigns with you in the unity
    of the Holy Spirit,
God for ever and ever.
—© ICEL

Sixteenth Sunday in Ordinary Time
O God, patient and forebearing,
you alone know fully
the goodness of what you have made.

Strengthen our spirit when we are slow
and temper our zeal when we are rash,
that in your own good time
you may produce in us a rich harvest
from the seed you have sown and tended.

We make our prayer through our Lord
    Jesus
Christ, your Son, who lives and reigns with
    you in the unity of the Holy Spirit,
God for ever and ever.
—© ICEL

Seventeenth Sunday in Ordinary Time
God of eternal wisdom,
you alone impart the gift of right judgment.

Grant us an understanding heart,
that we may value wisely
the treasure of your kingdom
and gladly forgo all lesser gifts
to possess that kingdom's incomparable joy.

We make our prayer through our Lord Jesus
    Christ, your Son,
who lives and reigns with you in the unity
    of the Holy Spirit,
God for ever and ever.
—© ICEL

Eighteenth Sunday in Ordinary Time:
Bountiful and compassionate God,
you place in the hands of your disciples
the food of life.

Nourish us at your holy table,

that we may bear Christ to others
and share with them
the gifts we have so richly received.

We make our prayer through our Lord Jesus
    Christ, your Son,
who lives and reigns with you in the unity
    of the Holy Spirit,
God for ever and ever.
—© ICEL

Nineteenth Sunday in Ordinary Time
God of all power,
your sovereign word comes to us in Christ.
When your church is in danger,
make firm our trust;
when your people falter,
steady our faith.
Show us in Jesus your power to save,
that we may always acclaim him as Lord,
who lives and reigns with you in the unity
    of the Holy Spirit,
God for ever and ever.
—© ICEL

Twentieth Sunday in Ordinary Time
God of the nations,
to your table all are invited
and in your family no one is a stranger.

Satisfy the hunger
of those gathered in this house of prayer,
and mercifully extend to all the peoples
    on earth
the joy of salvation and faith.

Grant this through our Lord Jesus Christ,
    your Son,
who lives and reigns with you in the unity
    of the Holy Spirit,
God for ever and ever.
—© ICEL

Twenty-first Sunday in Ordinary Time
Living God,
you sent your Son among us
to reveal your wisdom
and make known your ways.

Increase our faith,
that we may confess Jesus as your Son,
take up his work on earth,
and trust his promise to sustain the church.

We ask this through our Lord Jesus Christ,
    your Son,

who lives and reigns with you in the unity
    of the Holy Spirit,
God for ever and ever.
—© *ICEL*

TWENTY-SECOND SUNDAY IN ORDINARY TIME
O God,
whose word burns like a fire within us,
grant us a bold and faithful spirit,
that in your strength we may be unafraid
to speak your word
and follow where you lead.

We make our prayer through our Lord
    Jesus Christ, your Son,
who lives and reigns with you in the unity
    of the Holy Spirit,
God for ever and ever.
—© *ICEL*

TWENTY-THIRD SUNDAY IN ORDINARY TIME
Confirm, O God, in unity and truth
the Church you gather in Christ.
Encourage the fervent,
enlighten the doubtful,
and bring back the wayward.
Bind us together in mutual love,
that our prayer in Christ's name
may be pleasing to you.

Grant this through our Lord Jesus Christ,
    your Son,
who lives and reigns with you in the unity
    of the Holy Spirit,
God for ever and ever.
—© *ICEL*

TWENTY-FOURTH SUNDAY IN ORDINARY TIME
O God, most high,
you are slow to anger and rich
    in compassion.

Keep alive in us the memory of your mercy,
that our angers may be calmed
and our resentments dispelled.
May we discover the forgiveness
promised to those who forgive
and become a people rich in mercy.

We ask this through our Lord Jesus Christ,
    your Son,
who lives and reigns with you in the unity
    of the Holy Spirit,
God for ever and ever.
—© *ICEL*

TWENTY-FIFTH SUNDAY IN ORDINARY TIME
God most high,
your ways are not our ways,
for your kindness is lavished equally
    upon all.

Teach us to welcome your mercy toward
    others,
even as we hope to receive mercy ourselves.

We ask this through our Lord Jesus Christ,
    your Son,
who lives and reigns with you in the unity
    of the Holy Spirit,
God for ever and ever.
—© *ICEL*

TWENTY-SIXTH SUNDAY IN ORDINARY TIME
O God,
you alone judge rightly
and search the depths of the heart.

Make us swift to do your will
and slow to judge our neighbor,
that we may walk with those
who follow the way of repentance and faith
and so enter your heavenly kingdom.

Grant this through our Lord Jesus Christ,
    your Son,
who lives and reigns with you in the unity
    of the Holy Spirit,
God for ever and ever.
—© *ICEL*

TWENTY-SEVENTH SUNDAY IN ORDINARY TIME
Yours, O God, is the vineyard and
    its harvest,
yours the kingdom of justice and peace.
You call your people to tend its growth.

Bless the work entrusted to our hands,
that we may offer you
an abundance of just works,
a rich harvest of peace.

We ask this through our Lord Jesus Christ,
    your Son,
who lives and reigns with you in the unity
    of the Holy Spirit,
God for ever and ever.
—© *ICEL*

TWENTY-EIGHTH SUNDAY IN ORDINARY TIME
God of goodness and kindness,
you invite all peoples to the banquet
and offer them a feast beyond compare.

Give us your saving grace
to keep unstained the robe of our baptism
until that day when you welcome us
to heaven's joyful table.

We ask this through our Lord Jesus Christ,
    your Son,
who lives and reigns with you in the unity
    of the Holy Spirit,
God for ever and ever.
—© ICEL

TWENTY-NINTH SUNDAY IN ORDINARY TIME
O God, whose image we bear
and whose name we carry,
yours is the world and all it contains.

Recall us to our true allegiance,
so that above the powers and rulers
    of this world
you alone may claim our fullest loyalty
    and love.

We make our prayer through our Lord
    Jesus Christ, your Son,
who lives and reigns with you in the unity
    of the Holy Spirit,
God for ever and ever.
—© ICEL

THIRTIETH SUNDAY IN ORDINARY TIME
Your love, O God, is boundless.
We who were strangers
have been made your children.
We who were defenseless
have been brought into your household.

Keep us mindful of your deeds of mercy,
that we may love you with our whole heart
and love our neighbor as ourselves.

We ask this through our Lord Jesus Christ,
    your Son,
who lives and reigns with you in the unity
    of the Holy Spirit,
God for ever and ever.
—© ICEL

THIRTY-FIRST SUNDAY IN ORDINARY TIME
Sovereign God,
we have no father but you,
no teacher but Christ.

Conform our lives to the faith we profess,
preserve us from arrogance and pride,
and teach us in Christ the greatness
    of humility and service.

We make our prayer through our Lord
    Jesus Christ, your Son,
who lives and reigns with you in the unity
    of the Holy Spirit,
God for ever and ever.
—© ICEL

THIRTY-SECOND SUNDAY IN ORDINARY TIME
Brighten your Church, O God,
with the promise of your kingdom
and waken our hearts to its light.
Bid us hasten with faith undimmed
to greet the bridegroom's return
and to enter the wedding feast.

We ask this through our Lord Jesus Christ,
    your Son,
who lives and reigns with you in the unity
    of the Holy Spirit,
God for ever and ever.
—© ICEL

THIRTY-THIRD SUNDAY IN ORDINARY TIME
O God,
from whose own abundance
all gifts and skills are lavishly bestowed,
encourage us to use our talents
as generously as you have allotted them,
so that, being faithful to your purpose,
we may become sharers in your glory.

We make our prayer through our Lord Jesus
    Christ, your Son,
who lives and reigns with you in the unity
    of the Holy Spirit,
God for ever and ever.
—© ICEL

CHRIST THE KING
Almighty God,
you have conferred upon Christ Jesus
sovereignty over every age and nation.

Direct us, in the love of Christ,
to care for the least of his brothers and sisters,
that we may be subject to his dominion
and receive the inheritance of your kingdom.

Grant this through our Lord Jesus Christ,
    your Son,
who lives and reigns with you in the unity
    of the Holy Spirit,
God for ever and ever.
—© ICEL

LITURGY OF THE EUCHARIST

Eucharistic Prayer Inserts

SUNDAYS IN EUCHARISTIC PRAYERS II AND III: *See page 84.*

BIRTH OF JOHN THE BAPTIST (JUNE 24)
IN EUCHARISTIC PRAYER II:
> *Lord, you are holy indeed,*
> *the fountain of all holiness.*
> We gather here before you,
> and in communion with the whole church
> we celebrate the birth
> of Saint John, the forerunner
> who prepared the way
> for the Savior of all people, Christ Jesus,
> who came after John
>> but existed before him;
> we pray:
> *Let your Spirit come upon . . .*

BIRTH OF JOHN THE BAPTIST (JUNE 24)
IN EUCHARISTIC PRAYER III:
> *. . . a perfect offering may be made*
> *to the glory of your name.*
> This is why we gather before you,
> and in communion with the whole church
> we celebrate the birth
> of Saint John, the forerunner
> who prepared the way
> for the Savior of all people, Christ Jesus,
> who came after John
>> but existed before him.
> *And so, Father, we bring you . . .*

ASSUMPTION (AUGUST 15) IN EUCHARISTIC
PRAYER II:
> *Lord, you are holy indeed,*
> *the fountain of all holiness.*
> We gather here before you,
> and in communion with the whole church
> we celebrate the day the Virgin Mother
>> of God
> was assumed into heaven in the glory
>> of her son,
> Jesus Christ, our Lord.
> Through him, who gives life to our faith,
> we pray:
> *Let your Spirit come upon . . .*

ASSUMPTION (AUGUST 15) IN EUCHARISTIC
PRAYER III:
> *. . . a perfect offering may be made*
> *to the glory of your name.*
> This is why we gather before you,
> and in communion with the whole church
> we celebrate the day the Virgin Mother
>> of God
> was assumed into heaven in the glory
>> of her Son,
> Jesus Christ, our Lord.
> Through him, who gives life to our faith
>> and fulfills it,
> *we bring you these gifts . . .*

ALL SAINTS (NOVEMBER 1) IN EUCHARISTIC
PRAYER II:
> *Lord, you are holy indeed,*
> *the fountain of all holiness.*
> We gather here before you,
> and in communion with the whole church
> we celebrate the day set aside
> in memory of all the saints:
> they followed Christ through their life,
> and at death they received the crown
>> of glory.
> Through him, who gives life to our faith
>> and fulfills it,
> we pray:
> *Let your Spirit come upon . . .*

ALL SAINTS (NOVEMBER 1) IN EUCHARISTIC
PRAYER III:
> *. . . a perfect offering may be made*
> *to the glory of your name.*
> This is why we gather before you,
> and in communion with the whole church
> we celebrate the day set aside
> in memory of all the saints:
> They followed Christ through their life,
> and at death they received the crown
>> of glory.
> Through him, who gives life to our faith
>> and fulfills it,
> *we bring you these gifts . . .*